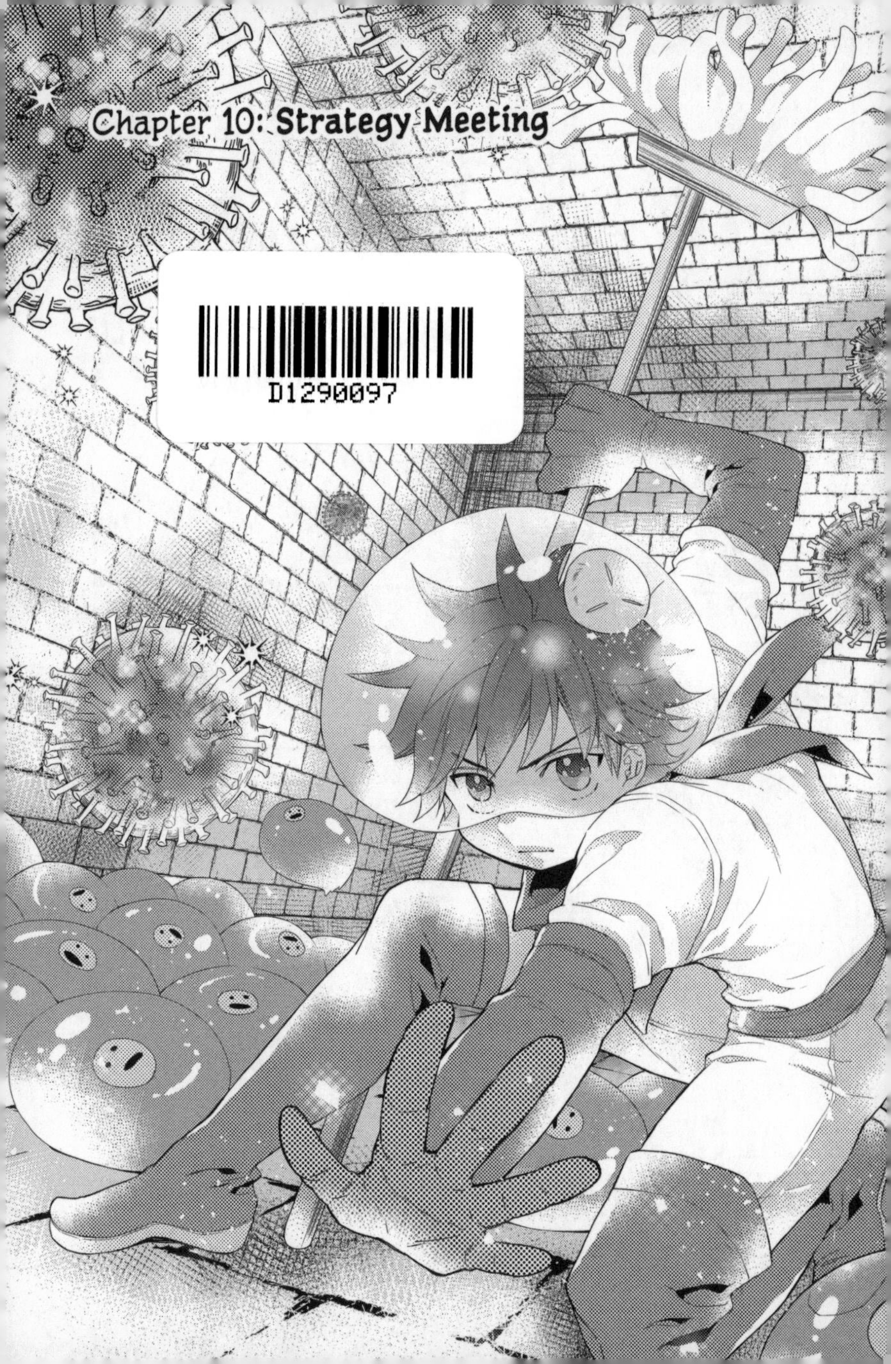
Chapter 10: Strategy Meeting

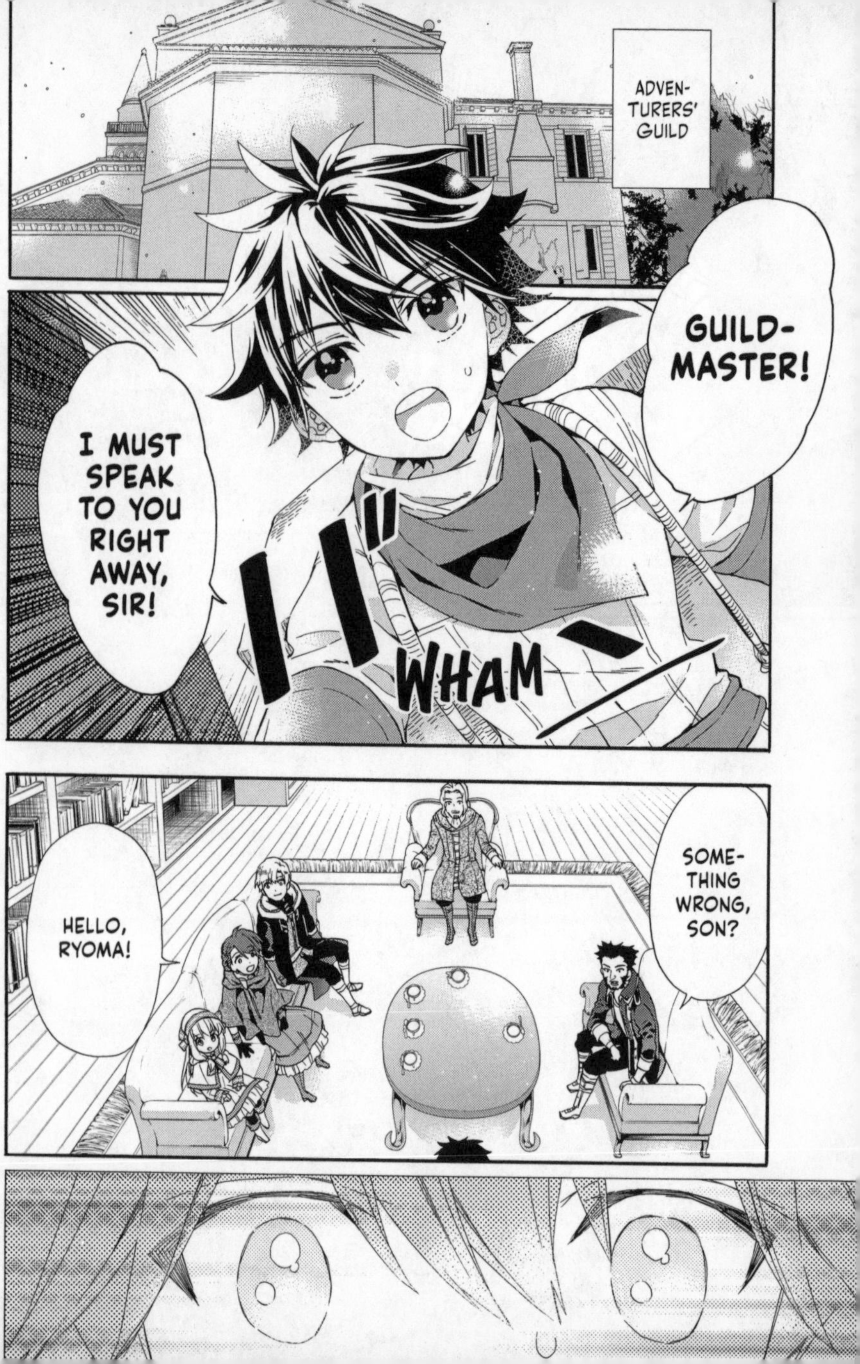
ADVEN-
TURERS'
GUILD
GUILD-
MASTER!
I MUST
SPEAK
TO YOU
RIGHT
AWAY,
SIR!
WHAM
SOME-
THING
WRONG,
SON?
HELLO,
RYOMA!

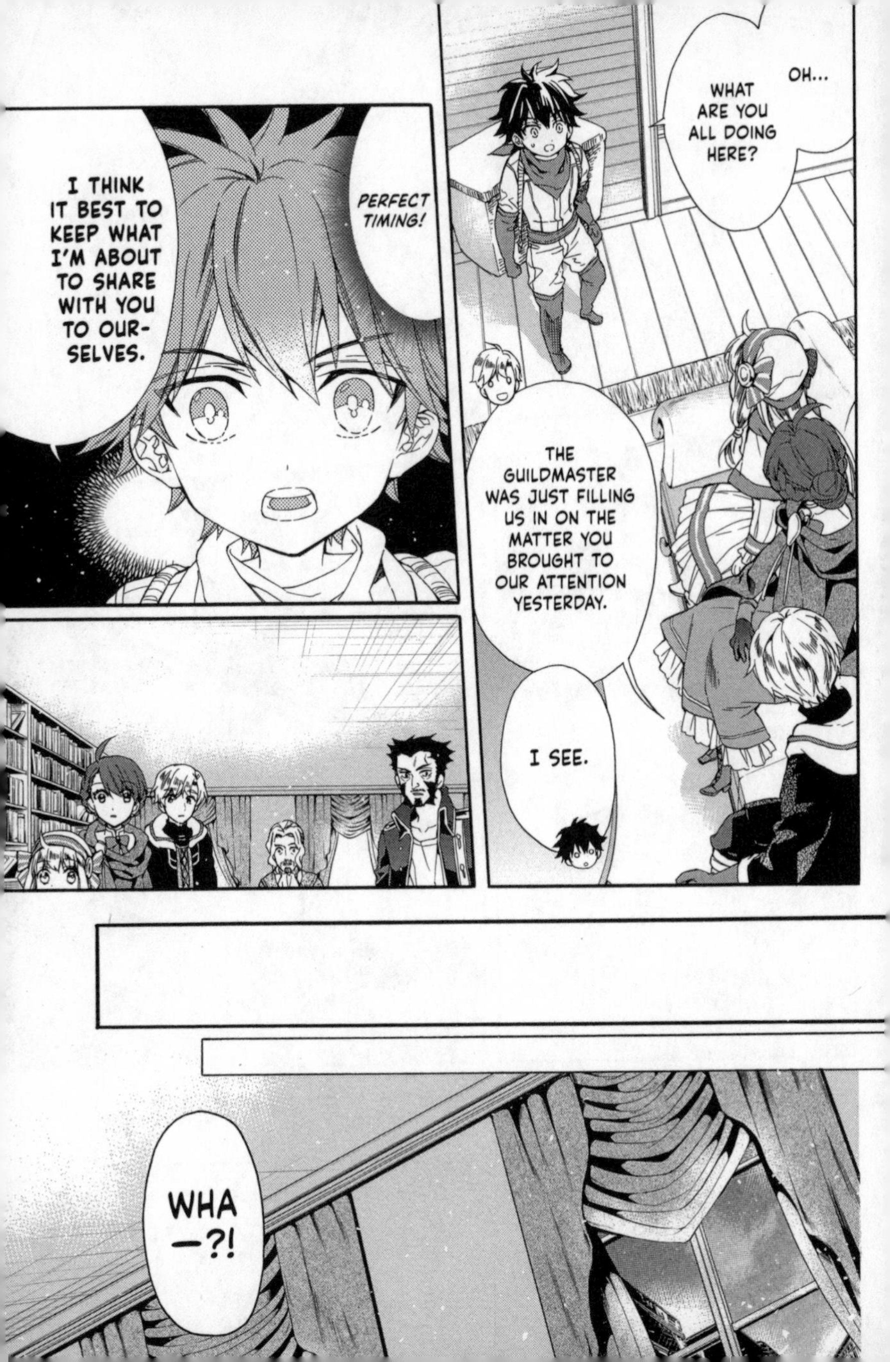
OH...
WHAT ARE YOU ALL DOING HERE?
THE GUILDMASTER WAS JUST FILLING US IN ON THE MATTER YOU BROUGHT TO OUR ATTENTION YESTERDAY.
I SEE.
PERFECT TIMING!
I THINK IT BEST TO KEEP WHAT I'M ABOUT TO SHARE WITH YOU TO OUR-SELVES.
WHA—?!

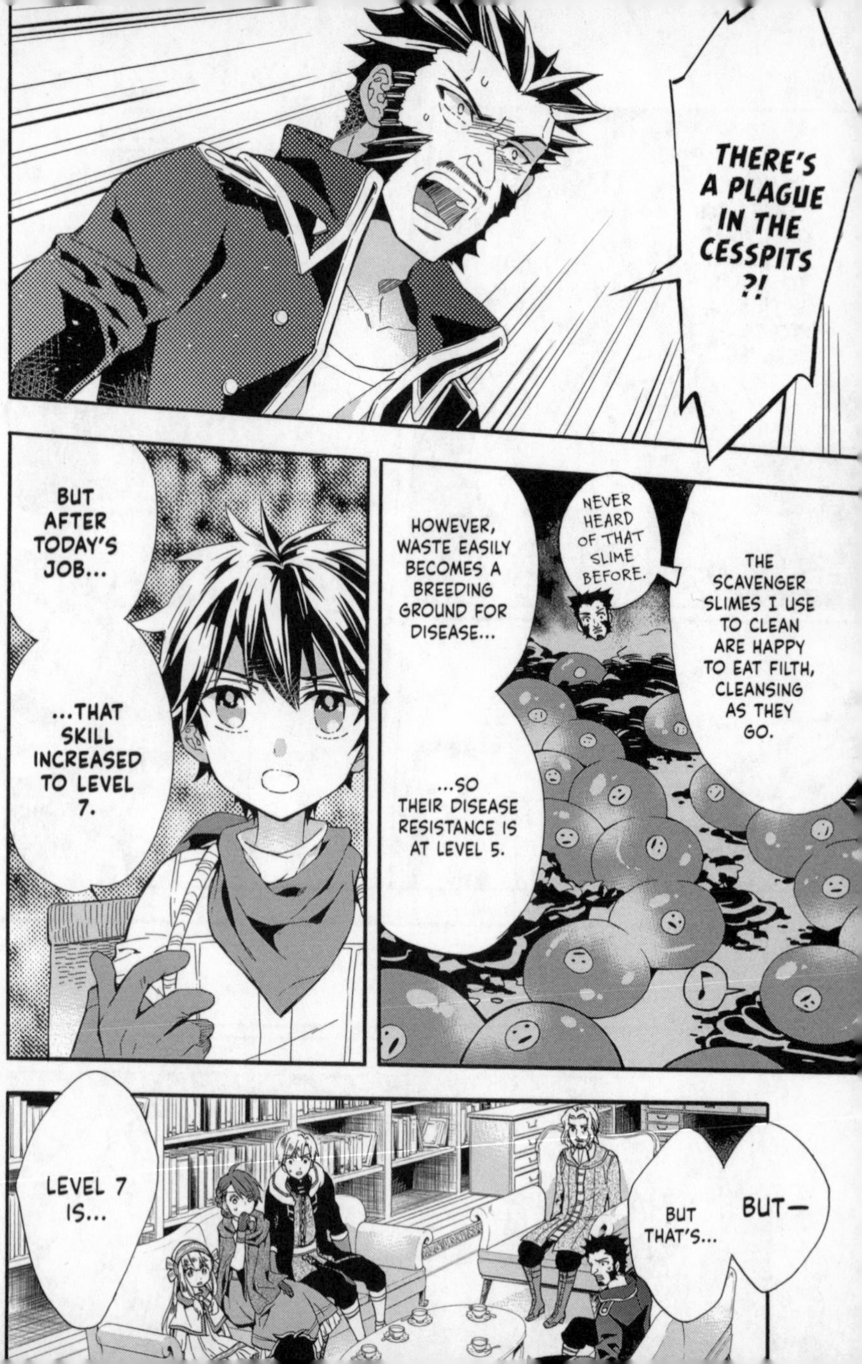
THERE'S A PLAGUE IN THE CESSPITS ?!
THE SCAVENGER SLIMES I USE TO CLEAN ARE HAPPY TO EAT FILTH, CLEANSING AS THEY GO.
NEVER HEARD OF THAT SLIME BEFORE.
HOWEVER, WASTE EASILY BECOMES A BREEDING GROUND FOR DISEASE...
...SO THEIR DISEASE RESISTANCE IS AT LEVEL 5.
BUT AFTER TODAY'S JOB...
...THAT SKILL INCREASED TO LEVEL 7.
BUT—
BUT THAT'S...
LEVEL 7 IS...

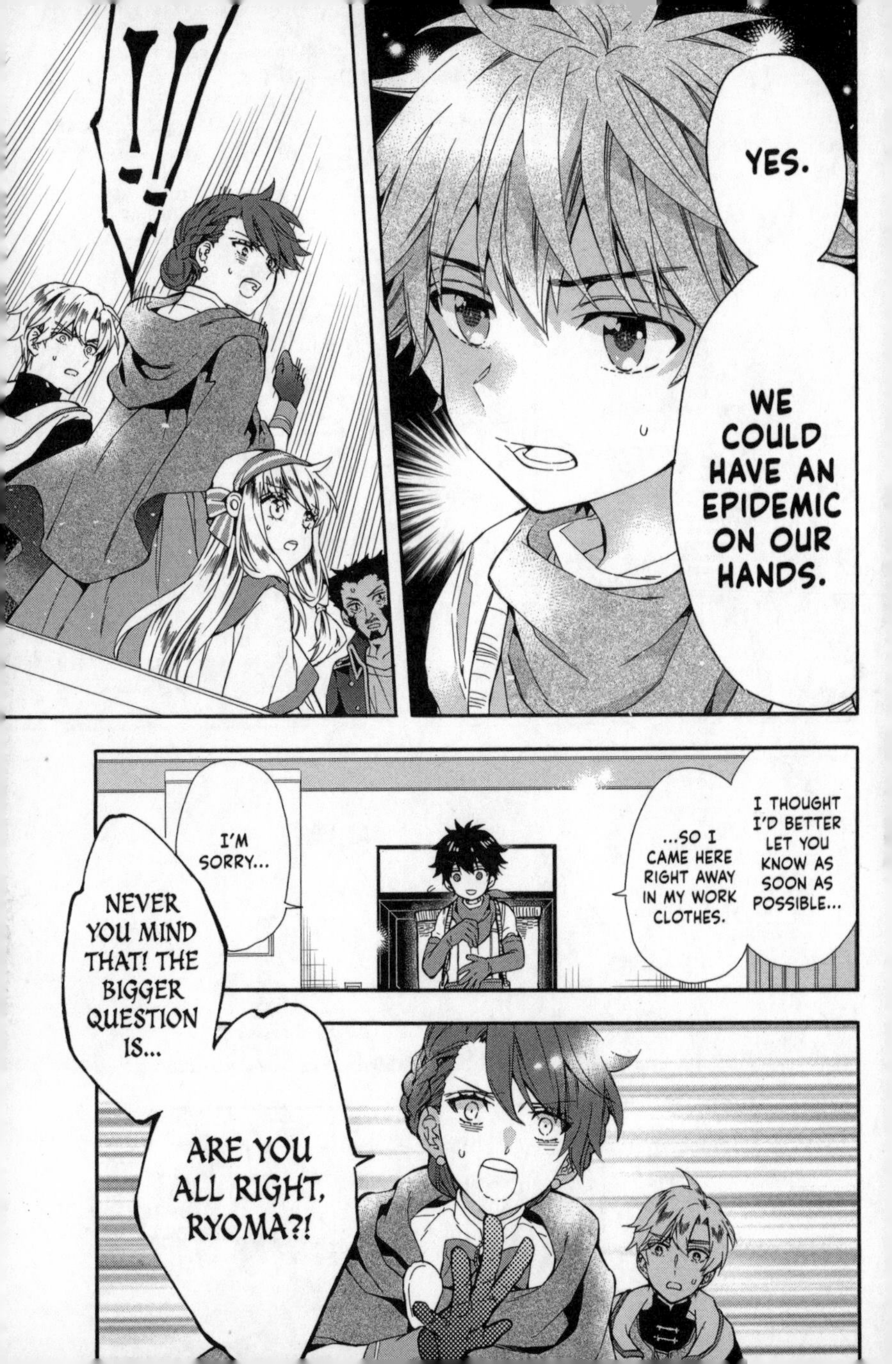
YES.
WE COULD HAVE AN EPIDEMIC ON OUR HANDS.
!!
I THOUGHT I'D BETTER LET YOU KNOW AS SOON AS POSSIBLE...
...SO I CAME HERE RIGHT AWAY IN MY WORK CLOTHES.
I'M SORRY...
NEVER YOU MIND THAT! THE BIGGER QUESTION IS...
ARE YOU ALL RIGHT, RYOMA?!

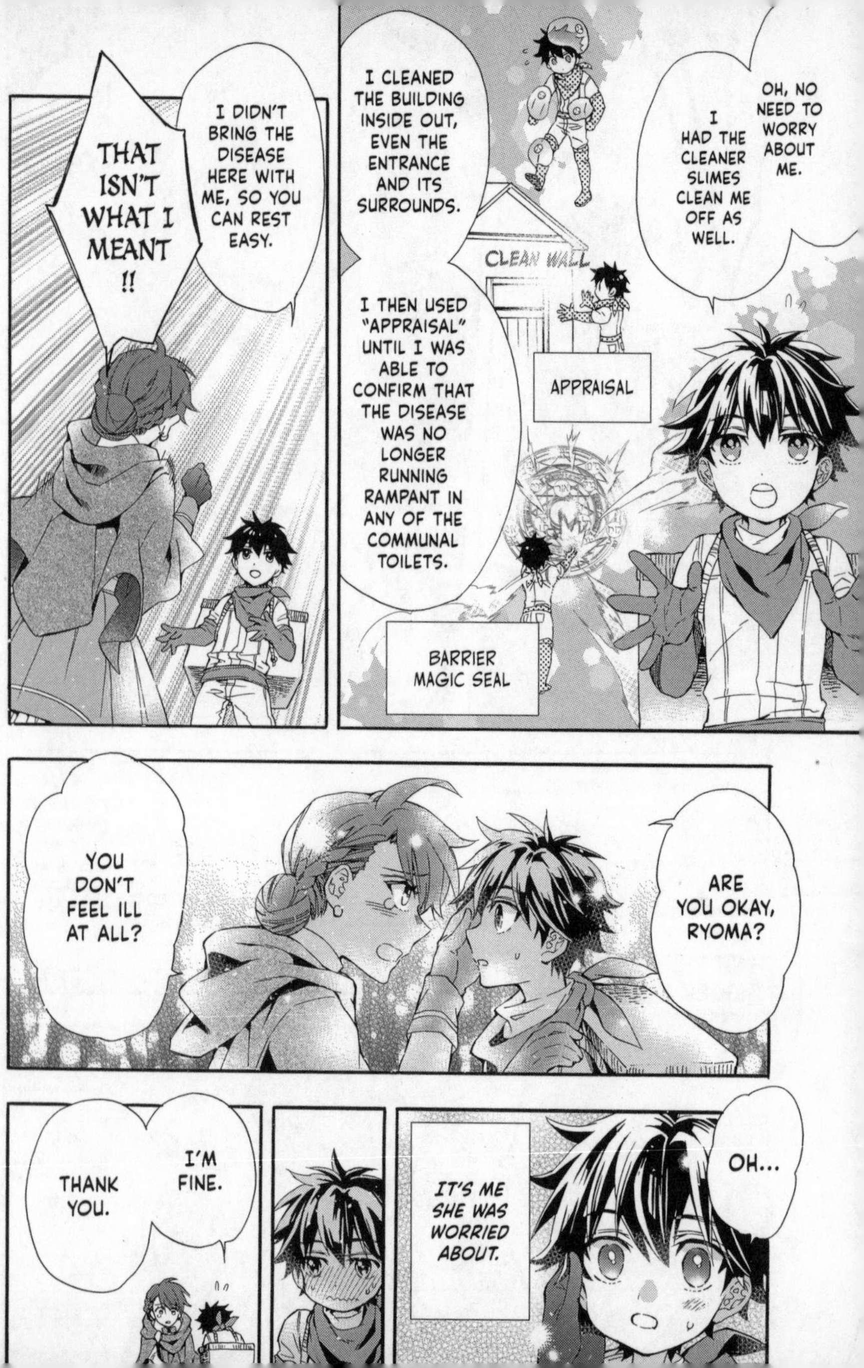
OH, NO NEED TO WORRY ABOUT ME.
I HAD THE CLEANER SLIMES CLEAN ME OFF AS WELL.
I CLEANED THE BUILDING INSIDE OUT, EVEN THE ENTRANCE AND ITS SURROUNDS.
CLEAN WALL
APPRAISAL
I THEN USED "APPRAISAL" UNTIL I WAS ABLE TO CONFIRM THAT THE DISEASE WAS NO LONGER RUNNING RAMPANT IN ANY OF THE COMMUNAL TOILETS.
BARRIER MAGIC SEAL
I DIDN'T BRING THE DISEASE HERE WITH ME, SO YOU CAN REST EASY.
THAT ISN'T WHAT I MEANT!!
ARE YOU OKAY, RYOMA?
YOU DON'T FEEL ILL AT ALL?
OH...
IT'S ME SHE WAS WORRIED ABOUT.
I'M FINE.
THANK YOU.

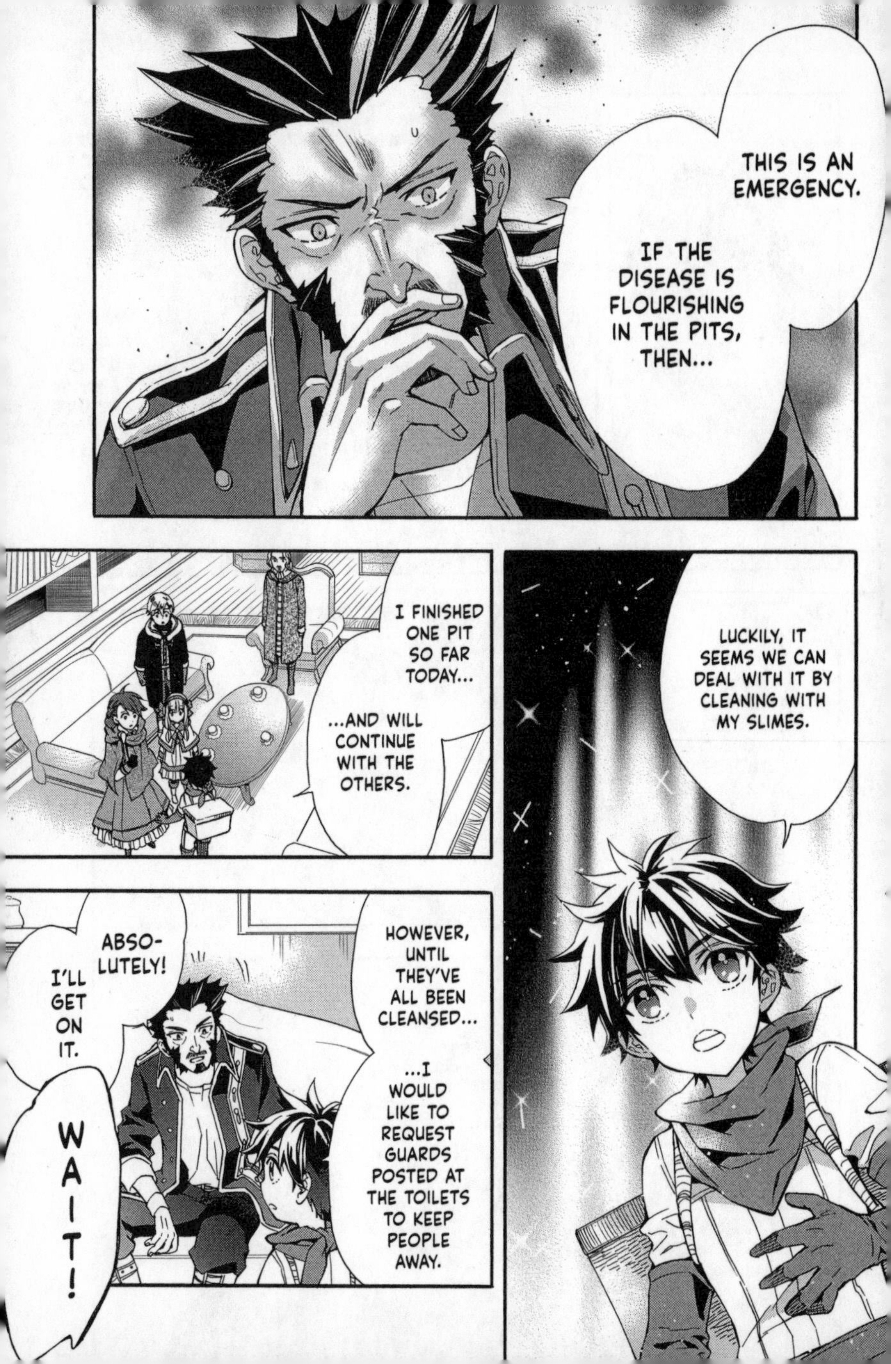
THIS IS AN EMERGENCY.
IF THE DISEASE IS FLOURISHING IN THE PITS, THEN...
LUCKILY, IT SEEMS WE CAN DEAL WITH IT BY CLEANING WITH MY SLIMES.
I FINISHED ONE PIT SO FAR TODAY...
...AND WILL CONTINUE WITH THE OTHERS.
HOWEVER, UNTIL THEY'VE ALL BEEN CLEANSED...
...I WOULD LIKE TO REQUEST GUARDS POSTED AT THE TOILETS TO KEEP PEOPLE AWAY.
ABSO-LUTELY!
I'LL GET ON IT.
WAIT!

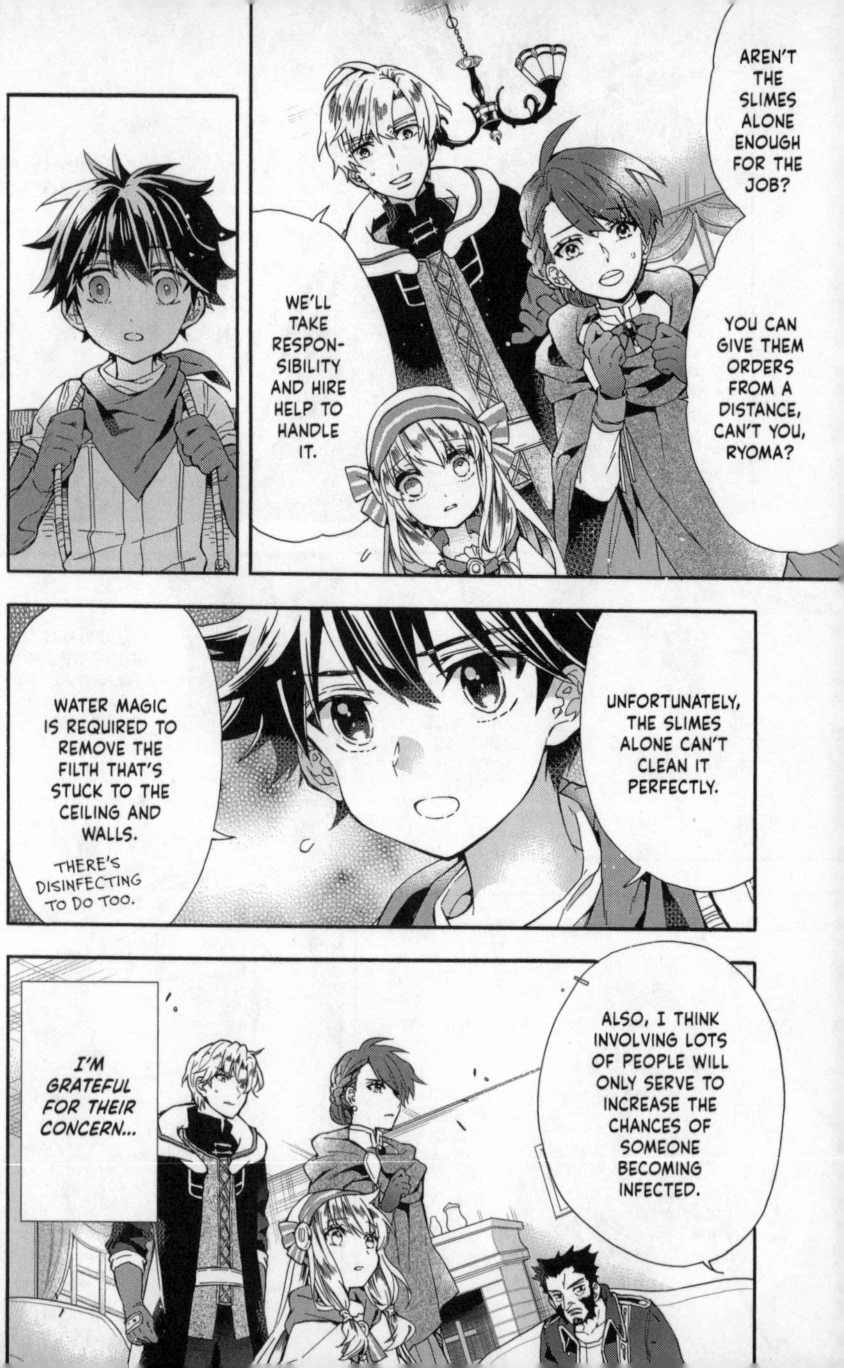
AREN'T THE SLIMES ALONE ENOUGH FOR THE JOB?
YOU CAN GIVE THEM ORDERS FROM A DISTANCE, CAN'T YOU, RYOMA?
WE'LL TAKE RESPON-SIBILITY AND HIRE HELP TO HANDLE IT.
UNFORTUNATELY, THE SLIMES ALONE CAN'T CLEAN IT PERFECTLY.
WATER MAGIC IS REQUIRED TO REMOVE THE FILTH THAT'S STUCK TO THE CEILING AND WALLS.
THERE'S DISINFECTING TO DO TOO.
ALSO, I THINK INVOLVING LOTS OF PEOPLE WILL ONLY SERVE TO INCREASE THE CHANCES OF SOMEONE BECOMING INFECTED.
I'M GRATEFUL FOR THEIR CONCERN...

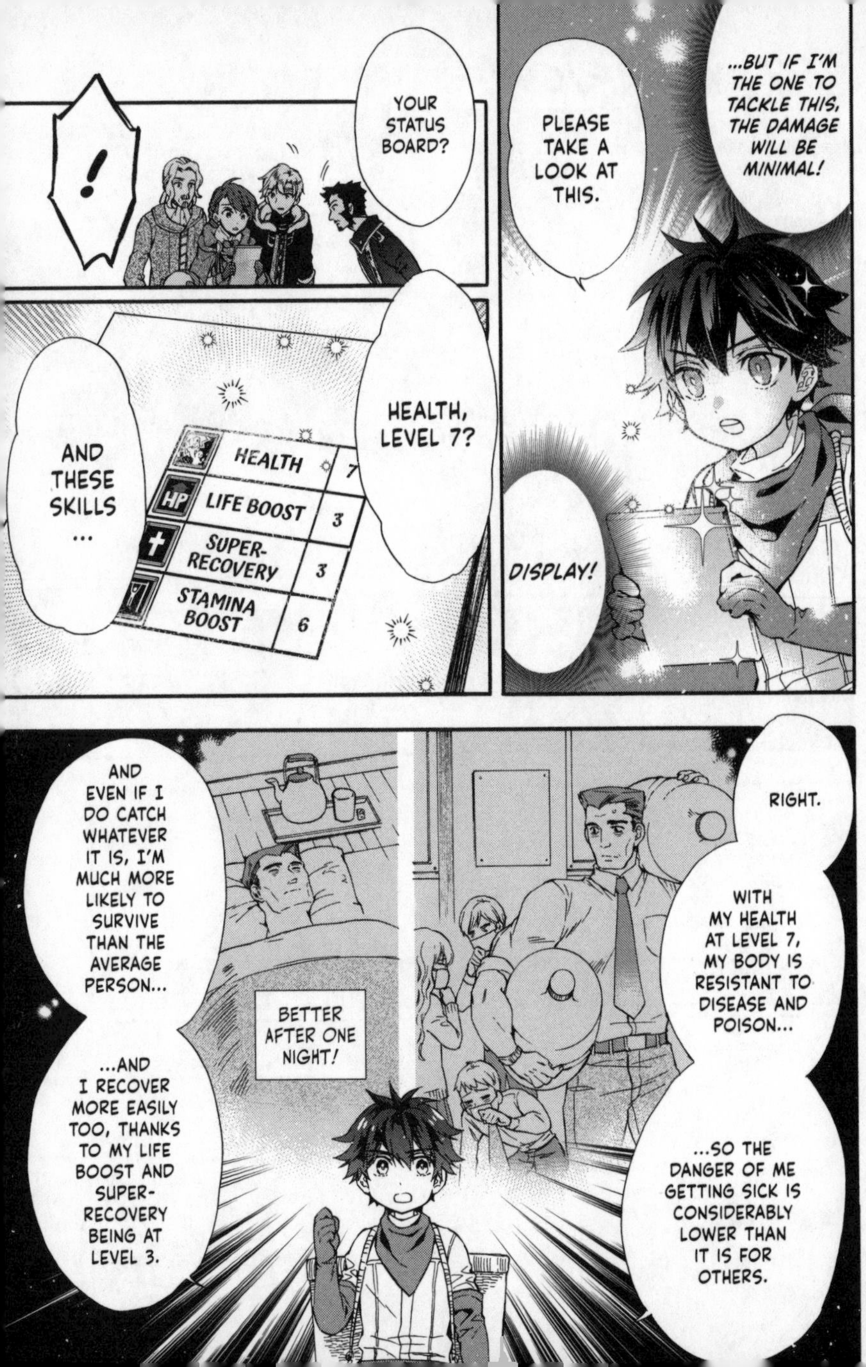
...BUT IF I'M THE ONE TO TACKLE THIS, THE DAMAGE WILL BE MINIMAL!
PLEASE TAKE A LOOK AT THIS.
DISPLAY!
YOUR STATUS BOARD?
!
HEALTH, LEVEL 7?
HEALTH 7
HP LIFE BOOST 3
SUPER-RECOVERY 3
STAMINA BOOST 6
AND THESE SKILLS ...
RIGHT.
WITH MY HEALTH AT LEVEL 7, MY BODY IS RESISTANT TO DISEASE AND POISON...
...SO THE DANGER OF ME GETTING SICK IS CONSIDERABLY LOWER THAN IT IS FOR OTHERS.
AND EVEN IF I DO CATCH WHATEVER IT IS, I'M MUCH MORE LIKELY TO SURVIVE THAN THE AVERAGE PERSON...
...AND I RECOVER MORE EASILY TOO, THANKS TO MY LIFE BOOST AND SUPER-RECOVERY BEING AT LEVEL 3.
BETTER AFTER ONE NIGHT!

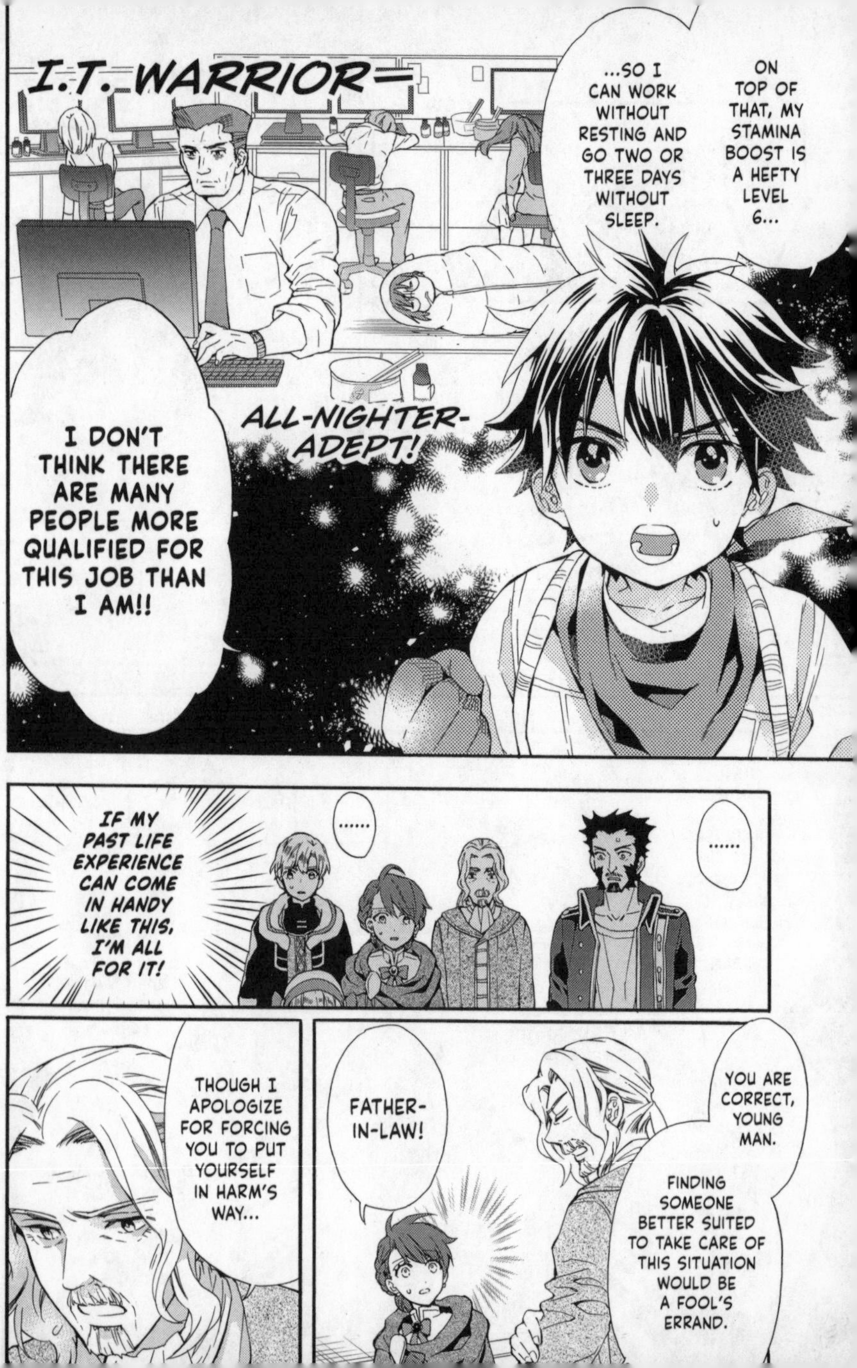
ON TOP OF THAT, MY STAMINA BOOST IS A HEFTY LEVEL 6...
...SO I CAN WORK WITHOUT RESTING AND GO TWO OR THREE DAYS WITHOUT SLEEP.
I.T. WARRIOR—
ALL-NIGHTER-ADEPT!
I DON'T THINK THERE ARE MANY PEOPLE MORE QUALIFIED FOR THIS JOB THAN I AM!!
......
......
IF MY PAST LIFE EXPERIENCE CAN COME IN HANDY LIKE THIS, I'M ALL FOR IT!
YOU ARE CORRECT, YOUNG MAN.
FINDING SOMEONE BETTER SUITED TO TAKE CARE OF THIS SITUATION WOULD BE A FOOL'S ERRAND.
FATHER-IN-LAW!
THOUGH I APOLOGIZE FOR FORCING YOU TO PUT YOURSELF IN HARM'S WAY...

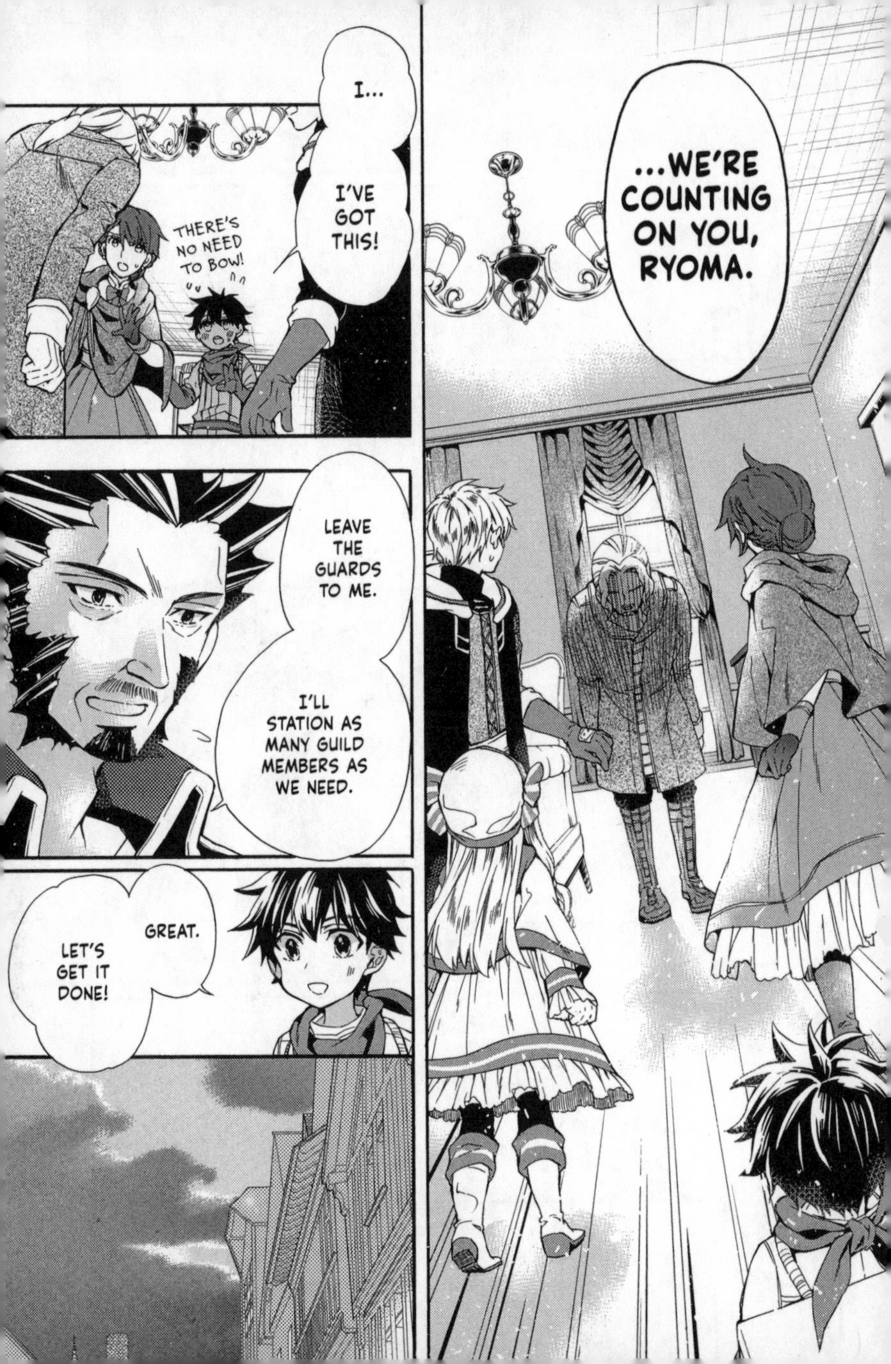
...WE'RE COUNTING ON YOU, RYOMA.
I...
I'VE GOT THIS!
THERE'S NO NEED TO BOW!
LEAVE THE GUARDS TO ME.
I'LL STATION AS MANY GUILD MEMBERS AS WE NEED.
GREAT.
LET'S GET IT DONE!

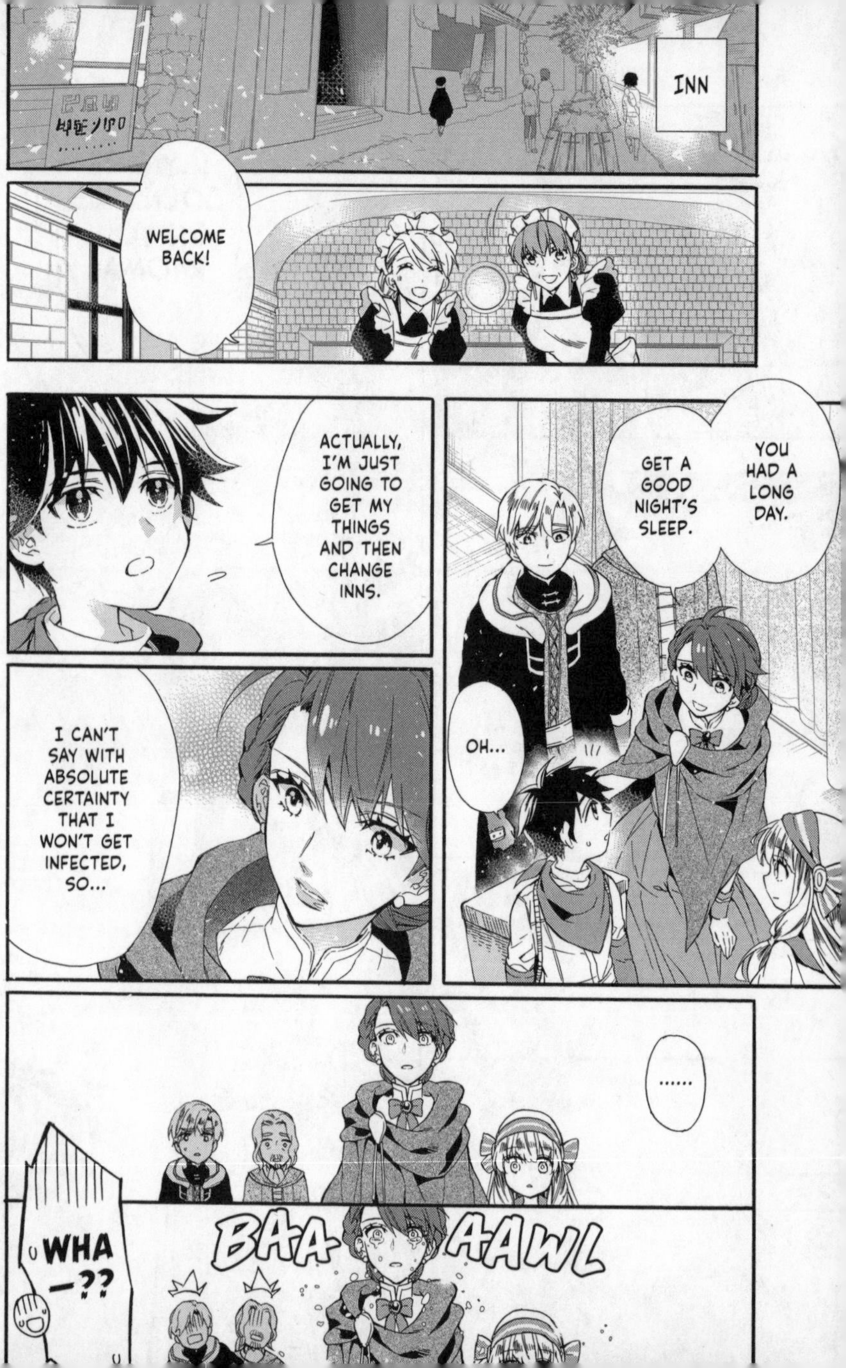
INN
WELCOME BACK!
YOU HAD A LONG DAY.
GET A GOOD NIGHT'S SLEEP.
OH...
ACTUALLY, I'M JUST GOING TO GET MY THINGS AND THEN CHANGE INNS.
I CAN'T SAY WITH ABSOLUTE CERTAINTY THAT I WON'T GET INFECTED, SO...
......
BAA AAWL
WHA—??

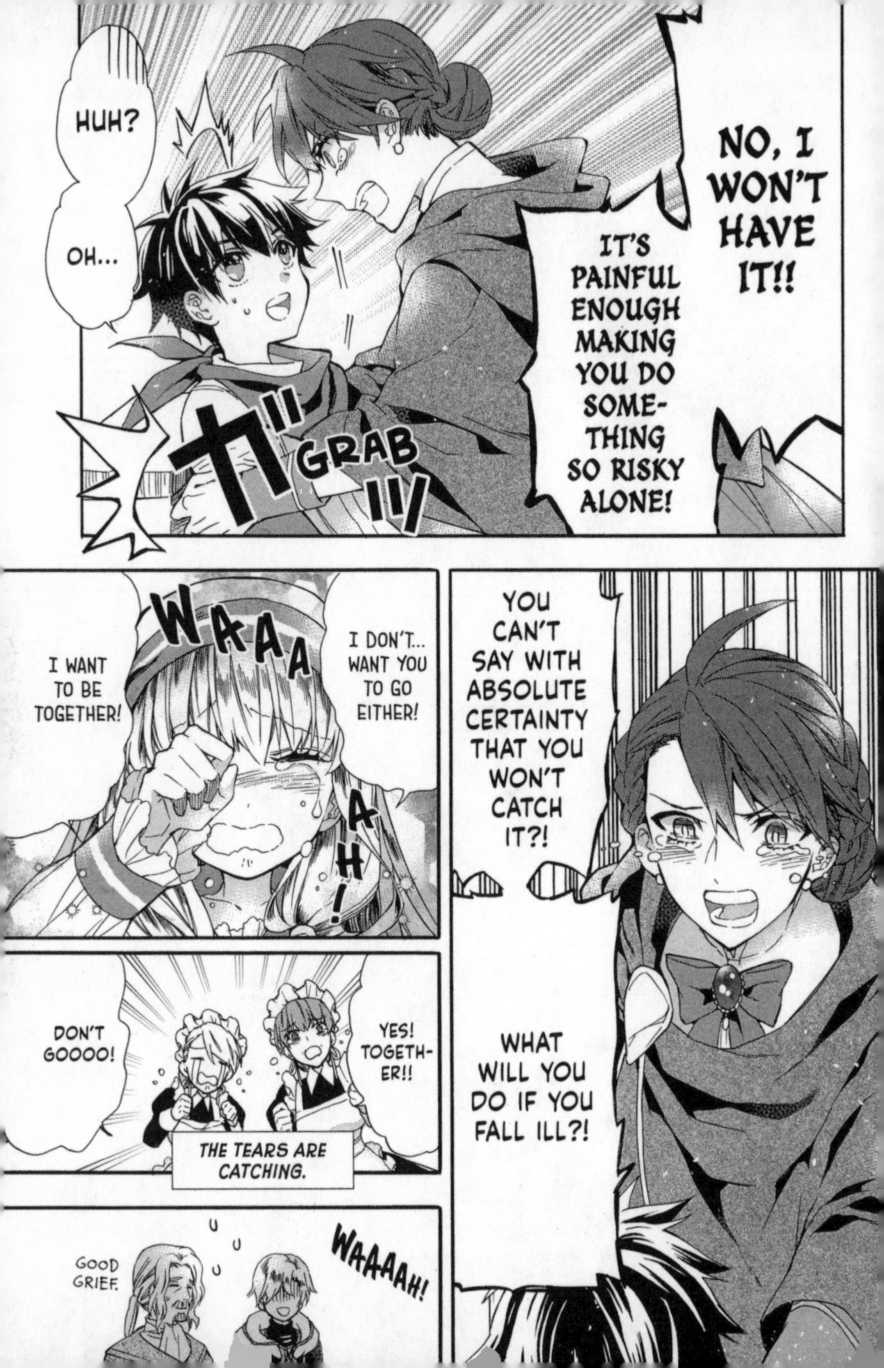
NO, I WON'T HAVE IT!!
IT'S PAINFUL ENOUGH MAKING YOU DO SOME-THING SO RISKY ALONE!
HUH?
OH...
GRAB
YOU CAN'T SAY WITH ABSOLUTE CERTAINTY THAT YOU WON'T CATCH IT?!
WHAT WILL YOU DO IF YOU FALL ILL?!
I DON'T... WANT YOU TO GO EITHER!
WAAAAH!
I WANT TO BE TOGETHER!
YES! TOGETH-ER!!
DON'T GOOOO!
THE TEARS ARE CATCHING.
WAAAAH!
GOOD GRIEF.

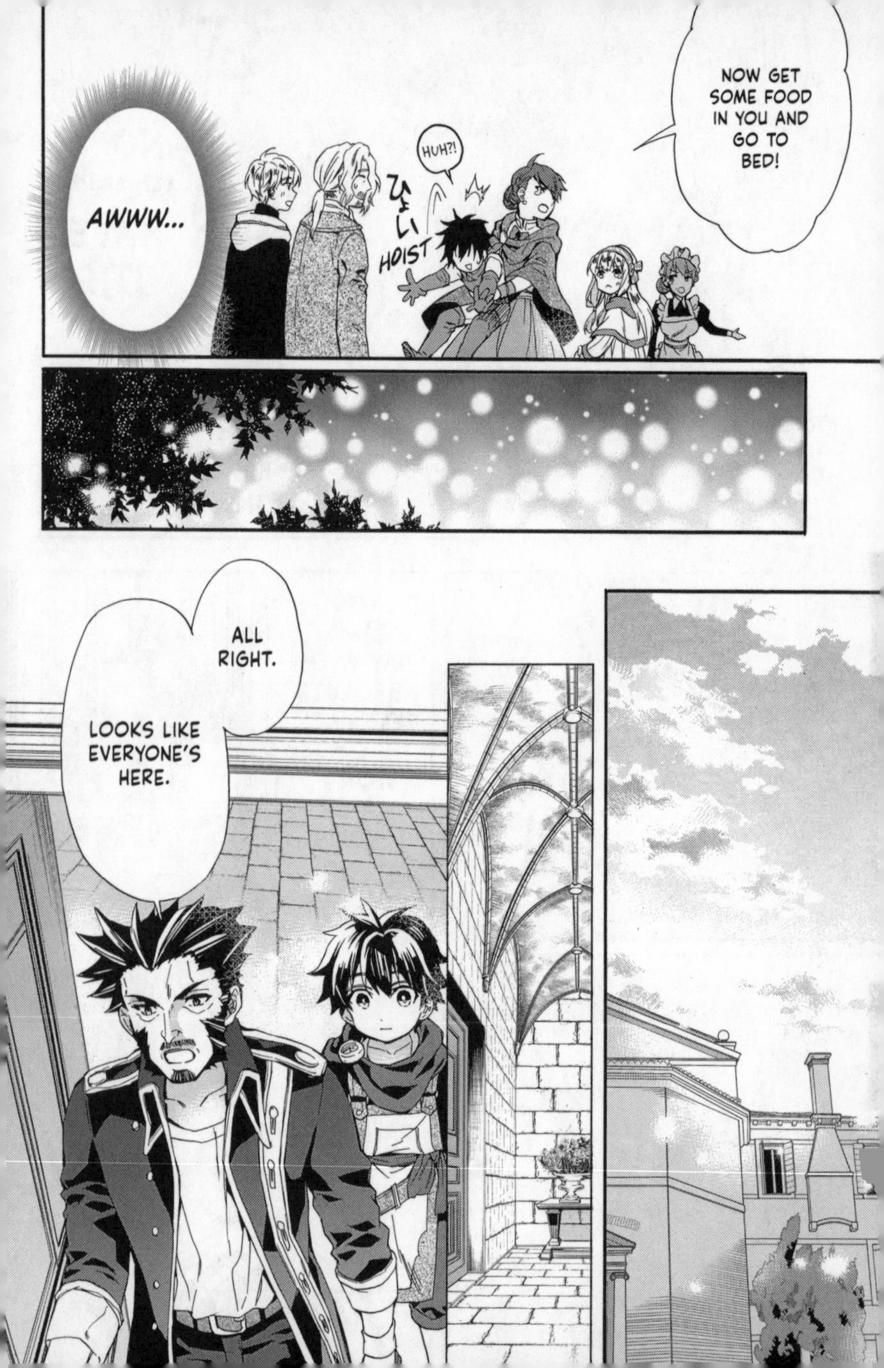
NOW GET SOME FOOD IN YOU AND GO TO BED!
HUH?!
ひょい
HOIST
AWWW...
ALL RIGHT.
LOOKS LIKE EVERYONE'S HERE.

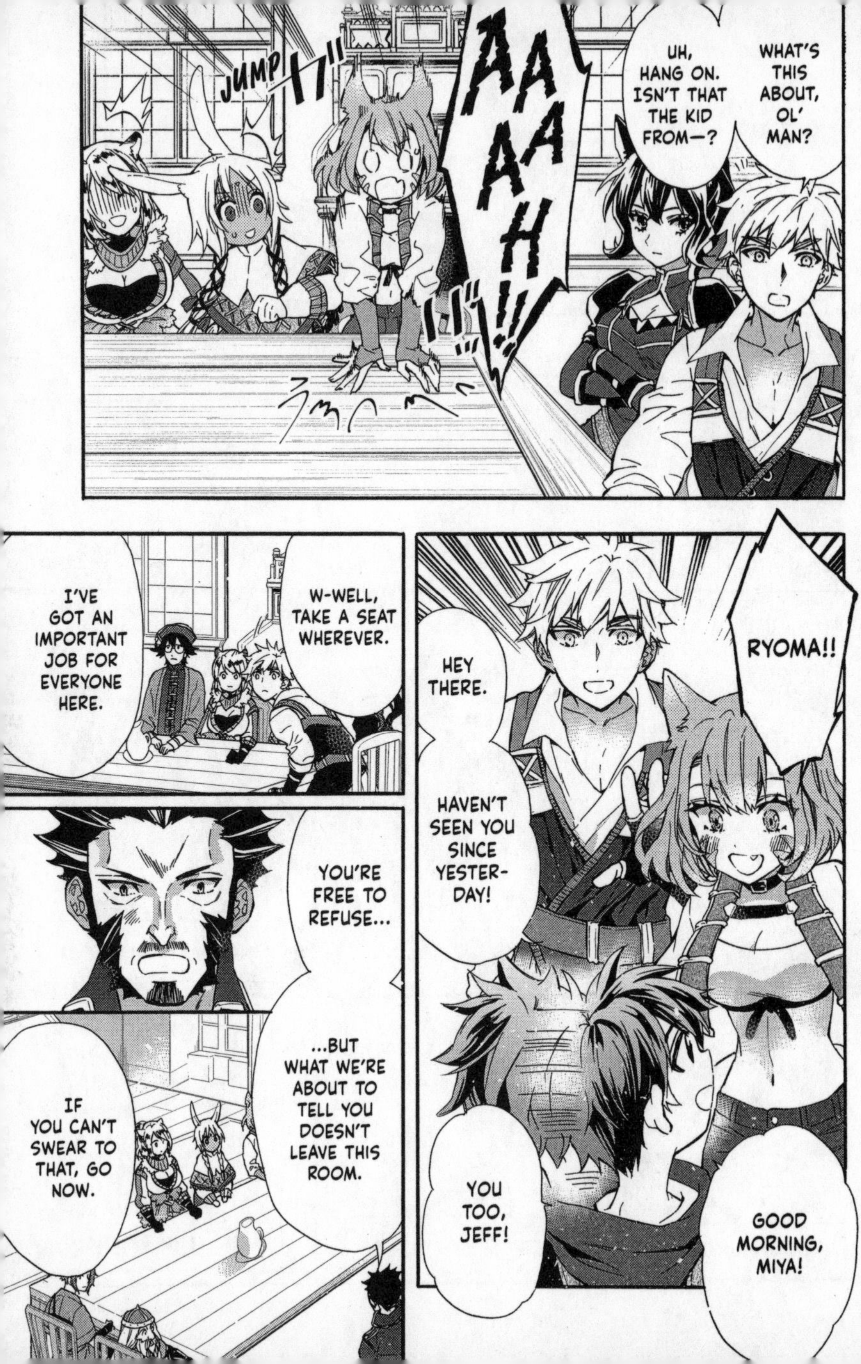
WHAT'S THIS ABOUT, OL' MAN?
UH, HANG ON. ISN'T THAT THE KID FROM—?
AAAAH!!
JUMP
RYOMA!!
HEY THERE.
HAVEN'T SEEN YOU SINCE YESTER-DAY!
GOOD MORNING, MIYA!
YOU TOO, JEFF!
W-WELL, TAKE A SEAT WHEREVER.
I'VE GOT AN IMPORTANT JOB FOR EVERYONE HERE.
YOU'RE FREE TO REFUSE...
...BUT WHAT WE'RE ABOUT TO TELL YOU DOESN'T LEAVE THIS ROOM.
IF YOU CAN'T SWEAR TO THAT, GO NOW.

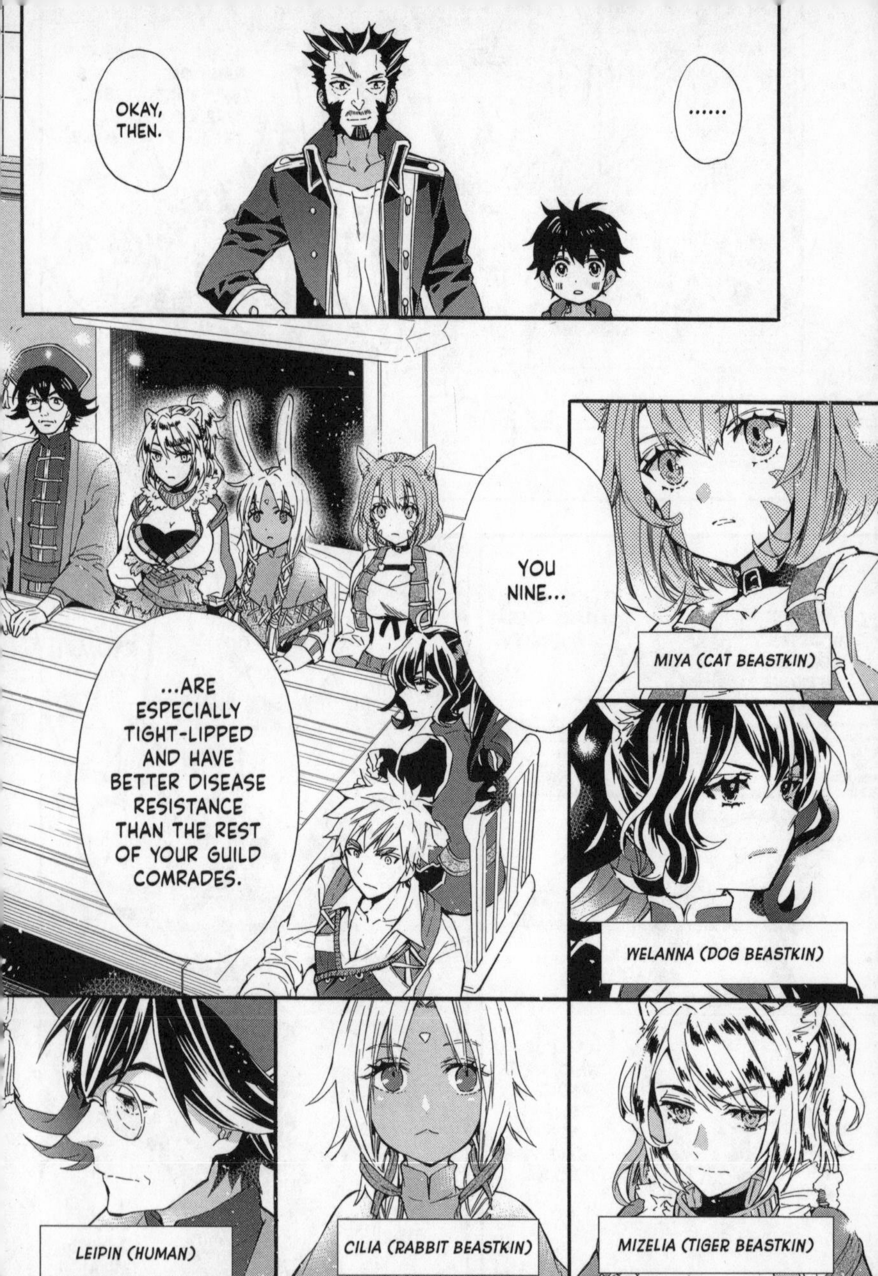
......
OKAY, THEN.
MIYA (CAT BEASTKIN)
WELANNA (DOG BEASTKIN)
YOU NINE...
...ARE ESPECIALLY TIGHT-LIPPED AND HAVE BETTER DISEASE RESISTANCE THAN THE REST OF YOUR GUILD COMRADES.
MIZELIA (TIGER BEASTKIN)
CILIA (RABBIT BEASTKIN)
LEIPIN (HUMAN)

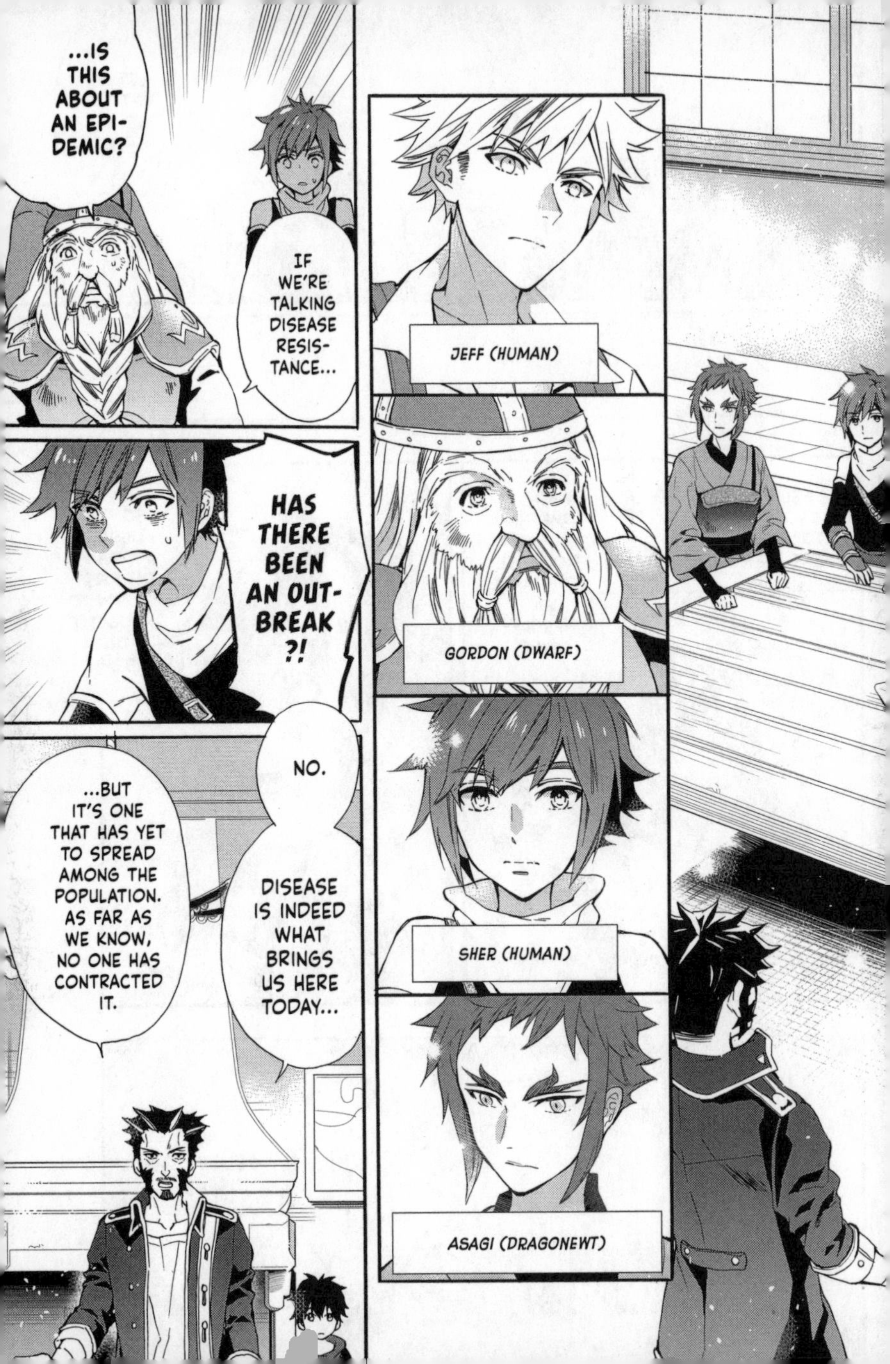
JEFF (HUMAN)
GORDON (DWARF)
SHER (HUMAN)
ASAGI (DRAGONEWT)
IF WE'RE TALKING DISEASE RESISTANCE...
...IS THIS ABOUT AN EPIDEMIC?
HAS THERE BEEN AN OUTBREAK?!
NO.
DISEASE IS INDEED WHAT BRINGS US HERE TODAY...
...BUT IT'S ONE THAT HAS YET TO SPREAD AMONG THE POPULATION. AS FAR AS WE KNOW, NO ONE HAS CONTRACTED IT.

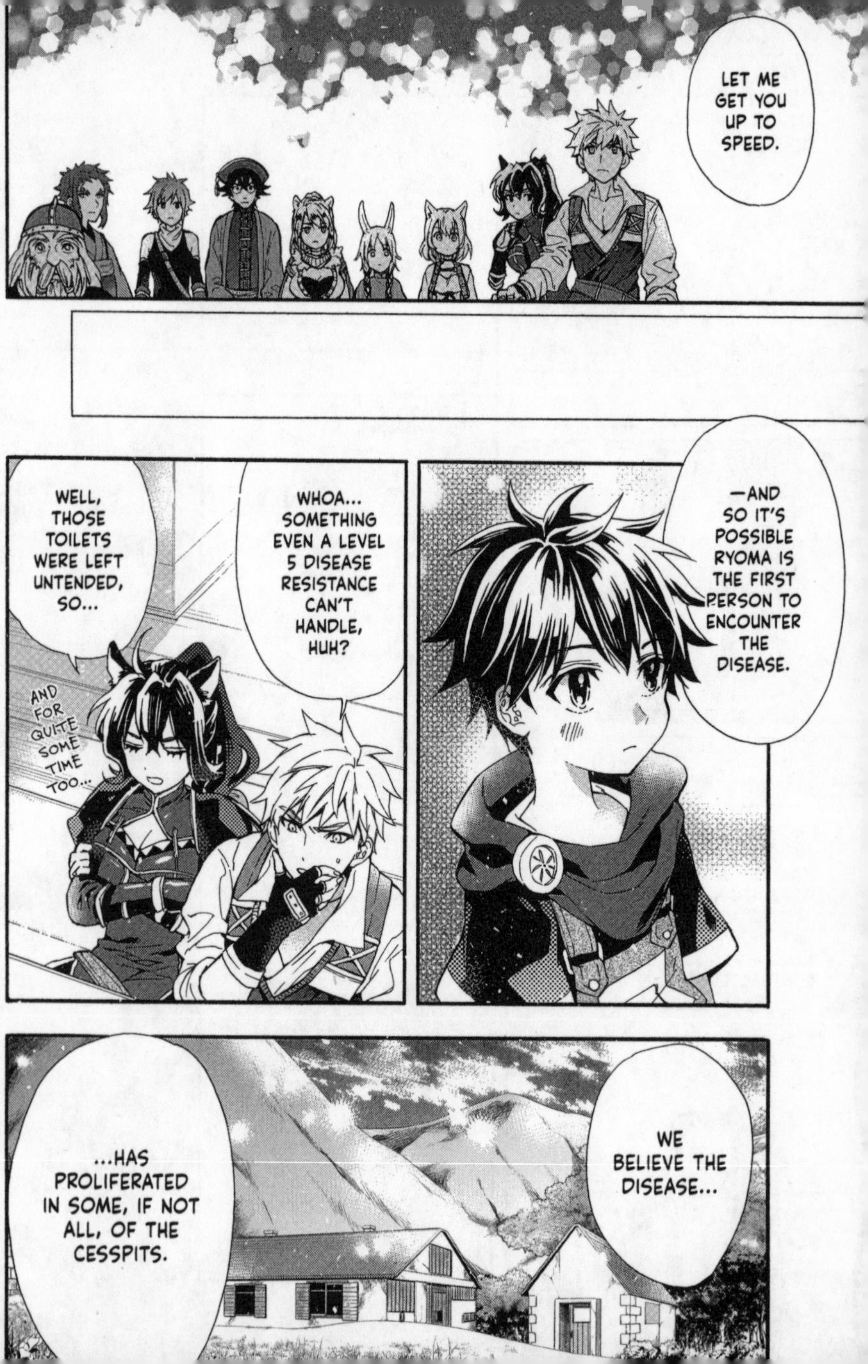
LET ME GET YOU UP TO SPEED.
—AND SO IT'S POSSIBLE RYOMA IS THE FIRST PERSON TO ENCOUNTER THE DISEASE.
WHOA... SOMETHING EVEN A LEVEL 5 DISEASE RESISTANCE CAN'T HANDLE, HUH?
WELL, THOSE TOILETS WERE LEFT UNTENDED, SO...
AND FOR QUITE SOME TIME TOO...
WE BELIEVE THE DISEASE...
...HAS PROLIFERATED IN SOME, IF NOT ALL, OF THE CESSPITS.

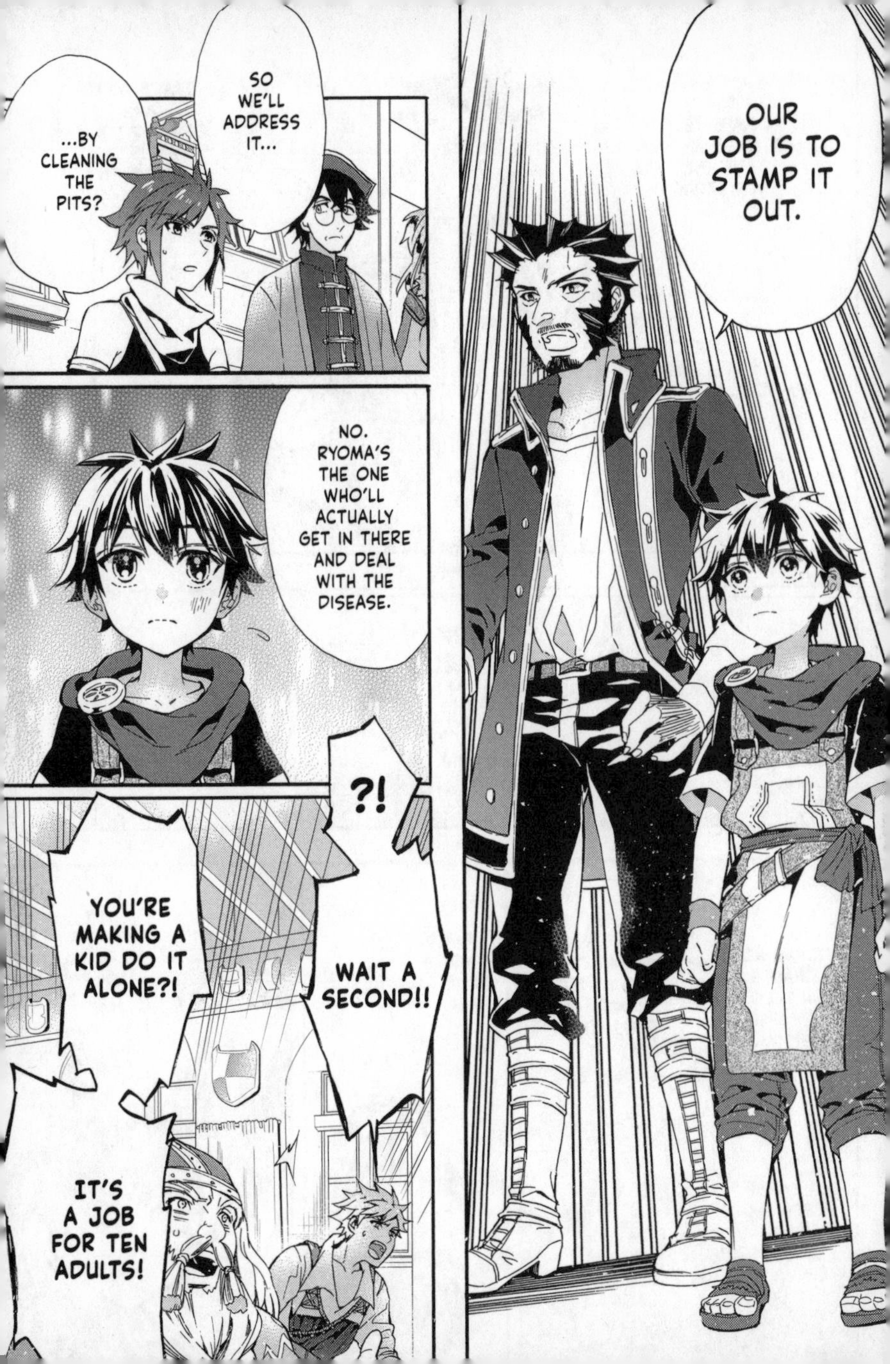
OUR JOB IS TO STAMP IT OUT.
SO WE'LL ADDRESS IT...
...BY CLEANING THE PITS?
NO. RYOMA'S THE ONE WHO'LL ACTUALLY GET IN THERE AND DEAL WITH THE DISEASE.
?!
WAIT A SECOND!!
YOU'RE MAKING A KID DO IT ALONE?!
IT'S A JOB FOR TEN ADULTS!

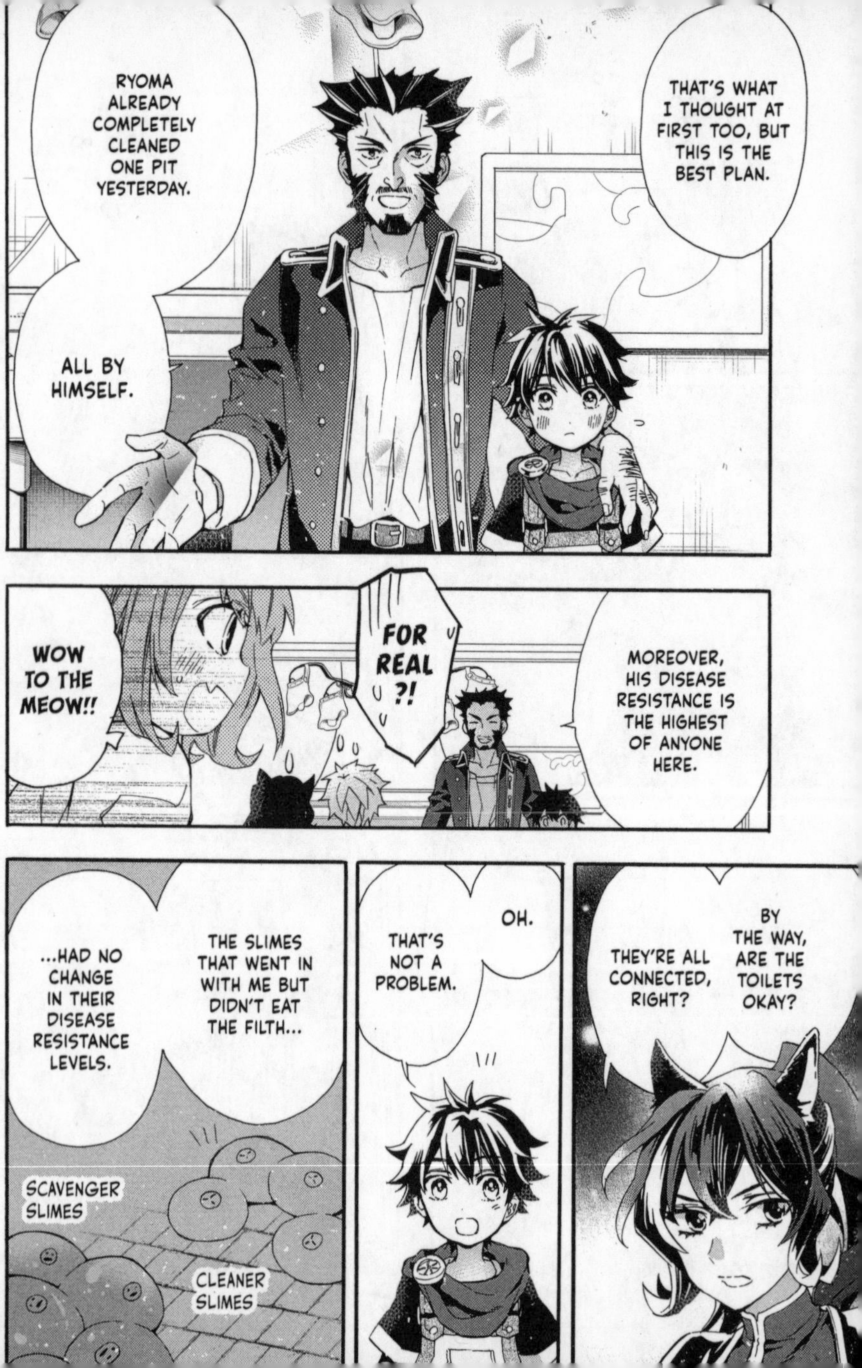
THAT'S WHAT I THOUGHT AT FIRST TOO, BUT THIS IS THE BEST PLAN.
RYOMA ALREADY COMPLETELY CLEANED ONE PIT YESTERDAY.
ALL BY HIMSELF.
MOREOVER, HIS DISEASE RESISTANCE IS THE HIGHEST OF ANYONE HERE.
FOR REAL ?!
WOW TO THE MEOW!!
BY THE WAY, ARE THE TOILETS OKAY?
THEY'RE ALL CONNECTED, RIGHT?
OH.
THAT'S NOT A PROBLEM.
THE SLIMES THAT WENT IN WITH ME BUT DIDN'T EAT THE FILTH...
...HAD NO CHANGE IN THEIR DISEASE RESISTANCE LEVELS.
SCAVENGER SLIMES
CLEANER SLIMES

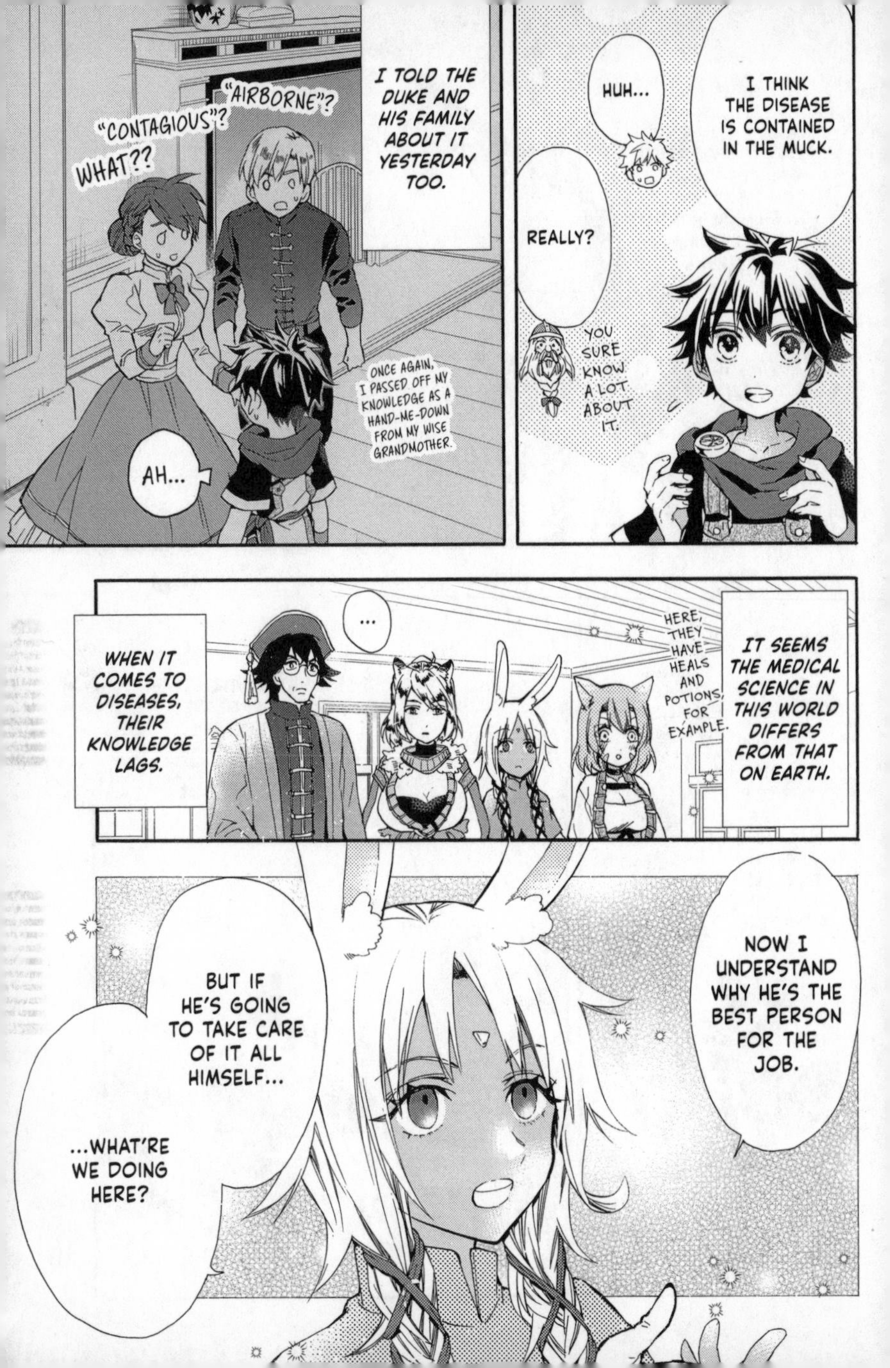
I THINK THE DISEASE IS CONTAINED IN THE MUCK.
HUH...
REALLY?
YOU SURE KNOW A LOT ABOUT IT.
I TOLD THE DUKE AND HIS FAMILY ABOUT IT YESTERDAY TOO.
"AIRBORNE"?
"CONTAGIOUS"?
WHAT??
ONCE AGAIN, I PASSED OFF MY KNOWLEDGE AS A HAND-ME-DOWN FROM MY WISE GRANDMOTHER.
AH...
IT SEEMS THE MEDICAL SCIENCE IN THIS WORLD DIFFERS FROM THAT ON EARTH.
HERE, THEY HAVE HEALS AND POTIONS, FOR EXAMPLE.
...
WHEN IT COMES TO DISEASES, THEIR KNOWLEDGE LAGS.
NOW I UNDERSTAND WHY HE'S THE BEST PERSON FOR THE JOB.
BUT IF HE'S GOING TO TAKE CARE OF IT ALL HIMSELF...
...WHAT'RE WE DOING HERE?

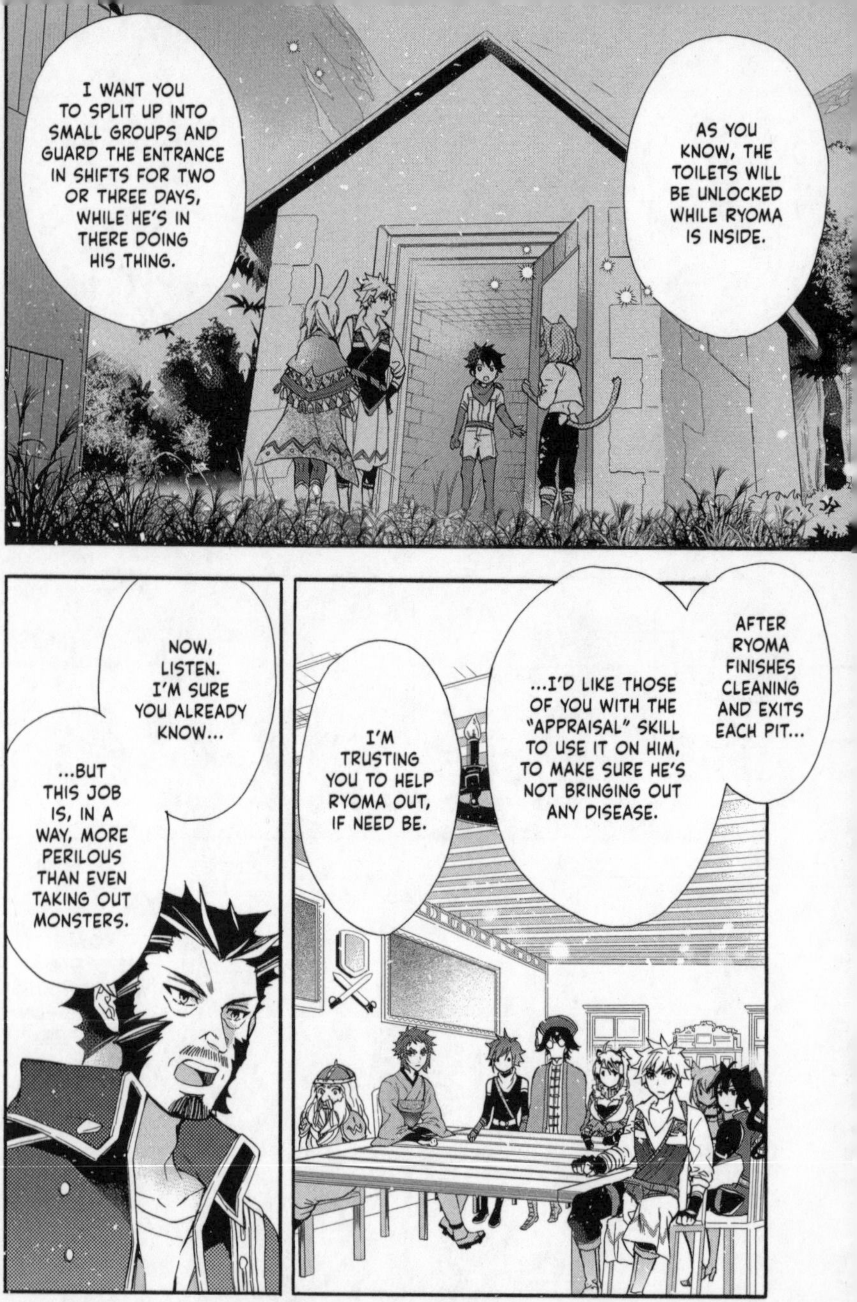
AS YOU KNOW, THE TOILETS WILL BE UNLOCKED WHILE RYOMA IS INSIDE.
I WANT YOU TO SPLIT UP INTO SMALL GROUPS AND GUARD THE ENTRANCE IN SHIFTS FOR TWO OR THREE DAYS, WHILE HE'S IN THERE DOING HIS THING.
AFTER RYOMA FINISHES CLEANING AND EXITS EACH PIT...
...I'D LIKE THOSE OF YOU WITH THE "APPRAISAL" SKILL TO USE IT ON HIM, TO MAKE SURE HE'S NOT BRINGING OUT ANY DISEASE.
I'M TRUSTING YOU TO HELP RYOMA OUT, IF NEED BE.
NOW, LISTEN. I'M SURE YOU ALREADY KNOW...
...BUT THIS JOB IS, IN A WAY, MORE PERILOUS THAN EVEN TAKING OUT MONSTERS.

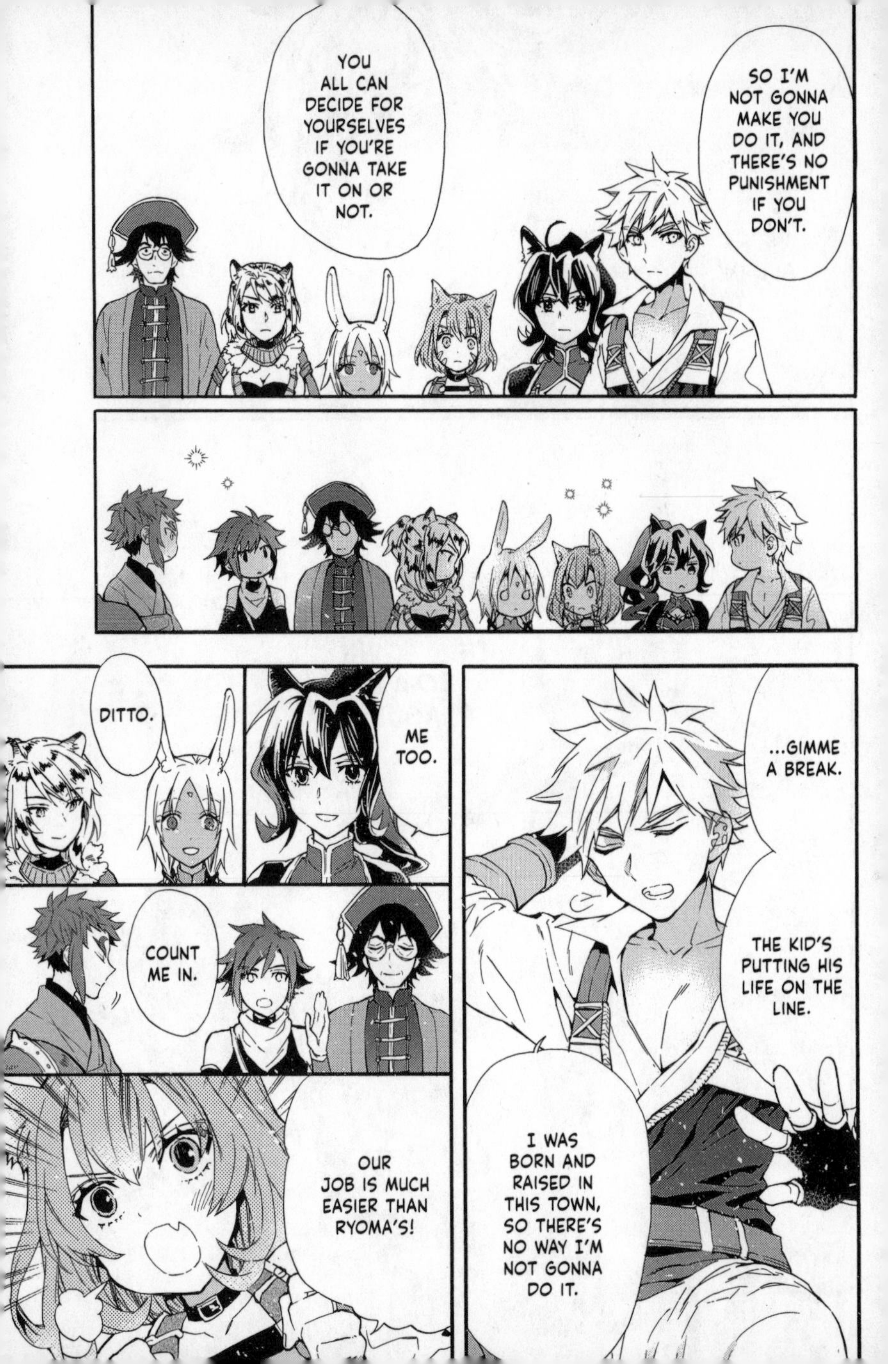
SO I'M NOT GONNA MAKE YOU DO IT, AND THERE'S NO PUNISHMENT IF YOU DON'T.
YOU ALL CAN DECIDE FOR YOURSELVES IF YOU'RE GONNA TAKE IT ON OR NOT.
...GIMME A BREAK.
THE KID'S PUTTING HIS LIFE ON THE LINE.
I WAS BORN AND RAISED IN THIS TOWN, SO THERE'S NO WAY I'M NOT GONNA DO IT.
ME TOO.
DITTO.
COUNT ME IN.
OUR JOB IS MUCH EASIER THAN RYOMA'S!

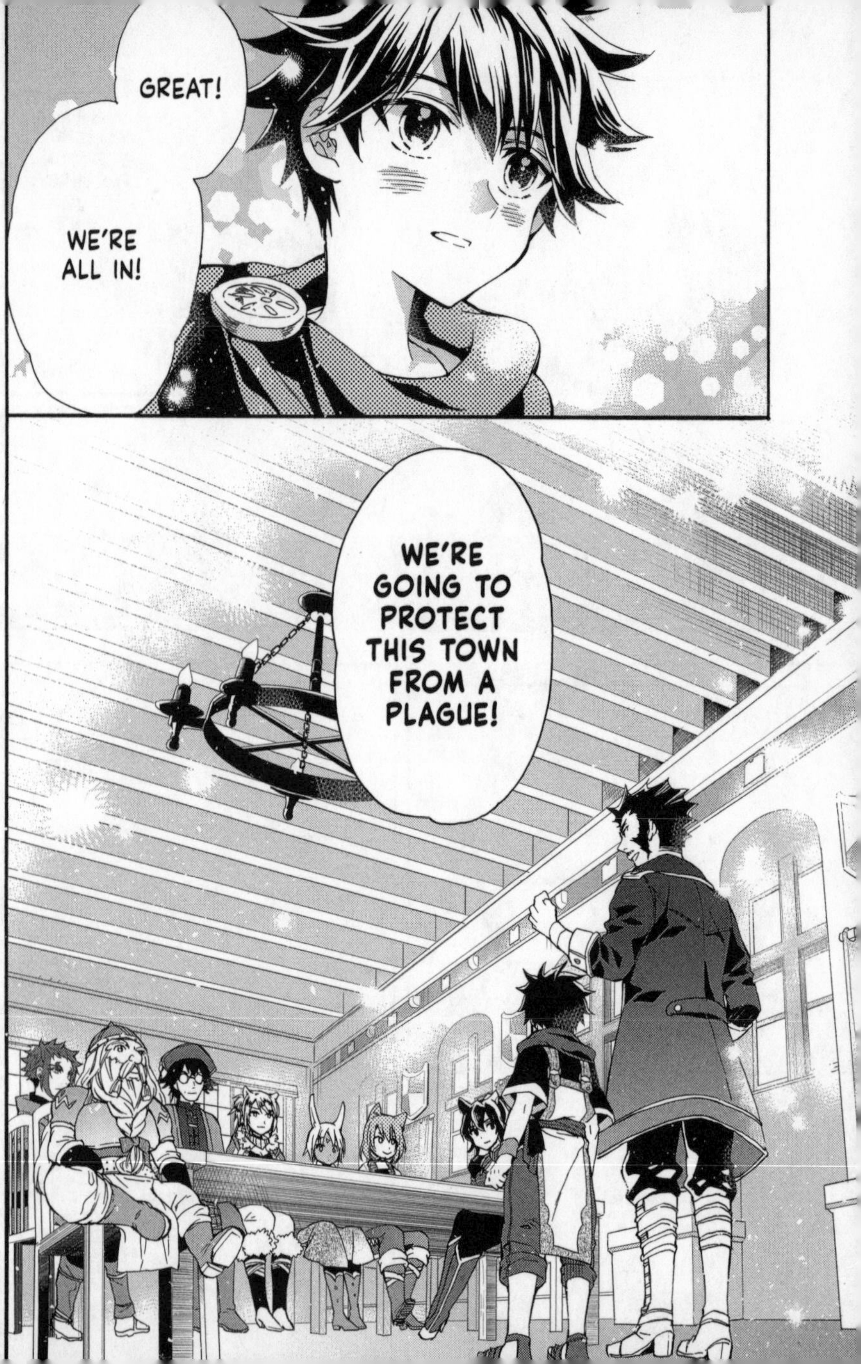
GREAT!
WE'RE ALL IN!
WE'RE GOING TO PROTECT THIS TOWN FROM A PLAGUE!

Chapter 11: Cleanup Work

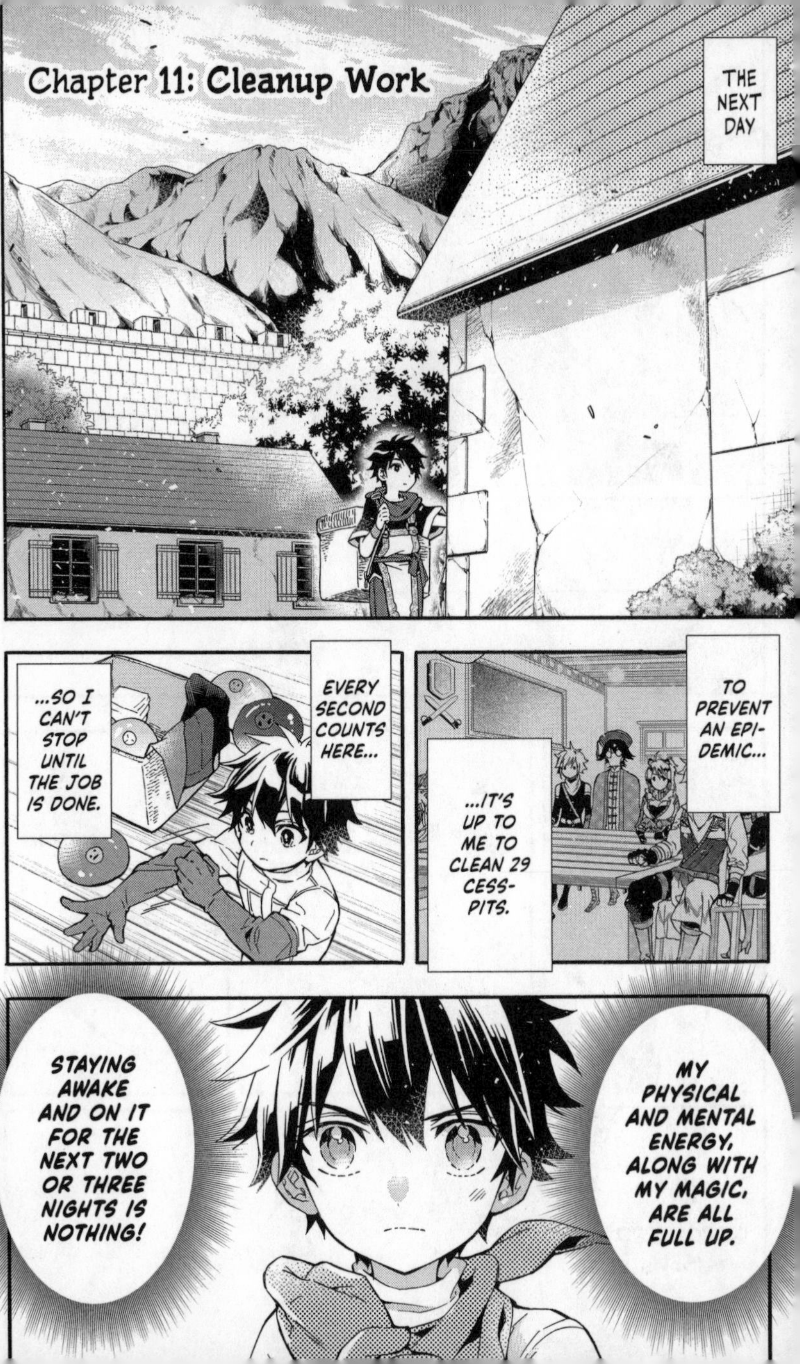
THE NEXT DAY
TO PREVENT AN EPI-DEMIC...
...IT'S UP TO ME TO CLEAN 29 CESS-PITS.
EVERY SECOND COUNTS HERE...
...SO I CAN'T STOP UNTIL THE JOB IS DONE.
MY PHYSICAL AND MENTAL ENERGY, ALONG WITH MY MAGIC, ARE ALL FULL UP.
STAYING AWAKE AND ON IT FOR THE NEXT TWO OR THREE NIGHTS IS NOTHING!

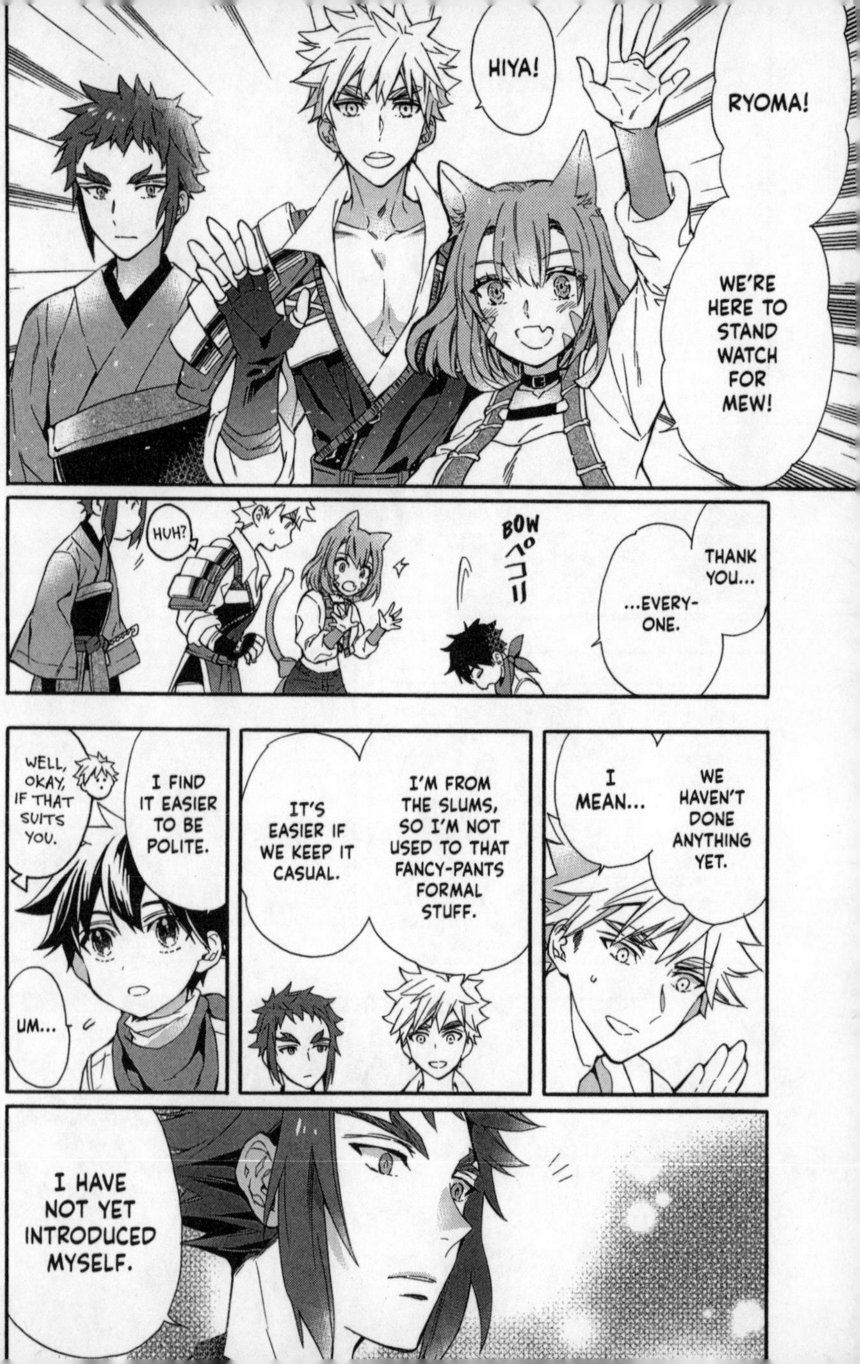
RYOMA!
HIYA!
WE'RE HERE TO STAND WATCH FOR MEW!
THANK YOU...
...EVERY-ONE.
BOW
ペコリ
HUH?
WE HAVEN'T DONE ANYTHING YET.
I MEAN...
I'M FROM THE SLUMS, SO I'M NOT USED TO THAT FANCY-PANTS FORMAL STUFF.
IT'S EASIER IF WE KEEP IT CASUAL.
I FIND IT EASIER TO BE POLITE.
WELL, OKAY, IF THAT SUITS YOU.
UM...
I HAVE NOT YET INTRODUCED MYSELF.

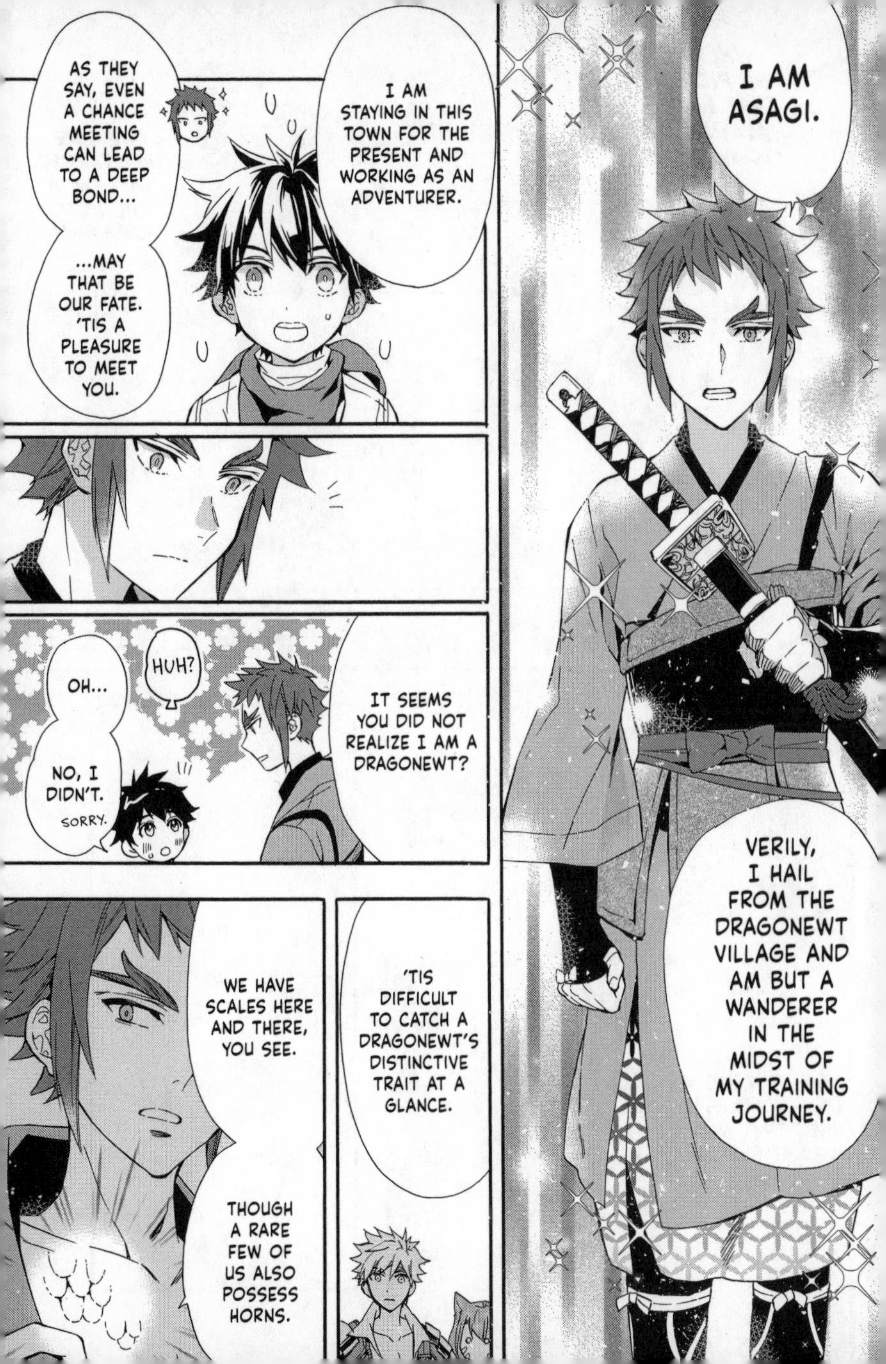
I AM ASAGI.
VERILY, I HAIL FROM THE DRAGONEWT VILLAGE AND AM BUT A WANDERER IN THE MIDST OF MY TRAINING JOURNEY.
I AM STAYING IN THIS TOWN FOR THE PRESENT AND WORKING AS AN ADVENTURER.
AS THEY SAY, EVEN A CHANCE MEETING CAN LEAD TO A DEEP BOND...
...MAY THAT BE OUR FATE. 'TIS A PLEASURE TO MEET YOU.
IT SEEMS YOU DID NOT REALIZE I AM A DRAGONEWT?
HUH?
OH...
NO, I DIDN'T.
SORRY.
'TIS DIFFICULT TO CATCH A DRAGONEWT'S DISTINCTIVE TRAIT AT A GLANCE.
WE HAVE SCALES HERE AND THERE, YOU SEE.
THOUGH A RARE FEW OF US ALSO POSSESS HORNS.

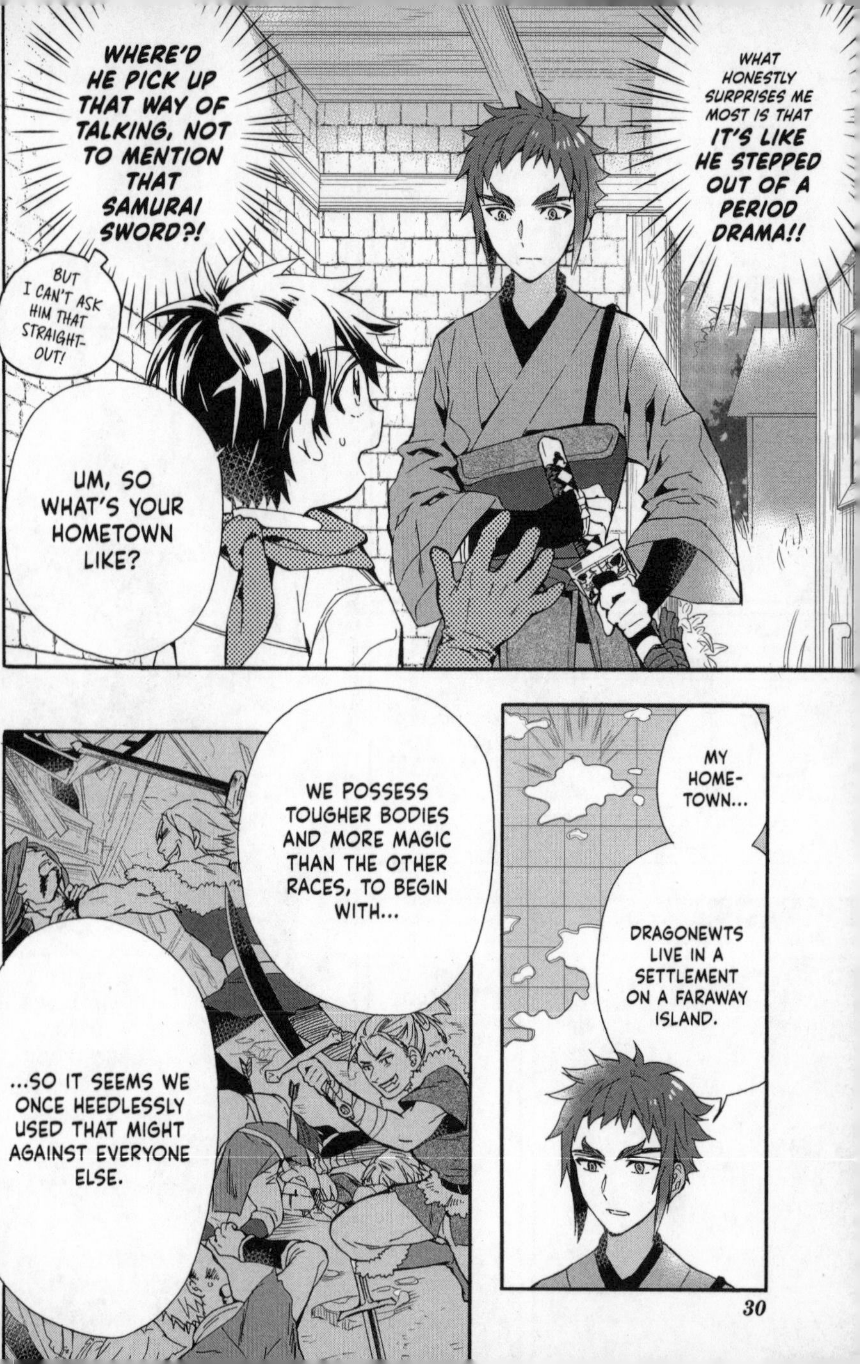
WHAT HONESTLY SURPRISES ME MOST IS THAT IT'S LIKE HE STEPPED OUT OF A PERIOD DRAMA!!
WHERE'D HE PICK UP THAT WAY OF TALKING, NOT TO MENTION THAT SAMURAI SWORD?!
BUT I CAN'T ASK HIM THAT STRAIGHT-OUT!
UM, SO WHAT'S YOUR HOMETOWN LIKE?
MY HOME-TOWN...
DRAGONEWTS LIVE IN A SETTLEMENT ON A FARAWAY ISLAND.
WE POSSESS TOUGHER BODIES AND MORE MAGIC THAN THE OTHER RACES, TO BEGIN WITH...
...SO IT SEEMS WE ONCE HEEDLESSLY USED THAT MIGHT AGAINST EVERYONE ELSE.

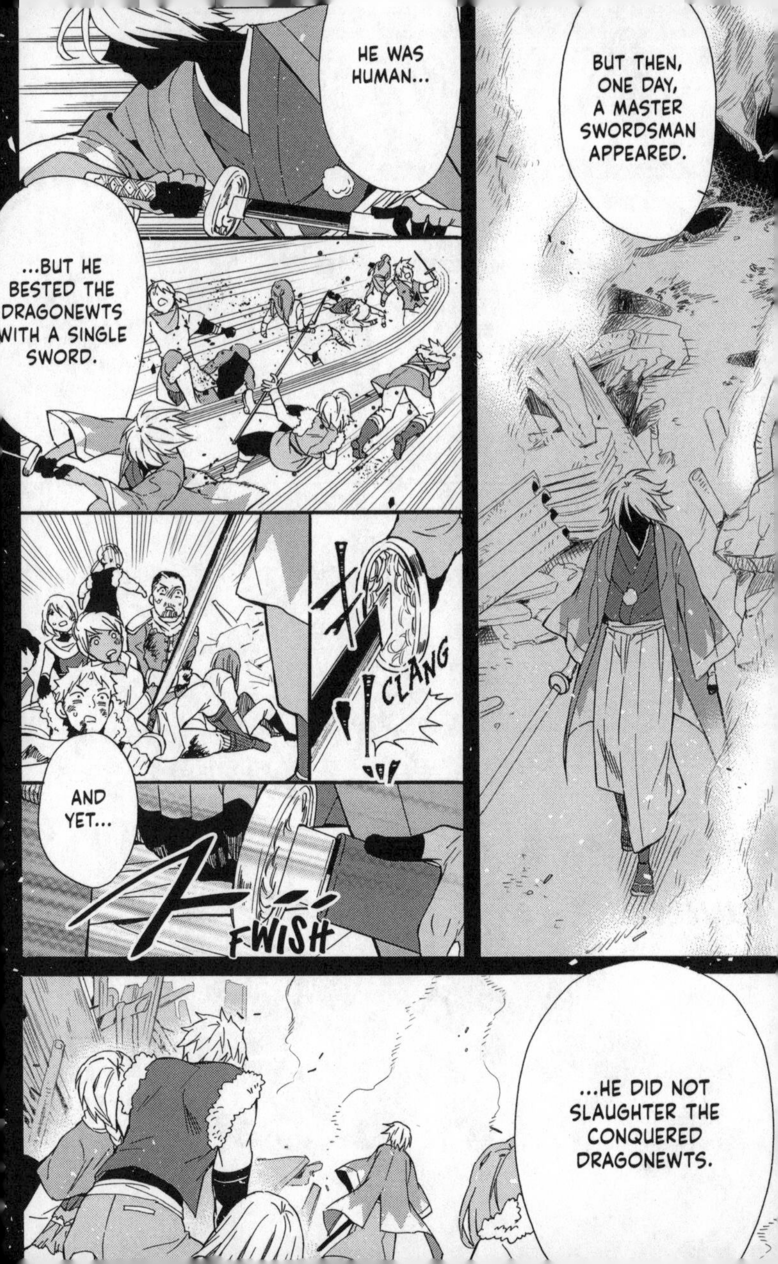
BUT THEN, ONE DAY, A MASTER SWORDSMAN APPEARED.
HE WAS HUMAN...
...BUT HE BESTED THE DRAGONEWTS WITH A SINGLE SWORD.
CLANG
AND YET...
FWISH
...HE DID NOT SLAUGHTER THE CONQUERED DRAGONEWTS.

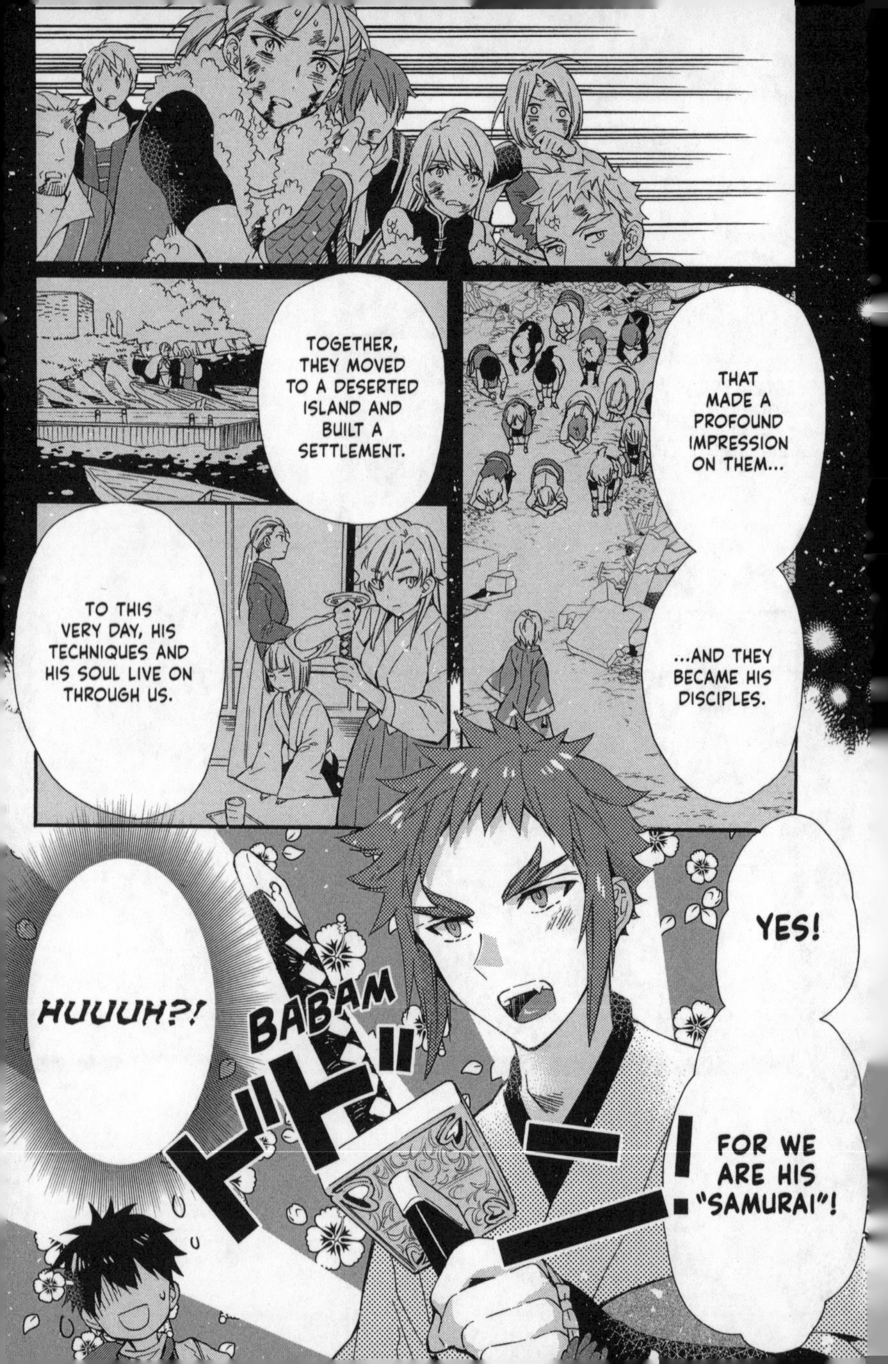
THAT MADE A PROFOUND IMPRESSION ON THEM...
...AND THEY BECAME HIS DISCIPLES.
TOGETHER, THEY MOVED TO A DESERTED ISLAND AND BUILT A SETTLEMENT.
TO THIS VERY DAY, HIS TECHNIQUES AND HIS SOUL LIVE ON THROUGH US.
YES!
FOR WE ARE HIS "SAMURAI"!
BABAM
HUUUH?!

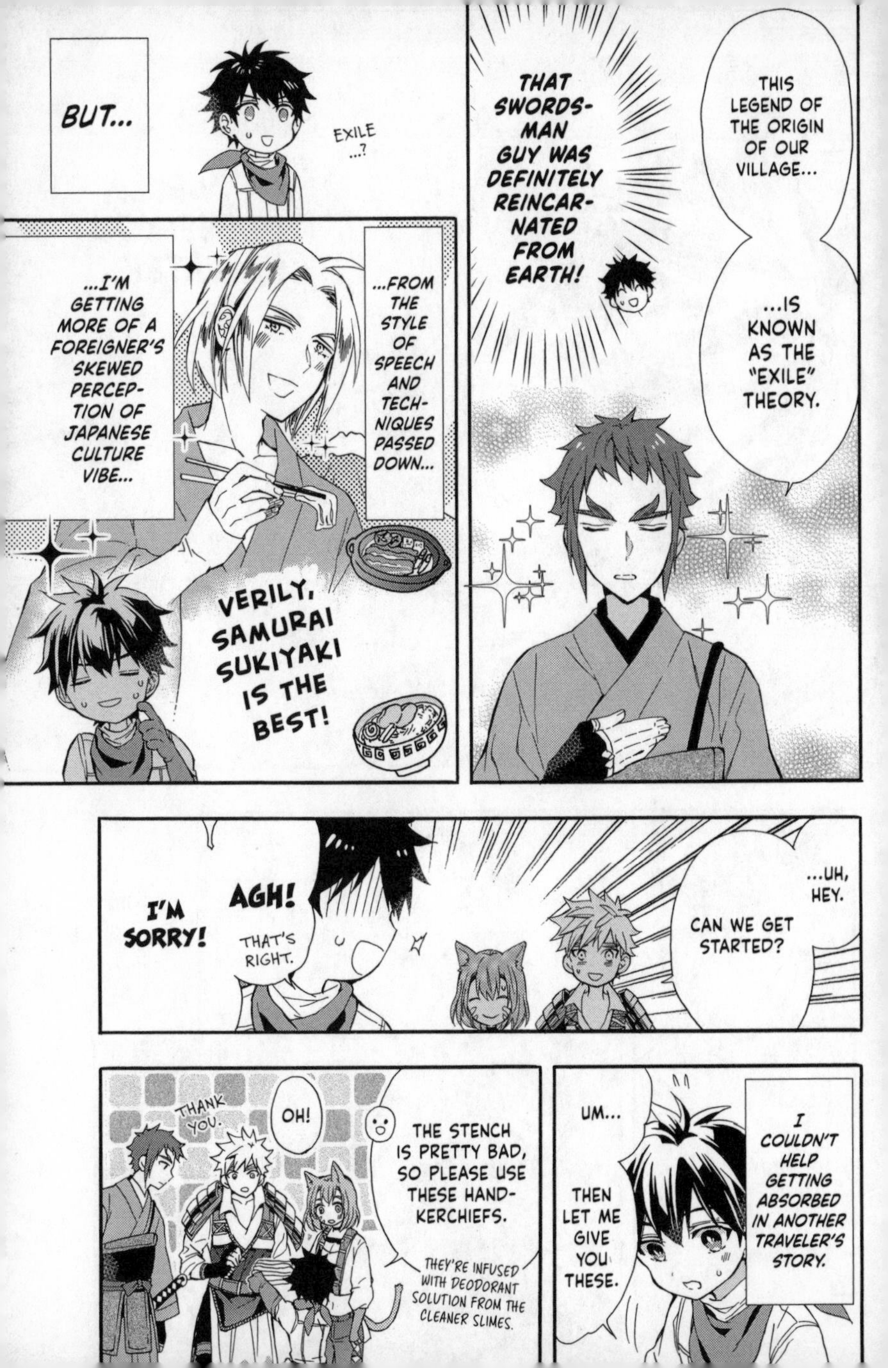
THIS LEGEND OF THE ORIGIN OF OUR VILLAGE...
...IS KNOWN AS THE "EXILE" THEORY.
THAT SWORDS-MAN GUY WAS DEFINITELY REINCAR-NATED FROM EARTH!
BUT...
EXILE ...?
...FROM THE STYLE OF SPEECH AND TECH-NIQUES PASSED DOWN...
...I'M GETTING MORE OF A FOREIGNER'S SKEWED PERCEP-TION OF JAPANESE CULTURE VIBE...
VERILY, SAMURAI SUKIYAKI IS THE BEST!
...UH, HEY.
CAN WE GET STARTED?
AGH!
THAT'S RIGHT.
I'M SORRY!
I COULDN'T HELP GETTING ABSORBED IN ANOTHER TRAVELER'S STORY.
UM...
THEN LET ME GIVE YOU THESE.
THE STENCH IS PRETTY BAD, SO PLEASE USE THESE HAND-KERCHIEFS.
THEY'RE INFUSED WITH DEODORANT SOLUTION FROM THE CLEANER SLIMES.
OH!
THANK YOU.

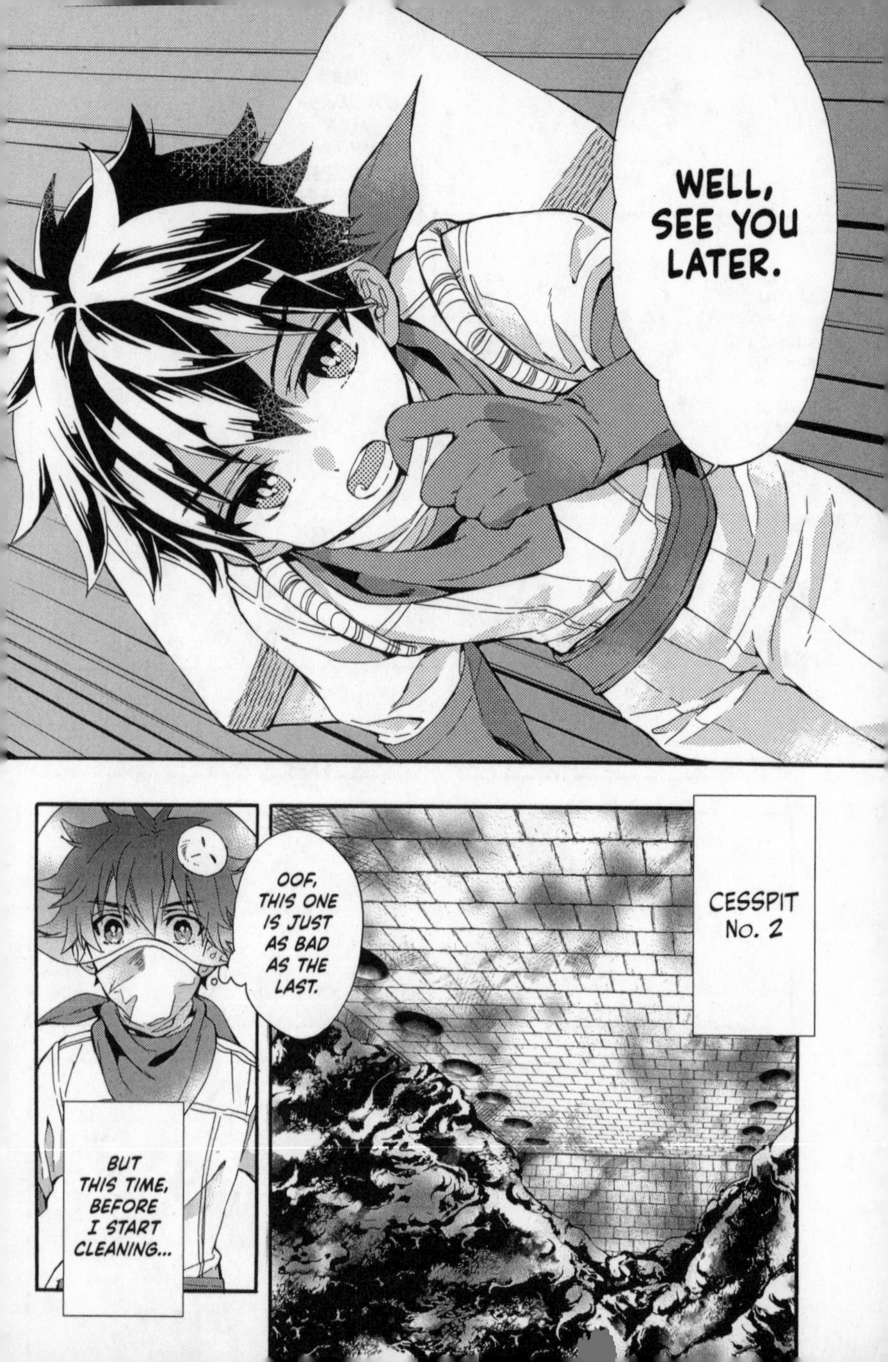
WELL, SEE YOU LATER.
CESSPIT No. 2
OOF, THIS ONE IS JUST AS BAD AS THE LAST.
BUT THIS TIME, BEFORE I START CLEANING...

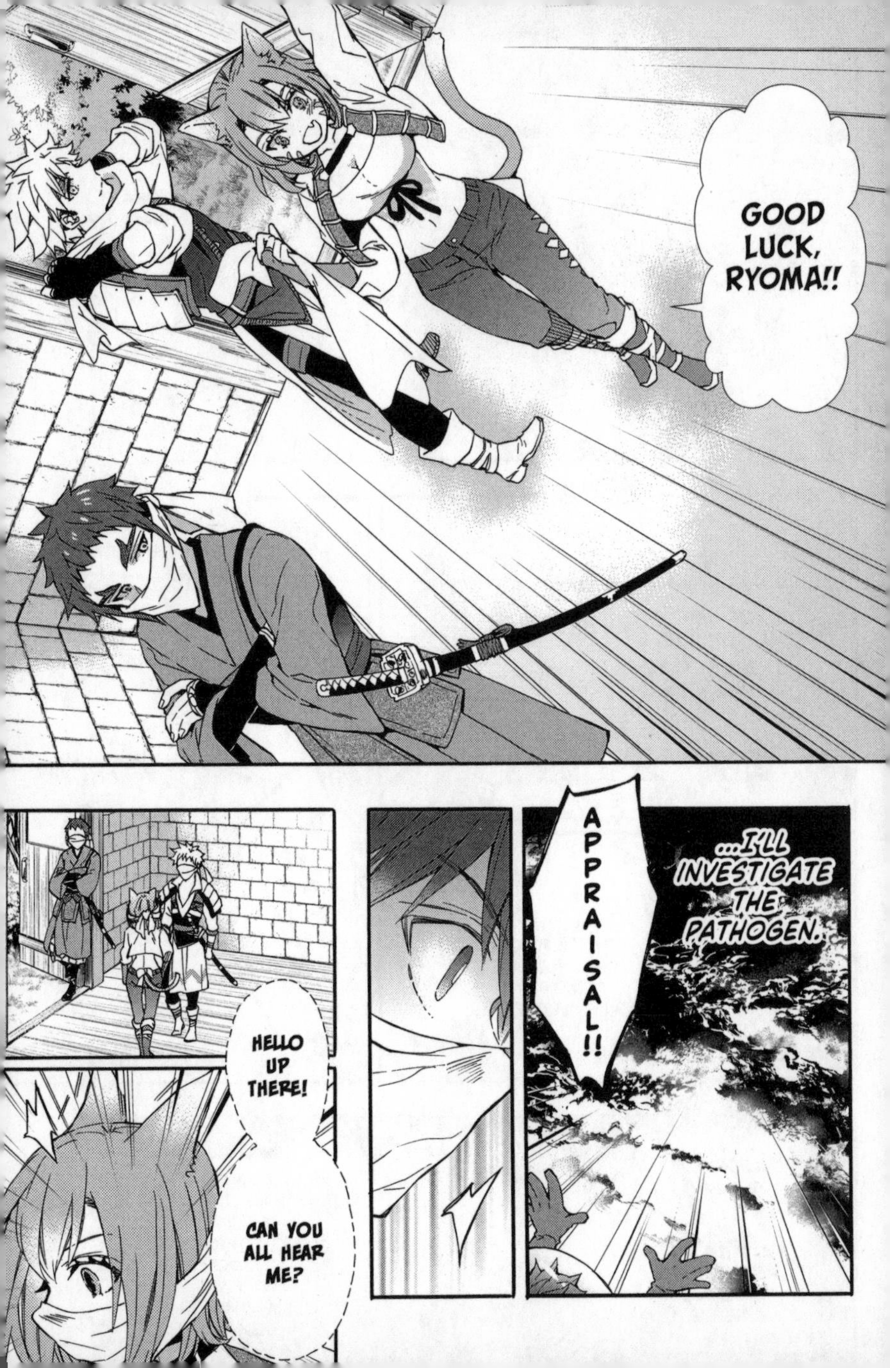
GOOD LUCK, RYOMA!!
...I'LL INVESTIGATE THE PATHOGEN.
APPRAISAL!!
HELLO UP THERE!
CAN YOU ALL HEAR ME?

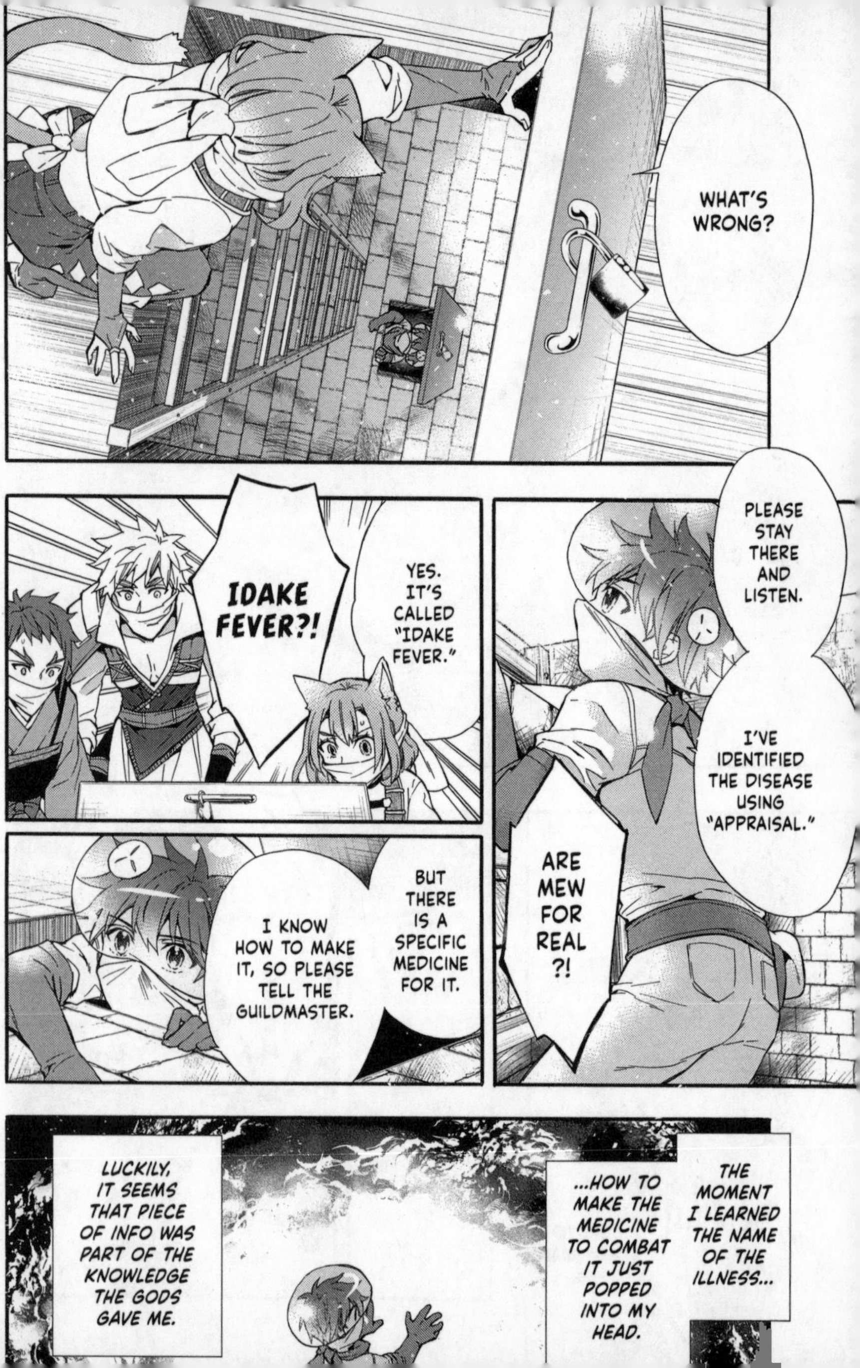
WHAT'S WRONG?
PLEASE STAY THERE AND LISTEN.
I'VE IDENTIFIED THE DISEASE USING "APPRAISAL."
ARE MEW FOR REAL ?!
YES. IT'S CALLED "IDAKE FEVER."
IDAKE FEVER?!
BUT THERE IS A SPECIFIC MEDICINE FOR IT.
I KNOW HOW TO MAKE IT, SO PLEASE TELL THE GUILDMASTER.
THE MOMENT I LEARNED THE NAME OF THE ILLNESS...
...HOW TO MAKE THE MEDICINE TO COMBAT IT JUST POPPED INTO MY HEAD.
LUCKILY, IT SEEMS THAT PIECE OF INFO WAS PART OF THE KNOWLEDGE THE GODS GAVE ME.

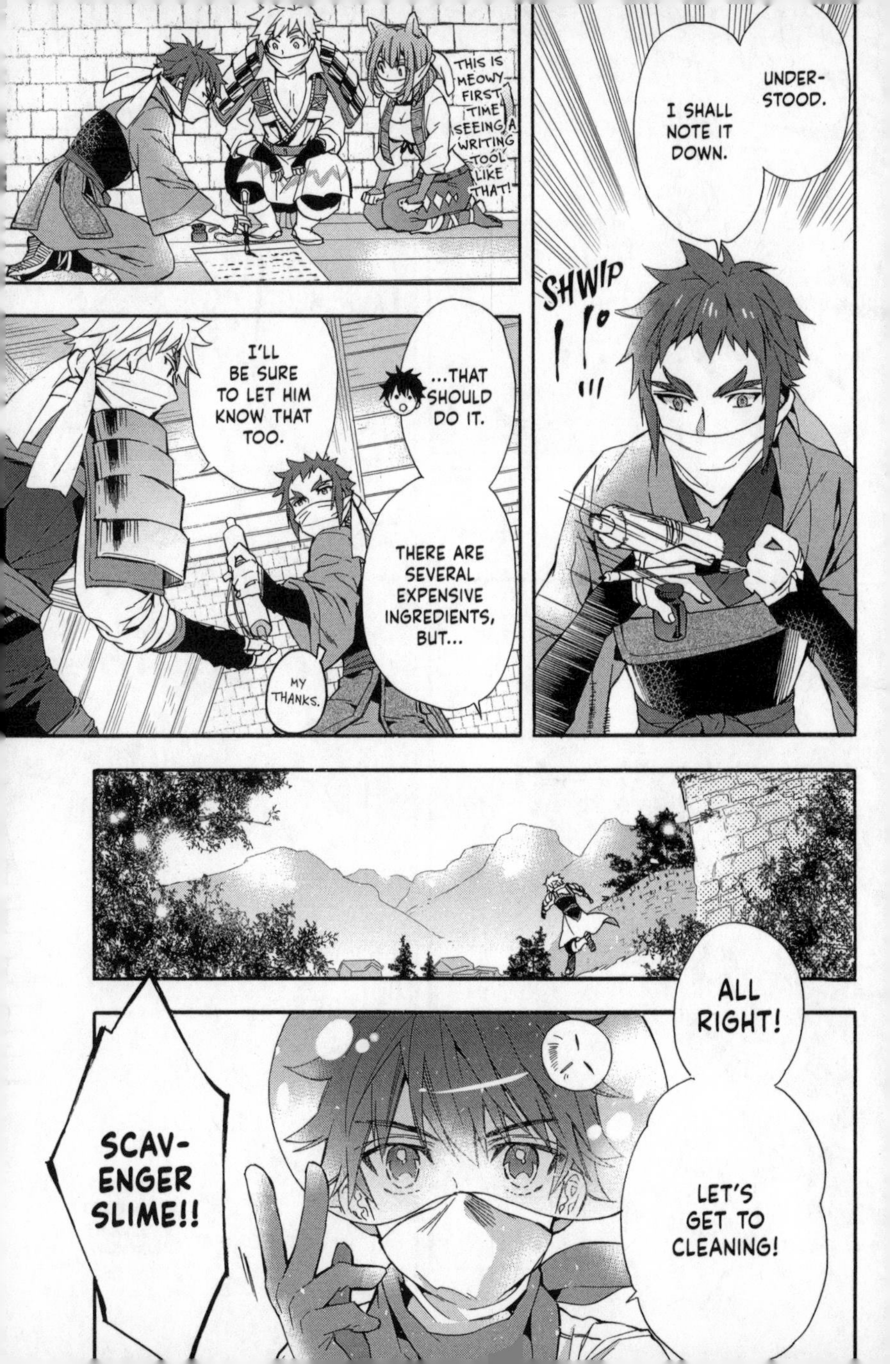

UNDER-STOOD.
I SHALL NOTE IT DOWN.
SHWIP
THIS IS MEOWY FIRST TIME SEEING A WRITING TOOL LIKE THAT!
...THAT SHOULD DO IT.
THERE ARE SEVERAL EXPENSIVE INGREDIENTS, BUT...
I'LL BE SURE TO LET HIM KNOW THAT TOO.
MY THANKS.
ALL RIGHT!
LET'S GET TO CLEANING!
SCAV-ENGER SLIME!!

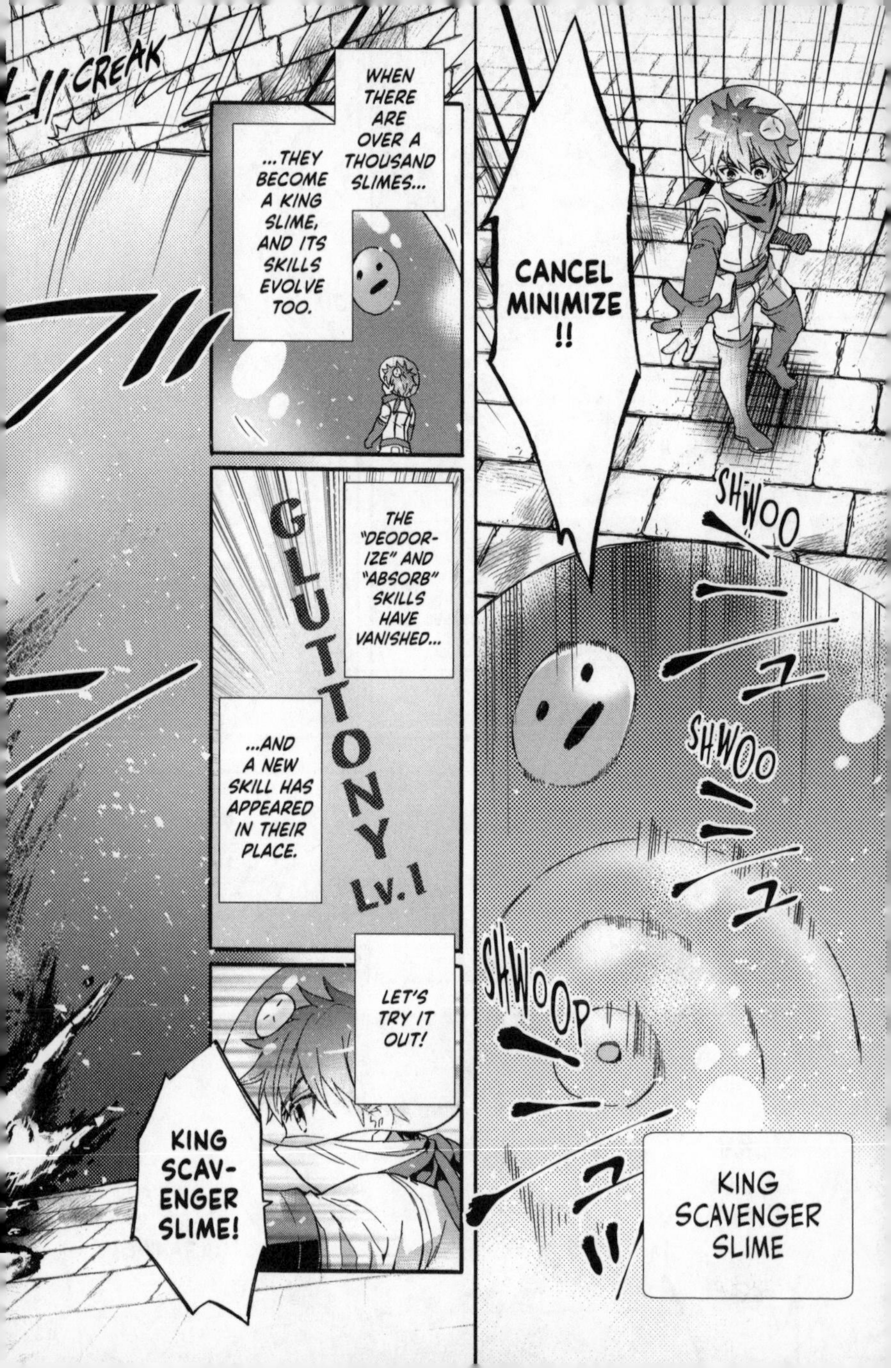
CANCEL MINIMIZE!!
SHWOO
SHWOO
SHWOOP
KING SCAVENGER SLIME
CREAK
WHEN THERE ARE OVER A THOUSAND SLIMES...
...THEY BECOME A KING SLIME, AND ITS SKILLS EVOLVE TOO.
THE "DEODORIZE" AND "ABSORB" SKILLS HAVE VANISHED...
GLUTTONY Lv.1
...AND A NEW SKILL HAS APPEARED IN THEIR PLACE.
LET'S TRY IT OUT!
KING SCAVENGER SLIME!

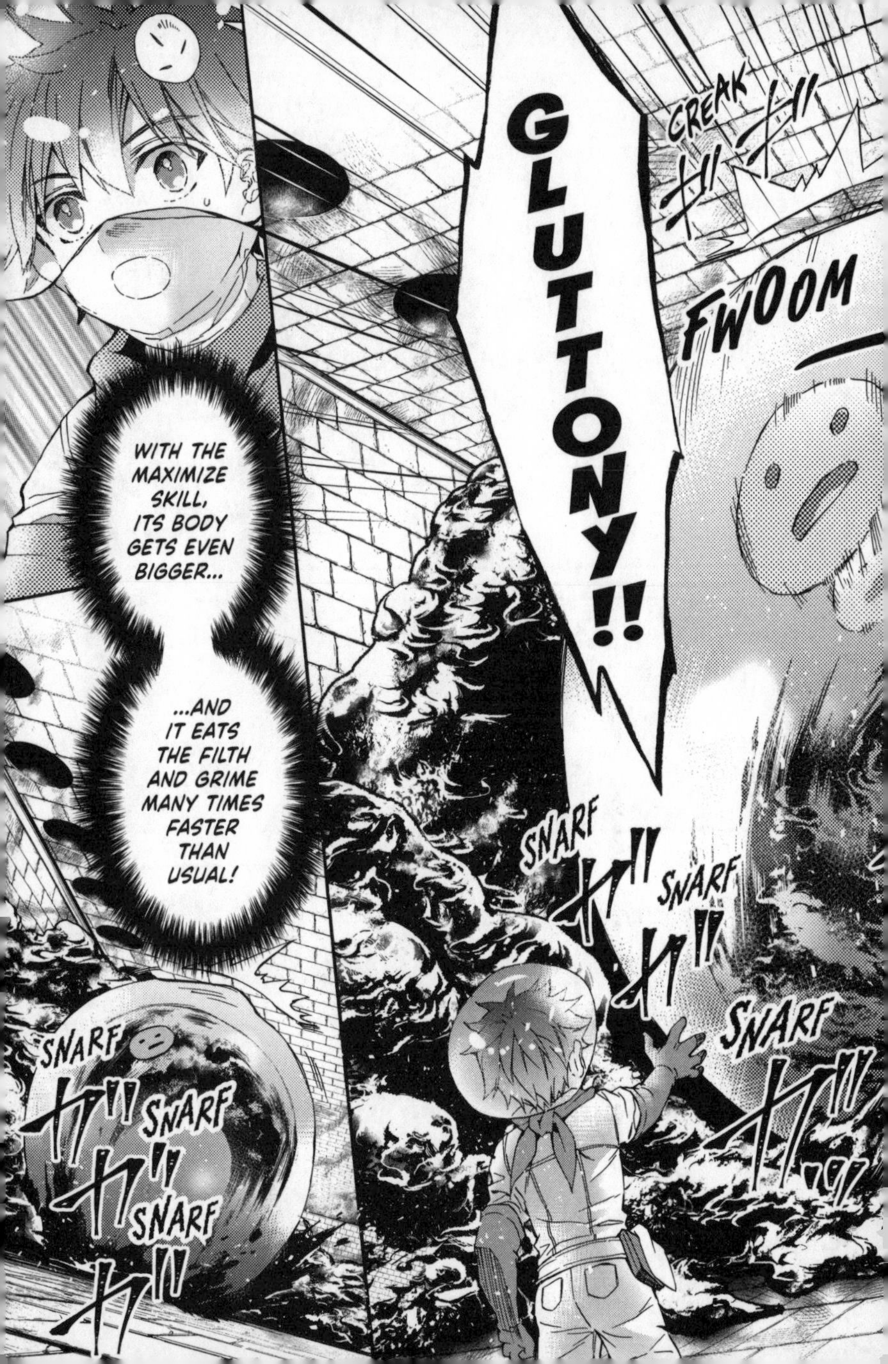
CREAK
GLUTTONY!!
FWOOM
SNARF
SNARF
SNARF
WITH THE MAXIMIZE SKILL, ITS BODY GETS EVEN BIGGER...
...AND IT EATS THE FILTH AND GRIME MANY TIMES FASTER THAN USUAL!
SNARF
SNARF
SNARF

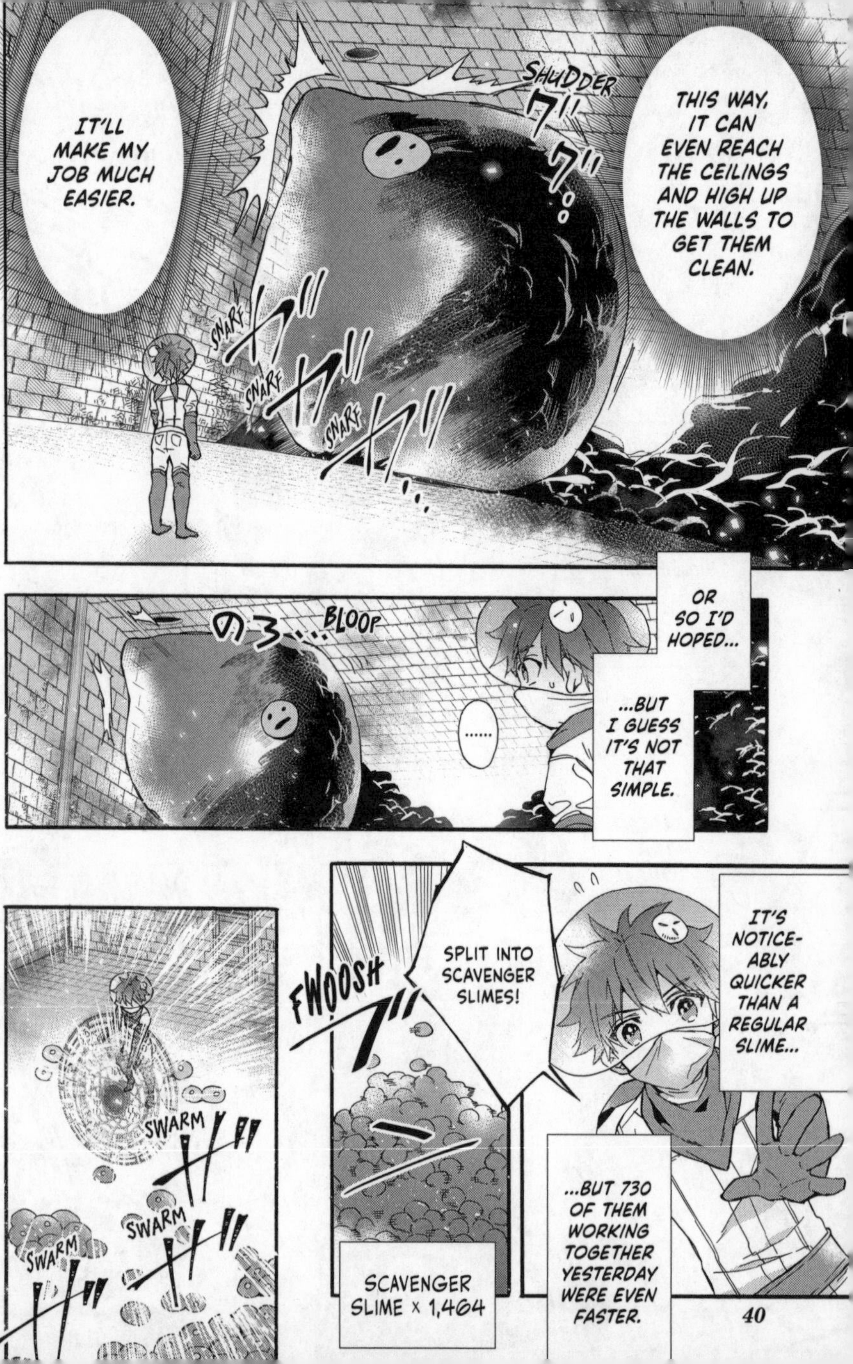
SHUDDER
THIS WAY, IT CAN EVEN REACH THE CEILINGS AND HIGH UP THE WALLS TO GET THEM CLEAN.
IT'LL MAKE MY JOB MUCH EASIER.
SNARF
SNARF
SNARF
OR SO I'D HOPED...
...BUT I GUESS IT'S NOT THAT SIMPLE.
BLOOP
......
IT'S NOTICE-ABLY QUICKER THAN A REGULAR SLIME...
...BUT 730 OF THEM WORKING TOGETHER YESTERDAY WERE EVEN FASTER.
SPLIT INTO SCAVENGER SLIMES!
FWOOSH
SCAVENGER SLIME x 1,464
SWARM
SWARM
SWARM

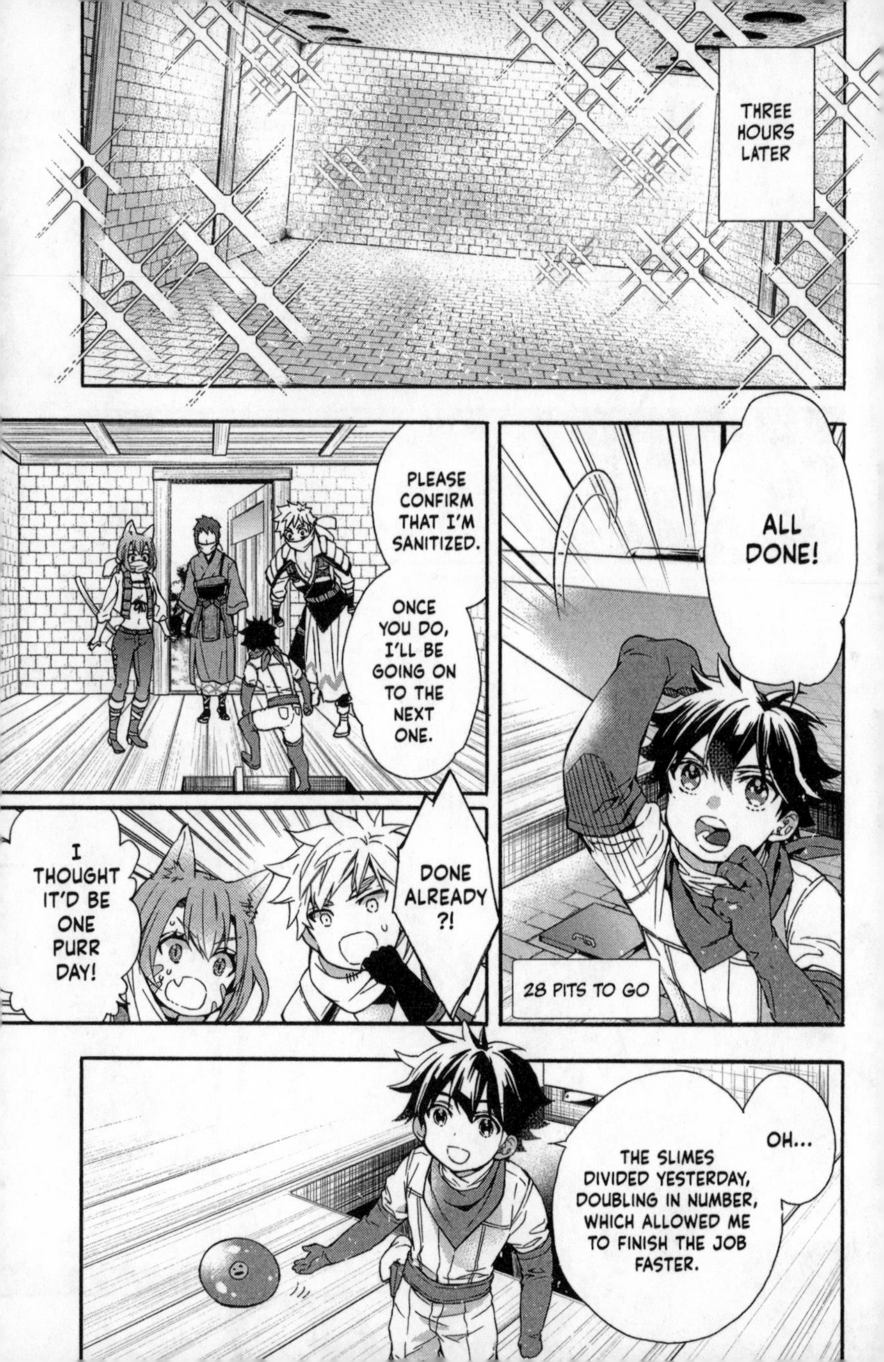
THREE HOURS LATER
ALL DONE!
28 PITS TO GO
PLEASE CONFIRM THAT I'M SANITIZED.
ONCE YOU DO, I'LL BE GOING ON TO THE NEXT ONE.
DONE ALREADY?!
I THOUGHT IT'D BE ONE PURR DAY!
OH...
THE SLIMES DIVIDED YESTERDAY, DOUBLING IN NUMBER, WHICH ALLOWED ME TO FINISH THE JOB FASTER.

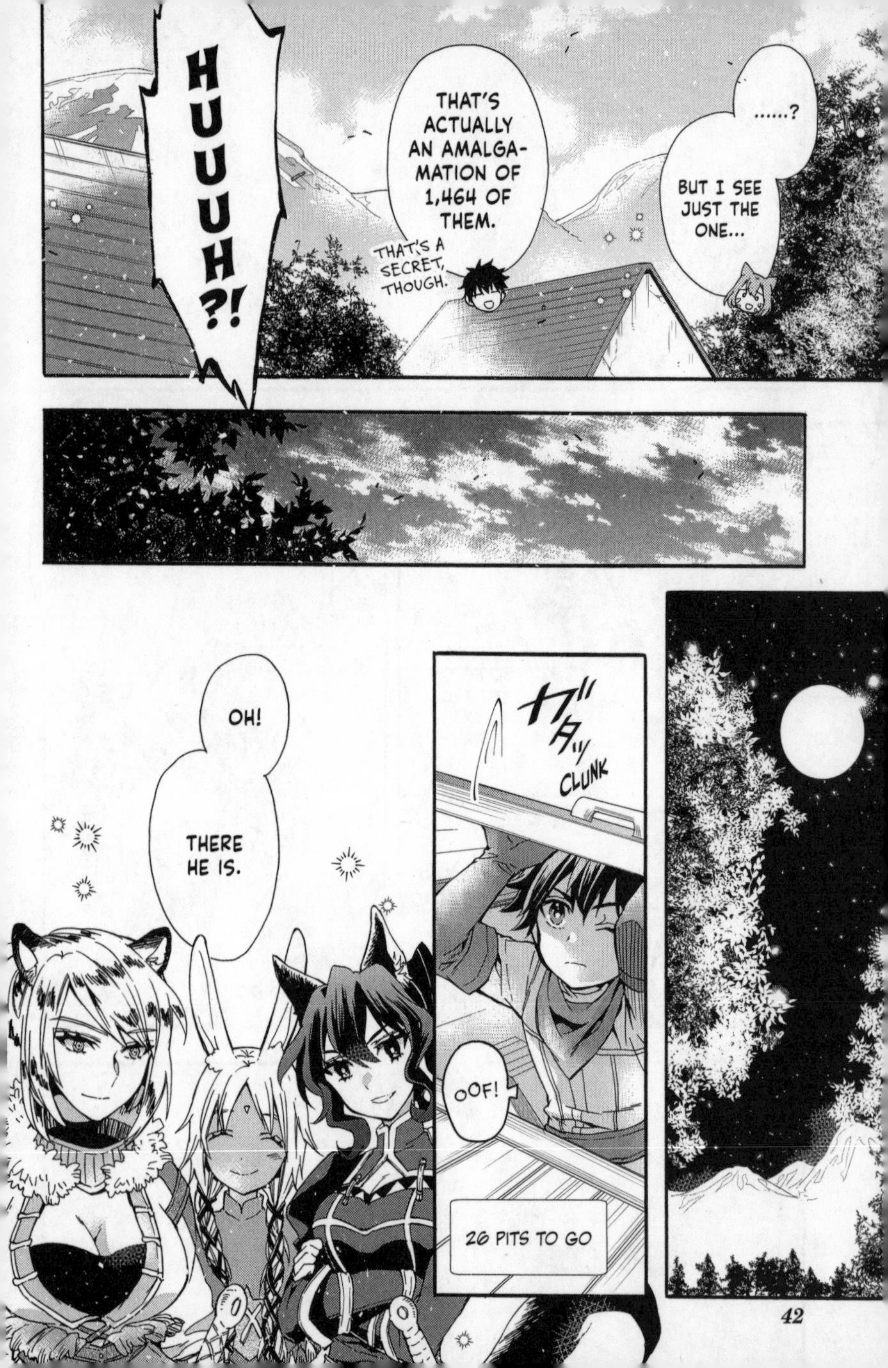
......?
BUT I SEE JUST THE ONE...
THAT'S ACTUALLY AN AMALGAMATION OF 1,464 OF THEM.
THAT'S A SECRET, THOUGH.
HUUUH?!
CLUNK
OOF!
26 PITS TO GO
OH!
THERE HE IS.

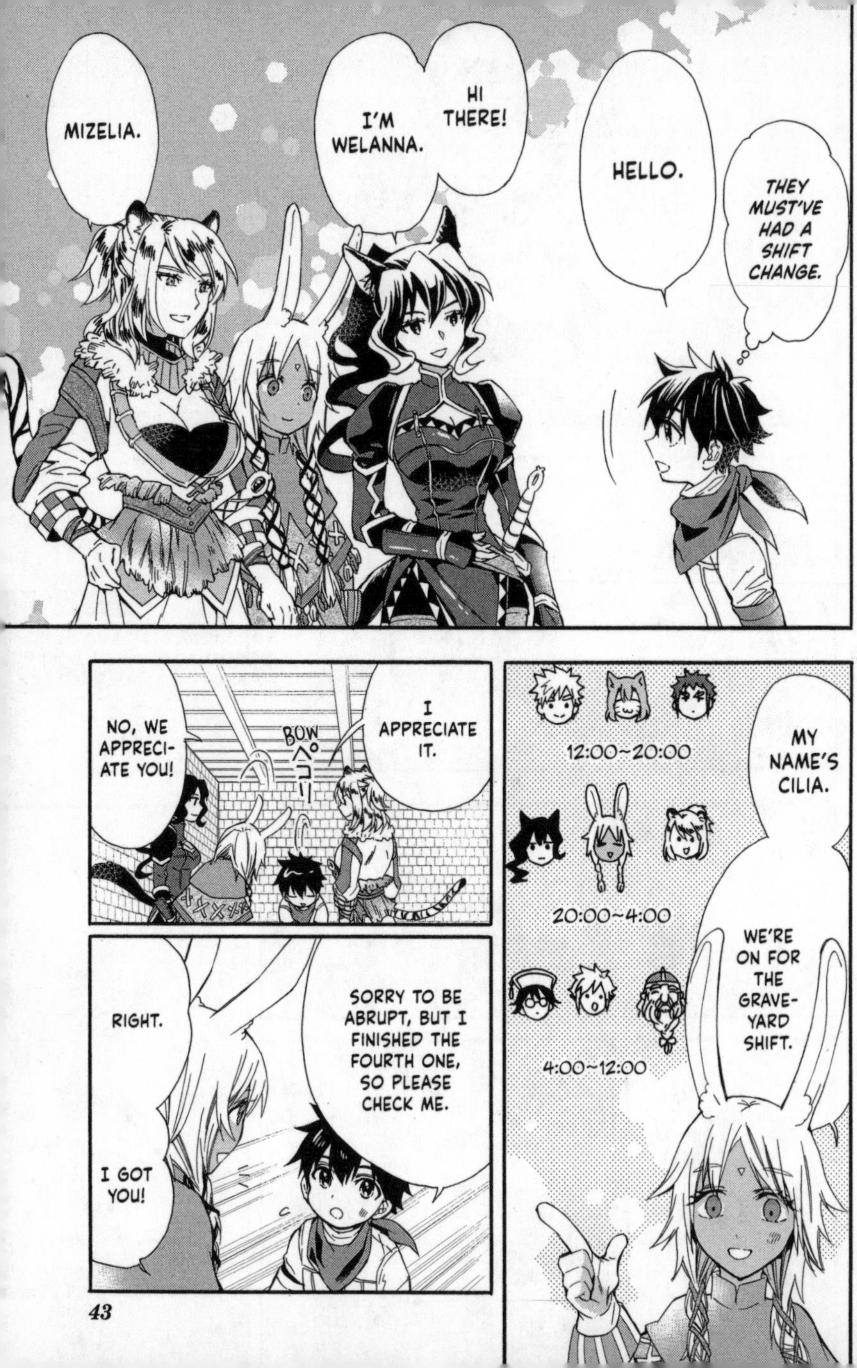
THEY MUST'VE HAD A SHIFT CHANGE.
HELLO.
HI THERE!
I'M WELANNA.
MIZELIA.
MY NAME'S CILIA.
12:00~20:00
20:00~4:00
WE'RE ON FOR THE GRAVEYARD SHIFT.
4:00~12:00
I APPRECIATE IT.
BOW
NO, WE APPRECIATE YOU!
SORRY TO BE ABRUPT, BUT I FINISHED THE FOURTH ONE, SO PLEASE CHECK ME.
RIGHT.
I GOT YOU!

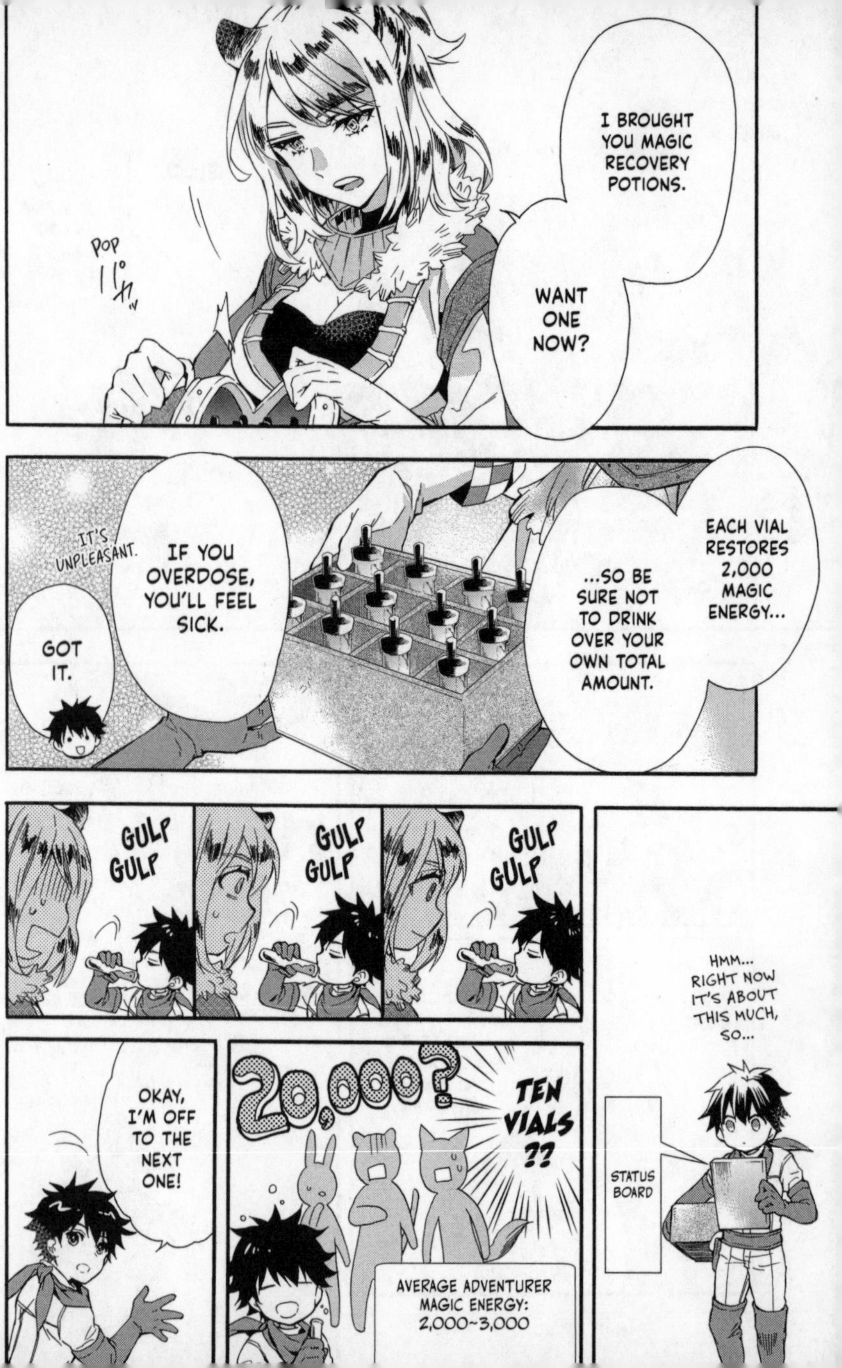
I BROUGHT YOU MAGIC RECOVERY POTIONS.
WANT ONE NOW?
POP
EACH VIAL RESTORES 2,000 MAGIC ENERGY...
...SO BE SURE NOT TO DRINK OVER YOUR OWN TOTAL AMOUNT.
IF YOU OVERDOSE, YOU'LL FEEL SICK.
IT'S UNPLEASANT.
GOT IT.
HMM... RIGHT NOW IT'S ABOUT THIS MUCH, SO...
STATUS BOARD
GULP GULP
GULP GULP
GULP GULP
20,000?
TEN VIALS??
AVERAGE ADVENTURER MAGIC ENERGY: 2,000~3,000
OKAY, I'M OFF TO THE NEXT ONE!

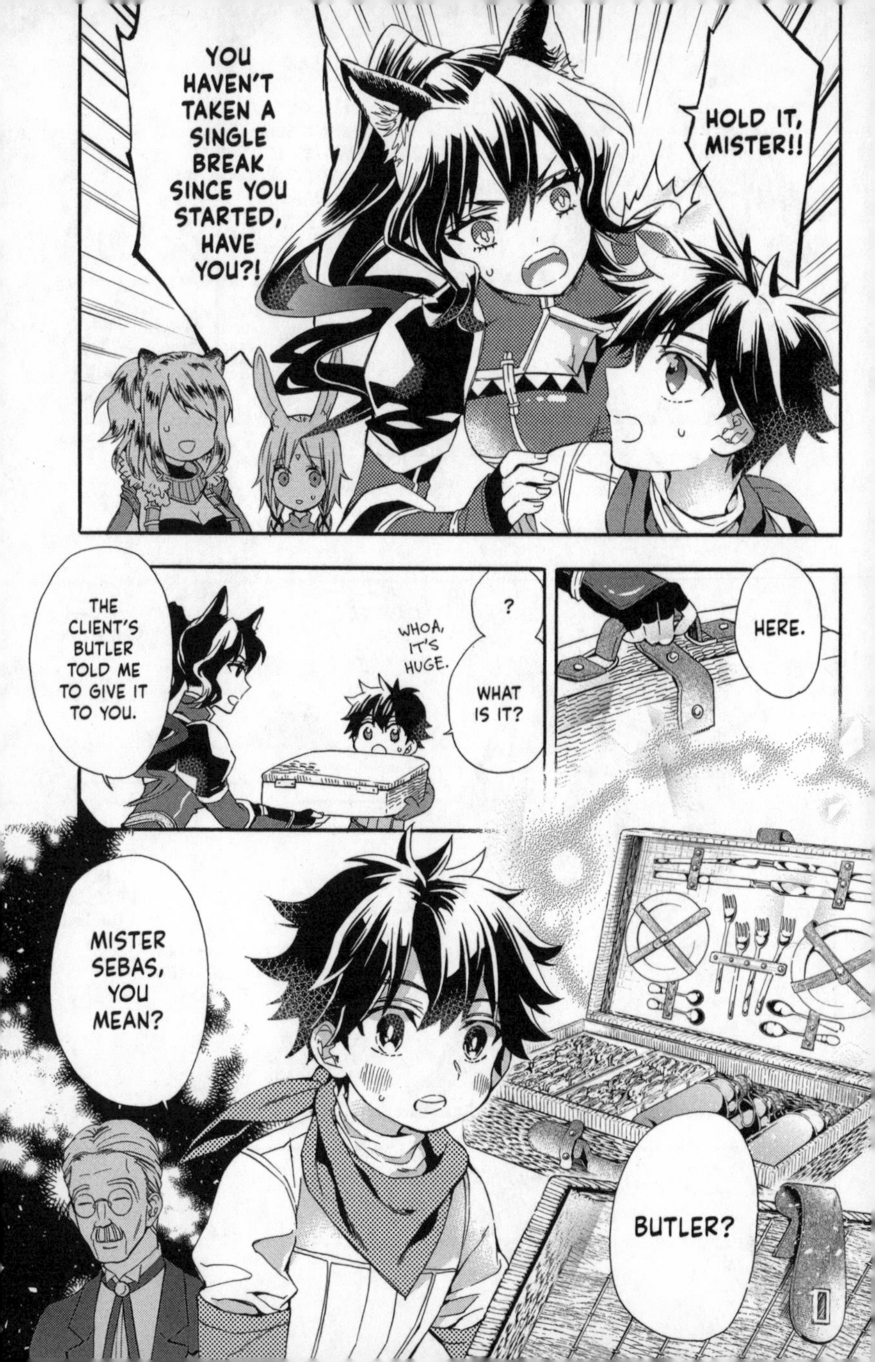
HOLD IT, MISTER!!
YOU HAVEN'T TAKEN A SINGLE BREAK SINCE YOU STARTED, HAVE YOU?!
HERE.
?
WHAT IS IT?
WHOA, IT'S HUGE.
THE CLIENT'S BUTLER TOLD ME TO GIVE IT TO YOU.
BUTLER?
MISTER SEBAS, YOU MEAN?

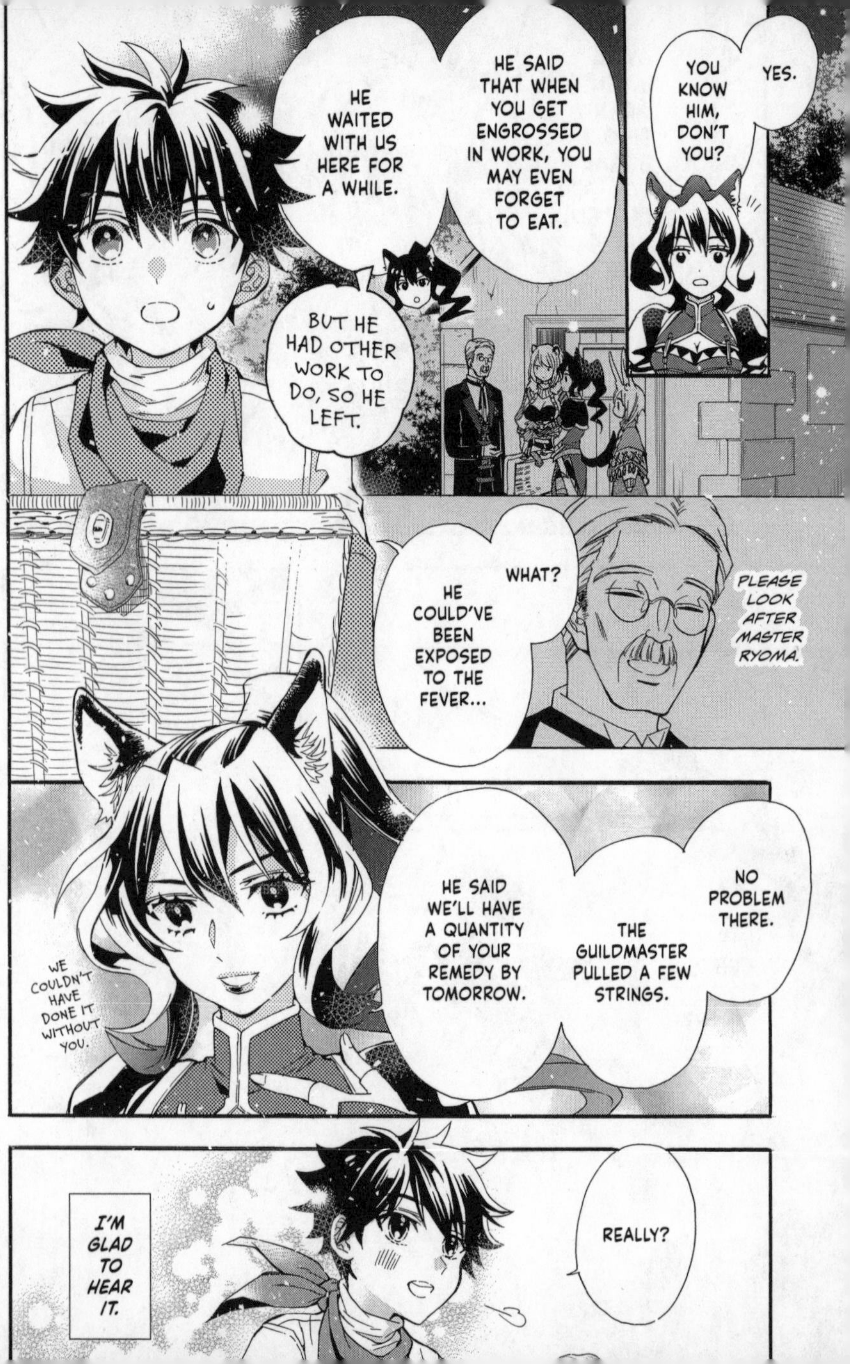
YES.
YOU KNOW HIM, DON'T YOU?
HE SAID THAT WHEN YOU GET ENGROSSED IN WORK, YOU MAY EVEN FORGET TO EAT.
HE WAITED WITH US HERE FOR A WHILE.
BUT HE HAD OTHER WORK TO DO, SO HE LEFT.
PLEASE LOOK AFTER MASTER RYOMA.
WHAT?
HE COULD'VE BEEN EXPOSED TO THE FEVER...
NO PROBLEM THERE.
THE GUILDMASTER PULLED A FEW STRINGS.
HE SAID WE'LL HAVE A QUANTITY OF YOUR REMEDY BY TOMORROW.
WE COULDN'T HAVE DONE IT WITHOUT YOU.
REALLY?
I'M GLAD TO HEAR IT.

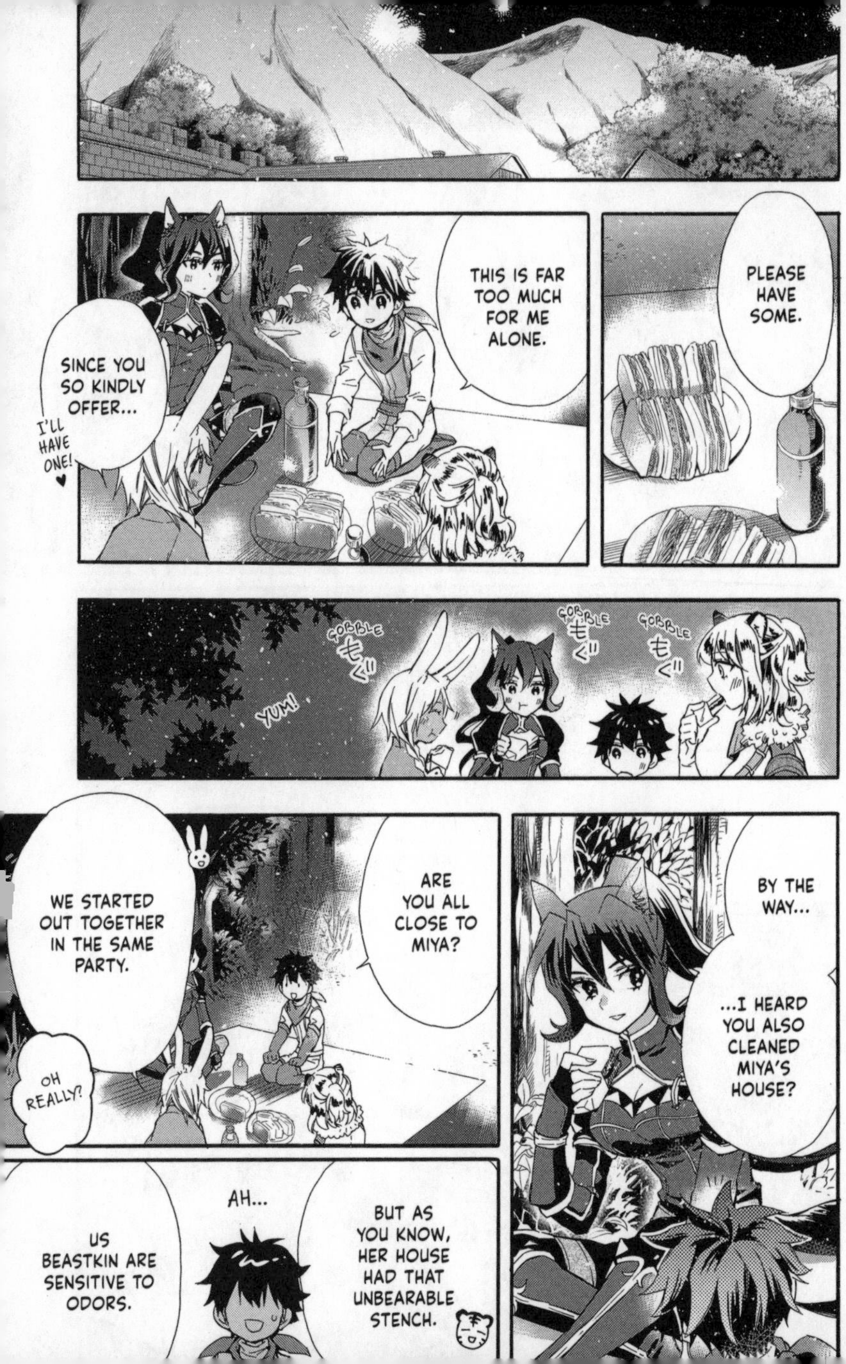
PLEASE HAVE SOME.
THIS IS FAR TOO MUCH FOR ME ALONE.
SINCE YOU SO KINDLY OFFER...
I'LL HAVE ONE! ♥
GOBBLE もぐ
GOBBLE もぐ
GOBBLE もぐ
YUM!
BY THE WAY...
...I HEARD YOU ALSO CLEANED MIYA'S HOUSE?
ARE YOU ALL CLOSE TO MIYA?
WE STARTED OUT TOGETHER IN THE SAME PARTY.
OH REALLY?
BUT AS YOU KNOW, HER HOUSE HAD THAT UNBEARABLE STENCH.
AH...
US BEASTKIN ARE SENSITIVE TO ODORS.

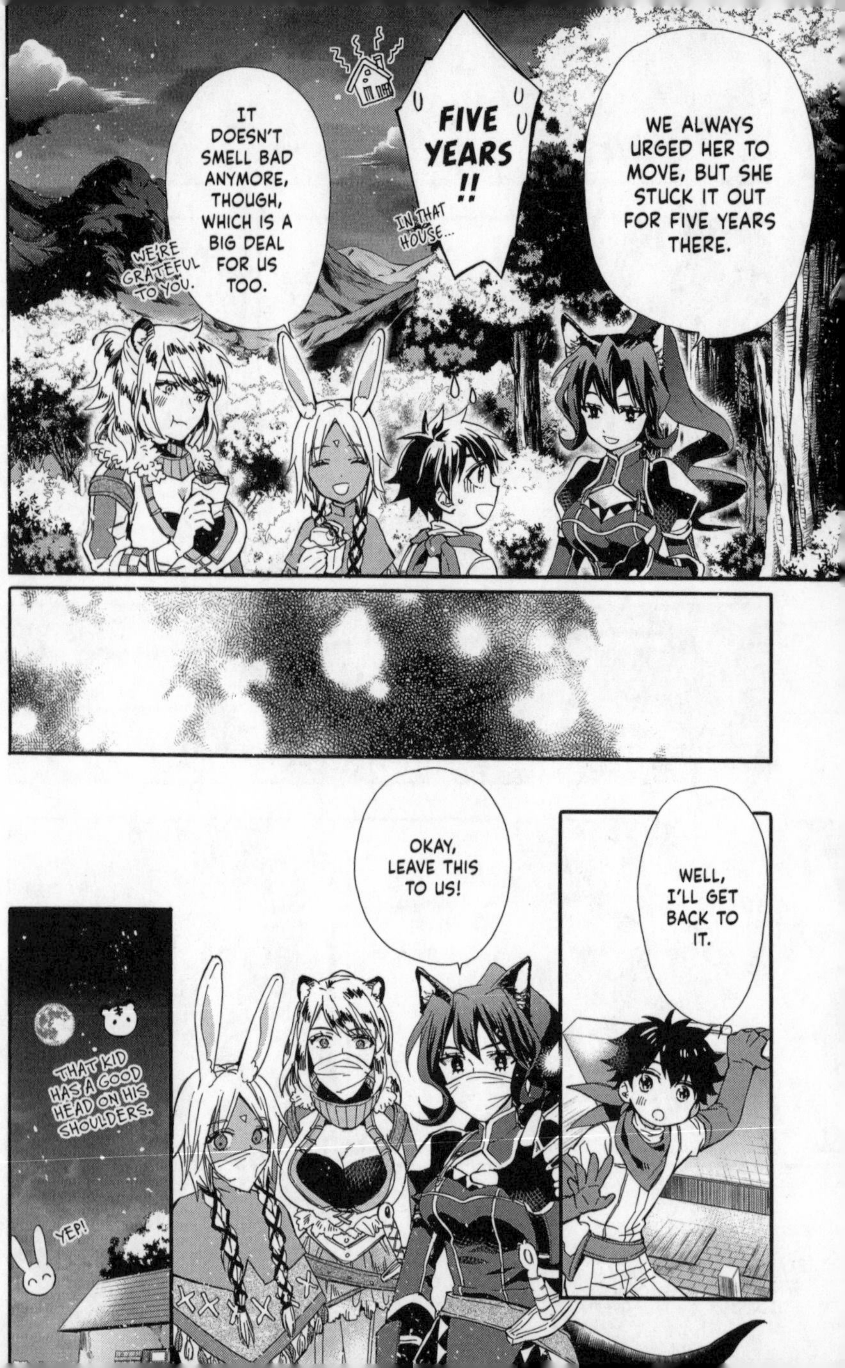
WE ALWAYS URGED HER TO MOVE, BUT SHE STUCK IT OUT FOR FIVE YEARS THERE.
FIVE YEARS!!
IN THAT HOUSE...
IT DOESN'T SMELL BAD ANYMORE, THOUGH, WHICH IS A BIG DEAL FOR US TOO.
WE'RE GRATEFUL TO YOU.
WELL, I'LL GET BACK TO IT.
OKAY, LEAVE THIS TO US!
THAT KID HAS A GOOD HEAD ON HIS SHOULDERS.
YEP!

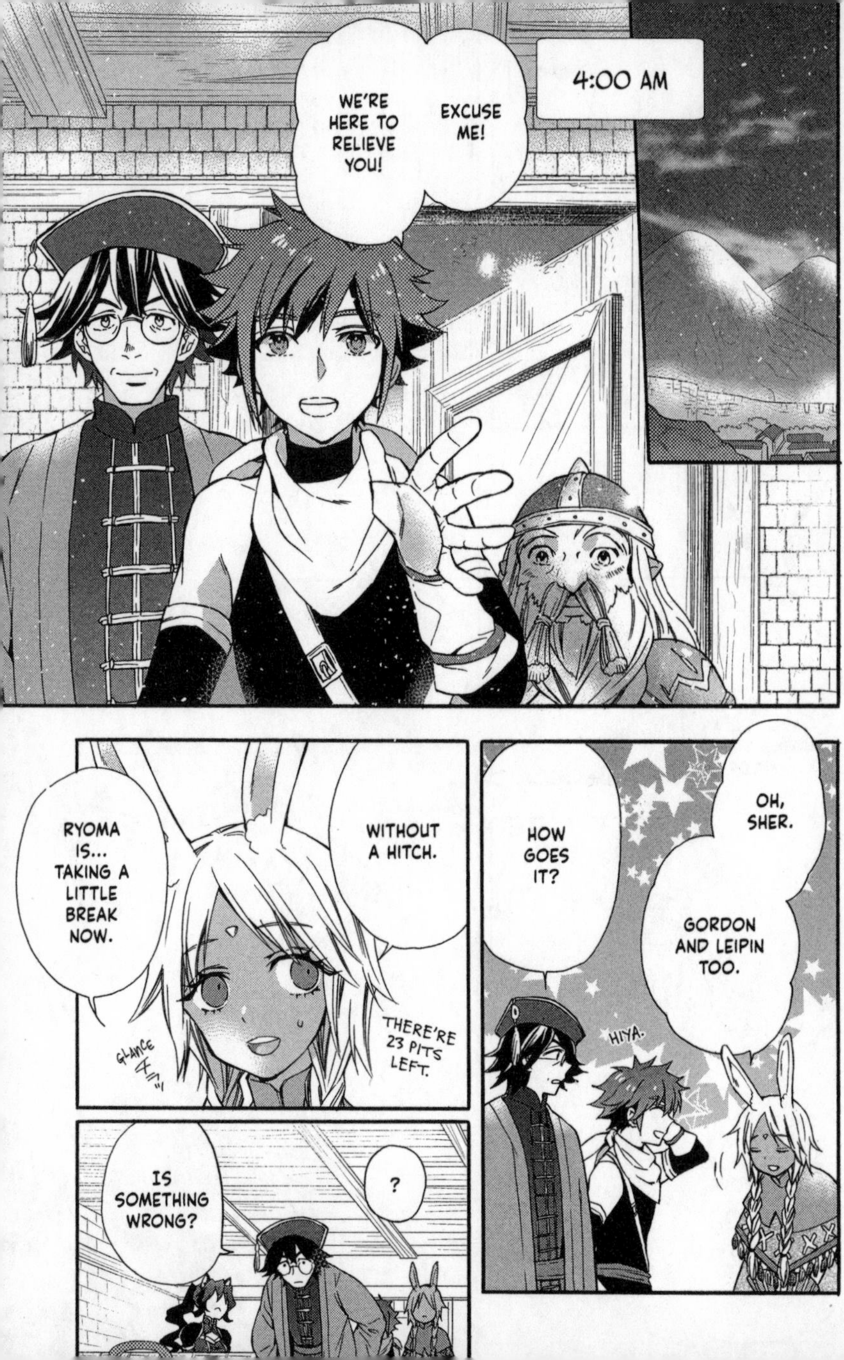
4:00 AM
EXCUSE ME!
WE'RE HERE TO RELIEVE YOU!
OH, SHER.
GORDON AND LEIPIN TOO.
HOW GOES IT?
HIYA.
WITHOUT A HITCH.
RYOMA IS... TAKING A LITTLE BREAK NOW.
THERE'RE 23 PITS LEFT.
GLANCE
?
IS SOMETHING WRONG?

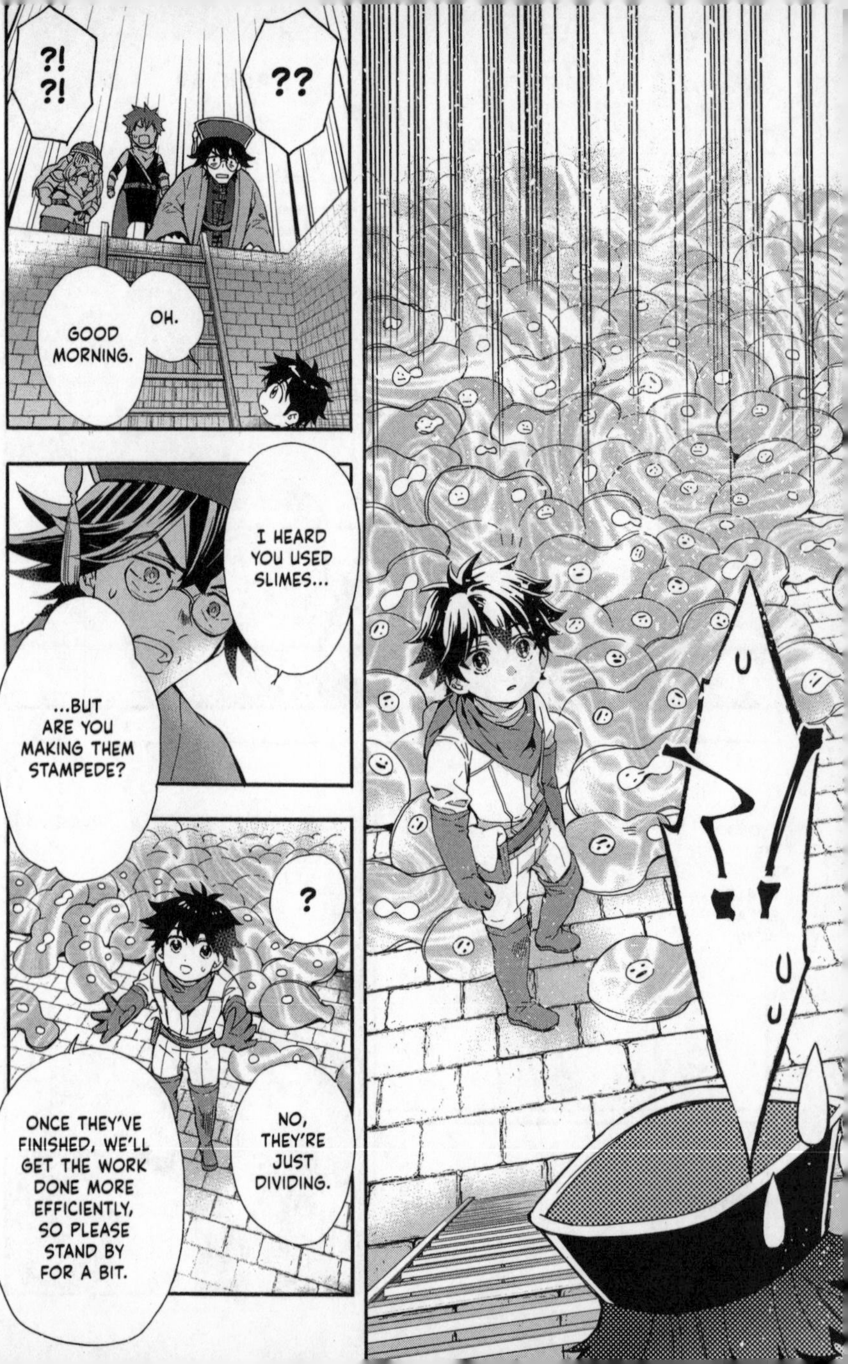
U U U
??
?!
?!
OH.
GOOD MORNING.
I HEARD YOU USED SLIMES...
...BUT ARE YOU MAKING THEM STAMPEDE?
?
NO, THEY'RE JUST DIVIDING.
ONCE THEY'VE FINISHED, WE'LL GET THE WORK DONE MORE EFFICIENTLY, SO PLEASE STAND BY FOR A BIT.

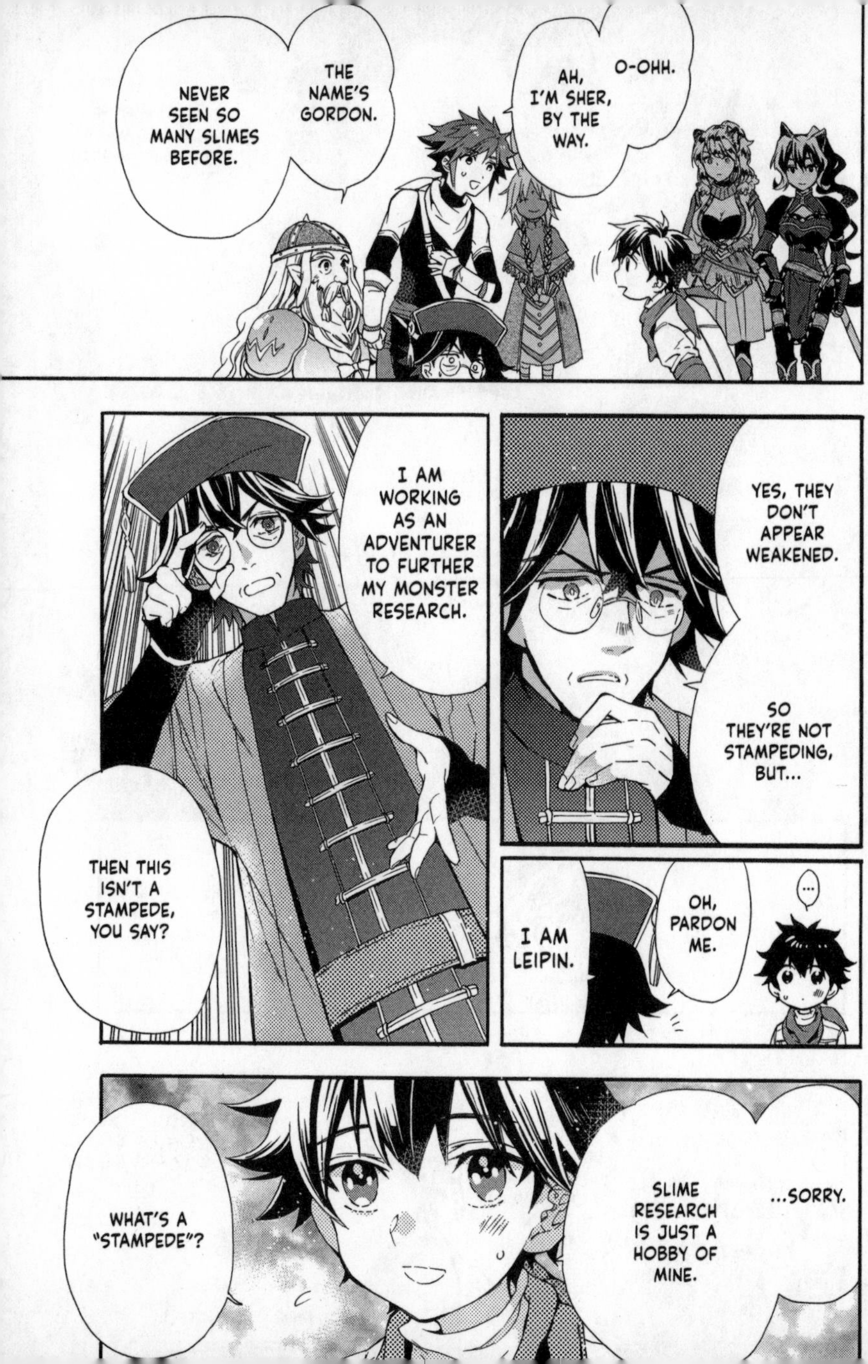
O-OHH.
AH, I'M SHER, BY THE WAY.
THE NAME'S GORDON.
NEVER SEEN SO MANY SLIMES BEFORE.
YES, THEY DON'T APPEAR WEAKENED.
SO THEY'RE NOT STAMPEDING, BUT...
...
OH, PARDON ME.
I AM LEIPIN.
I AM WORKING AS AN ADVENTURER TO FURTHER MY MONSTER RESEARCH.
THEN THIS ISN'T A STAMPEDE, YOU SAY?
...SORRY.
SLIME RESEARCH IS JUST A HOBBY OF MINE.
WHAT'S A "STAMPEDE"?

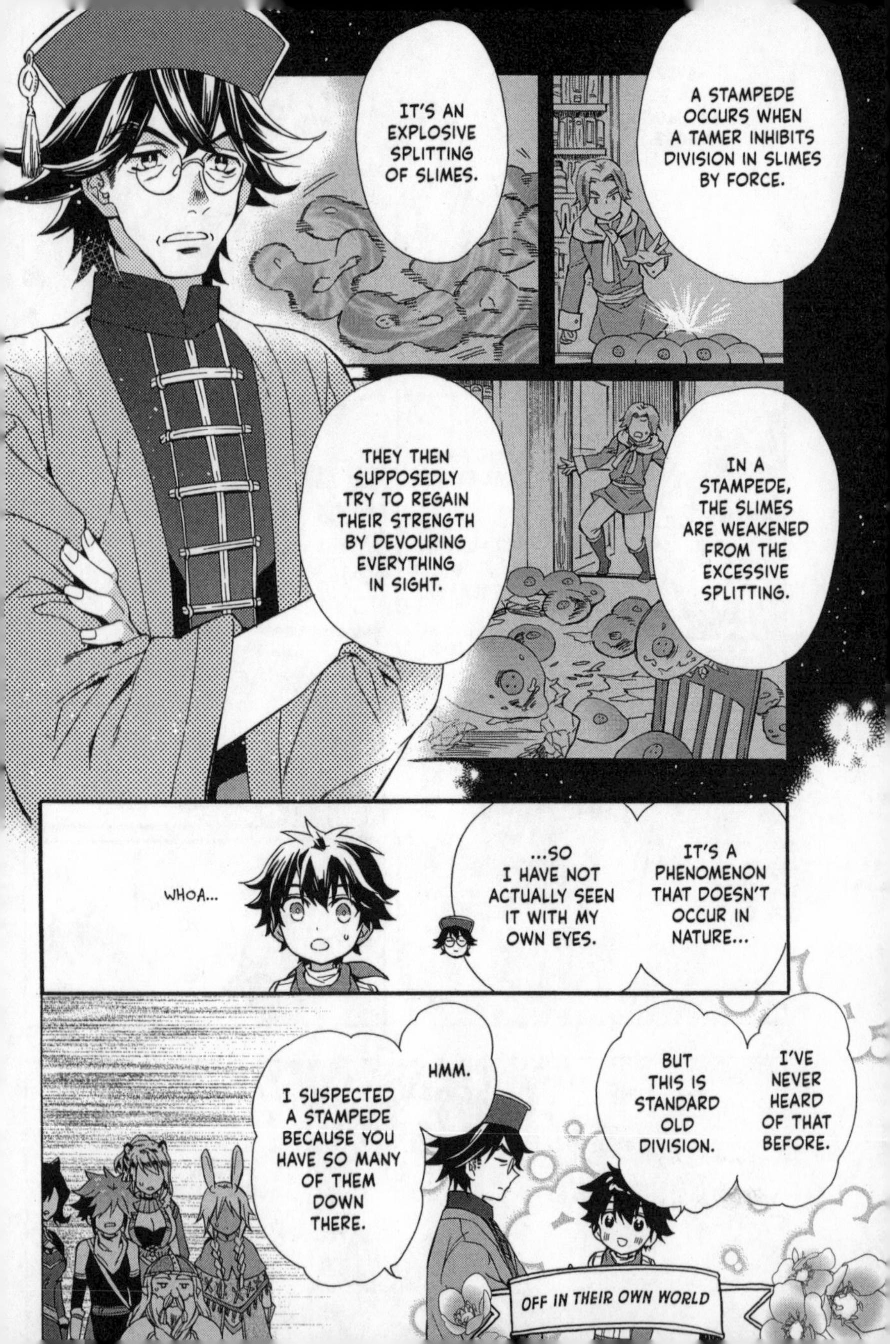
A STAMPEDE OCCURS WHEN A TAMER INHIBITS DIVISION IN SLIMES BY FORCE.
IT'S AN EXPLOSIVE SPLITTING OF SLIMES.
IN A STAMPEDE, THE SLIMES ARE WEAKENED FROM THE EXCESSIVE SPLITTING.
THEY THEN SUPPOSEDLY TRY TO REGAIN THEIR STRENGTH BY DEVOURING EVERYTHING IN SIGHT.
IT'S A PHENOMENON THAT DOESN'T OCCUR IN NATURE...
...SO I HAVE NOT ACTUALLY SEEN IT WITH MY OWN EYES.
WHOA...
I'VE NEVER HEARD OF THAT BEFORE.
BUT THIS IS STANDARD OLD DIVISION.
HMM.
I SUSPECTED A STAMPEDE BECAUSE YOU HAVE SO MANY OF THEM DOWN THERE.
OFF IN THEIR OWN WORLD

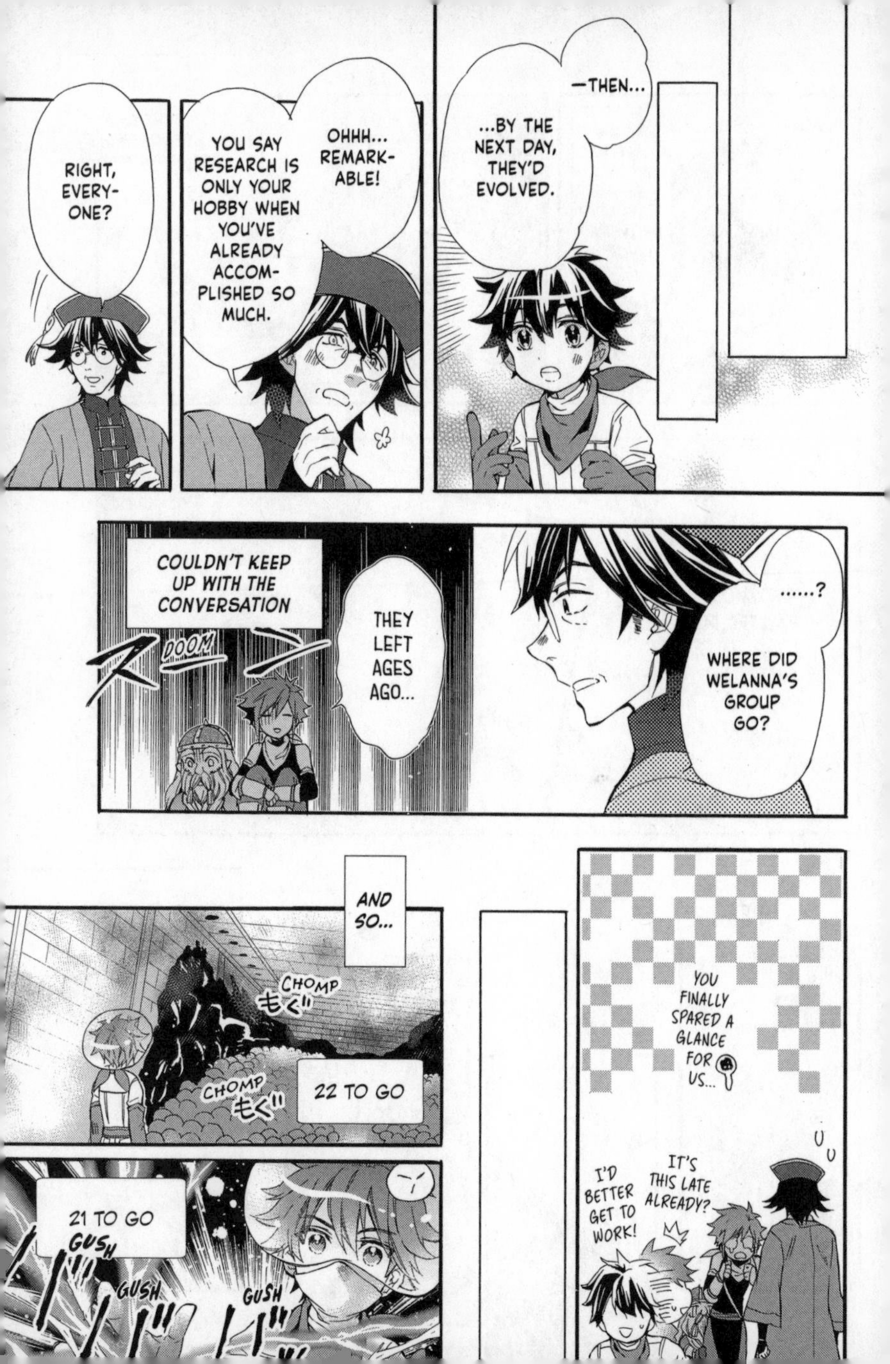
—THEN...
...BY THE NEXT DAY, THEY'D EVOLVED.
OHHH... REMARKABLE!
YOU SAY RESEARCH IS ONLY YOUR HOBBY WHEN YOU'VE ALREADY ACCOMPLISHED SO MUCH.
RIGHT, EVERYONE?
......?
WHERE DID WELANNA'S GROUP GO?
THEY LEFT AGES AGO...
COULDN'T KEEP UP WITH THE CONVERSATION
DOOM
YOU FINALLY SPARED A GLANCE FOR US...
IT'S THIS LATE ALREADY?
I'D BETTER GET TO WORK!
AND SO...
CHOMP もぐ
CHOMP もぐ
22 TO GO
21 TO GO
GUSH
GUSH
GUSH

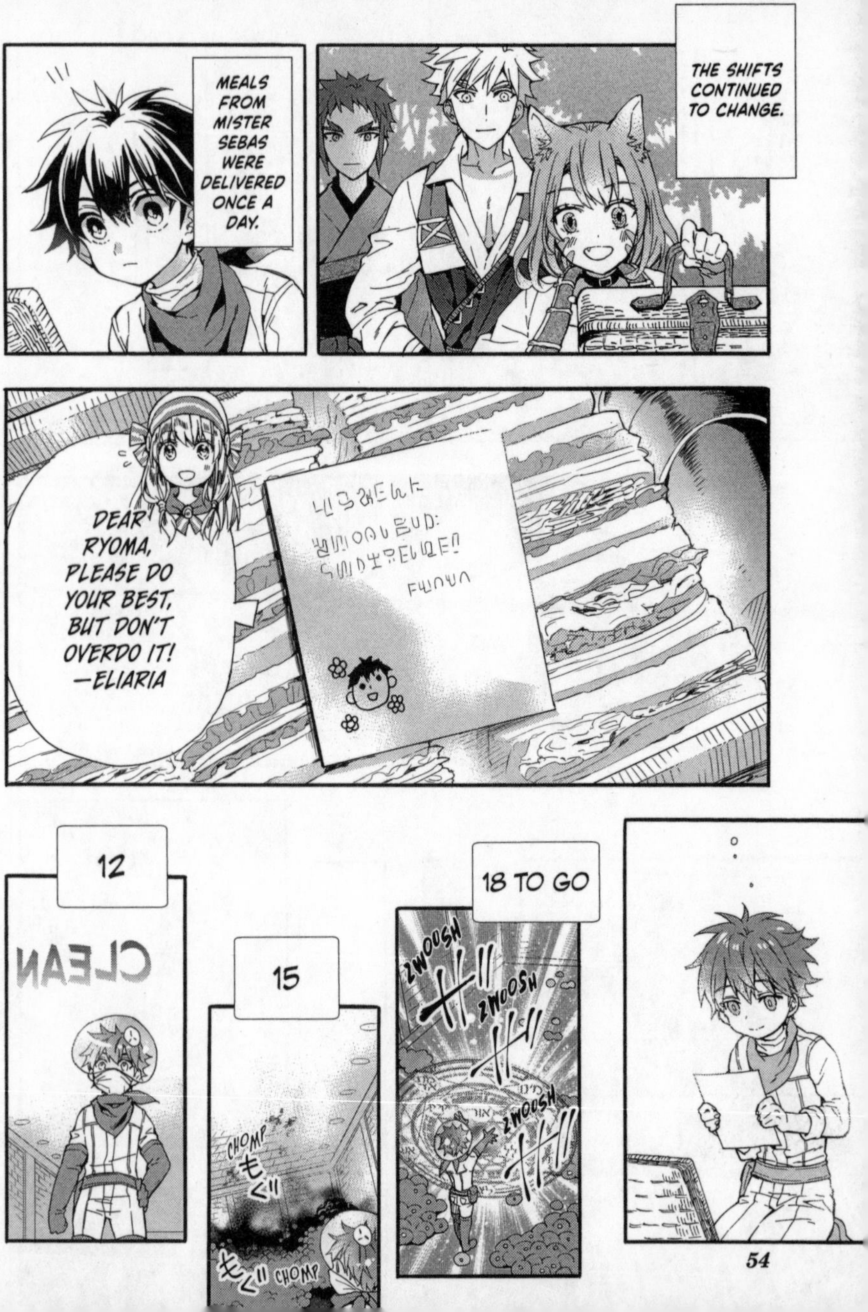
THE SHIFTS CONTINUED TO CHANGE.
MEALS FROM MISTER SEBAS WERE DELIVERED ONCE A DAY.
DEAR RYOMA, PLEASE DO YOUR BEST, BUT DON'T OVERDO IT! —ELIARIA
18 TO GO
ZWOOSH
ZWOOSH
ZWOOSH
15
CHOMP もぐ
もぐ CHOMP
12
CLEAN

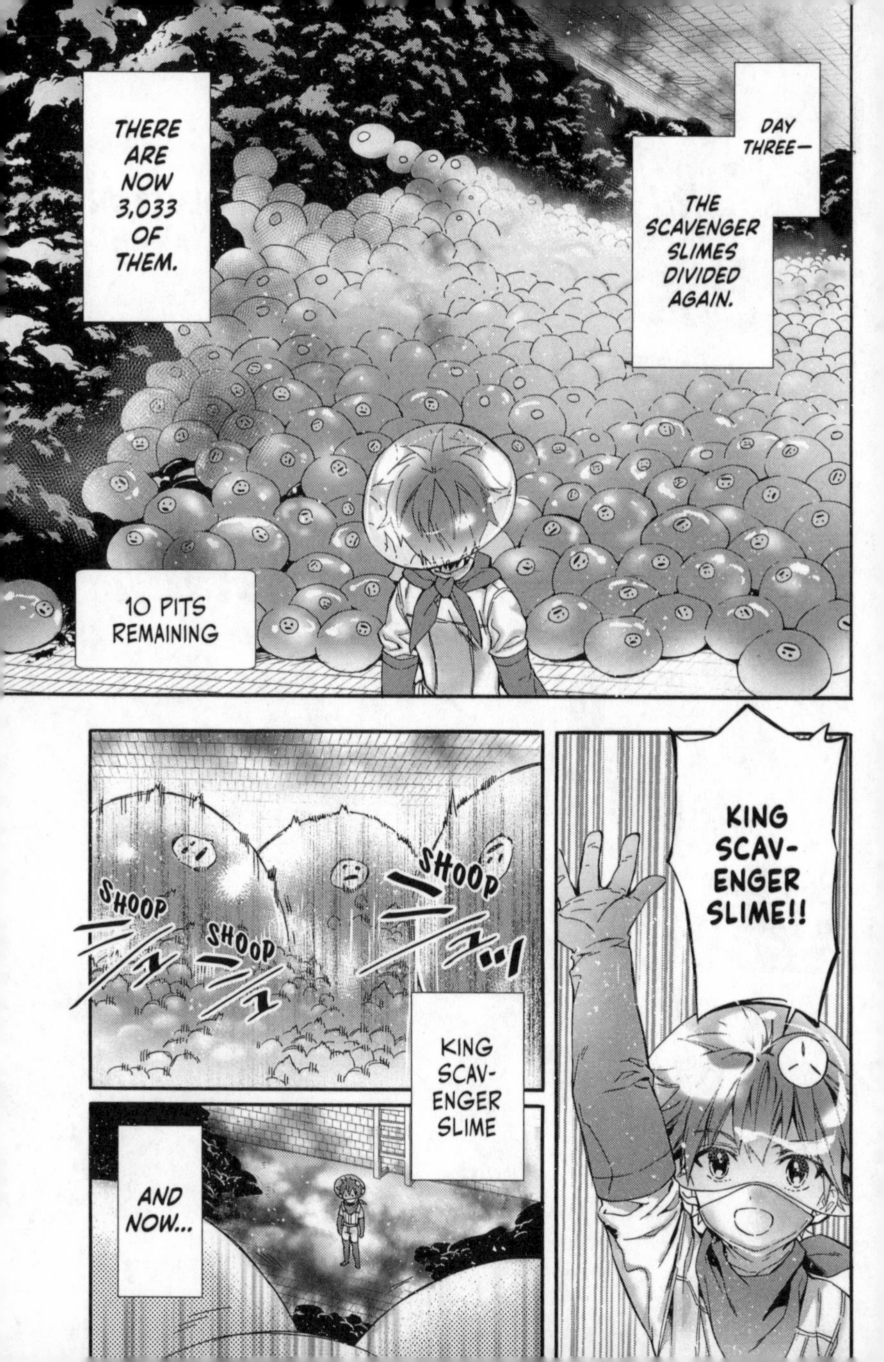
DAY THREE—
THE SCAVENGER SLIMES DIVIDED AGAIN.
THERE ARE NOW 3,033 OF THEM.
10 PITS REMAINING
KING SCAV-ENGER SLIME!!
SHOOP
SHOOP
SHOOP
KING SCAV-ENGER SLIME
AND NOW...

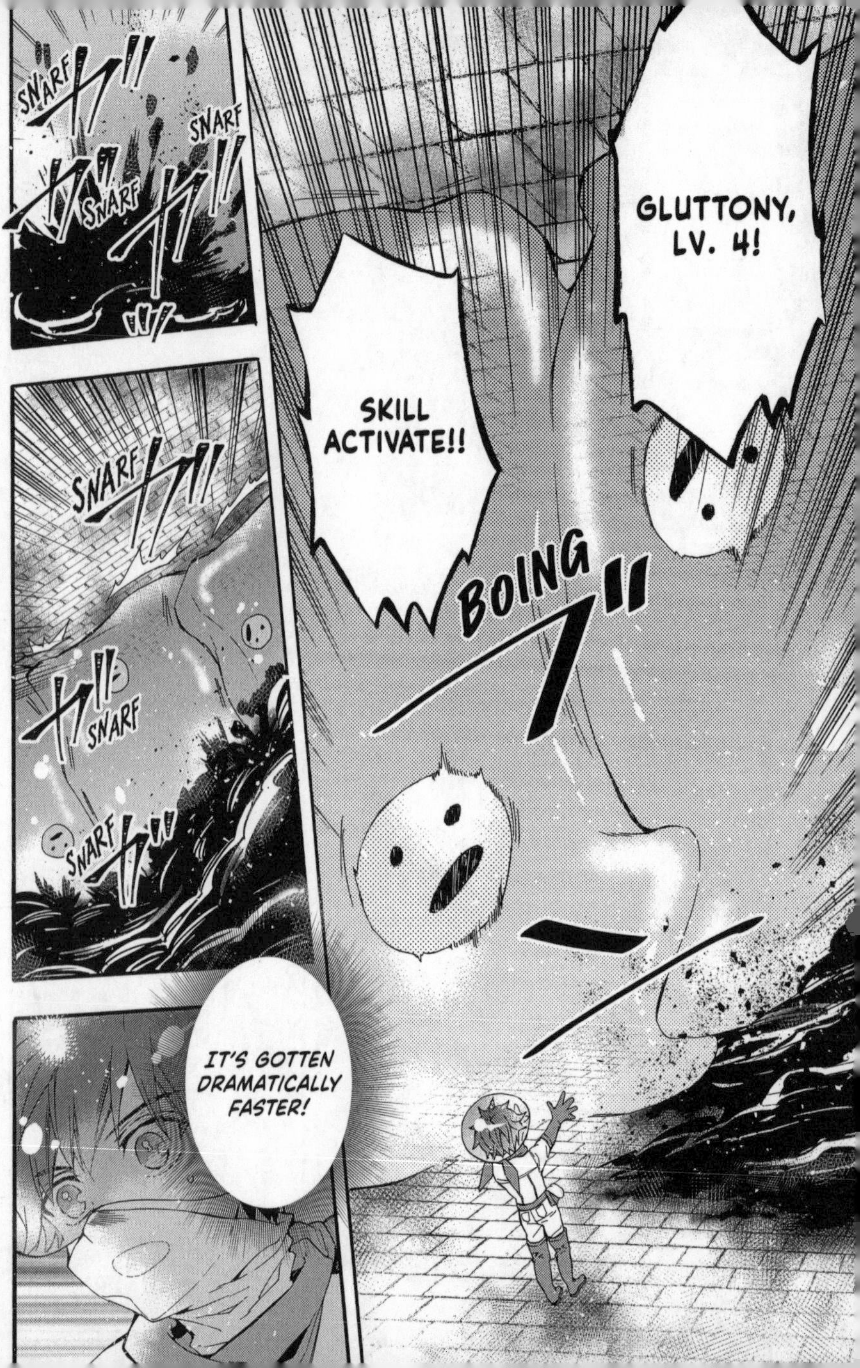
GLUTTONY, LV. 4!
SKILL ACTIVATE!!
BOING
SNARF
SNARF
SNARF
SNARF
SNARF
SNARF
IT'S GOTTEN DRAMATICALLY FASTER!

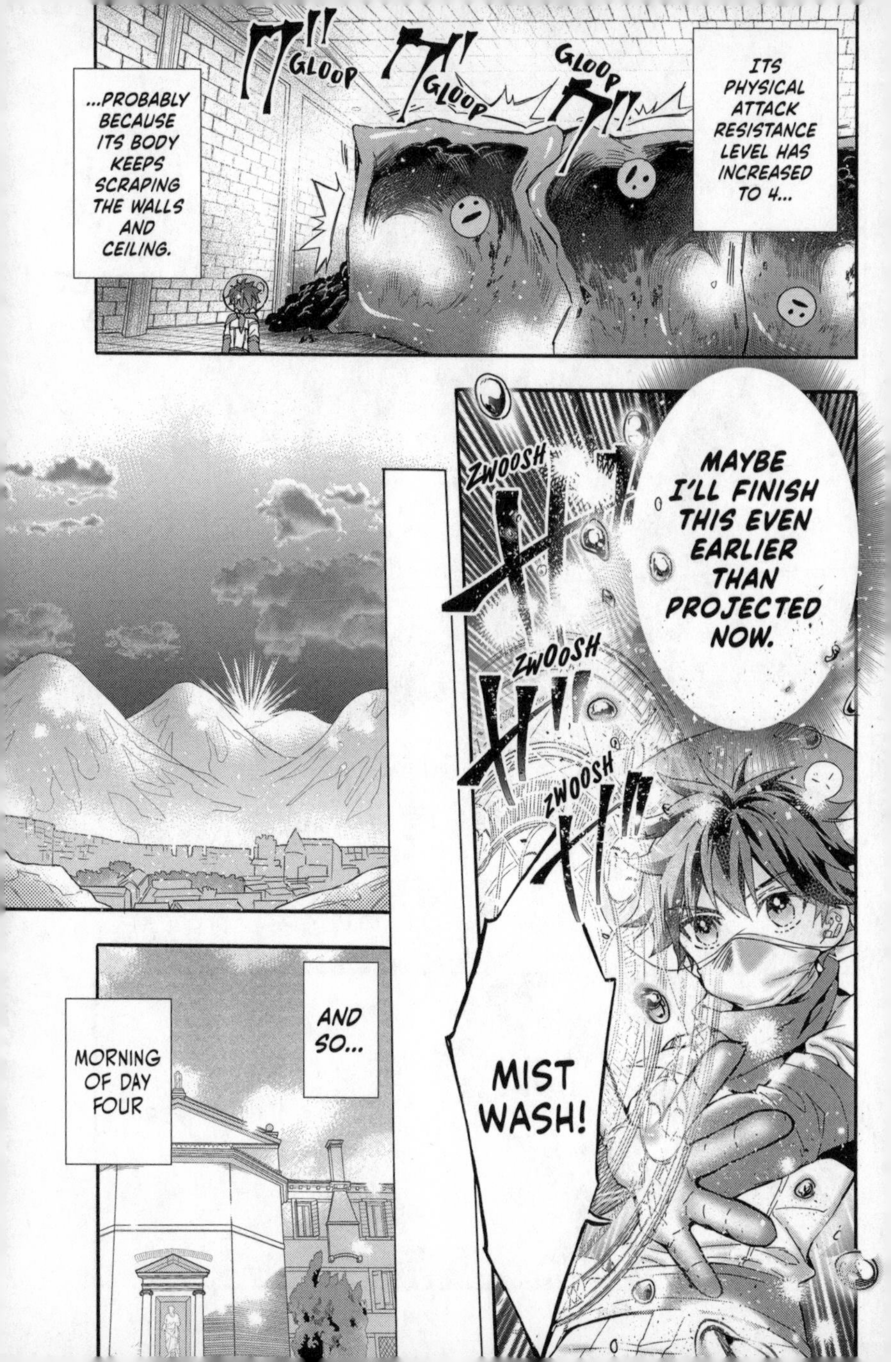
ITS PHYSICAL ATTACK RESISTANCE LEVEL HAS INCREASED TO 4...
GLOOP
GLOOP
GLOOP
...PROBABLY BECAUSE ITS BODY KEEPS SCRAPING THE WALLS AND CEILING.
MAYBE I'LL FINISH THIS EVEN EARLIER THAN PROJECTED NOW.
ZWOOSH
ZWOOSH
ZWOOSH
MIST WASH!
AND SO...
MORNING OF DAY FOUR

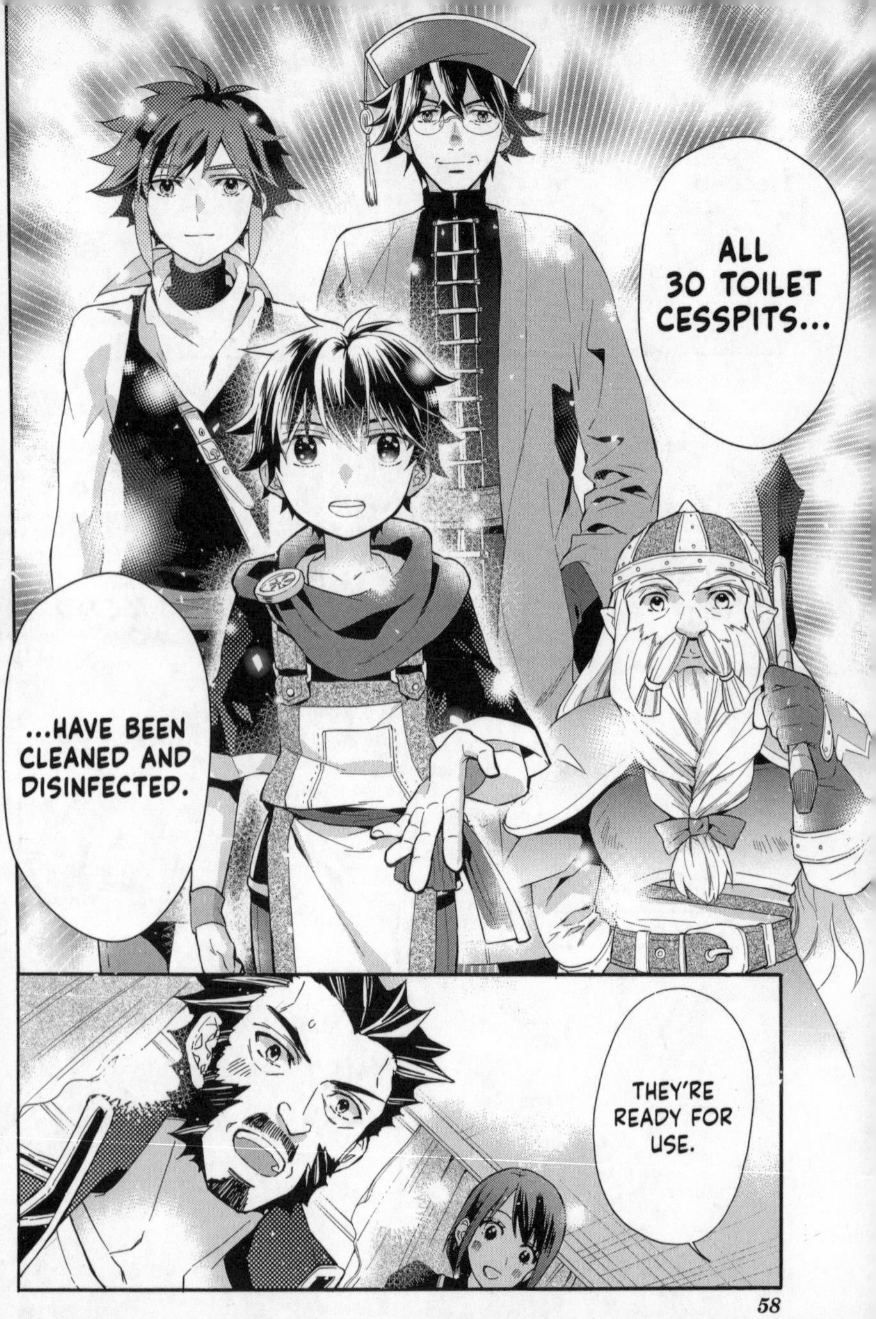
ALL 30 TOILET CESSPITS...
...HAVE BEEN CLEANED AND DISINFECTED.
THEY'RE READY FOR USE.

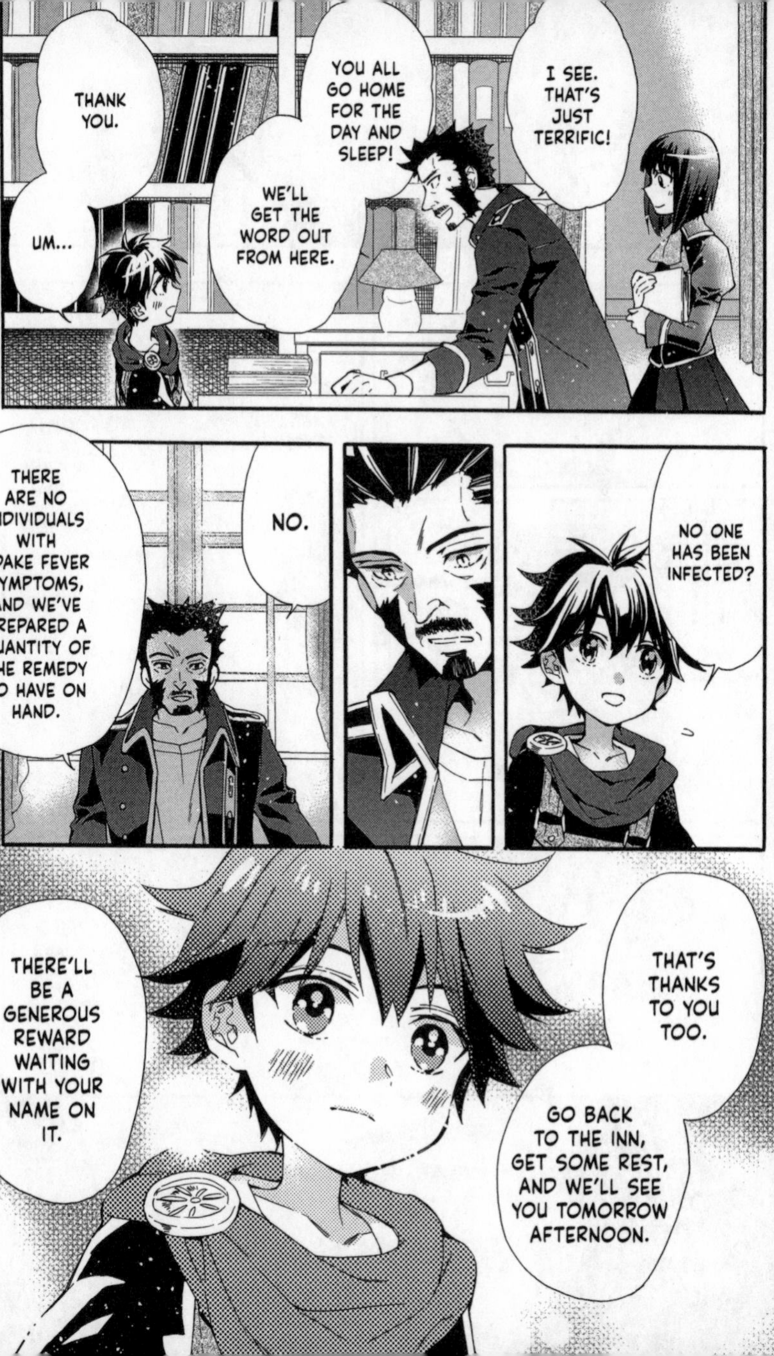
I SEE. THAT'S JUST TERRIFIC!
YOU ALL GO HOME FOR THE DAY AND SLEEP!
WE'LL GET THE WORD OUT FROM HERE.
THANK YOU.
UM...
NO ONE HAS BEEN INFECTED?
NO.
THERE ARE NO INDIVIDUALS WITH IDAKE FEVER SYMPTOMS, AND WE'VE PREPARED A QUANTITY OF THE REMEDY TO HAVE ON HAND.
THAT'S THANKS TO YOU TOO.
GO BACK TO THE INN, GET SOME REST, AND WE'LL SEE YOU TOMORROW AFTERNOON.
THERE'LL BE A GENEROUS REWARD WAITING WITH YOUR NAME ON IT.

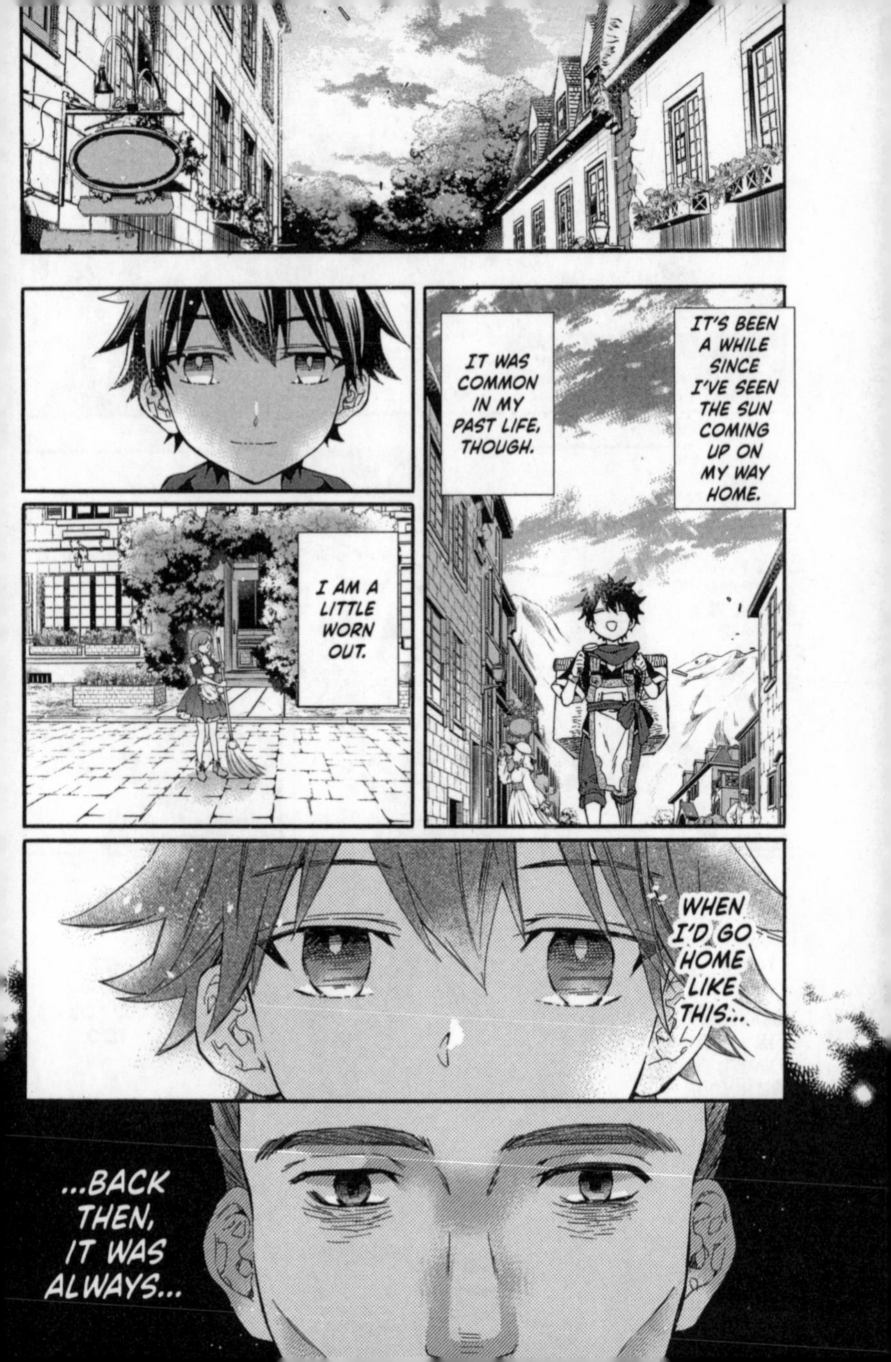
IT'S BEEN A WHILE SINCE I'VE SEEN THE SUN COMING UP ON MY WAY HOME.
IT WAS COMMON IN MY PAST LIFE, THOUGH.
I AM A LITTLE WORN OUT.
WHEN I'D GO HOME LIKE THIS...
...BACK THEN, IT WAS ALWAYS...

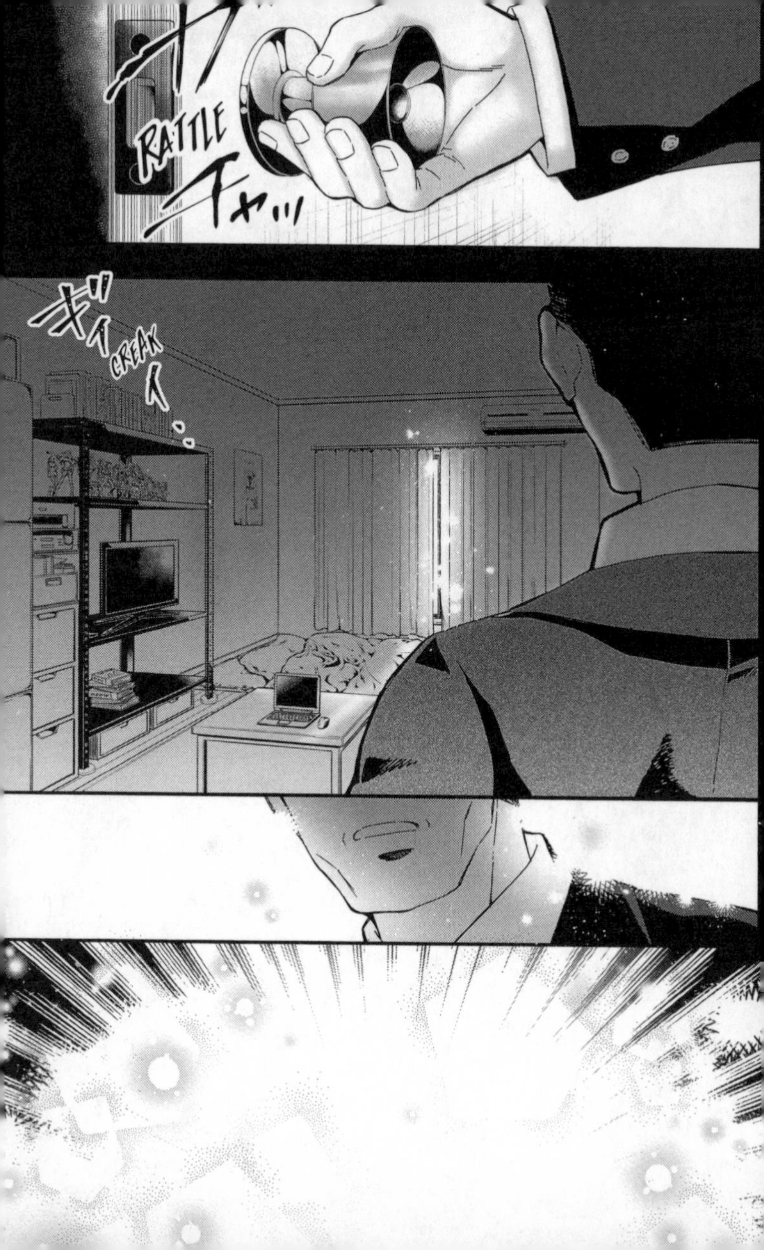
RATTLE
CREAK

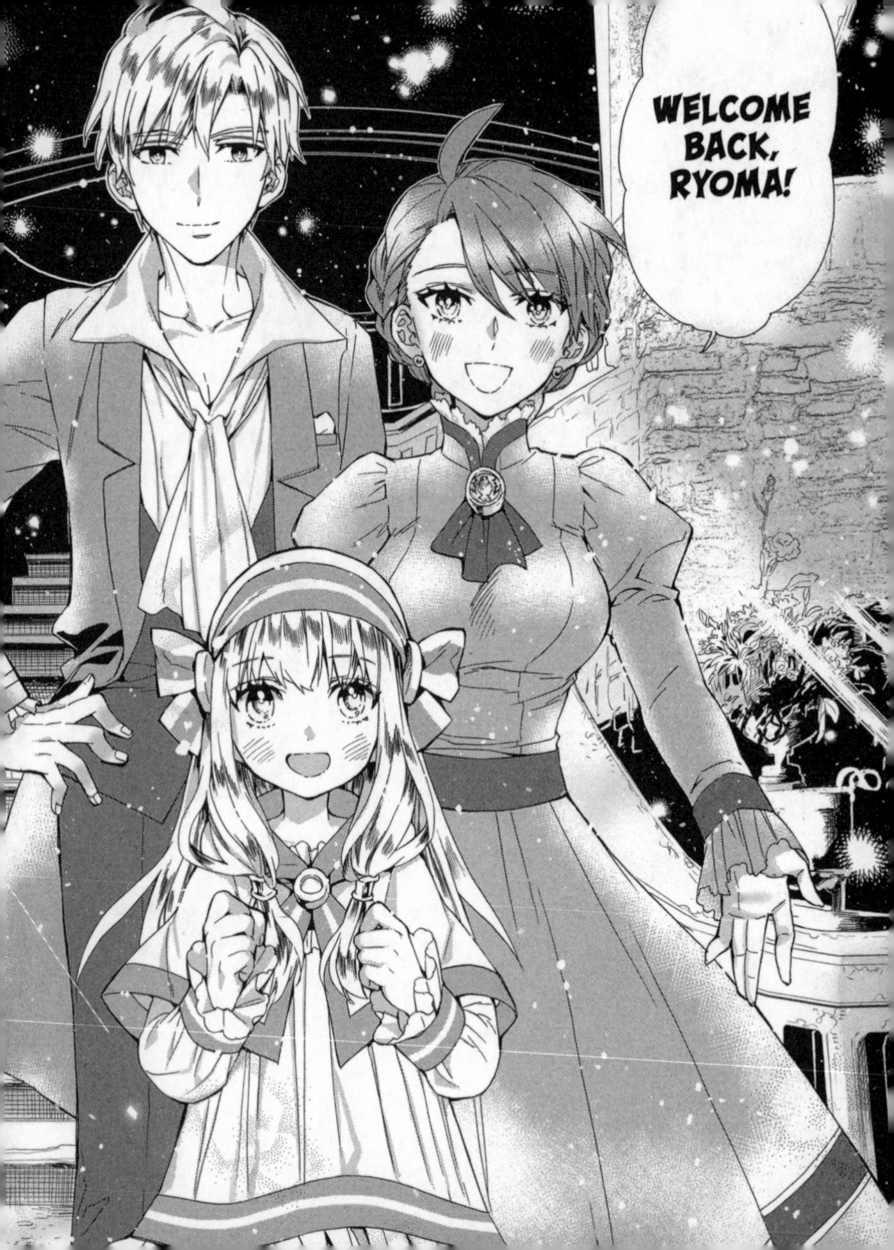
WELCOME BACK, RYOMA!

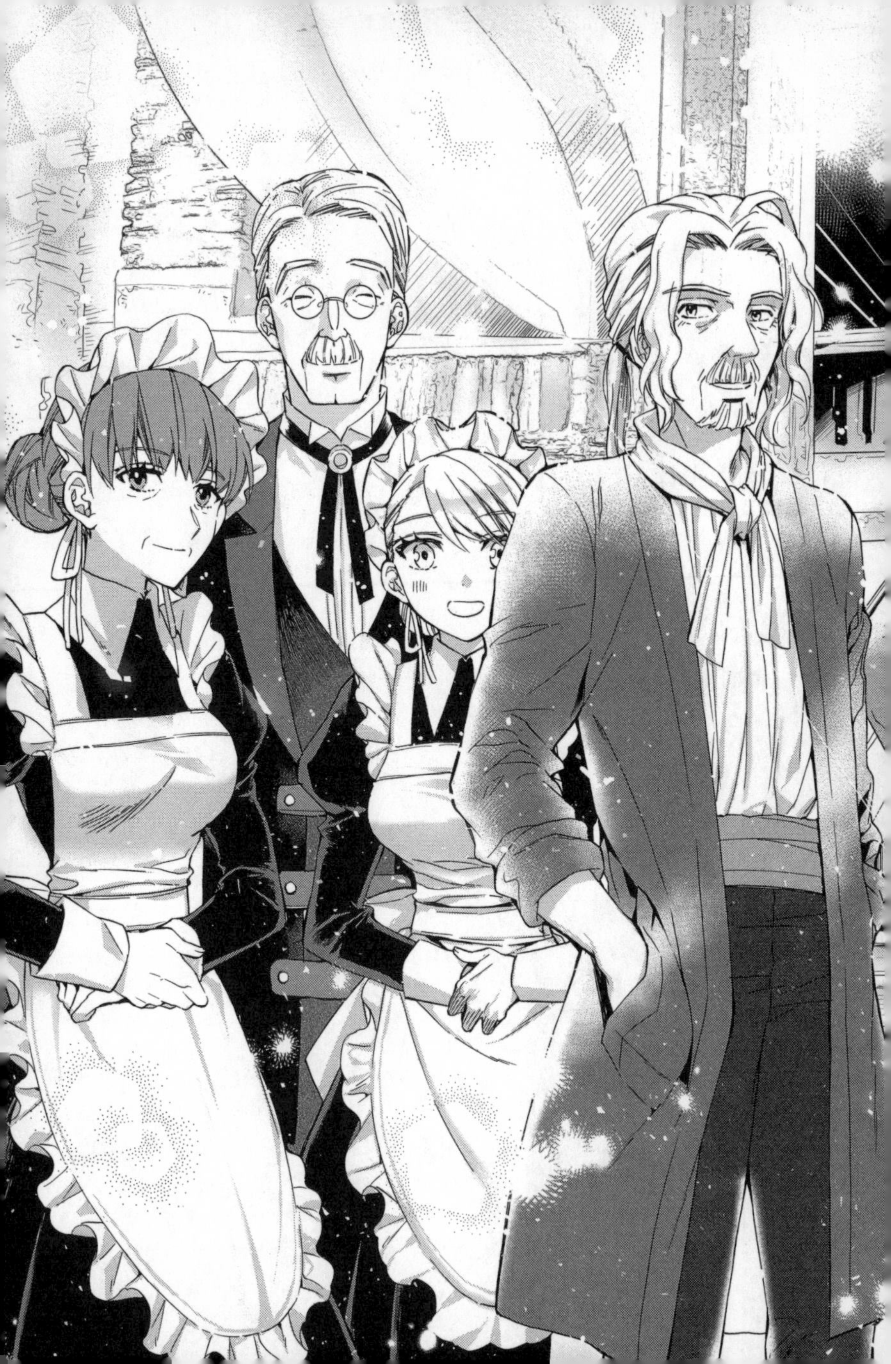

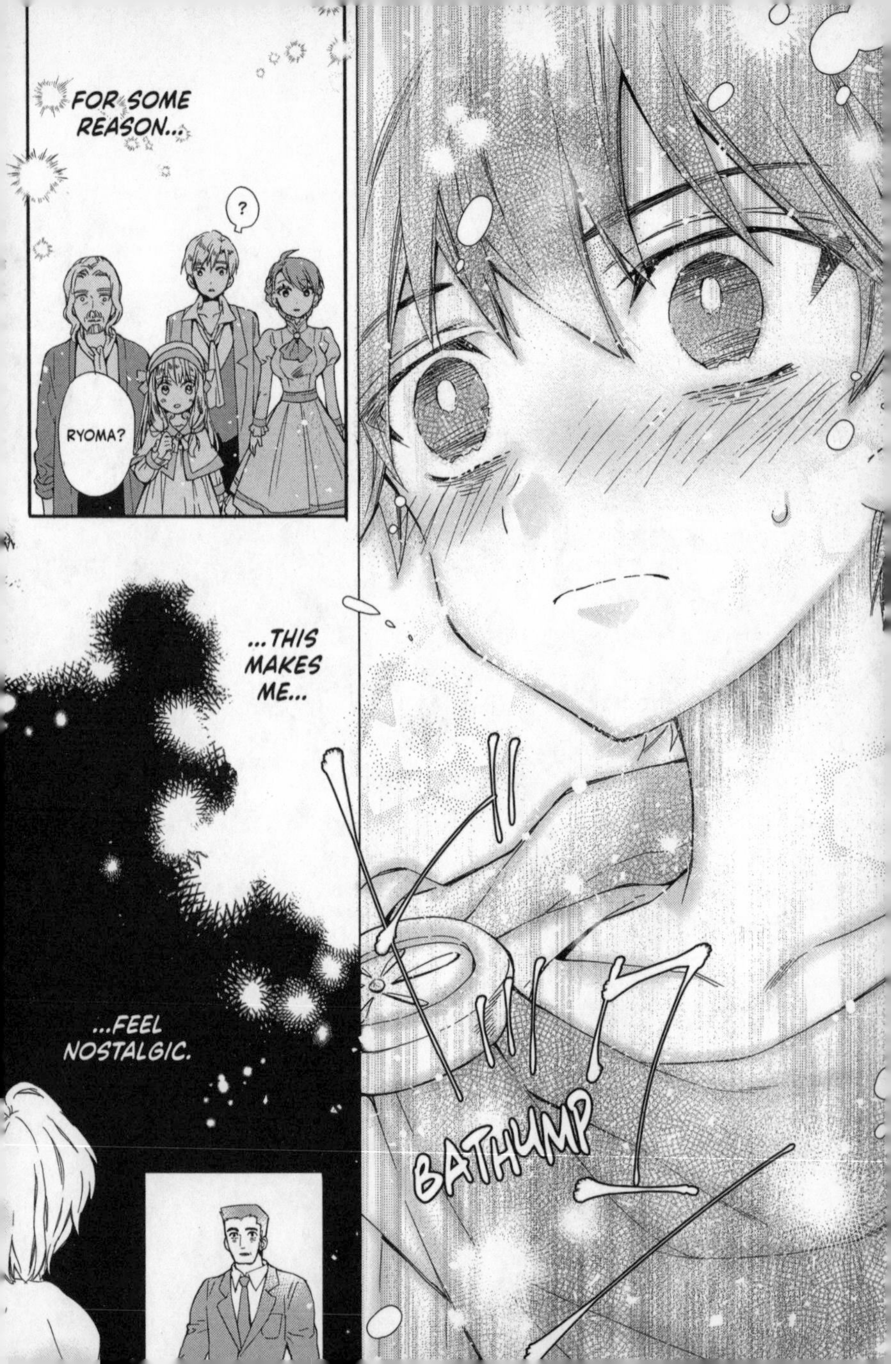
BATHUMP
FOR SOME REASON...
?
RYOMA?
...THIS MAKES ME...
...FEEL NOSTALGIC.

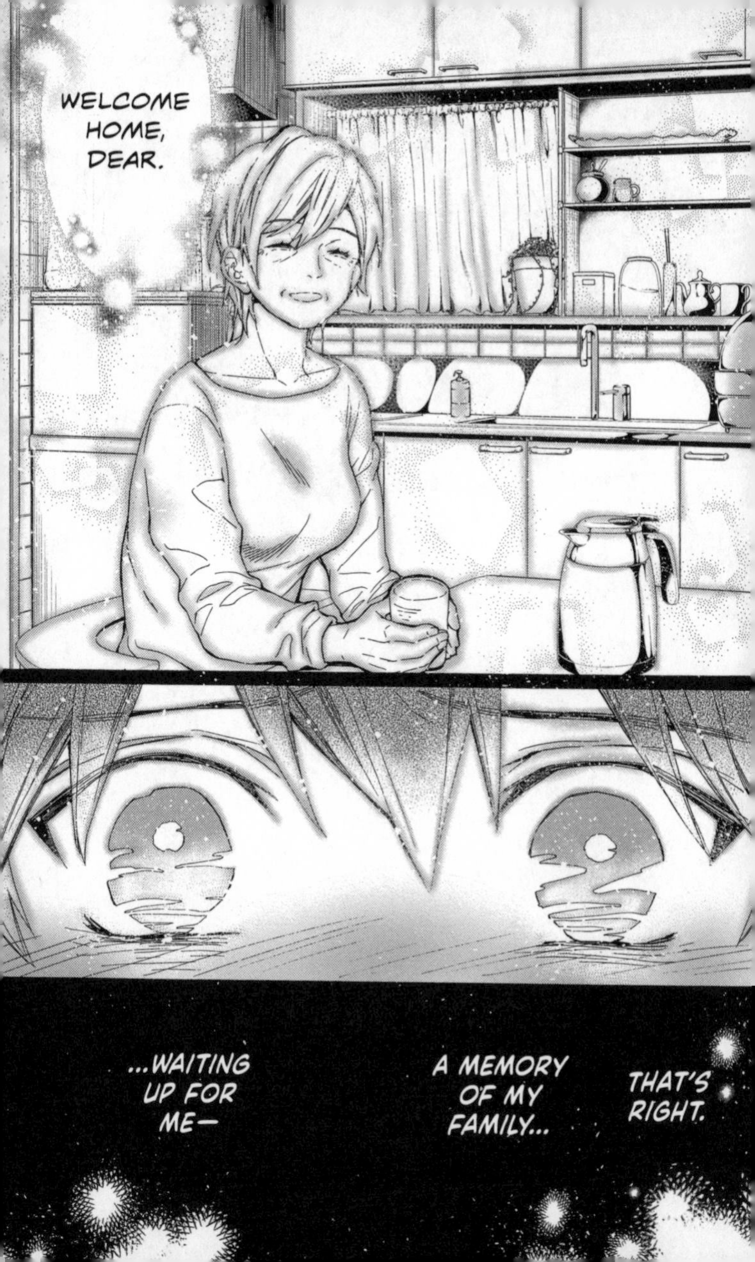
WELCOME HOME, DEAR.
THAT'S RIGHT.
A MEMORY OF MY FAMILY...
...WAITING UP FOR ME—

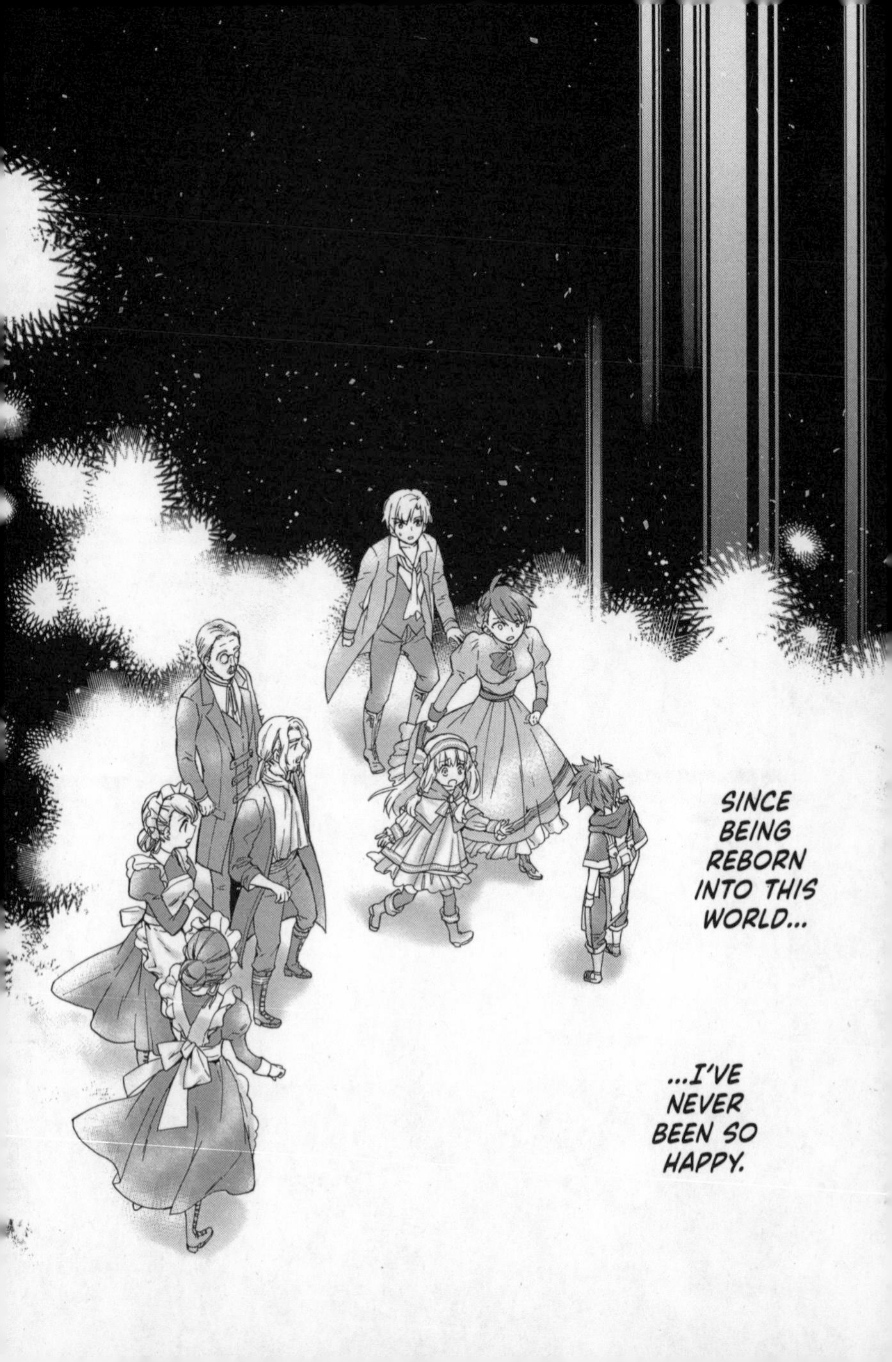
SINCE BEING REBORN INTO THIS WORLD...
...I'VE NEVER BEEN SO HAPPY.

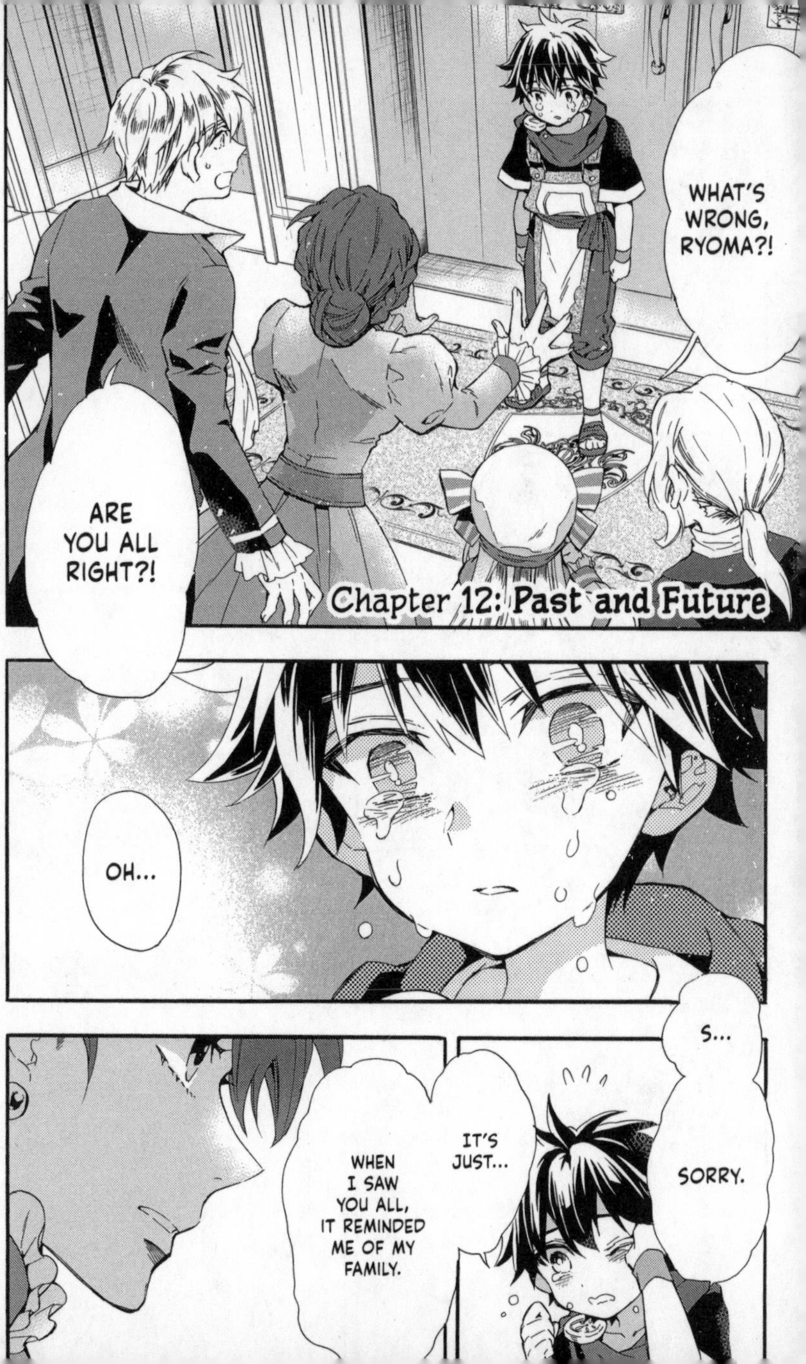
WHAT'S WRONG, RYOMA?!
ARE YOU ALL RIGHT?!
Chapter 12: Past and Future
OH...
S...
SORRY.
IT'S JUST...
WHEN I SAW YOU ALL, IT REMINDED ME OF MY FAMILY.

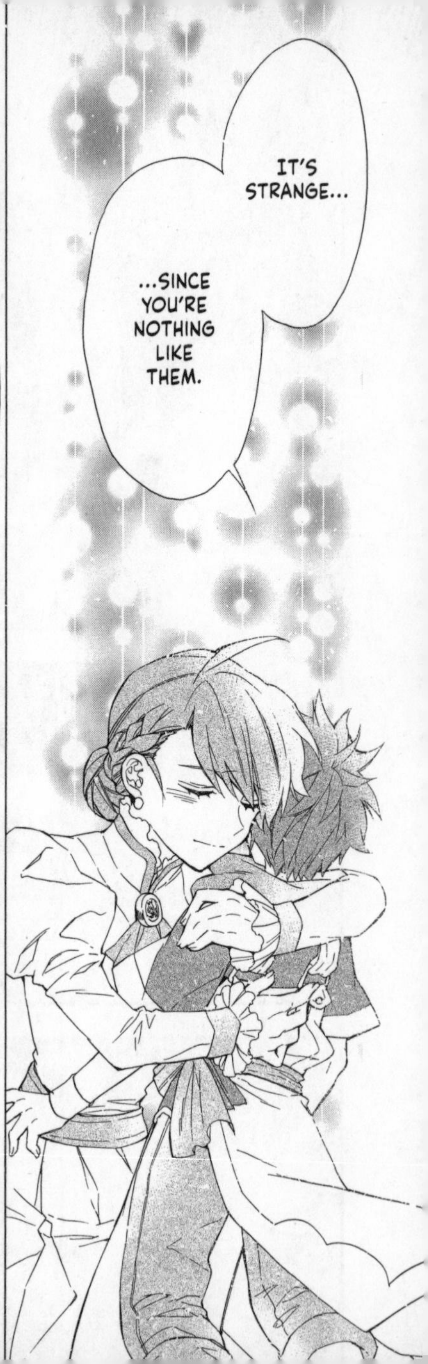
IT'S STRANGE...
...SINCE YOU'RE NOTHING LIKE THEM.

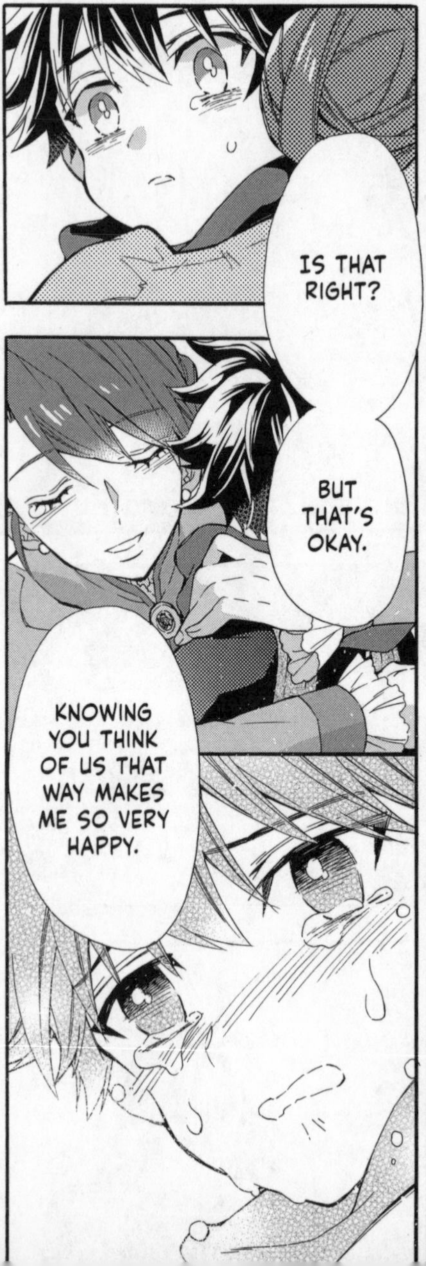
IS THAT RIGHT?
BUT THAT'S OKAY.
KNOWING YOU THINK OF US THAT WAY MAKES ME SO VERY HAPPY.

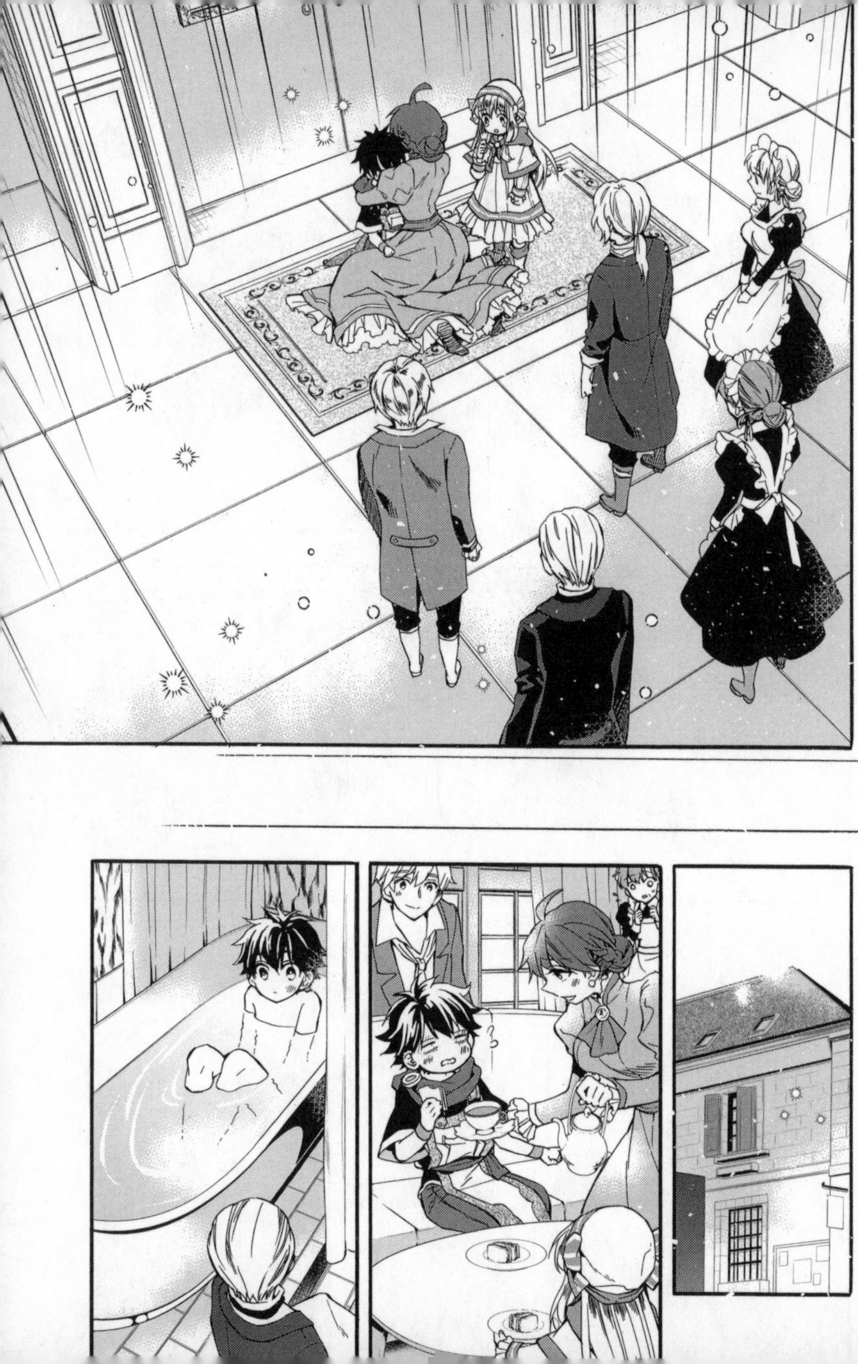

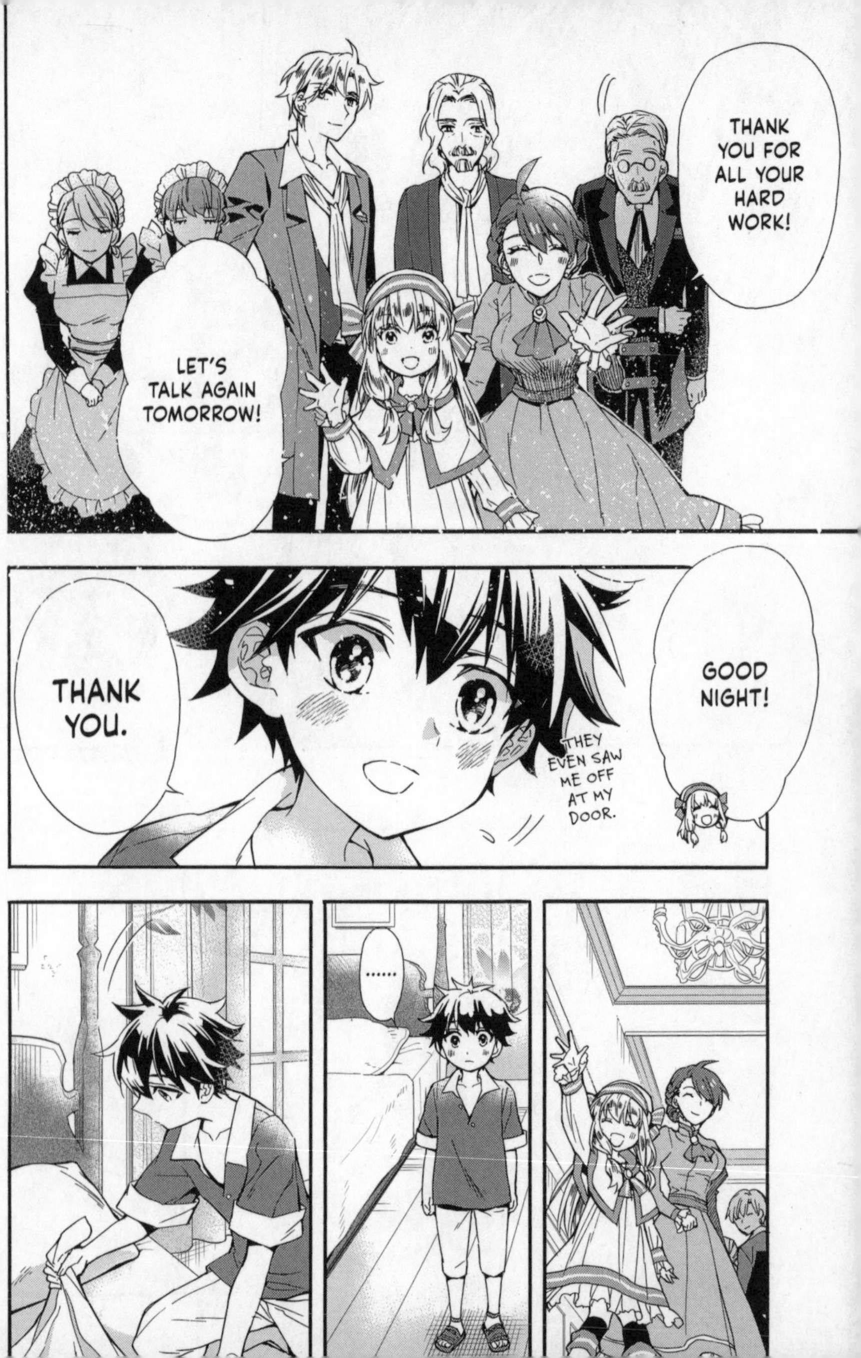
THANK YOU FOR ALL YOUR HARD WORK!
LET'S TALK AGAIN TOMORROW!
GOOD NIGHT!
THEY EVEN SAW ME OFF AT MY DOOR.
THANK YOU.
......

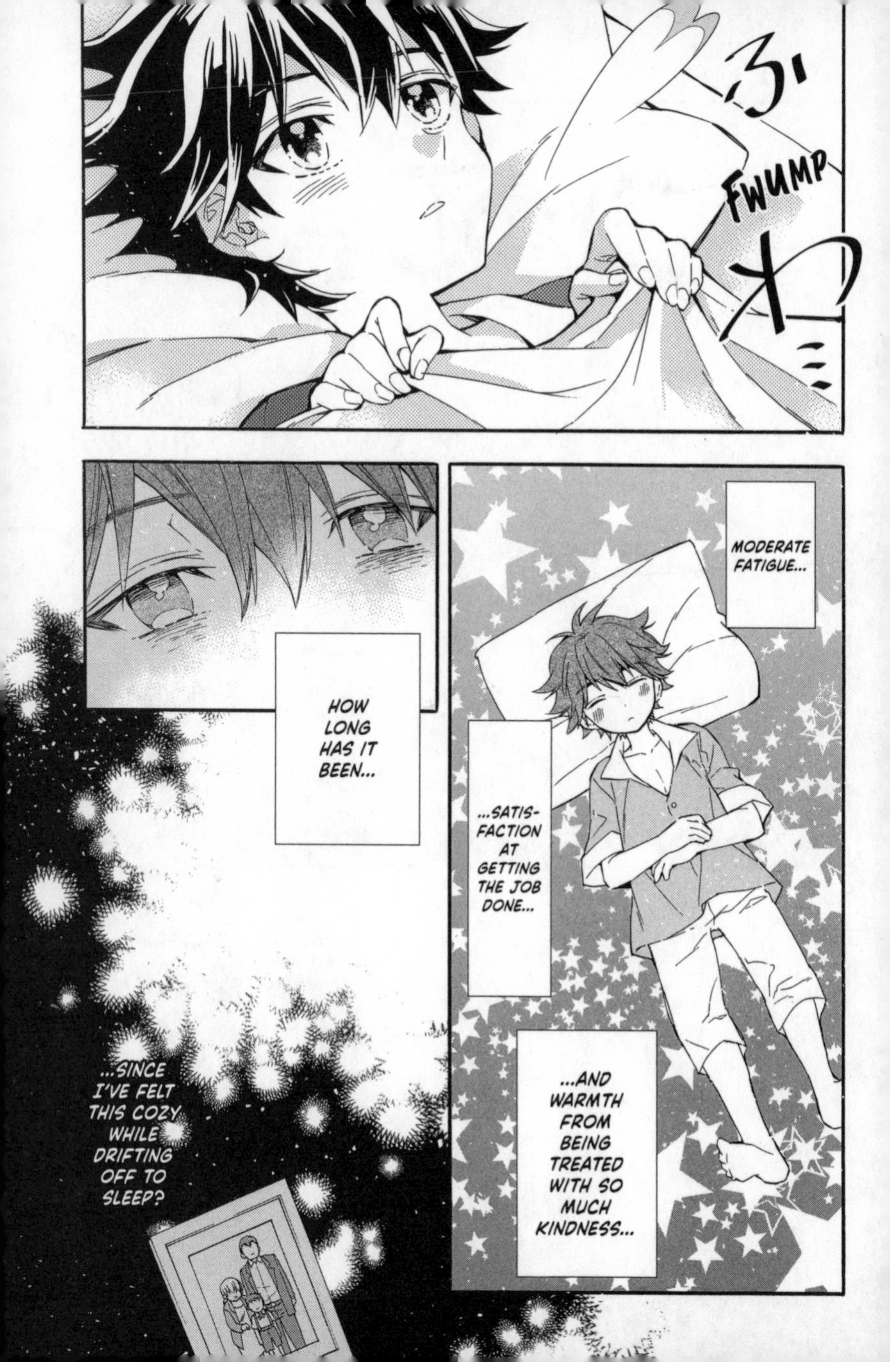
FWUMP
MODERATE FATIGUE...
...SATISFACTION AT GETTING THE JOB DONE...
...AND WARMTH FROM BEING TREATED WITH SO MUCH KINDNESS...
HOW LONG HAS IT BEEN...
...SINCE I'VE FELT THIS COZY WHILE DRIFTING OFF TO SLEEP?

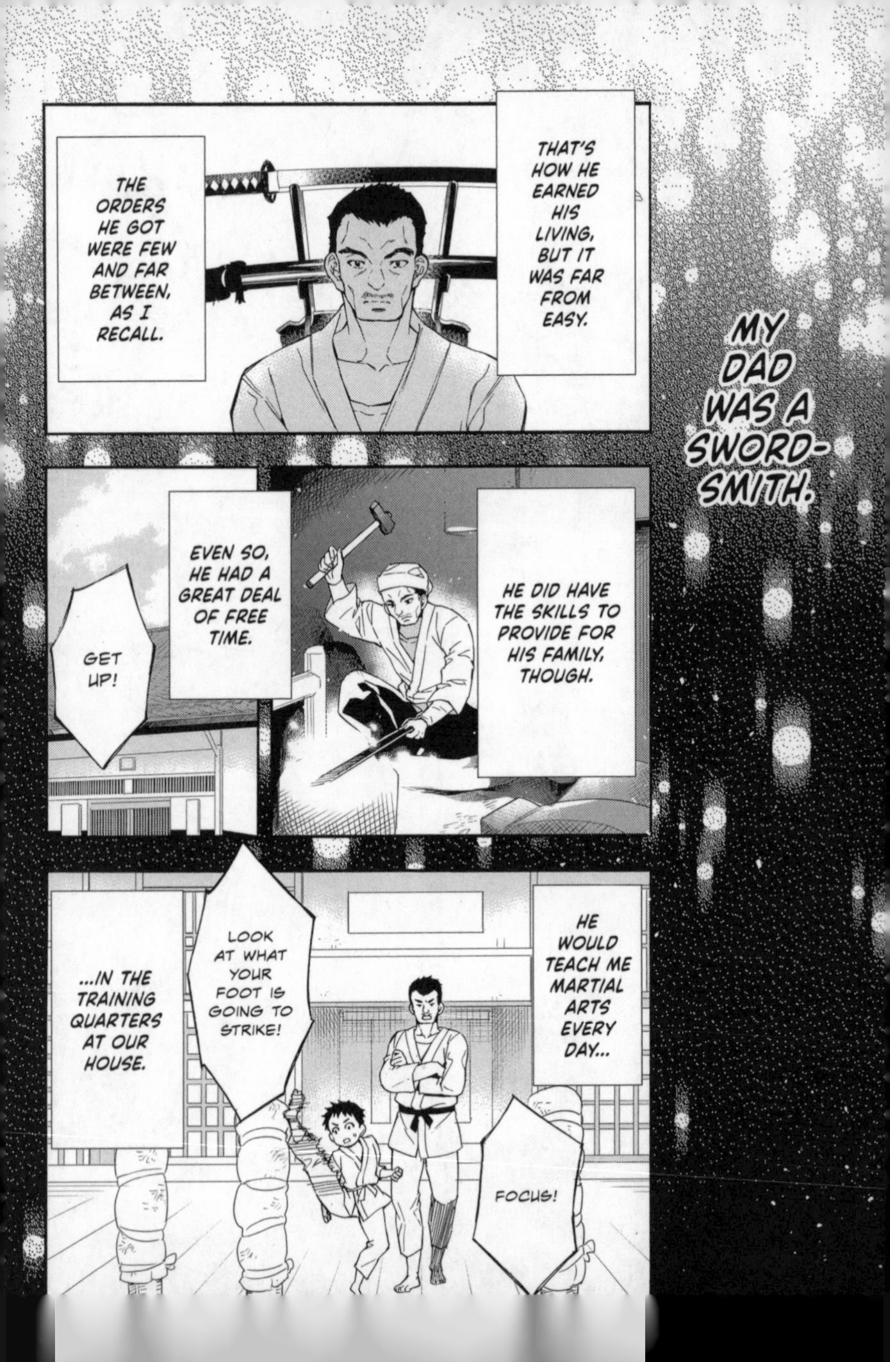
MY DAD WAS A SWORD-SMITH.
THAT'S HOW HE EARNED HIS LIVING, BUT IT WAS FAR FROM EASY.
THE ORDERS HE GOT WERE FEW AND FAR BETWEEN, AS I RECALL.
HE DID HAVE THE SKILLS TO PROVIDE FOR HIS FAMILY, THOUGH.
EVEN SO, HE HAD A GREAT DEAL OF FREE TIME.
GET UP!
HE WOULD TEACH ME MARTIAL ARTS EVERY DAY...
FOCUS!
LOOK AT WHAT YOUR FOOT IS GOING TO STRIKE!
...IN THE TRAINING QUARTERS AT OUR HOUSE.

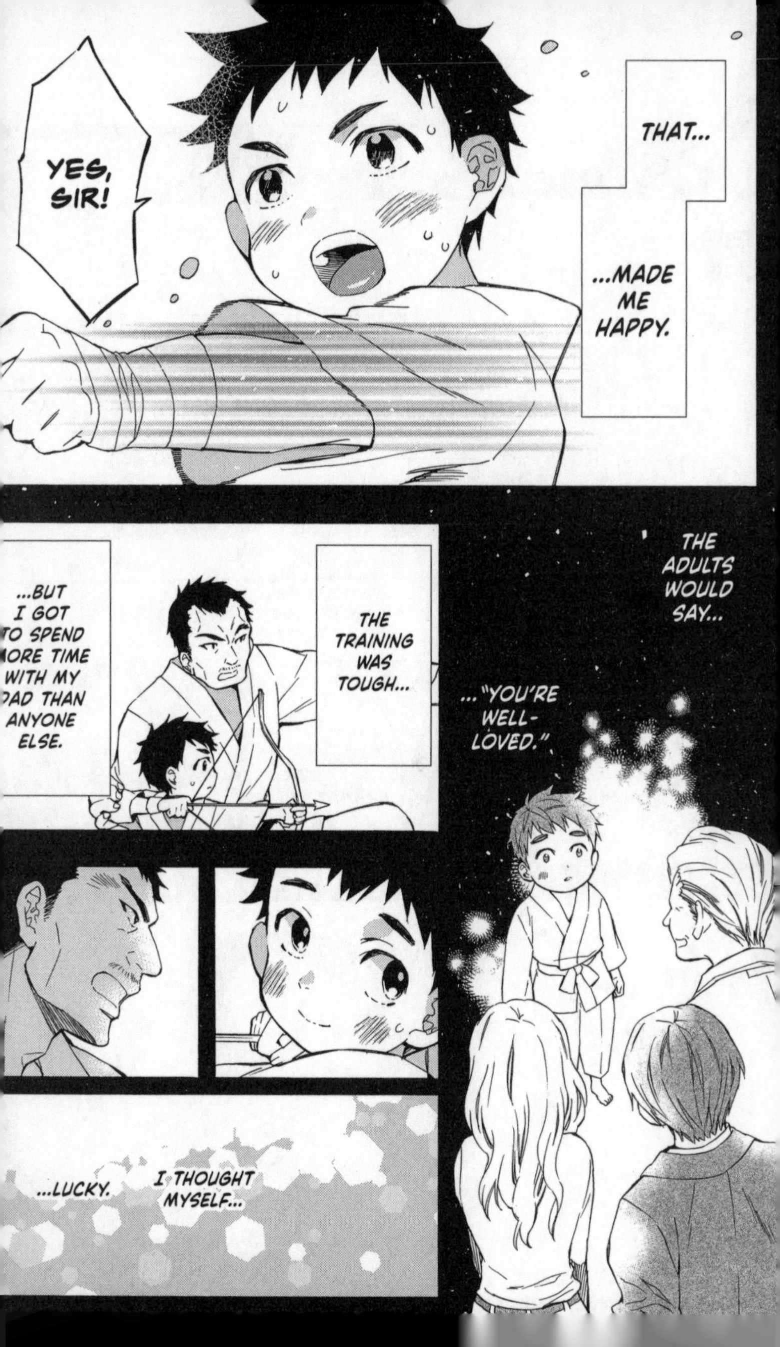
THAT...
YES, SIR!
...MADE ME HAPPY.
THE ADULTS WOULD SAY...
..."YOU'RE WELL-LOVED."
THE TRAINING WAS TOUGH...
...BUT I GOT TO SPEND MORE TIME WITH MY DAD THAN ANYONE ELSE.
I THOUGHT MYSELF...
...LUCKY.

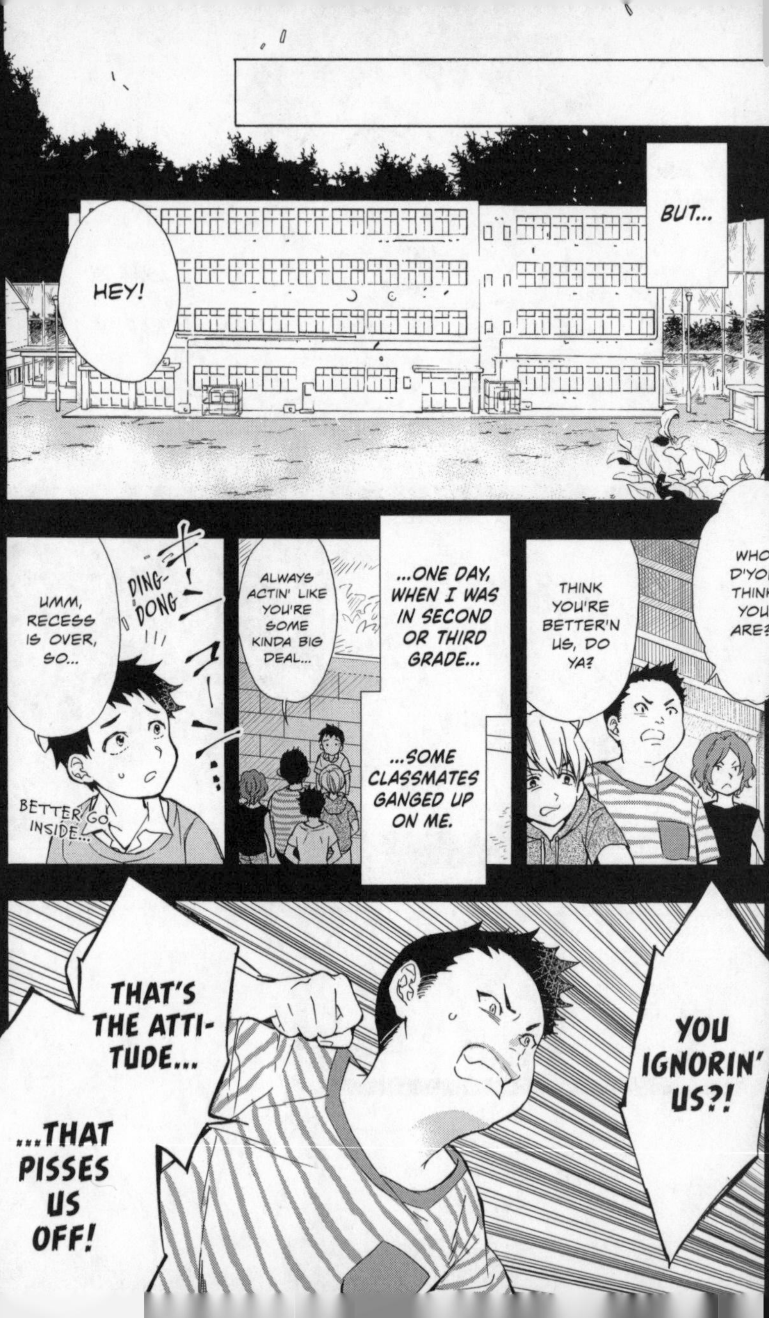
BUT...
HEY!
WHO D'YOU THINK YOU ARE?!
THINK YOU'RE BETTER'N US, DO YA?
...ONE DAY, WHEN I WAS IN SECOND OR THIRD GRADE...
...SOME CLASSMATES GANGED UP ON ME.
ALWAYS ACTIN' LIKE YOU'RE SOME KINDA BIG DEAL...
DING-DONG
UMM, RECESS IS OVER, SO...
BETTER GO INSIDE...
YOU IGNORIN' US?!
THAT'S THE ATTI-TUDE...
...THAT PISSES US OFF!

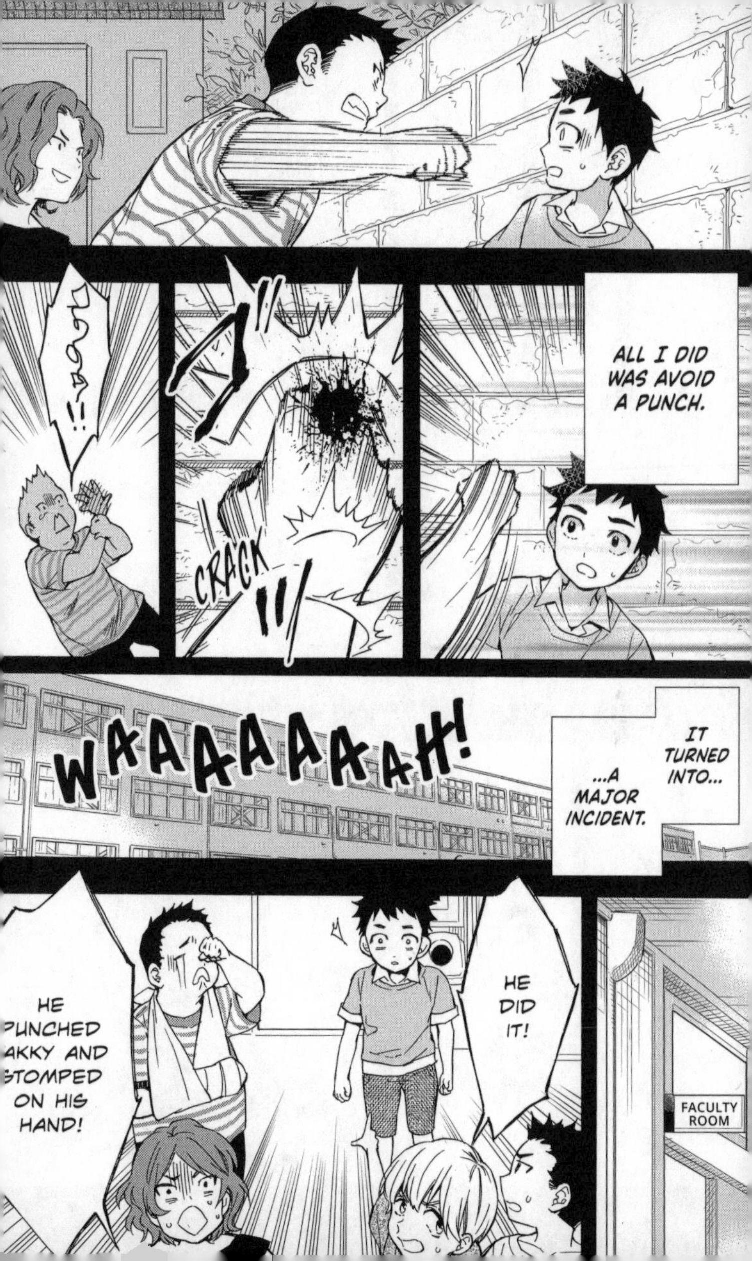

ALL I DID WAS AVOID A PUNCH.
CRACK!!
IT TURNED INTO...
...A MAJOR INCIDENT.
WAAAAAAAH!
FACULTY ROOM
HE DID IT!
HE PUNCHED AKKY AND STOMPED ON HIS HAND!

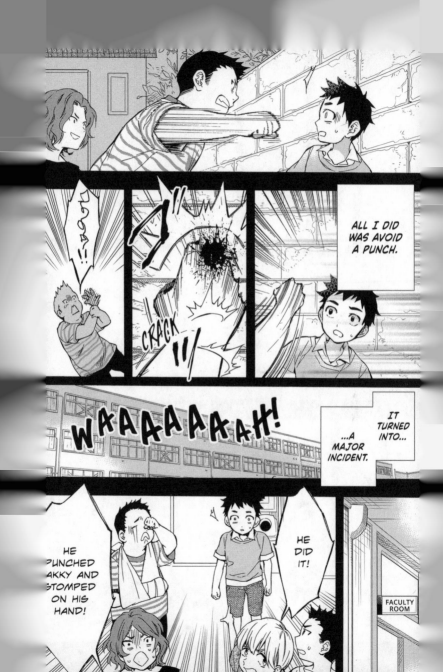

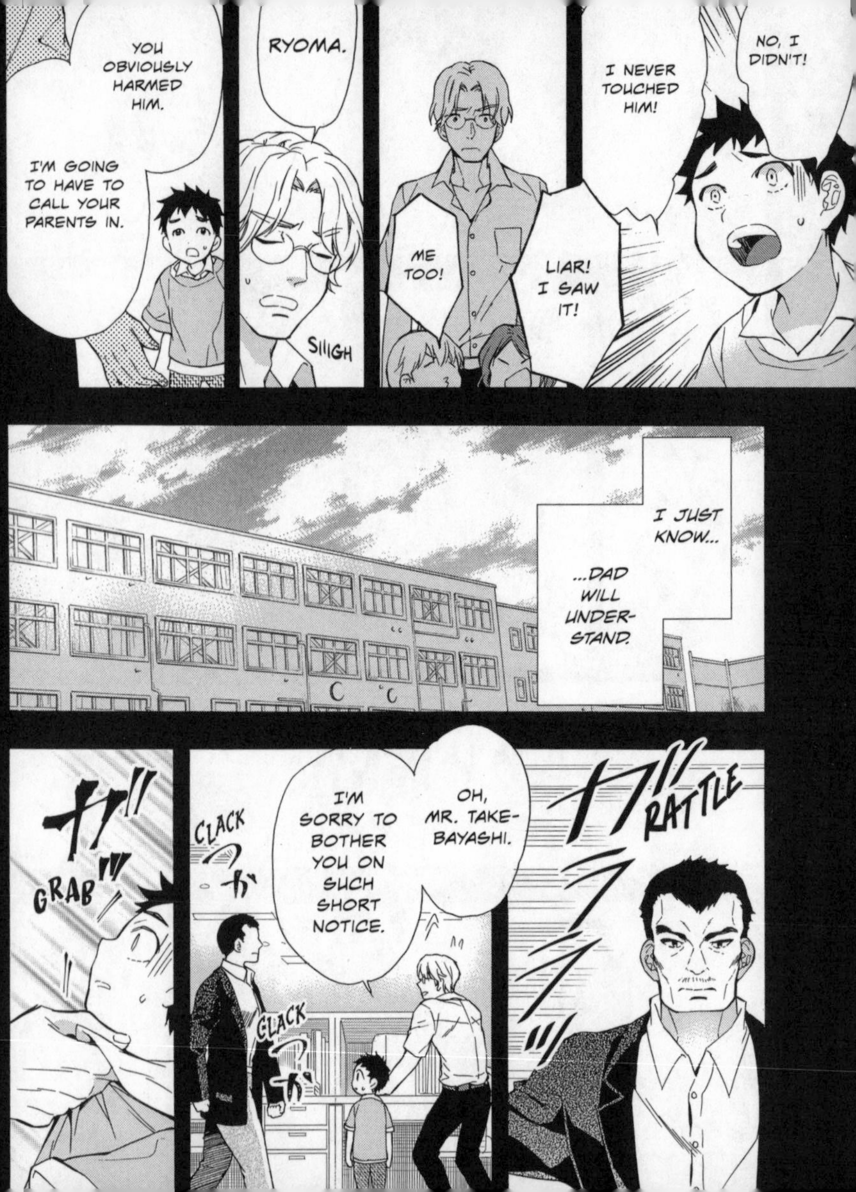

NO, I DIDN'T!
I NEVER TOUCHED HIM!
LIAR! I SAW IT!
ME TOO!
RYOMA.
SIIIGH
YOU OBVIOUSLY HARMED HIM.
I'M GOING TO HAVE TO CALL YOUR PARENTS IN.
I JUST KNOW...
...DAD WILL UNDER-STAND.
RATTLE
OH, MR. TAKE-BAYASHI.
I'M SORRY TO BOTHER YOU ON SUCH SHORT NOTICE.
CLACK
CLACK
GRAB

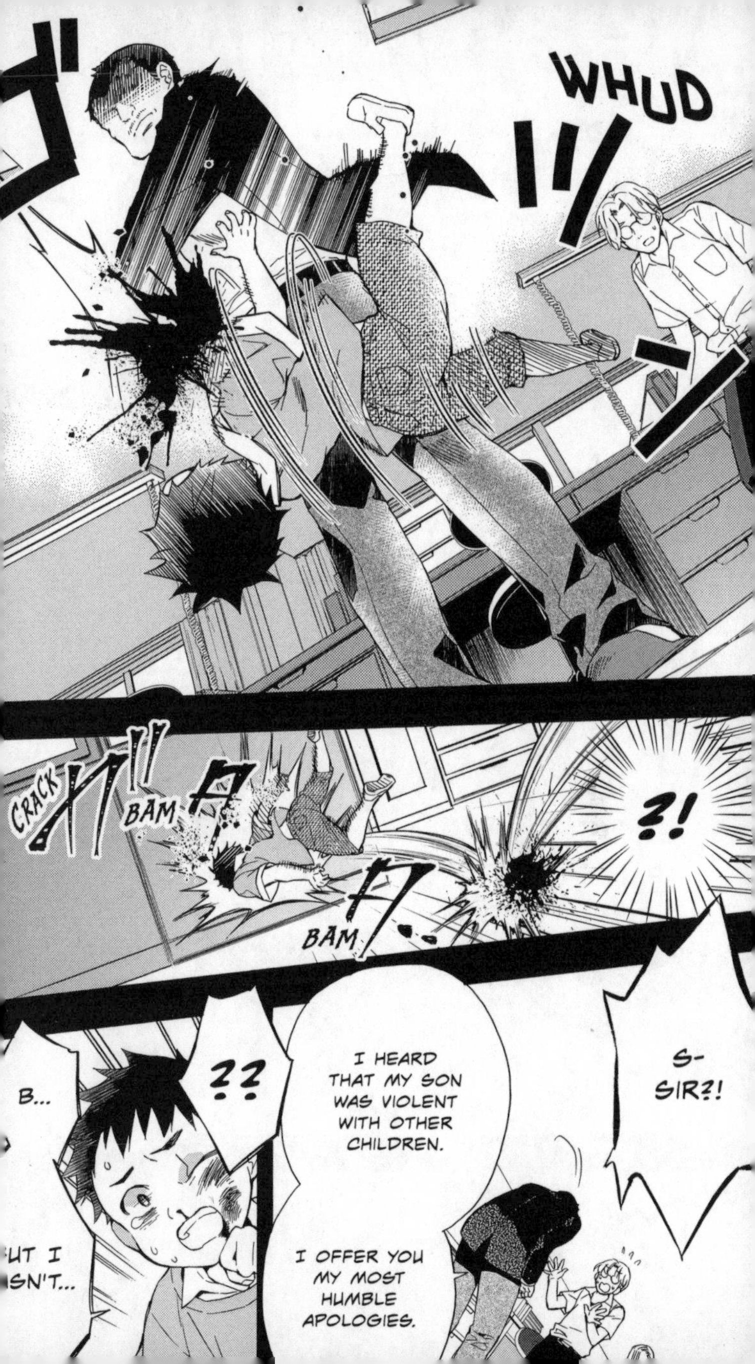
WHUD
?!
BAM
BAM
CRACK
S-SIR?!
I HEARD THAT MY SON WAS VIOLENT WITH OTHER CHILDREN.
I OFFER YOU MY MOST HUMBLE APOLOGIES.
??
B...
UT I SN'T...

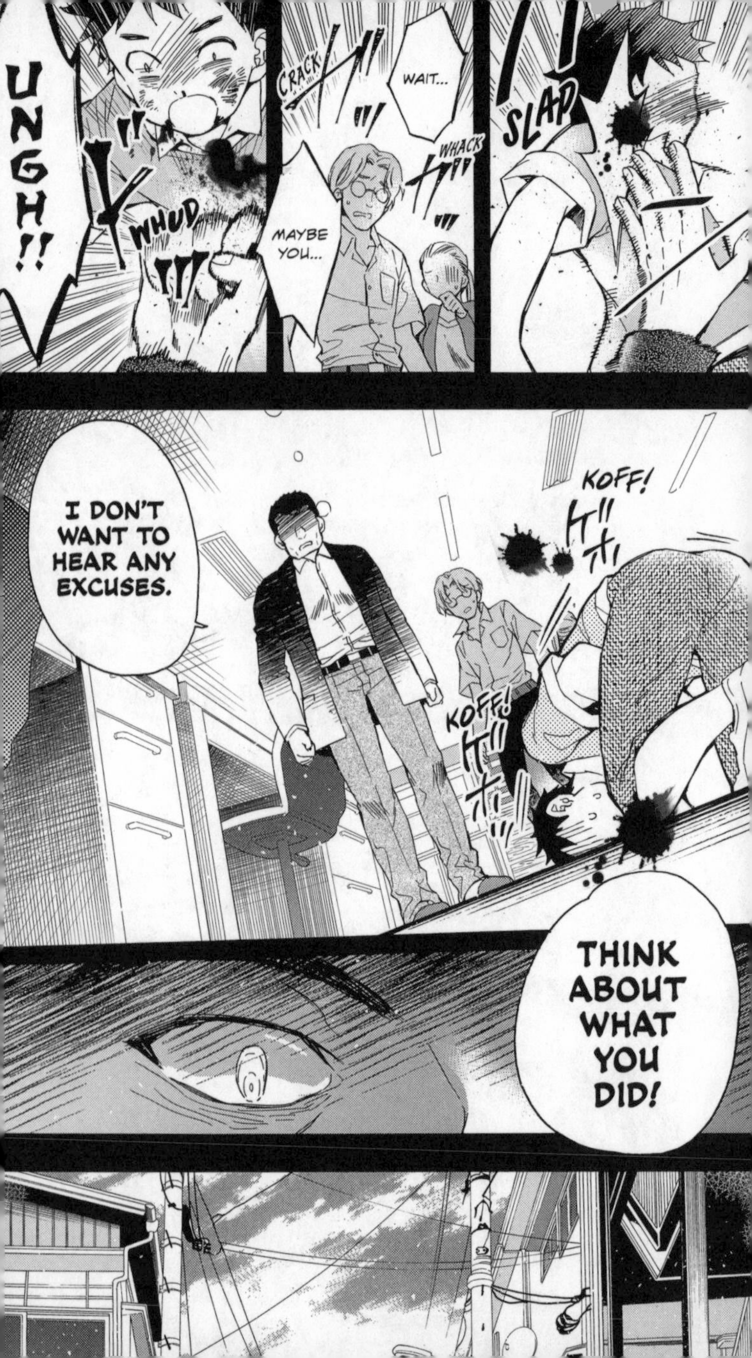
SLAP
WAIT...
CRACK
WHACK
MAYBE YOU...
UNGH!!
WHUD
KOFF!
I DON'T WANT TO HEAR ANY EXCUSES.
KOFF!
THINK ABOUT WHAT YOU DID!

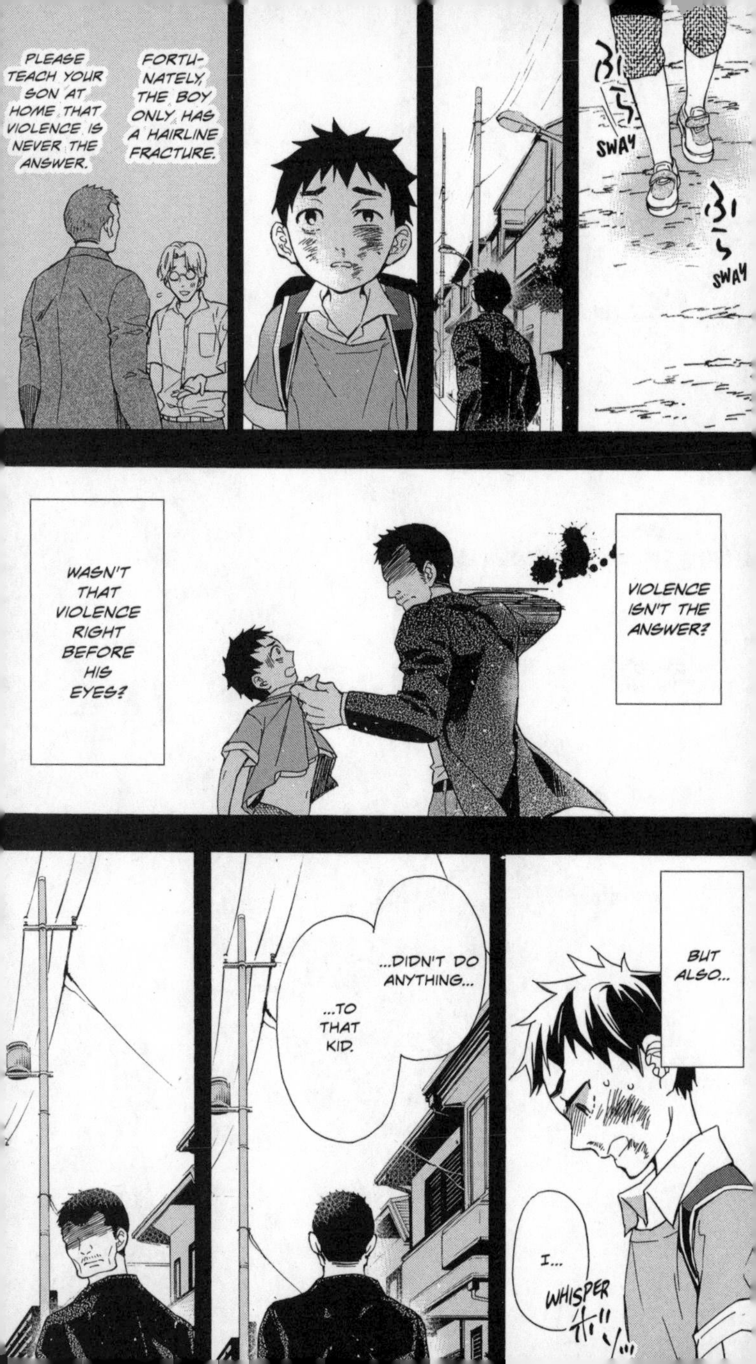
SWAY
SWAY
FORTUNATELY, THE BOY ONLY HAS A HAIRLINE FRACTURE.
PLEASE TEACH YOUR SON AT HOME THAT VIOLENCE IS NEVER THE ANSWER.
VIOLENCE ISN'T THE ANSWER?
WASN'T THAT VIOLENCE RIGHT BEFORE HIS EYES?
BUT ALSO...
I...
WHISPER
...DIDN'T DO ANYTHING...
...TO THAT KID.

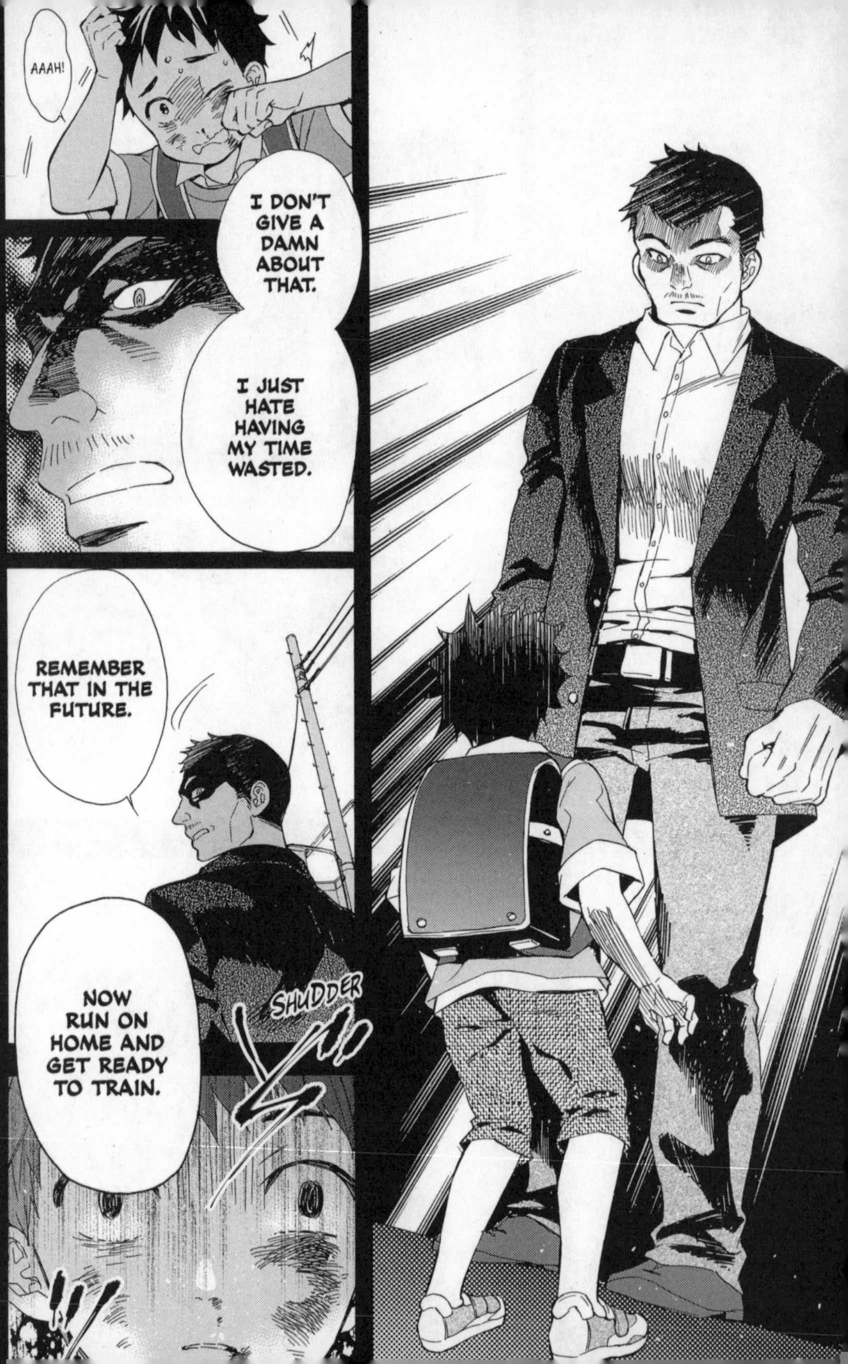
SHUDDER
AAAH!
I DON'T GIVE A DAMN ABOUT THAT.
I JUST HATE HAVING MY TIME WASTED.
REMEMBER THAT IN THE FUTURE.
NOW RUN ON HOME AND GET READY TO TRAIN.

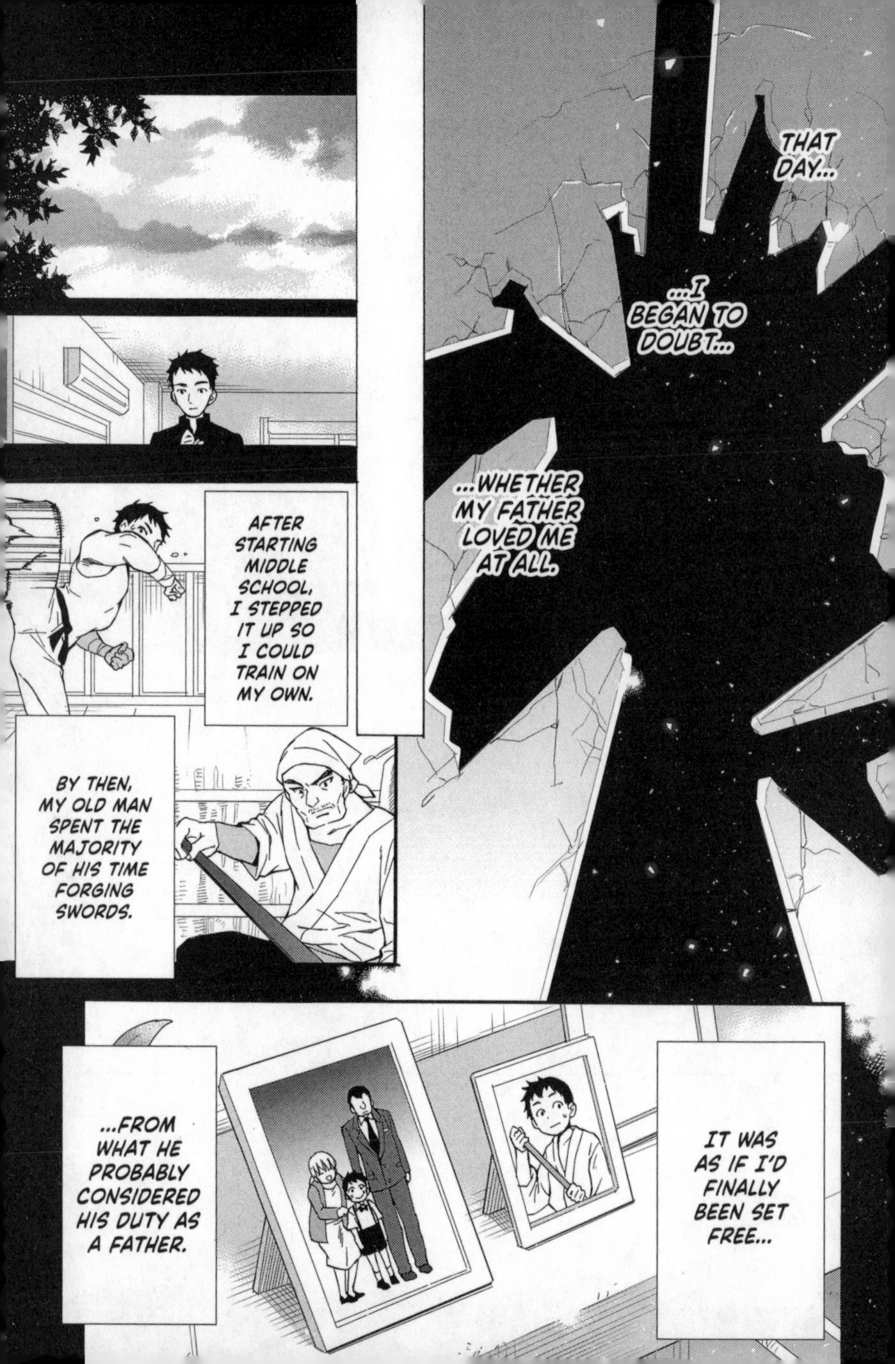
THAT DAY...
...I BEGAN TO DOUBT...
...WHETHER MY FATHER LOVED ME AT ALL.
AFTER STARTING MIDDLE SCHOOL, I STEPPED IT UP SO I COULD TRAIN ON MY OWN.
BY THEN, MY OLD MAN SPENT THE MAJORITY OF HIS TIME FORGING SWORDS.
IT WAS AS IF I'D FINALLY BEEN SET FREE...
...FROM WHAT HE PROBABLY CONSIDERED HIS DUTY AS A FATHER.

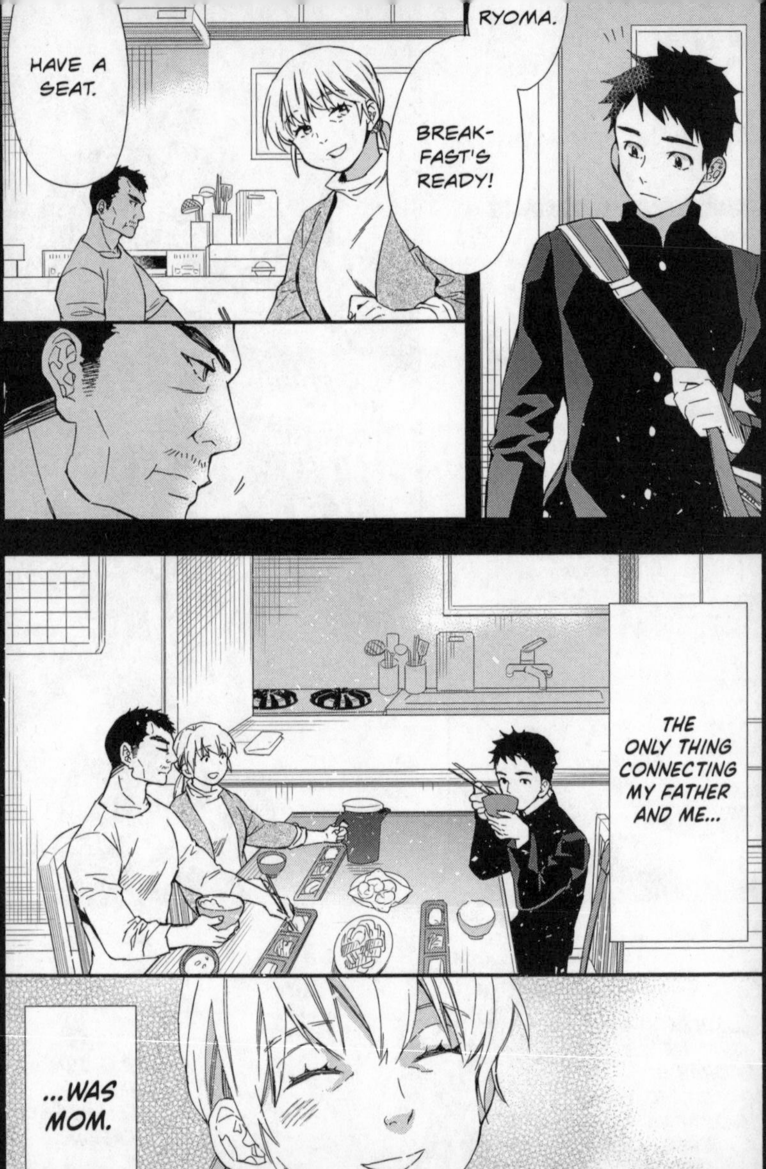
RYOMA.
BREAK-FAST'S READY!
HAVE A SEAT.
THE ONLY THING CONNECTING MY FATHER AND ME...
...WAS MOM.

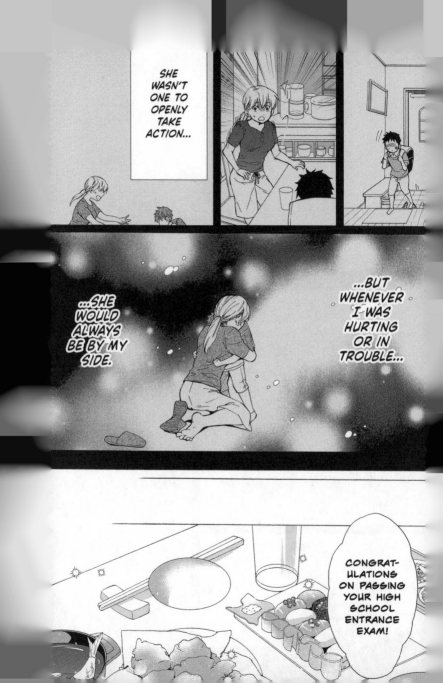

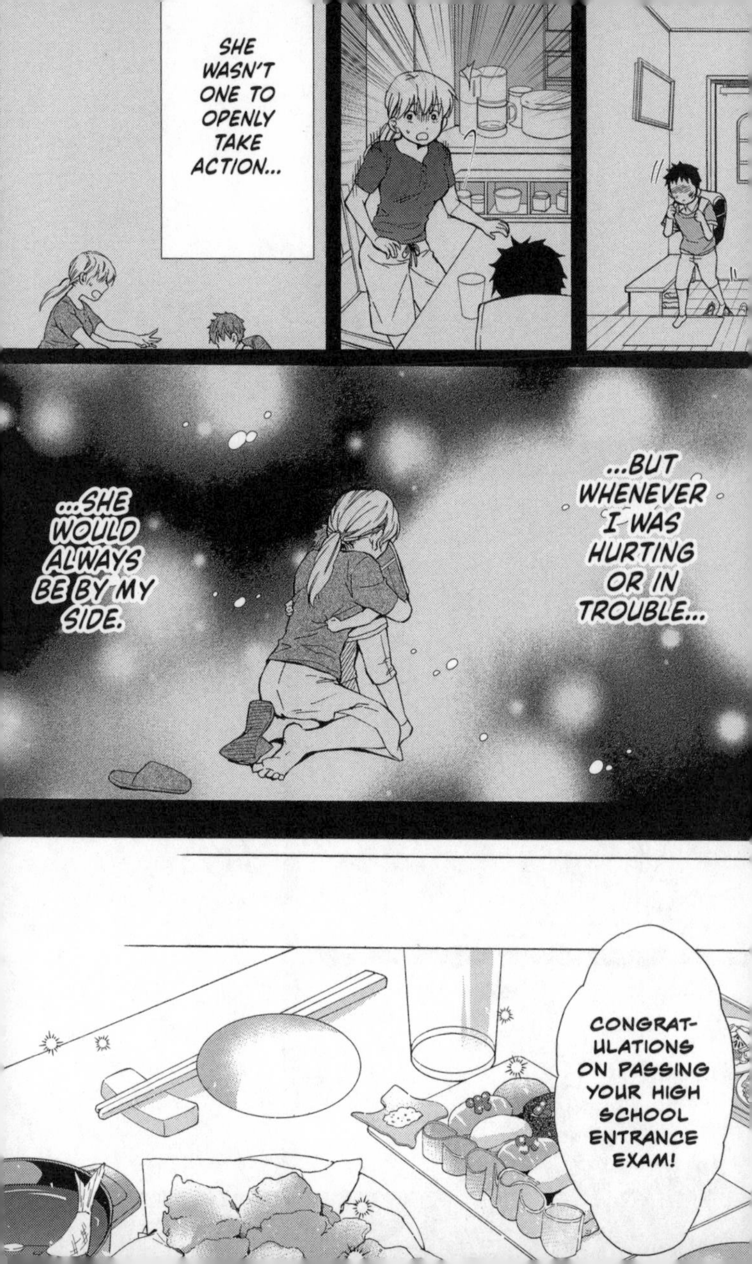
SHE WASN'T ONE TO OPENLY TAKE ACTION...
...BUT WHENEVER I WAS HURTING OR IN TROUBLE...
...SHE WOULD ALWAYS BE BY MY SIDE.
CONGRATULATIONS ON PASSING YOUR HIGH SCHOOL ENTRANCE EXAM!

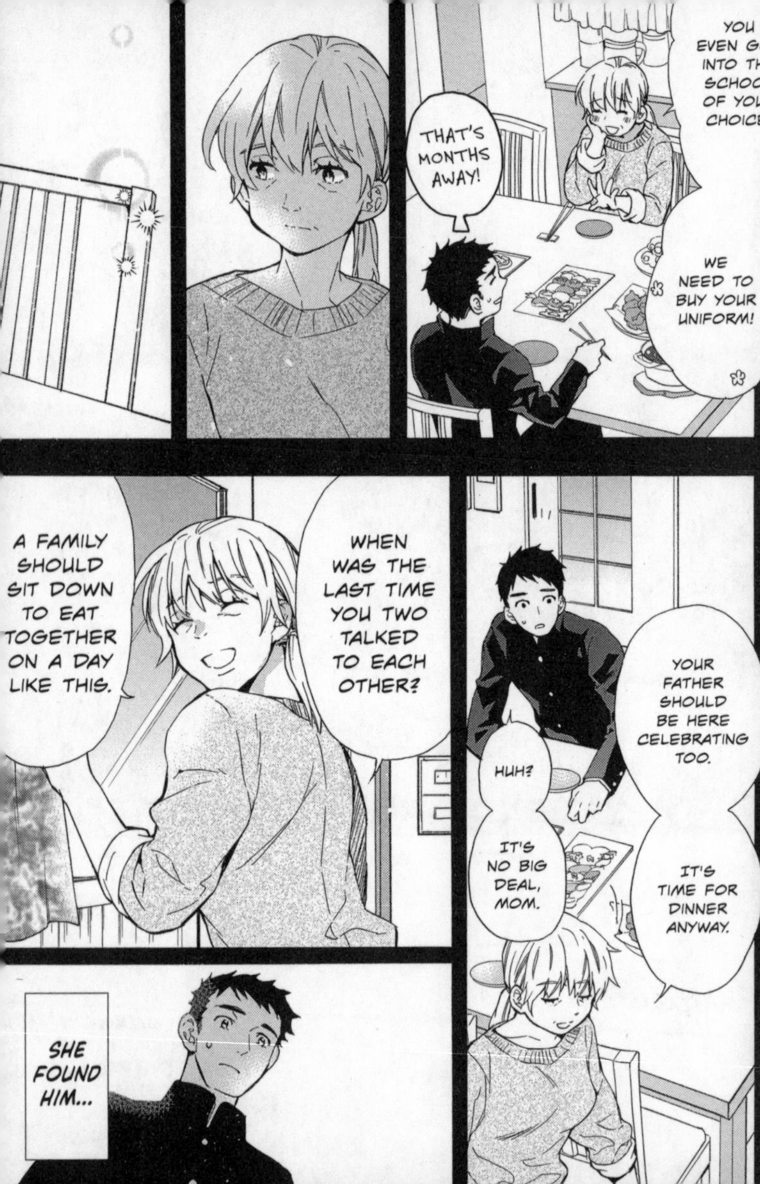
YOU EVEN GOT INTO THE SCHOOL OF YOUR CHOICE!
WE NEED TO BUY YOUR UNIFORM!
THAT'S MONTHS AWAY!
YOUR FATHER SHOULD BE HERE CELEBRATING TOO.
HUH?
IT'S NO BIG DEAL, MOM.
IT'S TIME FOR DINNER ANYWAY.
WHEN WAS THE LAST TIME YOU TWO TALKED TO EACH OTHER?
A FAMILY SHOULD SIT DOWN TO EAT TOGETHER ON A DAY LIKE THIS.
SHE FOUND HIM...

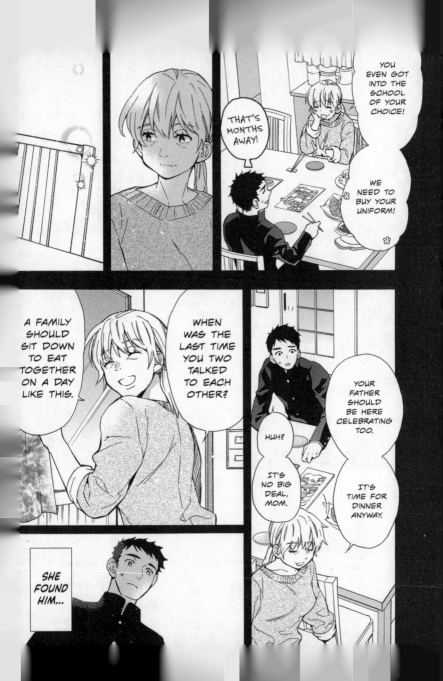

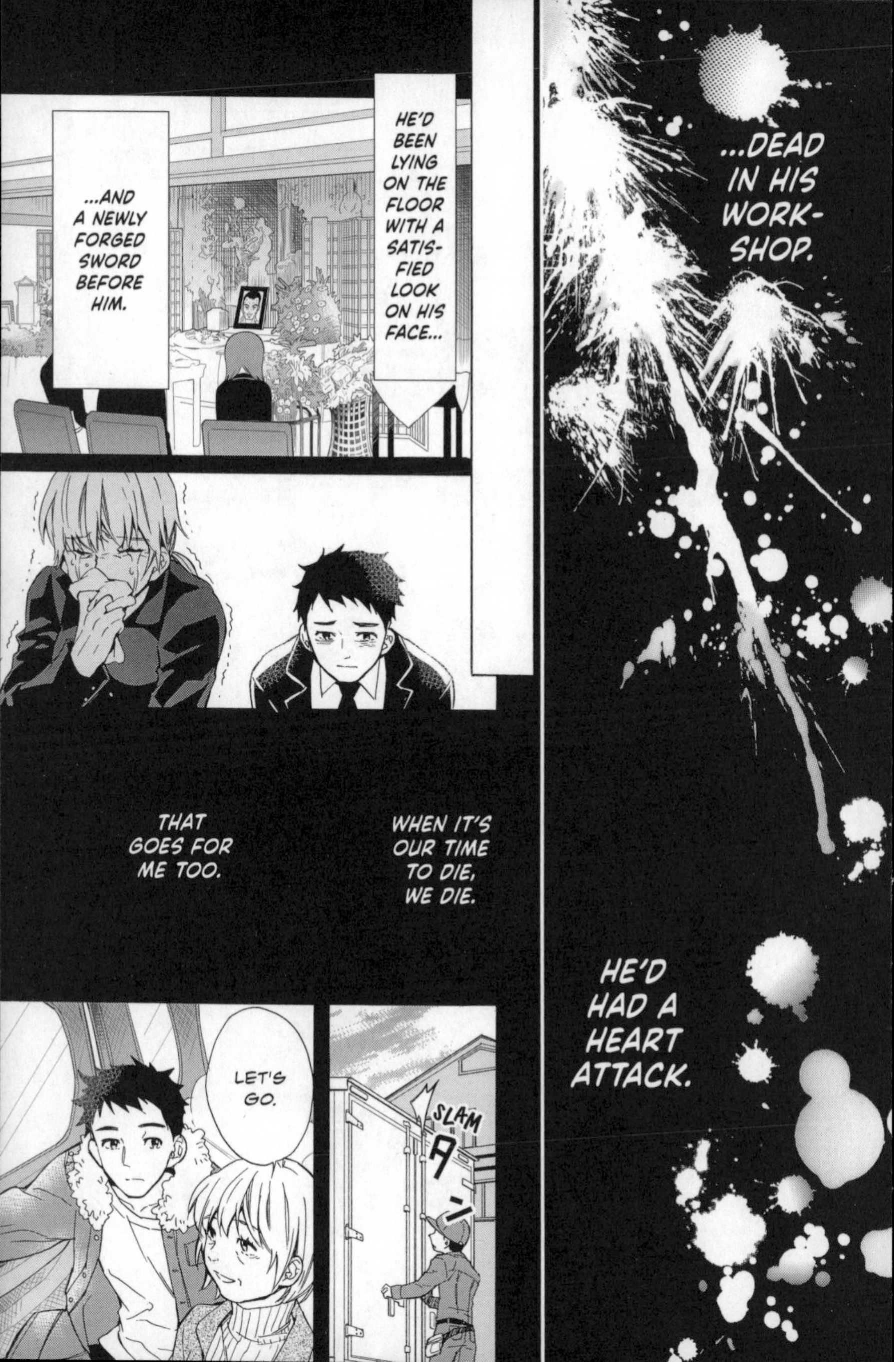

...DEAD IN HIS WORK-SHOP.
HE'D HAD A HEART ATTACK.
HE'D BEEN LYING ON THE FLOOR WITH A SATIS-FIED LOOK ON HIS FACE...
...AND A NEWLY FORGED SWORD BEFORE HIM.
WHEN IT'S OUR TIME TO DIE, WE DIE.
THAT GOES FOR ME TOO.
SLAM
LET'S GO.

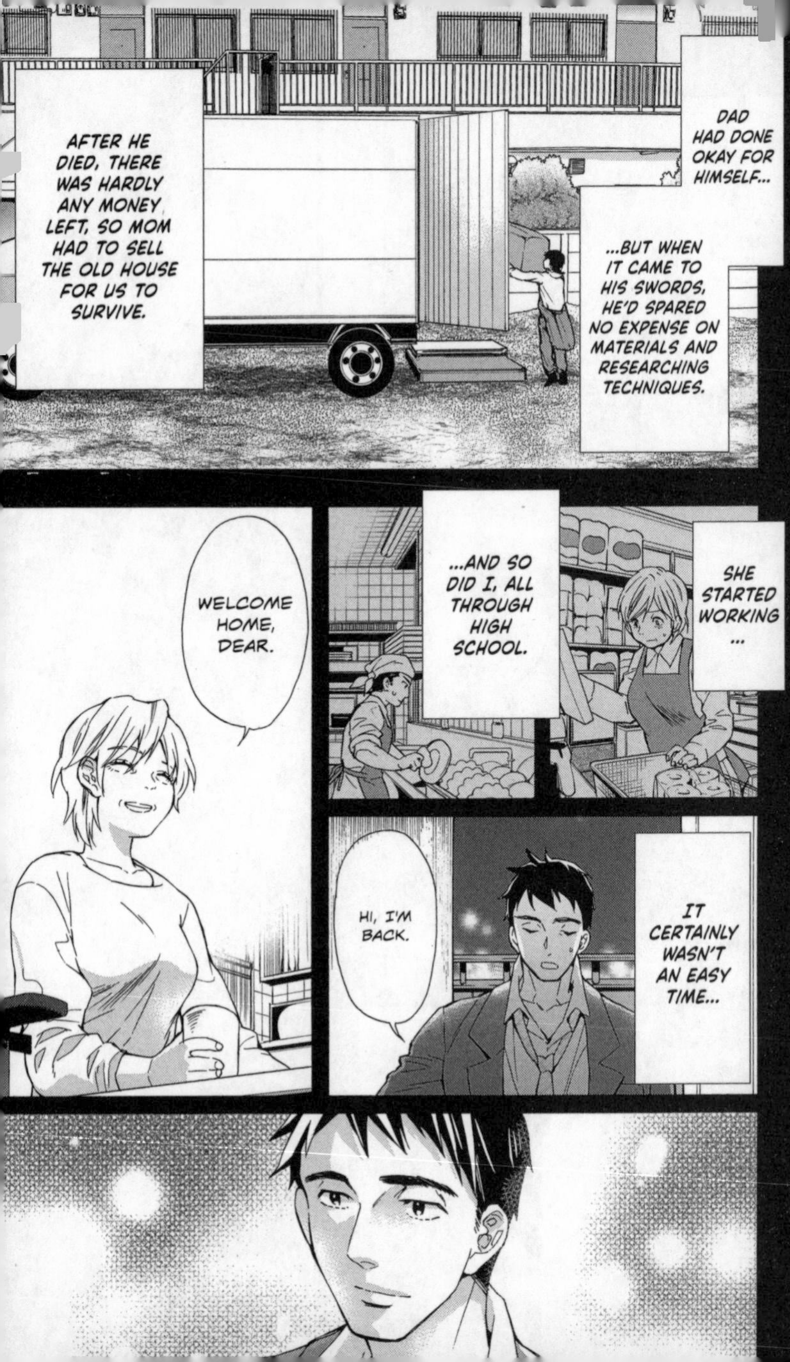
DAD HAD DONE OKAY FOR HIMSELF...
...BUT WHEN IT CAME TO HIS SWORDS, HE'D SPARED NO EXPENSE ON MATERIALS AND RESEARCHING TECHNIQUES.
AFTER HE DIED, THERE WAS HARDLY ANY MONEY LEFT, SO MOM HAD TO SELL THE OLD HOUSE FOR US TO SURVIVE.
SHE STARTED WORKING ...
...AND SO DID I, ALL THROUGH HIGH SCHOOL.
IT CERTAINLY WASN'T AN EASY TIME...
HI, I'M BACK.
WELCOME HOME, DEAR.

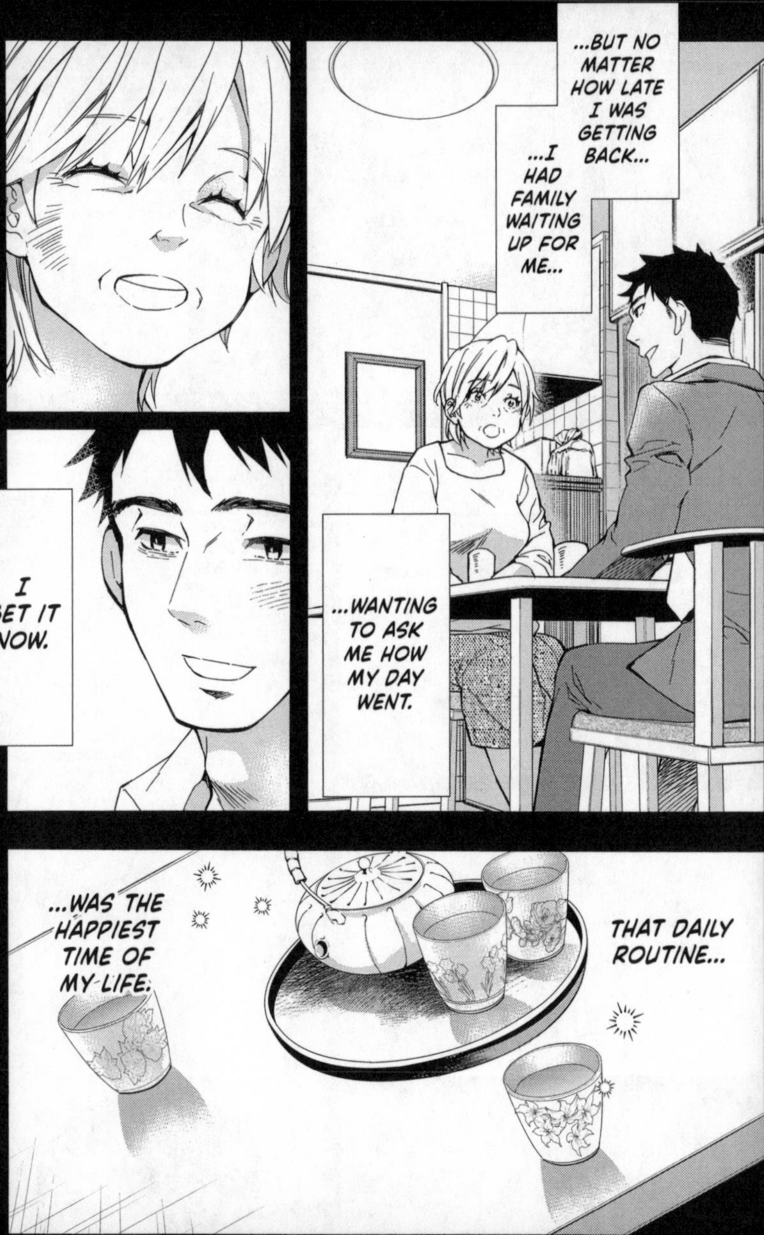
...BUT NO MATTER HOW LATE I WAS GETTING BACK...
...I HAD FAMILY WAITING UP FOR ME...
...WANTING TO ASK ME HOW MY DAY WENT.
I GET IT NOW.
THAT DAILY ROUTINE...
...WAS THE HAPPIEST TIME OF MY LIFE.

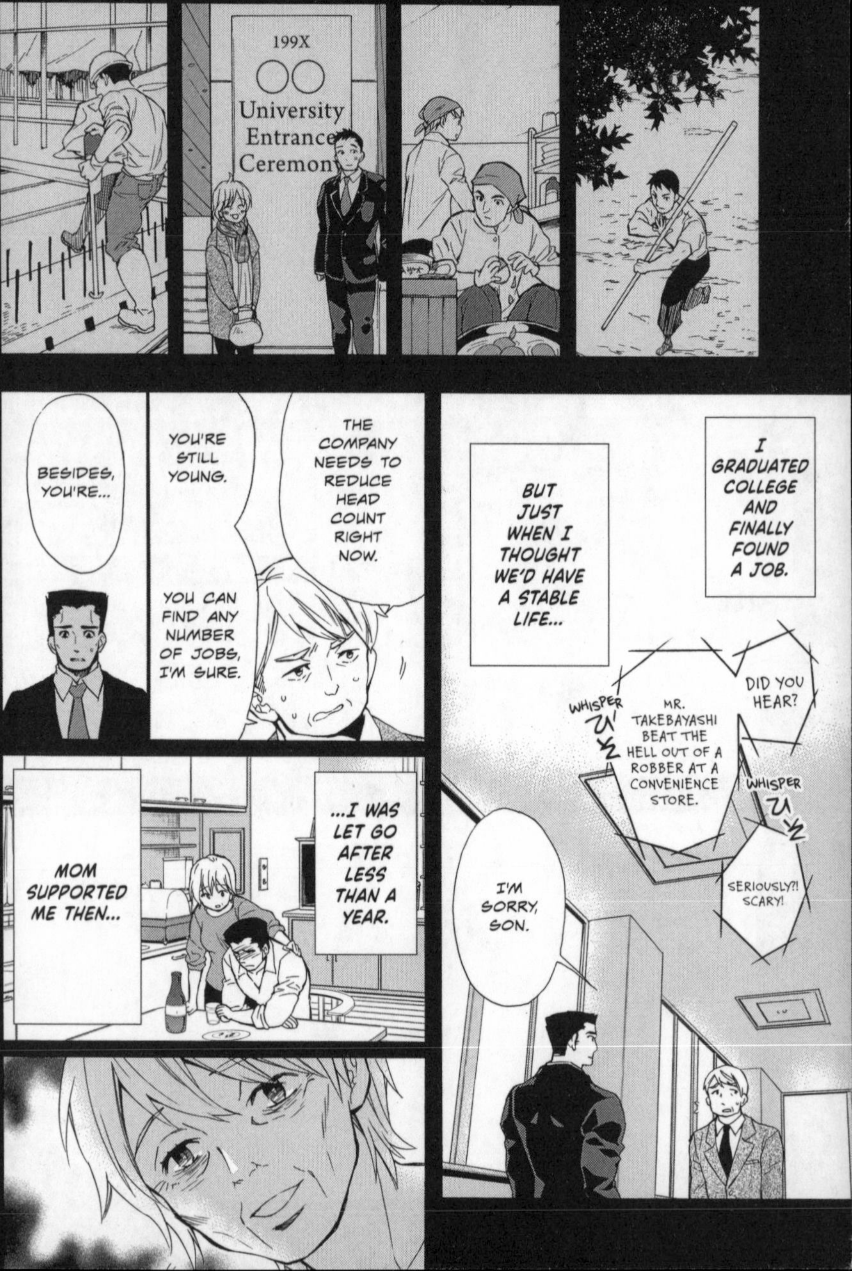
199X
○○
University
Entrance
Ceremon
I GRADUATED COLLEGE AND FINALLY FOUND A JOB.
BUT JUST WHEN I THOUGHT WE'D HAVE A STABLE LIFE...
DID YOU HEAR?
MR. TAKEBAYASHI BEAT THE HELL OUT OF A ROBBER AT A CONVENIENCE STORE.
WHISPER
WHISPER
SERIOUSLY?! SCARY!
I'M SORRY, SON.
THE COMPANY NEEDS TO REDUCE HEAD COUNT RIGHT NOW.
YOU'RE STILL YOUNG.
YOU CAN FIND ANY NUMBER OF JOBS, I'M SURE.
BESIDES, YOU'RE...
...I WAS LET GO AFTER LESS THAN A YEAR.
MOM SUPPORTED ME THEN...

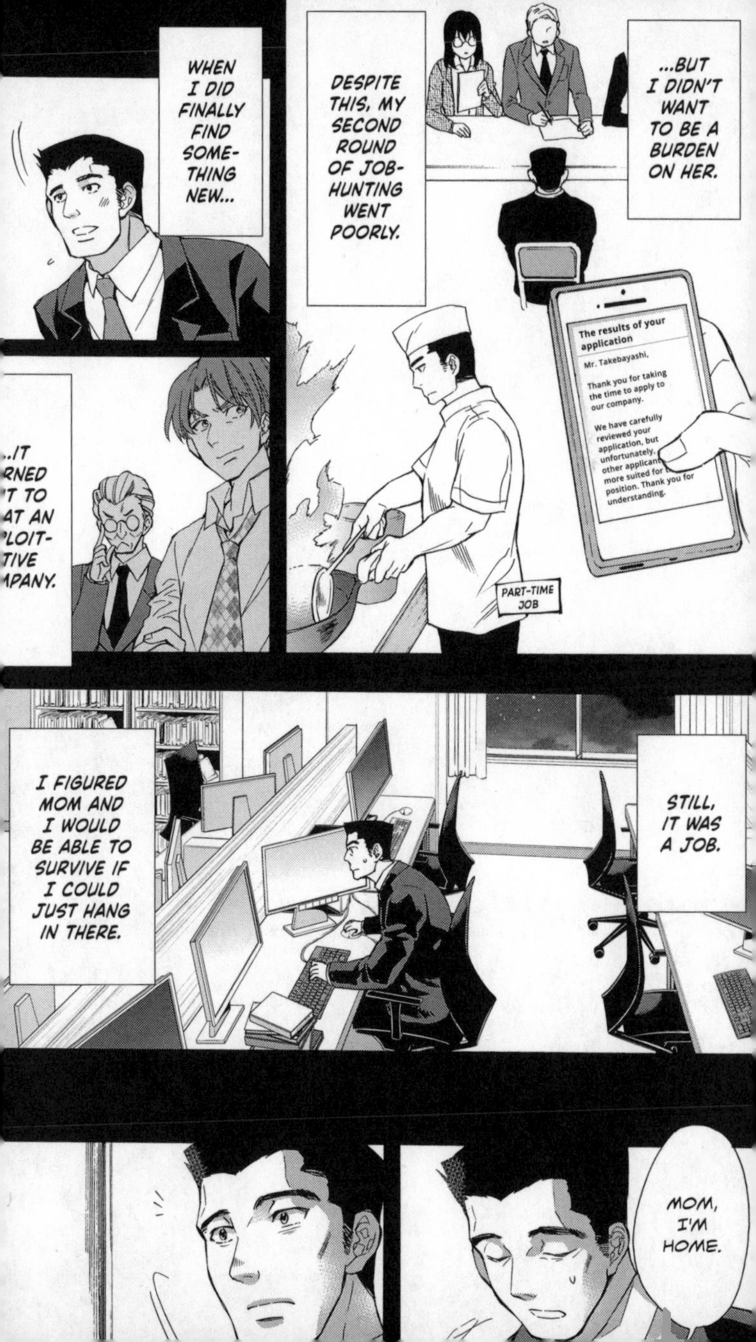
...BUT I DIDN'T WANT TO BE A BURDEN ON HER.
DESPITE THIS, MY SECOND ROUND OF JOB-HUNTING WENT POORLY.
The results of your application
Mr. Takebayashi,
Thank you for taking the time to apply to our company.
We have carefully reviewed your application, but unfortunately, other applicant more suited for t position. Thank you for understanding.
PART-TIME JOB
WHEN I DID FINALLY FIND SOME-THING NEW...
..IT RNED T TO AT AN PLOIT- TIVE MPANY.
STILL, IT WAS A JOB.
I FIGURED MOM AND I WOULD BE ABLE TO SURVIVE IF I COULD JUST HANG IN THERE.
MOM, I'M HOME.

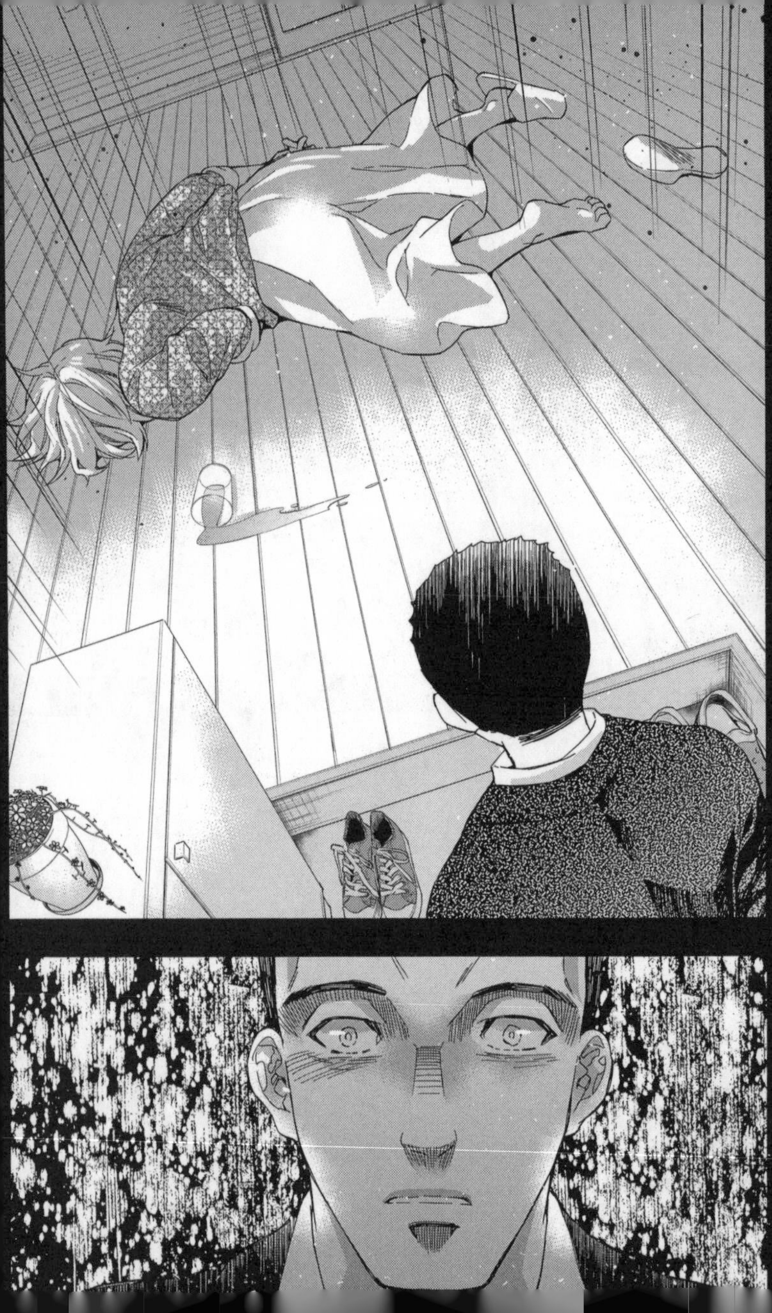

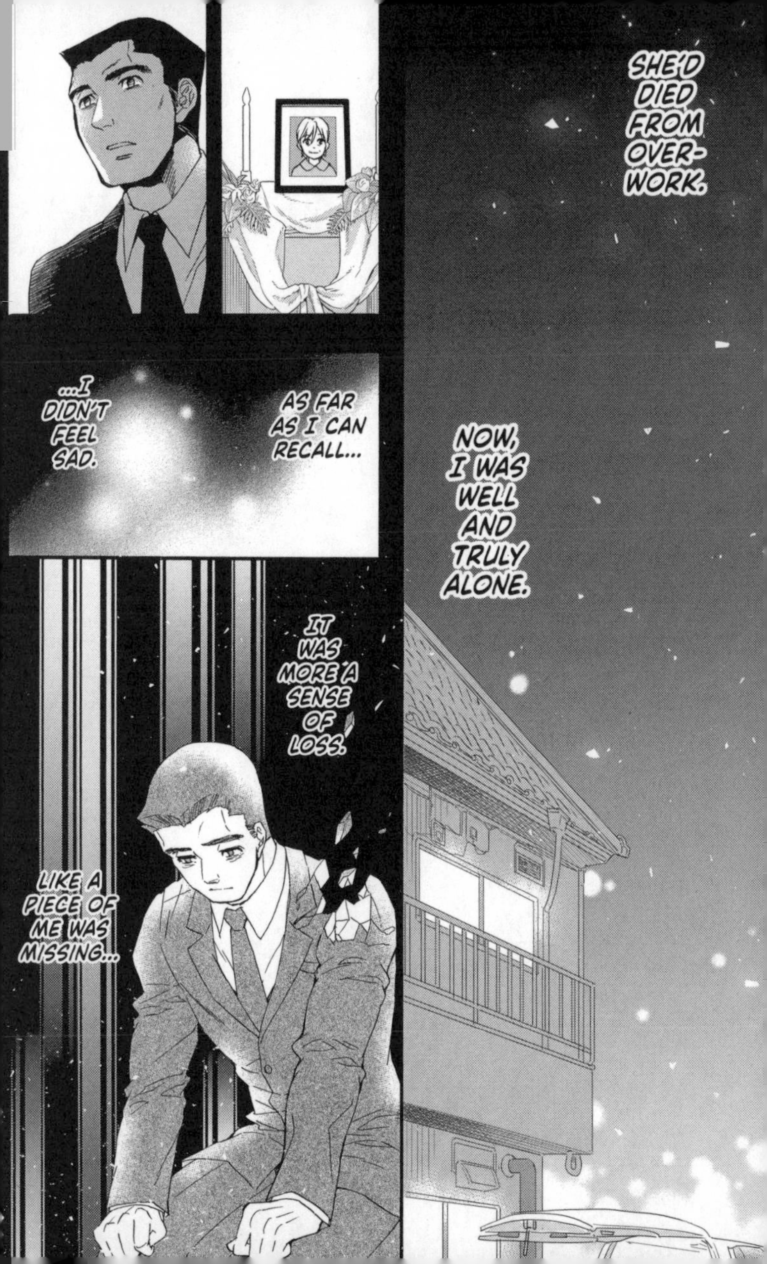
SHE'D DIED FROM OVER-WORK.
NOW, I WAS WELL AND TRULY ALONE.
AS FAR AS I CAN RECALL...
...I DIDN'T FEEL SAD.
IT WAS MORE A SENSE OF LOSS.
LIKE A PIECE OF ME WAS MISSING...

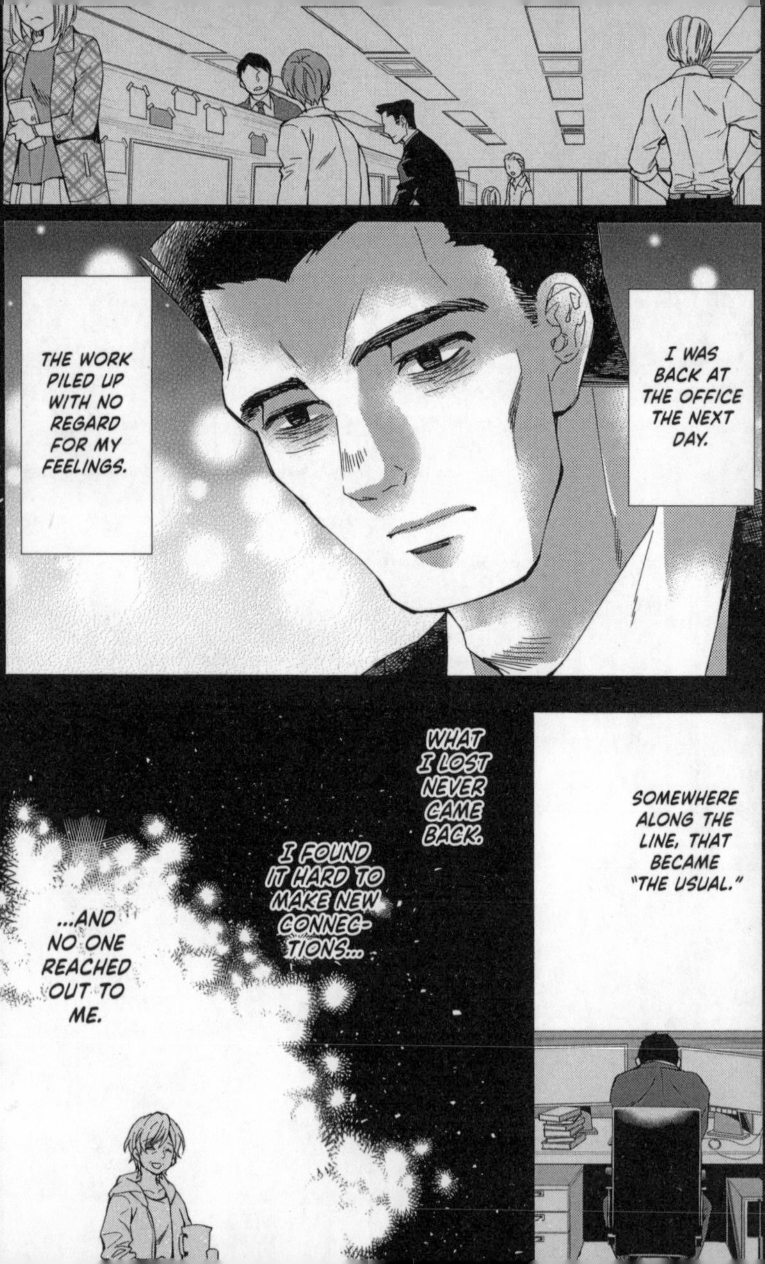
I WAS BACK AT THE OFFICE THE NEXT DAY.
THE WORK PILED UP WITH NO REGARD FOR MY FEELINGS.
SOMEWHERE ALONG THE LINE, THAT BECAME "THE USUAL."
WHAT I LOST NEVER CAME BACK.
I FOUND IT HARD TO MAKE NEW CONNEC-TIONS...
...AND NO ONE REACHED OUT TO ME.

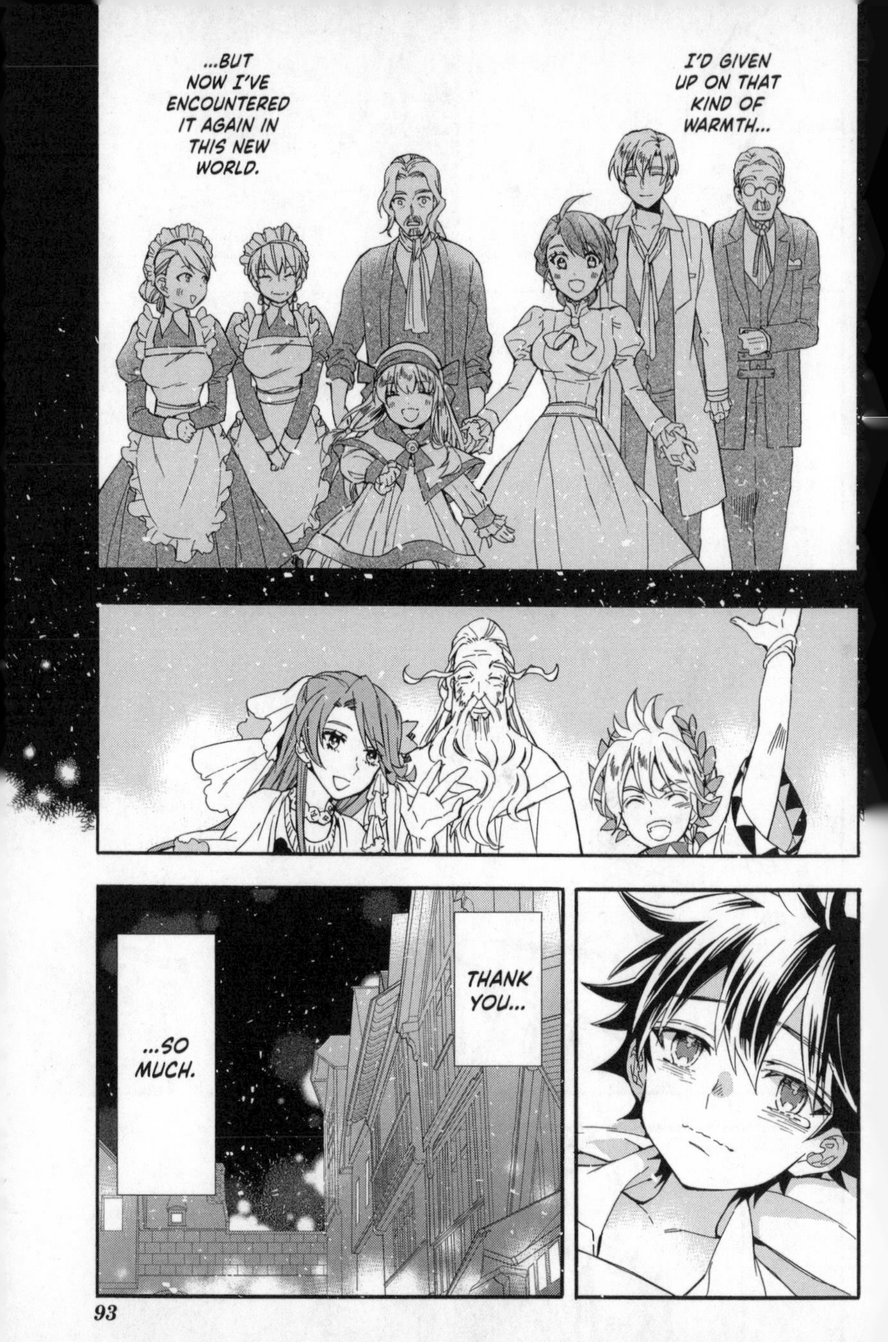
I'D GIVEN UP ON THAT KIND OF WARMTH...
...BUT NOW I'VE ENCOUNTERED IT AGAIN IN THIS NEW WORLD.
THANK YOU...
...SO MUCH.

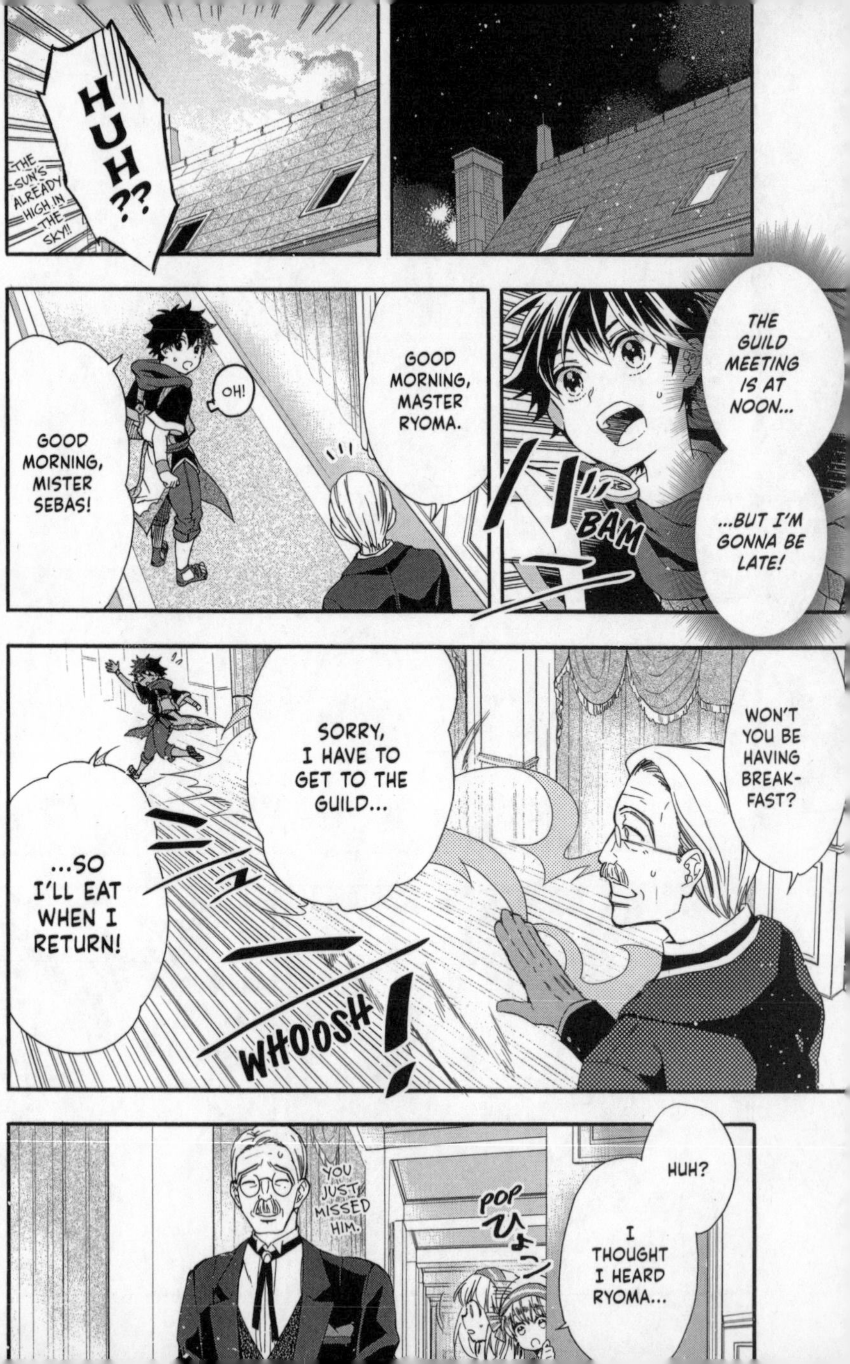
HUH??
THE SUN'S ALREADY HIGH IN THE SKY!!
THE GUILD MEETING IS AT NOON...
...BUT I'M GONNA BE LATE!
BAM
GOOD MORNING, MASTER RYOMA.
OH!
GOOD MORNING, MISTER SEBAS!
WON'T YOU BE HAVING BREAK-FAST?
SORRY, I HAVE TO GET TO THE GUILD...
...SO I'LL EAT WHEN I RETURN!
WHOOSH
HUH?
I THOUGHT I HEARD RYOMA...
POP
YOU JUST MISSED HIM.

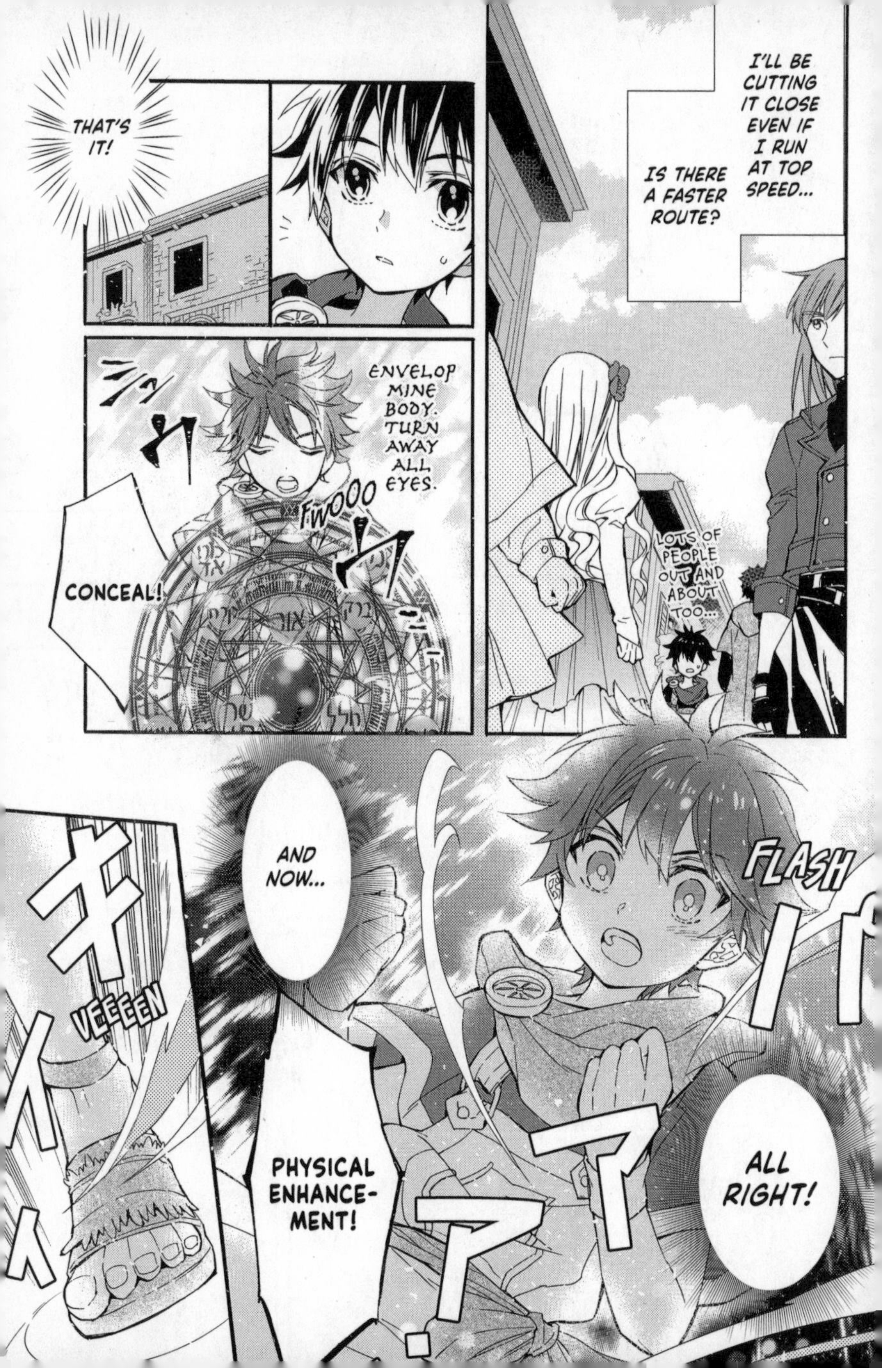
I'LL BE CUTTING IT CLOSE EVEN IF I RUN AT TOP SPEED...
IS THERE A FASTER ROUTE?
LOTS OF PEOPLE OUT AND ABOUT TOO...
THAT'S IT!
ENVELOP MINE BODY. TURN AWAY ALL EYES.
FWOOO
CONCEAL!
FLASH
ALL RIGHT!
AND NOW...
PHYSICAL ENHANCE-MENT!
VEEEEN

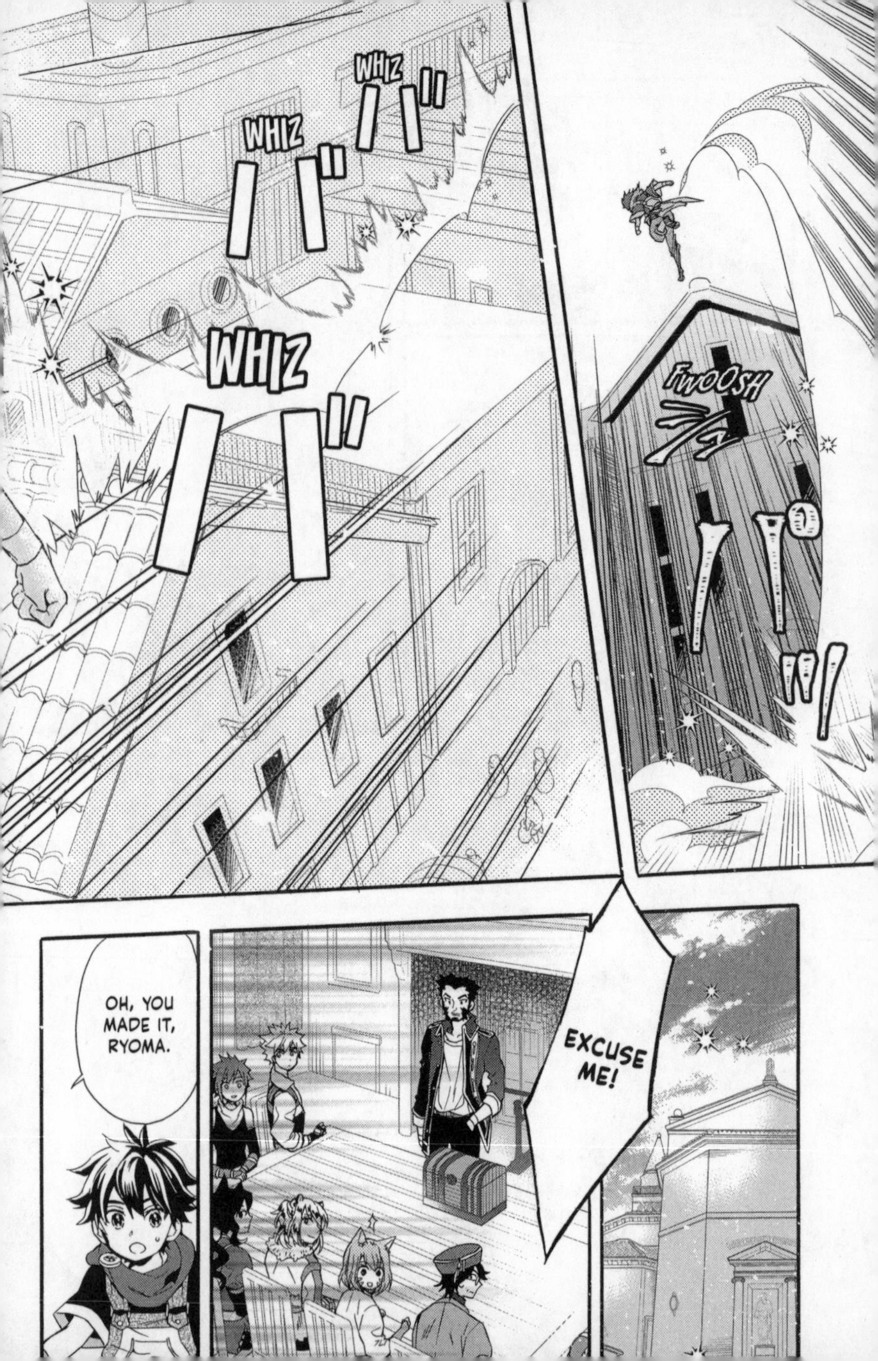
FWOOSH
WHIZ
WHIZ
WHIZ
EXCUSE ME!
OH, YOU MADE IT, RYOMA.

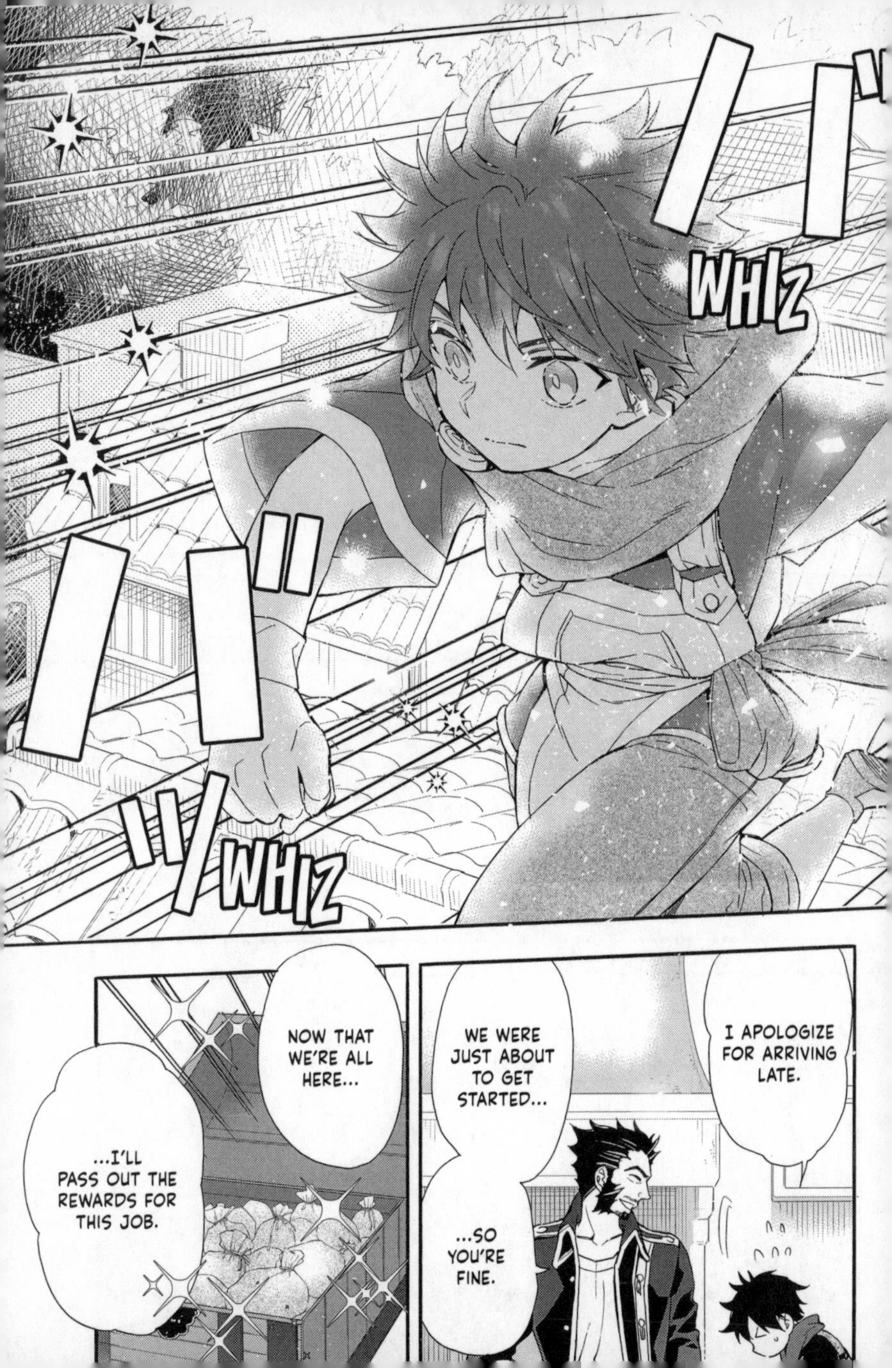
WHIZ
WHIZ
I APOLOGIZE FOR ARRIVING LATE.
WE WERE JUST ABOUT TO GET STARTED...
...SO YOU'RE FINE.
NOW THAT WE'RE ALL HERE...
...I'LL PASS OUT THE REWARDS FOR THIS JOB.

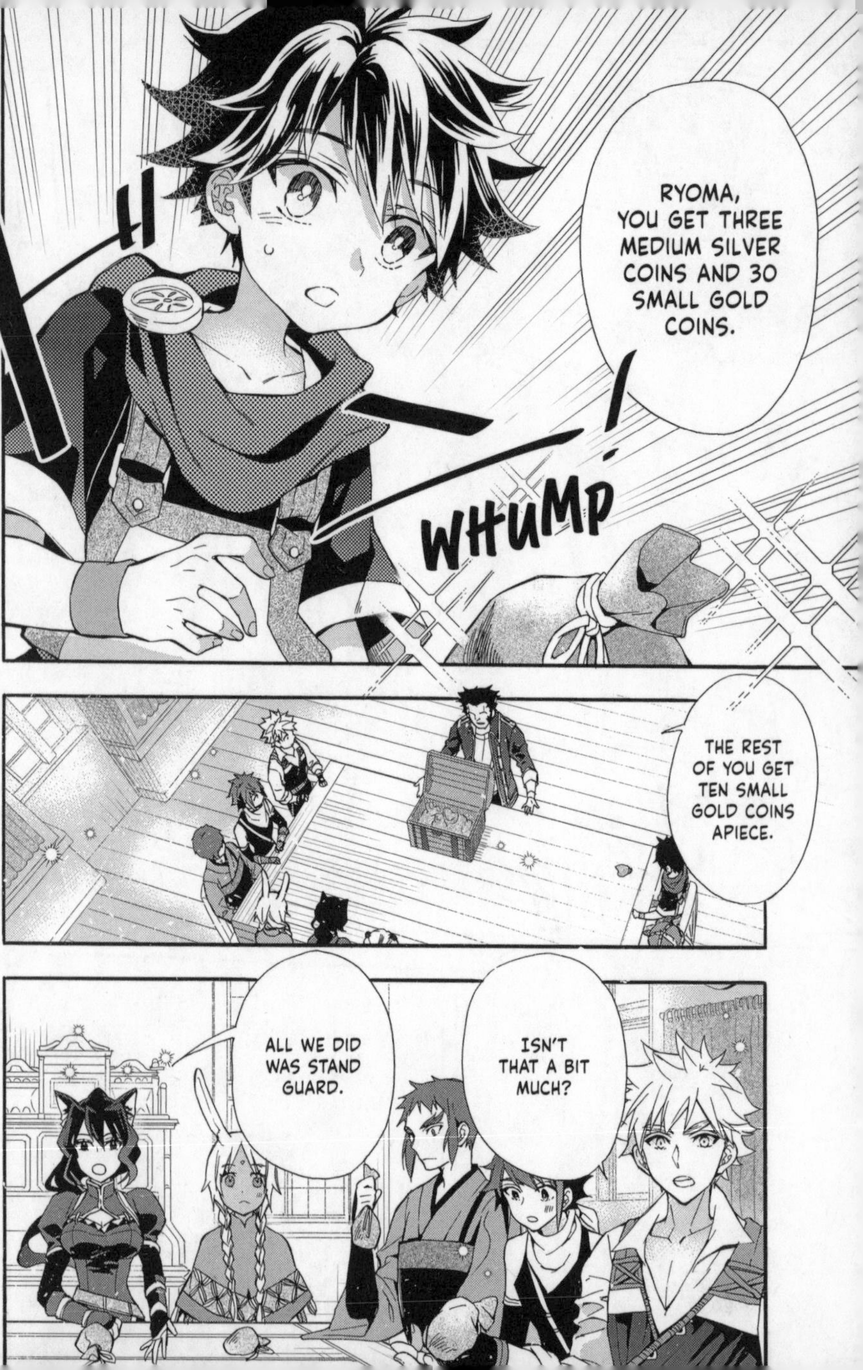
RYOMA, YOU GET THREE MEDIUM SILVER COINS AND 30 SMALL GOLD COINS.
!
WHUMP
THE REST OF YOU GET TEN SMALL GOLD COINS APIECE.
ISN'T THAT A BIT MUCH?
ALL WE DID WAS STAND GUARD.

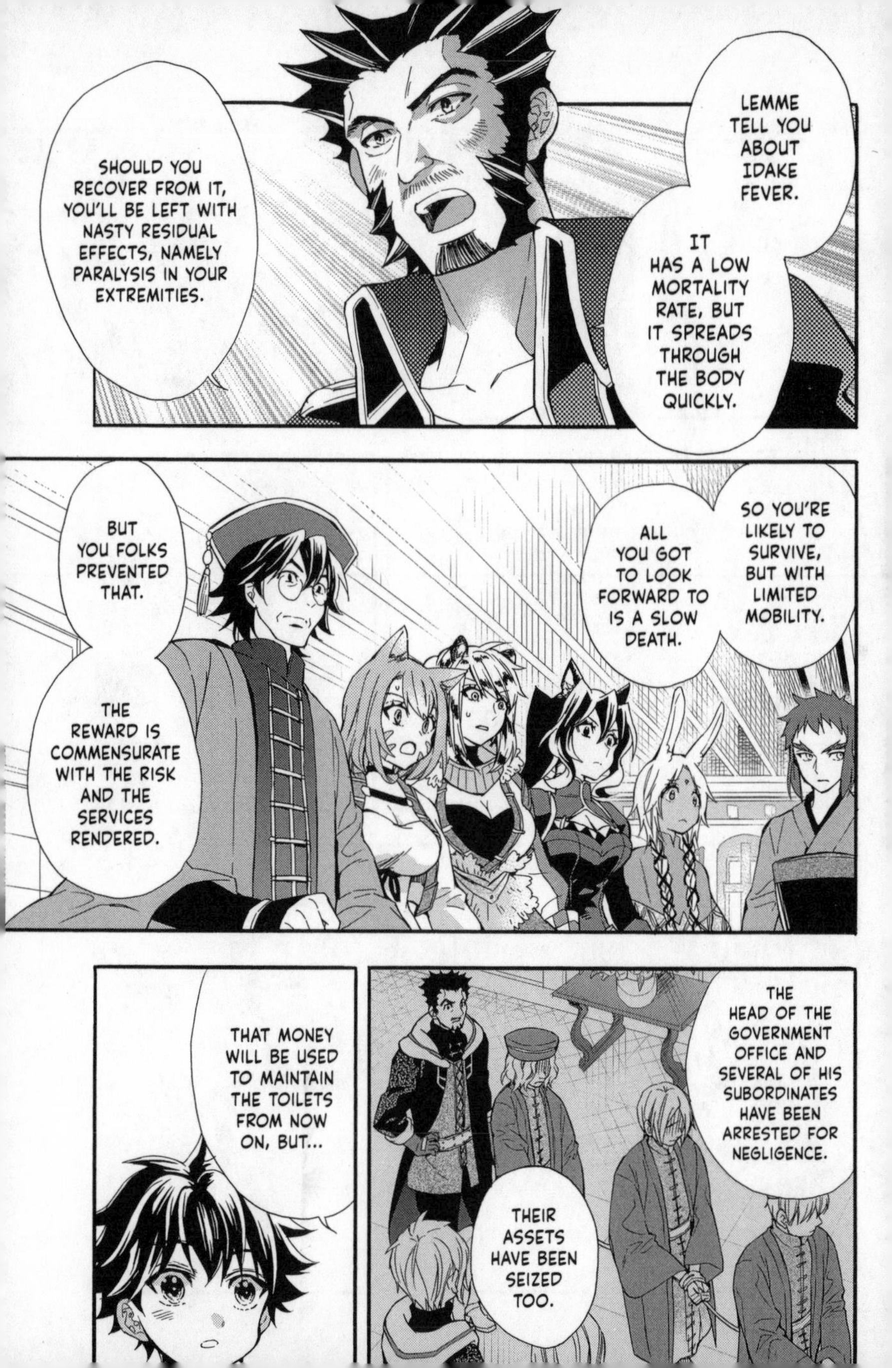
LEMME TELL YOU ABOUT IDAKE FEVER.
IT HAS A LOW MORTALITY RATE, BUT IT SPREADS THROUGH THE BODY QUICKLY.
SHOULD YOU RECOVER FROM IT, YOU'LL BE LEFT WITH NASTY RESIDUAL EFFECTS, NAMELY PARALYSIS IN YOUR EXTREMITIES.
SO YOU'RE LIKELY TO SURVIVE, BUT WITH LIMITED MOBILITY.
ALL YOU GOT TO LOOK FORWARD TO IS A SLOW DEATH.
BUT YOU FOLKS PREVENTED THAT.
THE REWARD IS COMMENSURATE WITH THE RISK AND THE SERVICES RENDERED.
THE HEAD OF THE GOVERNMENT OFFICE AND SEVERAL OF HIS SUBORDINATES HAVE BEEN ARRESTED FOR NEGLIGENCE.
THEIR ASSETS HAVE BEEN SEIZED TOO.
THAT MONEY WILL BE USED TO MAINTAIN THE TOILETS FROM NOW ON, BUT...

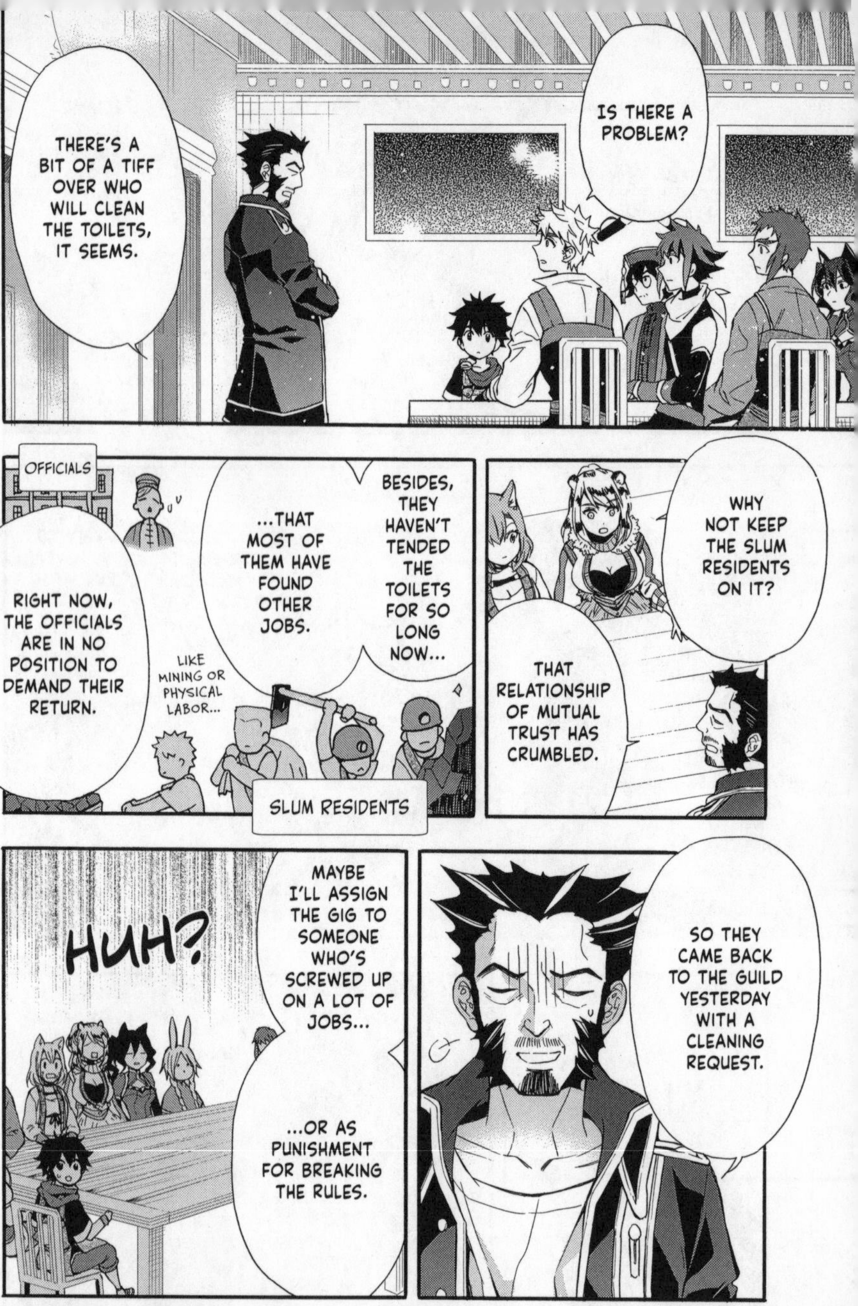
IS THERE A PROBLEM?
THERE'S A BIT OF A TIFF OVER WHO WILL CLEAN THE TOILETS, IT SEEMS.
WHY NOT KEEP THE SLUM RESIDENTS ON IT?
THAT RELATIONSHIP OF MUTUAL TRUST HAS CRUMBLED.
BESIDES, THEY HAVEN'T TENDED THE TOILETS FOR SO LONG NOW...
...THAT MOST OF THEM HAVE FOUND OTHER JOBS.
LIKE MINING OR PHYSICAL LABOR...
SLUM RESIDENTS
OFFICIALS
RIGHT NOW, THE OFFICIALS ARE IN NO POSITION TO DEMAND THEIR RETURN.
SO THEY CAME BACK TO THE GUILD YESTERDAY WITH A CLEANING REQUEST.
MAYBE I'LL ASSIGN THE GIG TO SOMEONE WHO'S SCREWED UP ON A LOT OF JOBS...
...OR AS PUNISHMENT FOR BREAKING THE RULES.
HUH?

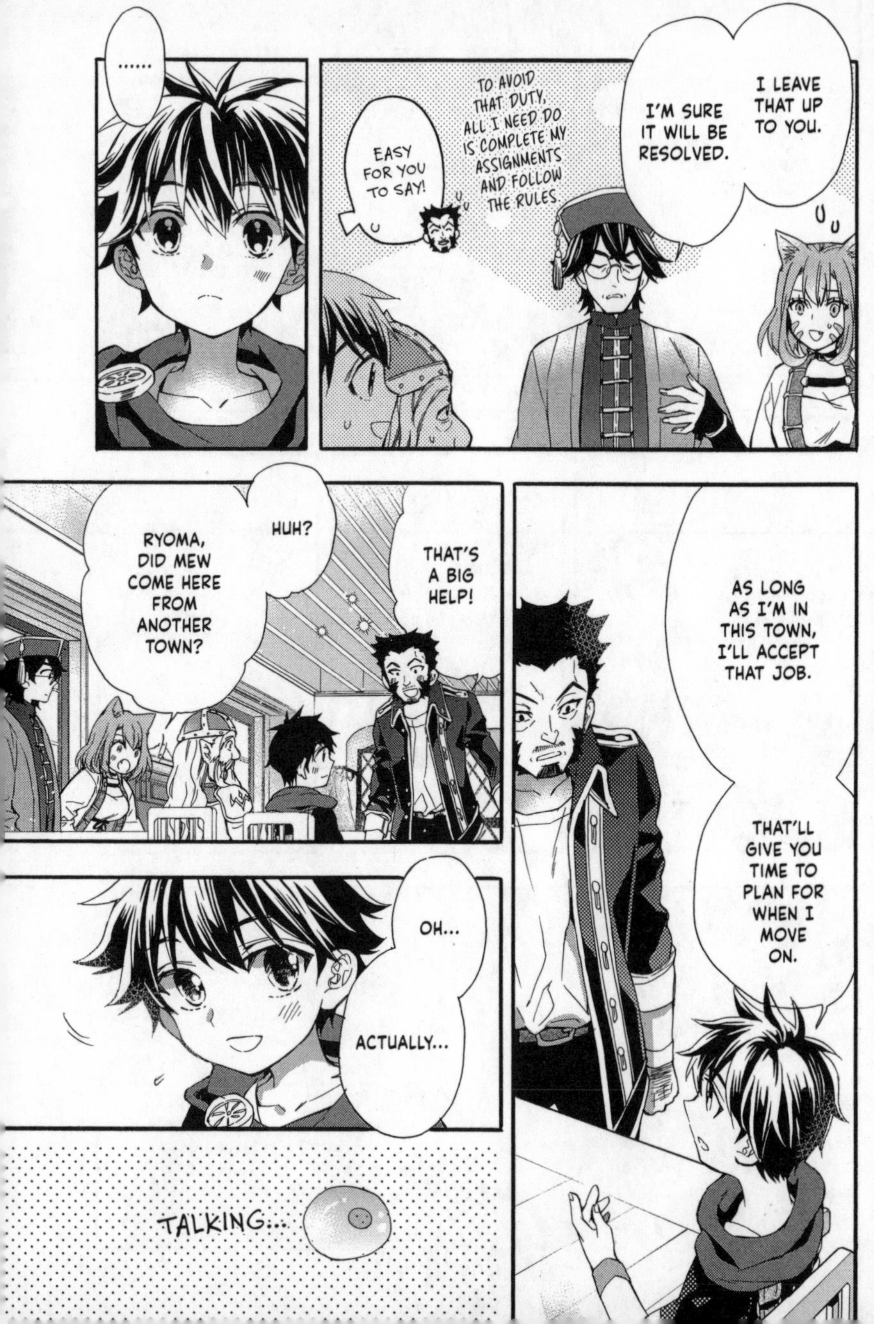
I LEAVE THAT UP TO YOU.
I'M SURE IT WILL BE RESOLVED.
TO AVOID THAT DUTY, ALL I NEED DO IS COMPLETE MY ASSIGNMENTS AND FOLLOW THE RULES.
EASY FOR YOU TO SAY!
......
AS LONG AS I'M IN THIS TOWN, I'LL ACCEPT THAT JOB.
THAT'LL GIVE YOU TIME TO PLAN FOR WHEN I MOVE ON.
THAT'S A BIG HELP!
HUH?
RYOMA, DID MEW COME HERE FROM ANOTHER TOWN?
OH...
ACTUALLY...
TALKING...

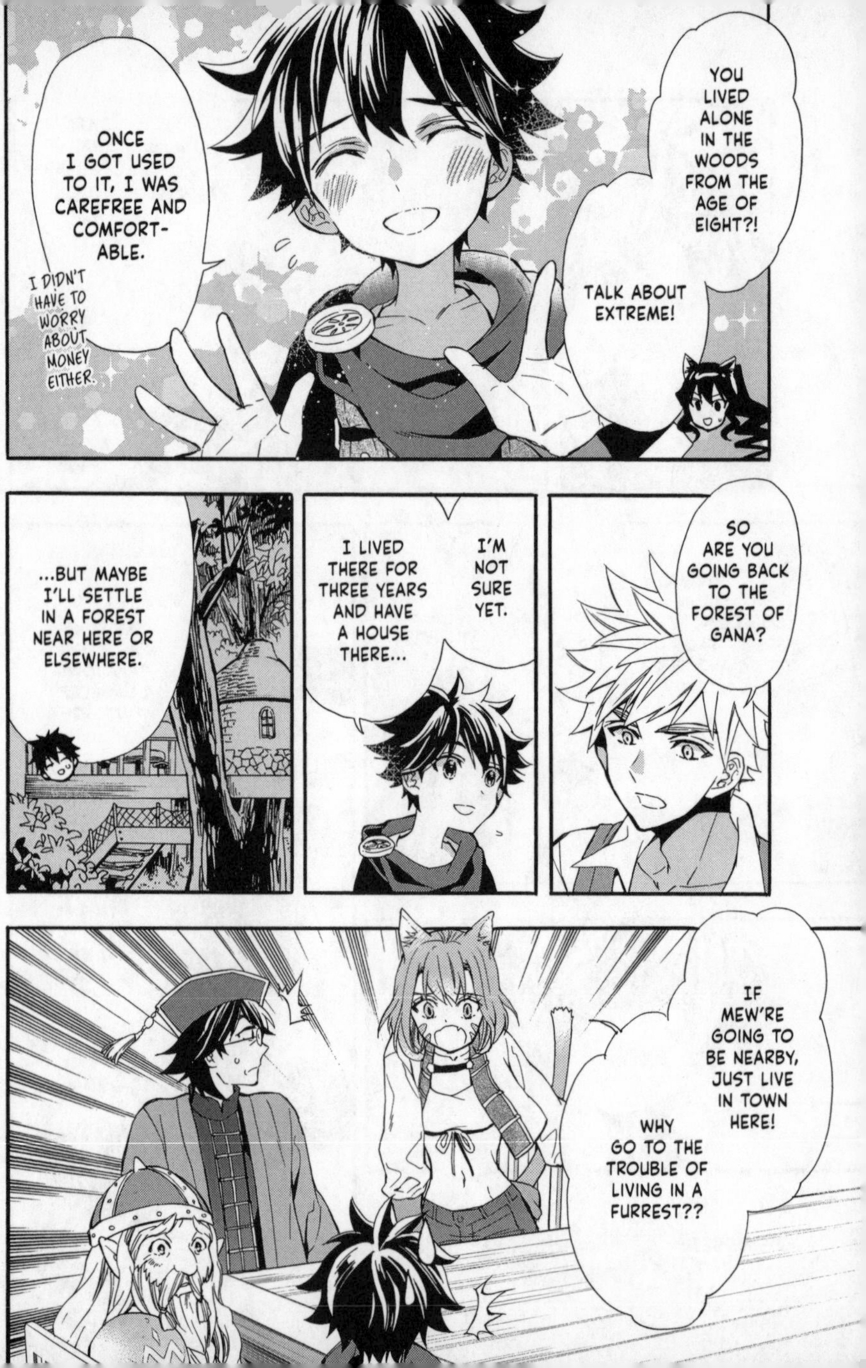
YOU LIVED ALONE IN THE WOODS FROM THE AGE OF EIGHT?!
TALK ABOUT EXTREME!
ONCE I GOT USED TO IT, I WAS CAREFREE AND COMFORT-ABLE.
I DIDN'T HAVE TO WORRY ABOUT MONEY EITHER.
SO ARE YOU GOING BACK TO THE FOREST OF GANA?
I'M NOT SURE YET.
I LIVED THERE FOR THREE YEARS AND HAVE A HOUSE THERE...
...BUT MAYBE I'LL SETTLE IN A FOREST NEAR HERE OR ELSEWHERE.
IF MEW'RE GOING TO BE NEARBY, JUST LIVE IN TOWN HERE!
WHY GO TO THE TROUBLE OF LIVING IN A FURREST??

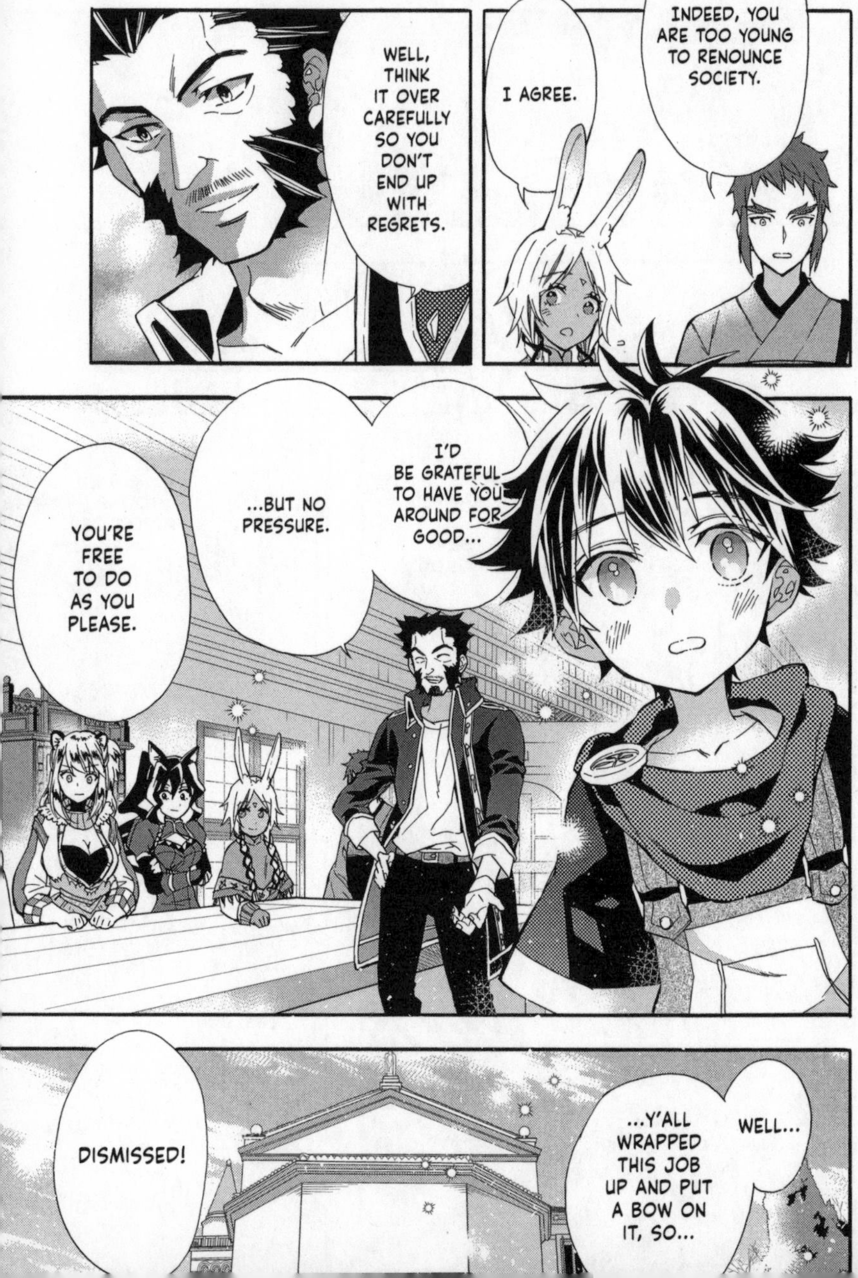
INDEED, YOU ARE TOO YOUNG TO RENOUNCE SOCIETY.
I AGREE.
WELL, THINK IT OVER CAREFULLY SO YOU DON'T END UP WITH REGRETS.
I'D BE GRATEFUL TO HAVE YOU AROUND FOR GOOD...
...BUT NO PRESSURE.
YOU'RE FREE TO DO AS YOU PLEASE.
WELL...
...Y'ALL WRAPPED THIS JOB UP AND PUT A BOW ON IT, SO...
DISMISSED!

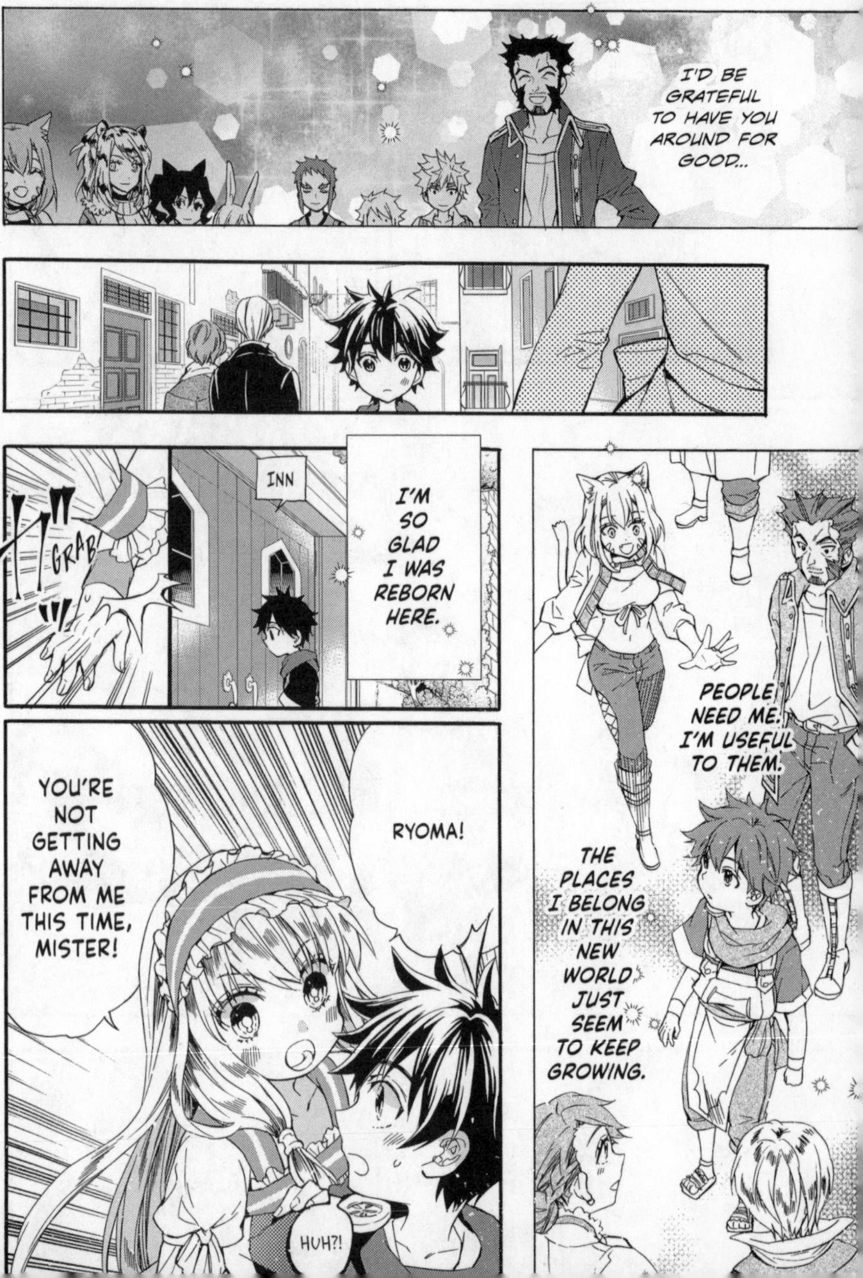
I'D BE GRATEFUL TO HAVE YOU AROUND FOR GOOD...
PEOPLE NEED ME. I'M USEFUL TO THEM.
THE PLACES I BELONG IN THIS NEW WORLD JUST SEEM TO KEEP GROWING.
INN
I'M SO GLAD I WAS REBORN HERE.
GRAB
RYOMA!
YOU'RE NOT GETTING AWAY FROM ME THIS TIME, MISTER!
HUH?!

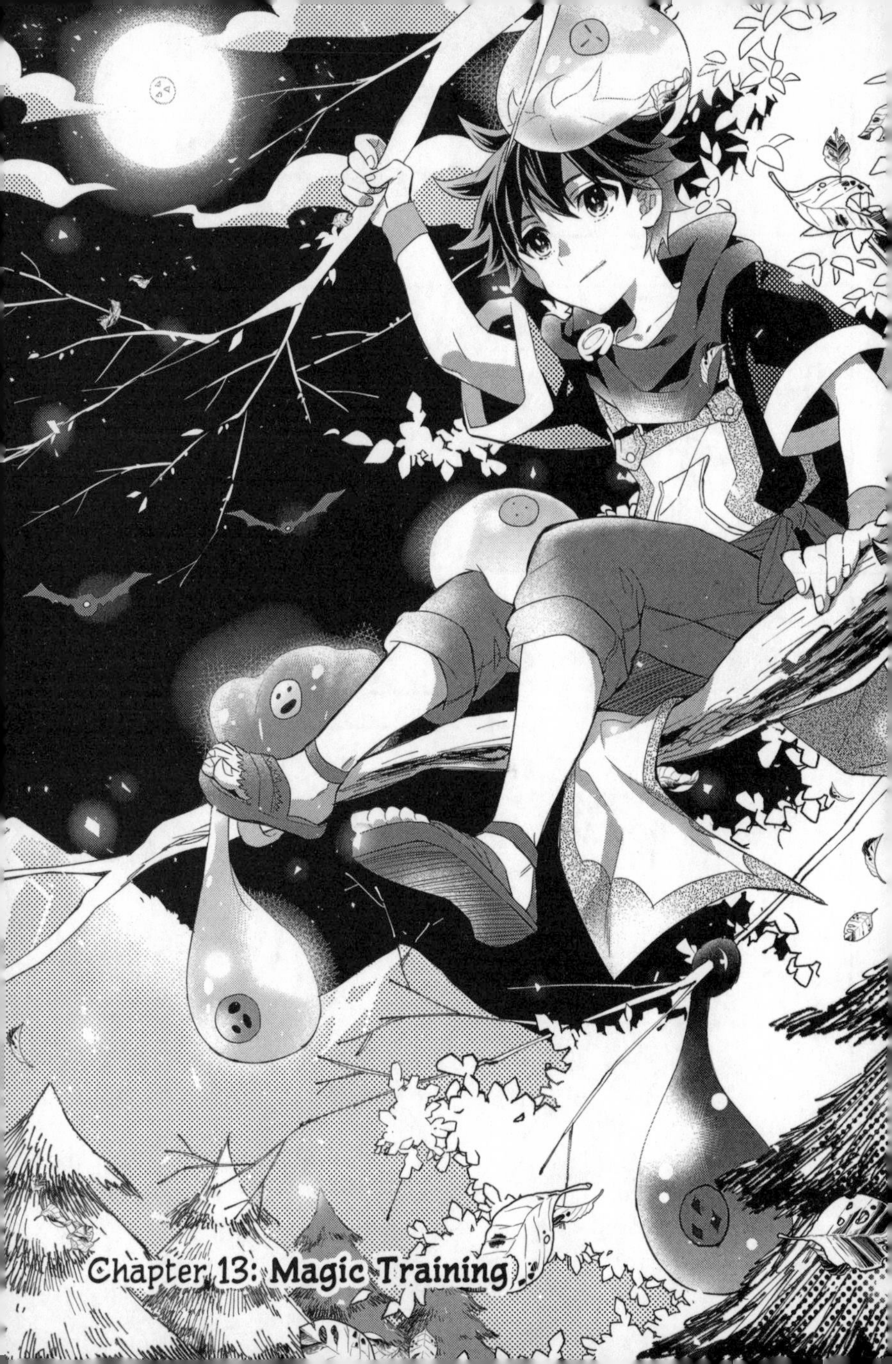
Chapter 13: Magic Training

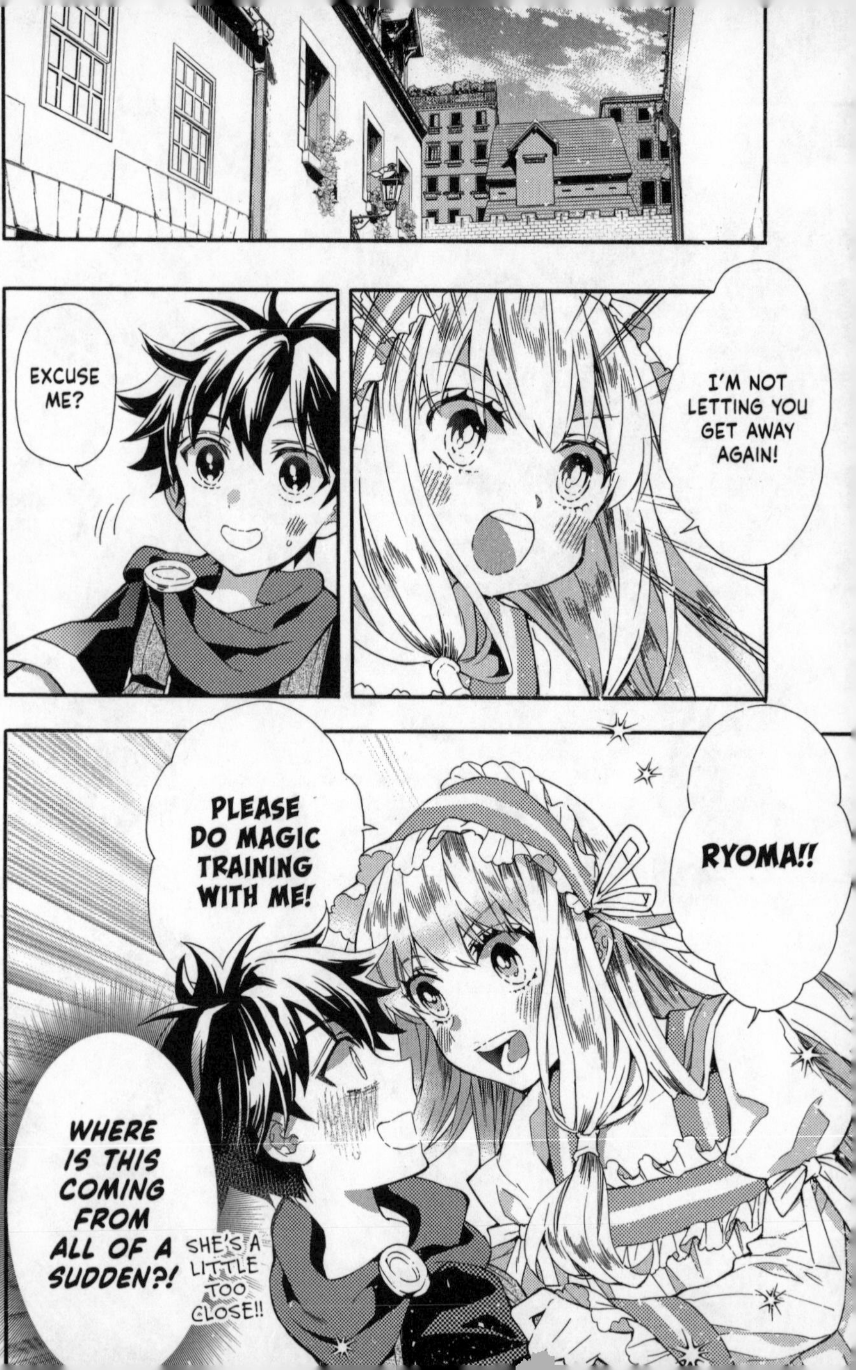
I'M NOT LETTING YOU GET AWAY AGAIN!
EXCUSE ME?
RYOMA!!
PLEASE DO MAGIC TRAINING WITH ME!
WHERE IS THIS COMING FROM ALL OF A SUDDEN?!
SHE'S A LITTLE TOO CLOSE!!

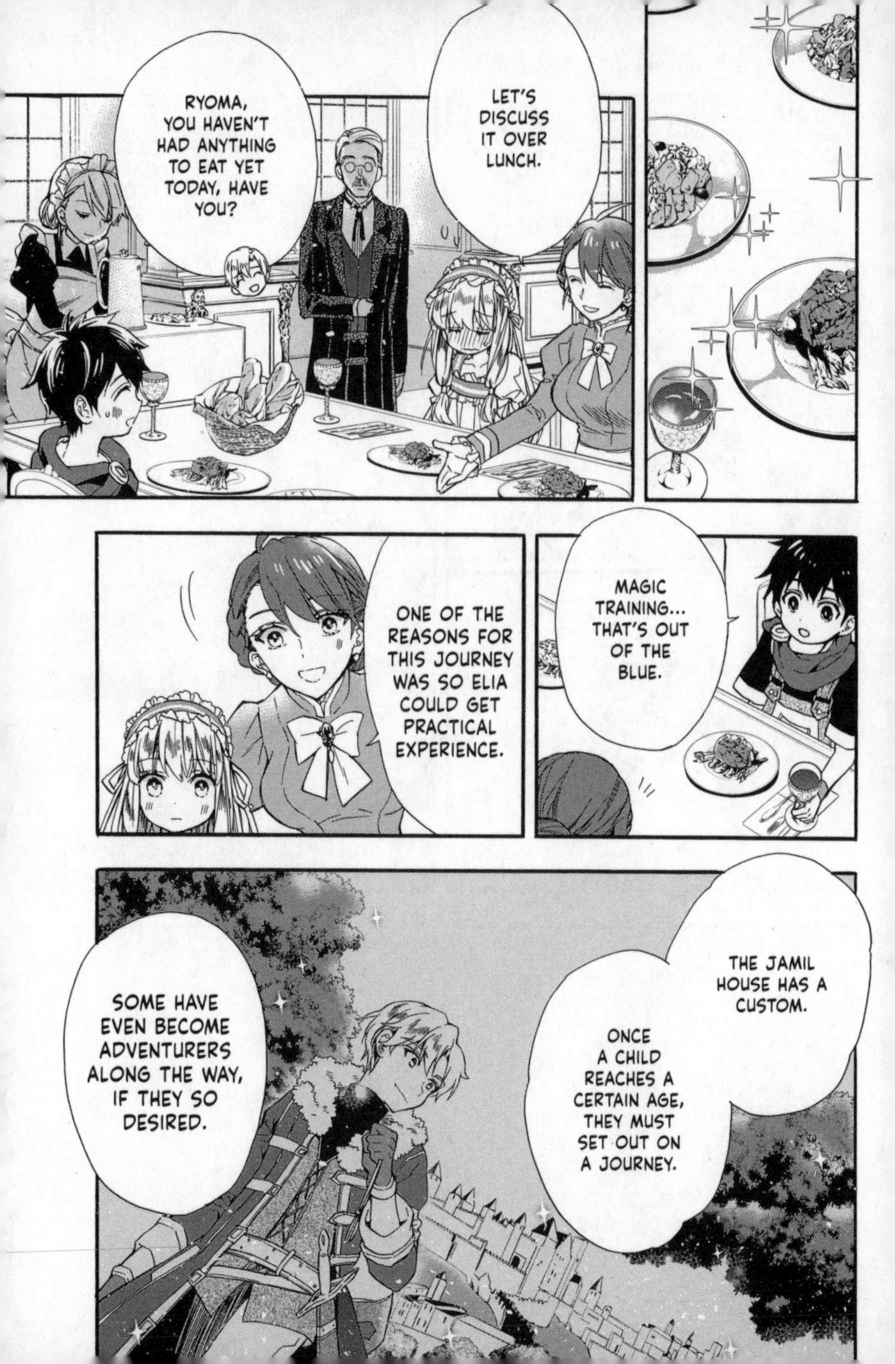
LET'S DISCUSS IT OVER LUNCH.
RYOMA, YOU HAVEN'T HAD ANYTHING TO EAT YET TODAY, HAVE YOU?
MAGIC TRAINING... THAT'S OUT OF THE BLUE.
ONE OF THE REASONS FOR THIS JOURNEY WAS SO ELIA COULD GET PRACTICAL EXPERIENCE.
THE JAMIL HOUSE HAS A CUSTOM.
ONCE A CHILD REACHES A CERTAIN AGE, THEY MUST SET OUT ON A JOURNEY.
SOME HAVE EVEN BECOME ADVENTURERS ALONG THE WAY, IF THEY SO DESIRED.

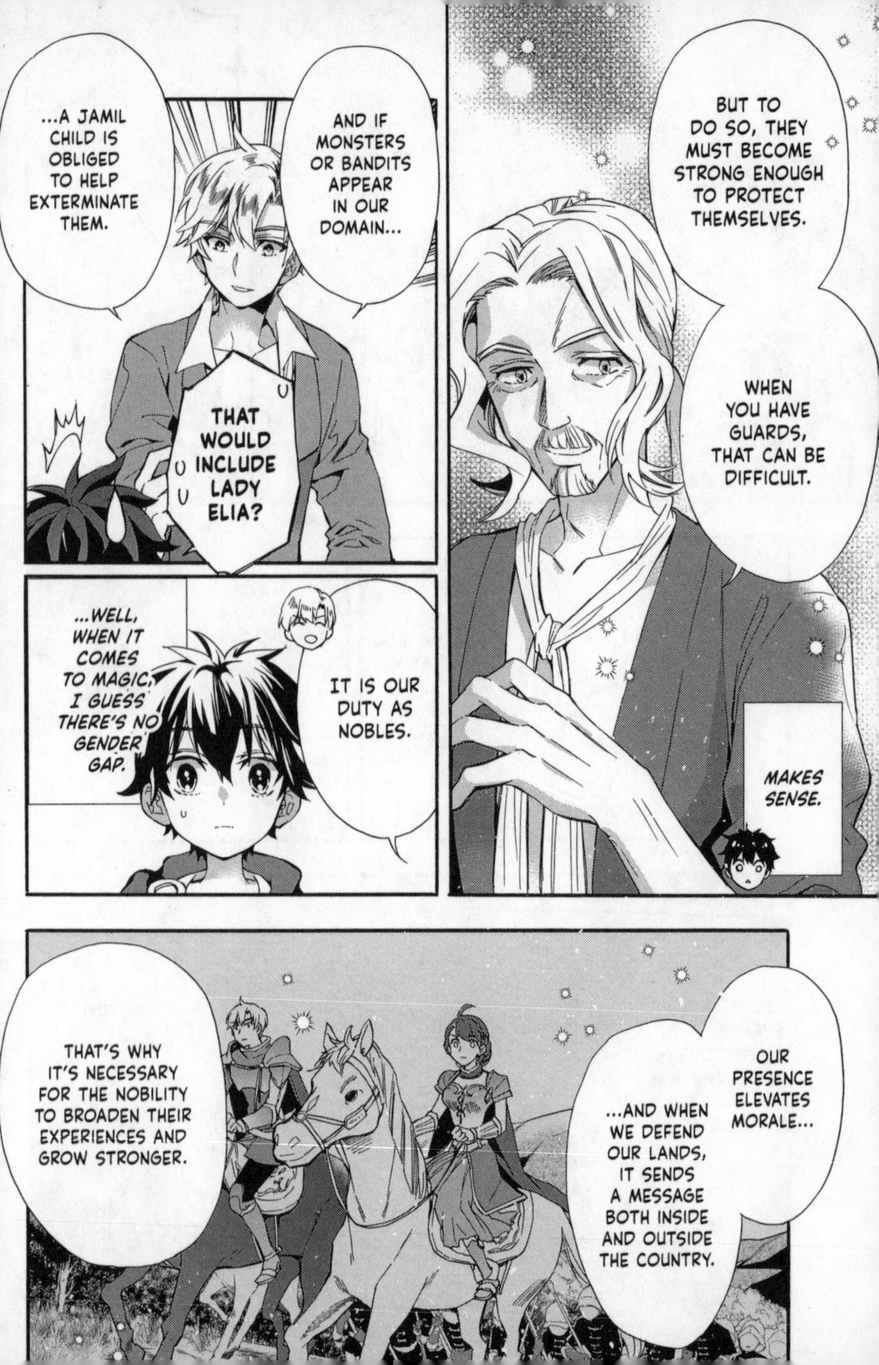
BUT TO DO SO, THEY MUST BECOME STRONG ENOUGH TO PROTECT THEMSELVES.
WHEN YOU HAVE GUARDS, THAT CAN BE DIFFICULT.
MAKES SENSE.
AND IF MONSTERS OR BANDITS APPEAR IN OUR DOMAIN...
...A JAMIL CHILD IS OBLIGED TO HELP EXTERMINATE THEM.
THAT WOULD INCLUDE LADY ELIA?
IT IS OUR DUTY AS NOBLES.
...WELL, WHEN IT COMES TO MAGIC, I GUESS THERE'S NO GENDER GAP.
OUR PRESENCE ELEVATES MORALE...
...AND WHEN WE DEFEND OUR LANDS, IT SENDS A MESSAGE BOTH INSIDE AND OUTSIDE THE COUNTRY.
THAT'S WHY IT'S NECESSARY FOR THE NOBILITY TO BROADEN THEIR EXPERIENCES AND GROW STRONGER.

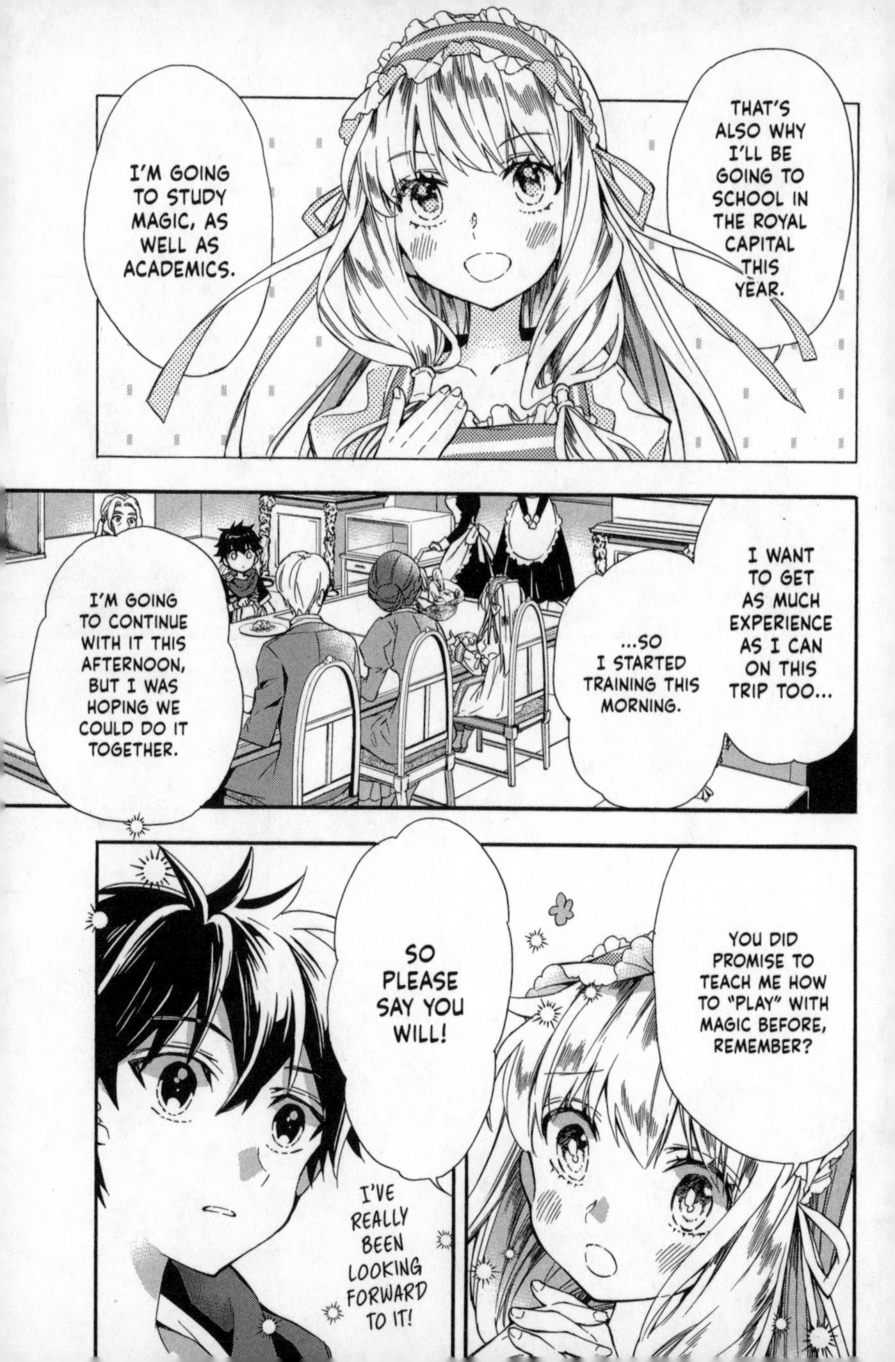
THAT'S ALSO WHY I'LL BE GOING TO SCHOOL IN THE ROYAL CAPITAL THIS YEAR.
I'M GOING TO STUDY MAGIC, AS WELL AS ACADEMICS.
I WANT TO GET AS MUCH EXPERIENCE AS I CAN ON THIS TRIP TOO...
...SO I STARTED TRAINING THIS MORNING.
I'M GOING TO CONTINUE WITH IT THIS AFTERNOON, BUT I WAS HOPING WE COULD DO IT TOGETHER.
YOU DID PROMISE TO TEACH ME HOW TO "PLAY" WITH MAGIC BEFORE, REMEMBER?
SO PLEASE SAY YOU WILL!
I'VE REALLY BEEN LOOKING FORWARD TO IT!

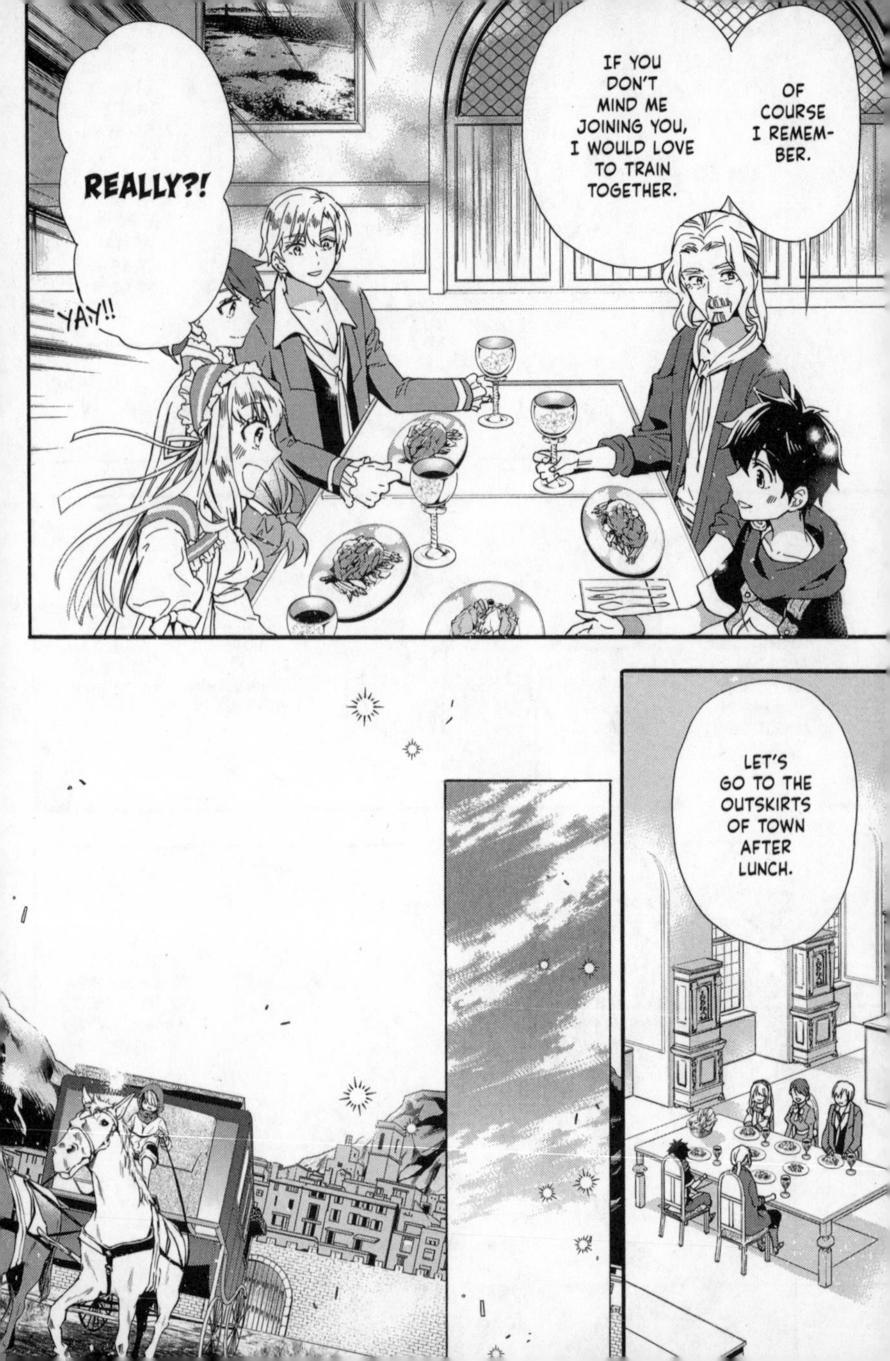
OF COURSE I REMEMBER.
IF YOU DON'T MIND ME JOINING YOU, I WOULD LOVE TO TRAIN TOGETHER.
REALLY?!
YAY!!
LET'S GO TO THE OUTSKIRTS OF TOWN AFTER LUNCH.

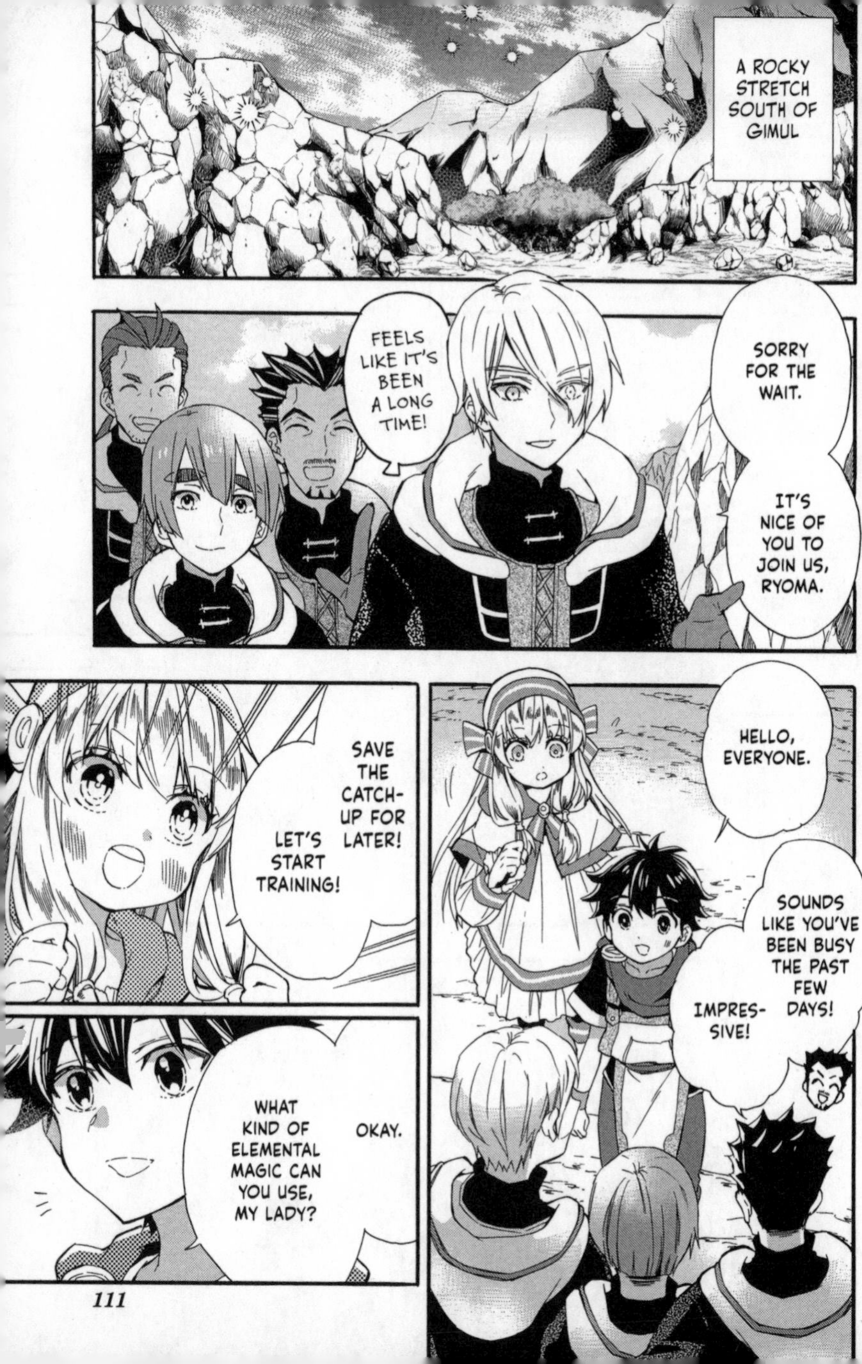
A ROCKY STRETCH SOUTH OF GIMUL
SORRY FOR THE WAIT.
IT'S NICE OF YOU TO JOIN US, RYOMA.
FEELS LIKE IT'S BEEN A LONG TIME!
HELLO, EVERYONE.
SOUNDS LIKE YOU'VE BEEN BUSY THE PAST FEW DAYS!
IMPRES-SIVE!
SAVE THE CATCH-UP FOR LATER!
LET'S START TRAINING!
OKAY.
WHAT KIND OF ELEMENTAL MAGIC CAN YOU USE, MY LADY?

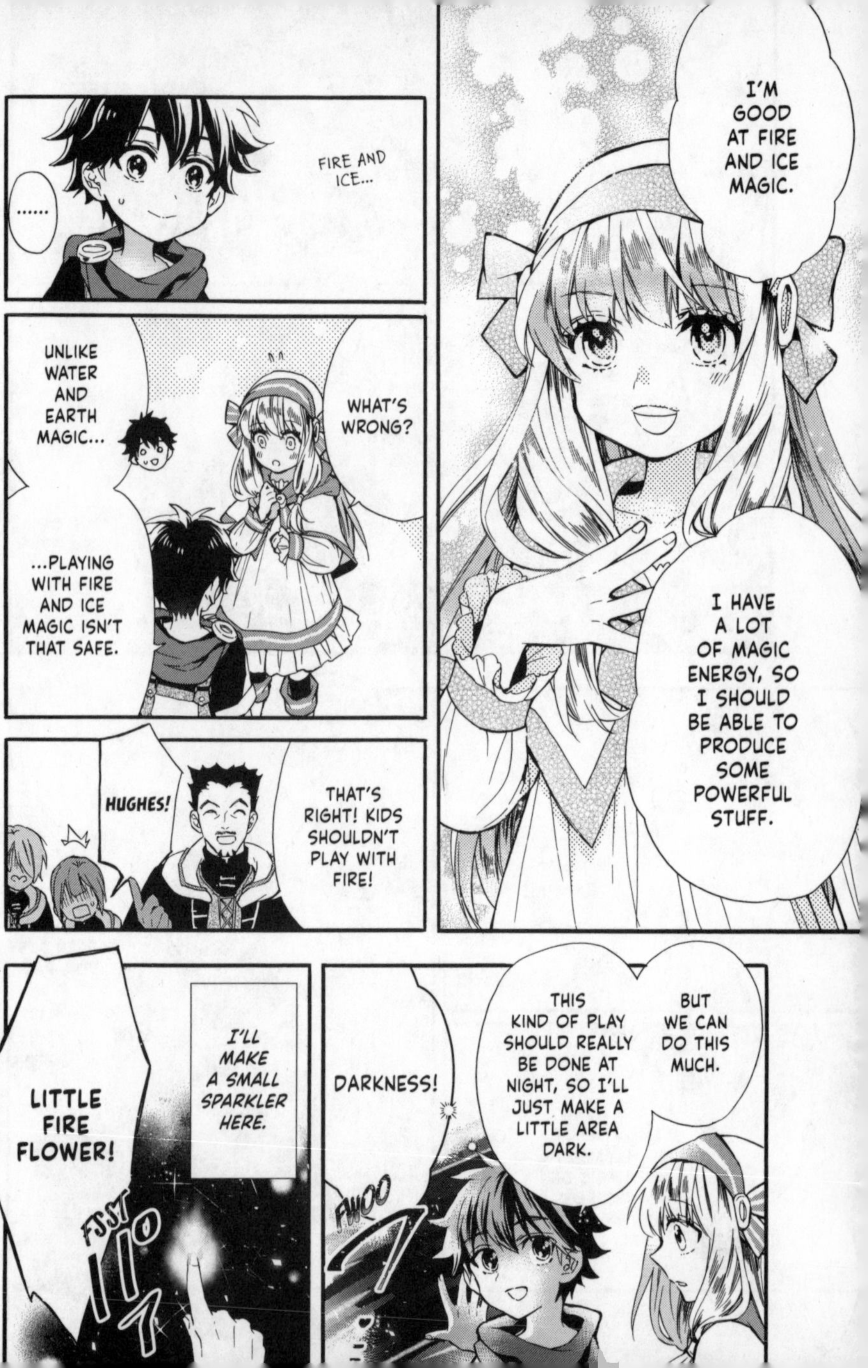
I'M GOOD AT FIRE AND ICE MAGIC.
I HAVE A LOT OF MAGIC ENERGY, SO I SHOULD BE ABLE TO PRODUCE SOME POWERFUL STUFF.
FIRE AND ICE...
......
WHAT'S WRONG?
UNLIKE WATER AND EARTH MAGIC...
...PLAYING WITH FIRE AND ICE MAGIC ISN'T THAT SAFE.
THAT'S RIGHT! KIDS SHOULDN'T PLAY WITH FIRE!
HUGHES!
BUT WE CAN DO THIS MUCH.
THIS KIND OF PLAY SHOULD REALLY BE DONE AT NIGHT, SO I'LL JUST MAKE A LITTLE AREA DARK.
DARKNESS!
FWOO
I'LL MAKE A SMALL SPARKLER HERE.
LITTLE FIRE FLOWER!
FSST

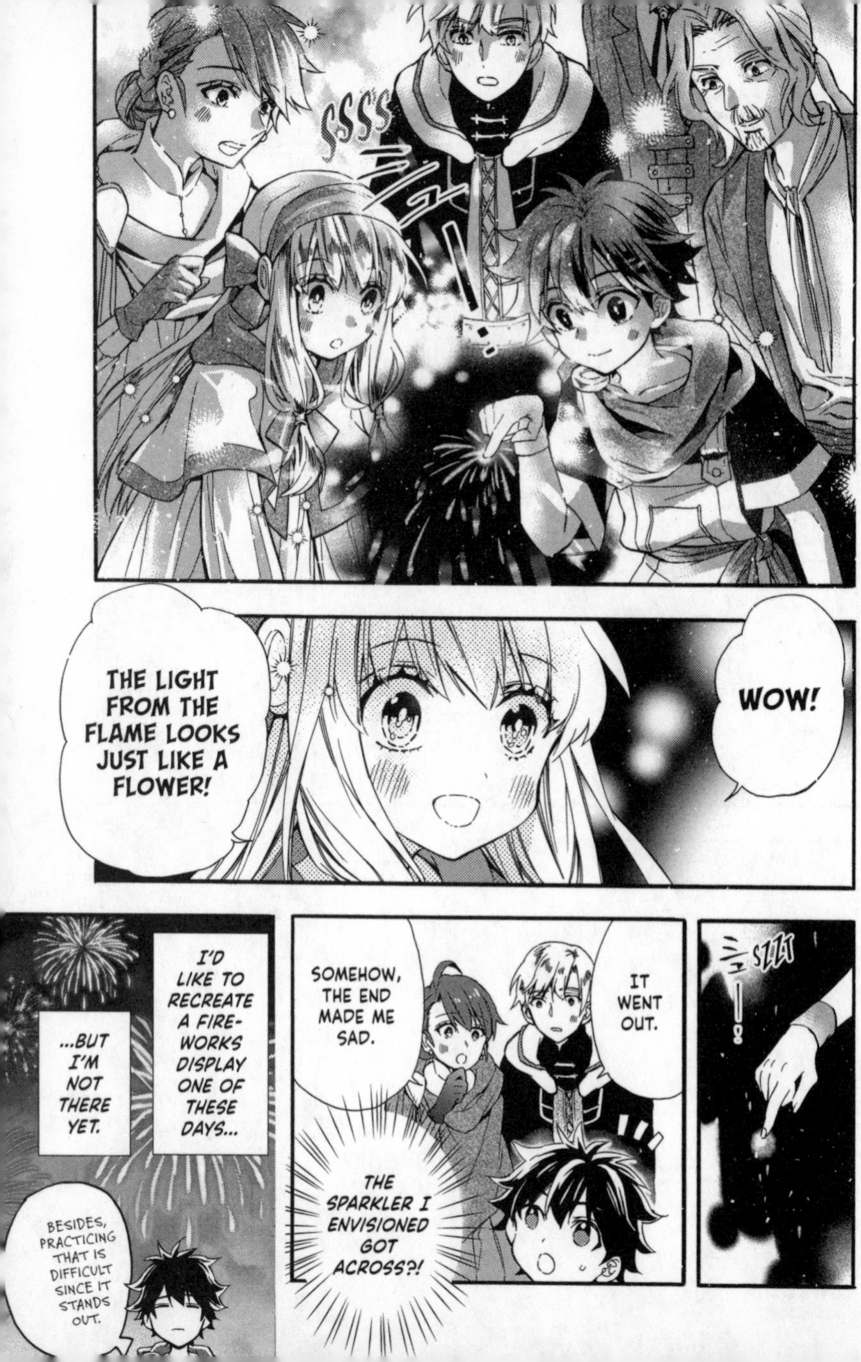
SSSS
WOW!
THE LIGHT FROM THE FLAME LOOKS JUST LIKE A FLOWER!
SZZT
IT WENT OUT.
SOMEHOW, THE END MADE ME SAD.
THE SPARKLER I ENVISIONED GOT ACROSS?!
I'D LIKE TO RECREATE A FIRE-WORKS DISPLAY ONE OF THESE DAYS...
...BUT I'M NOT THERE YET.
BESIDES, PRACTICING THAT IS DIFFICULT SINCE IT STANDS OUT.

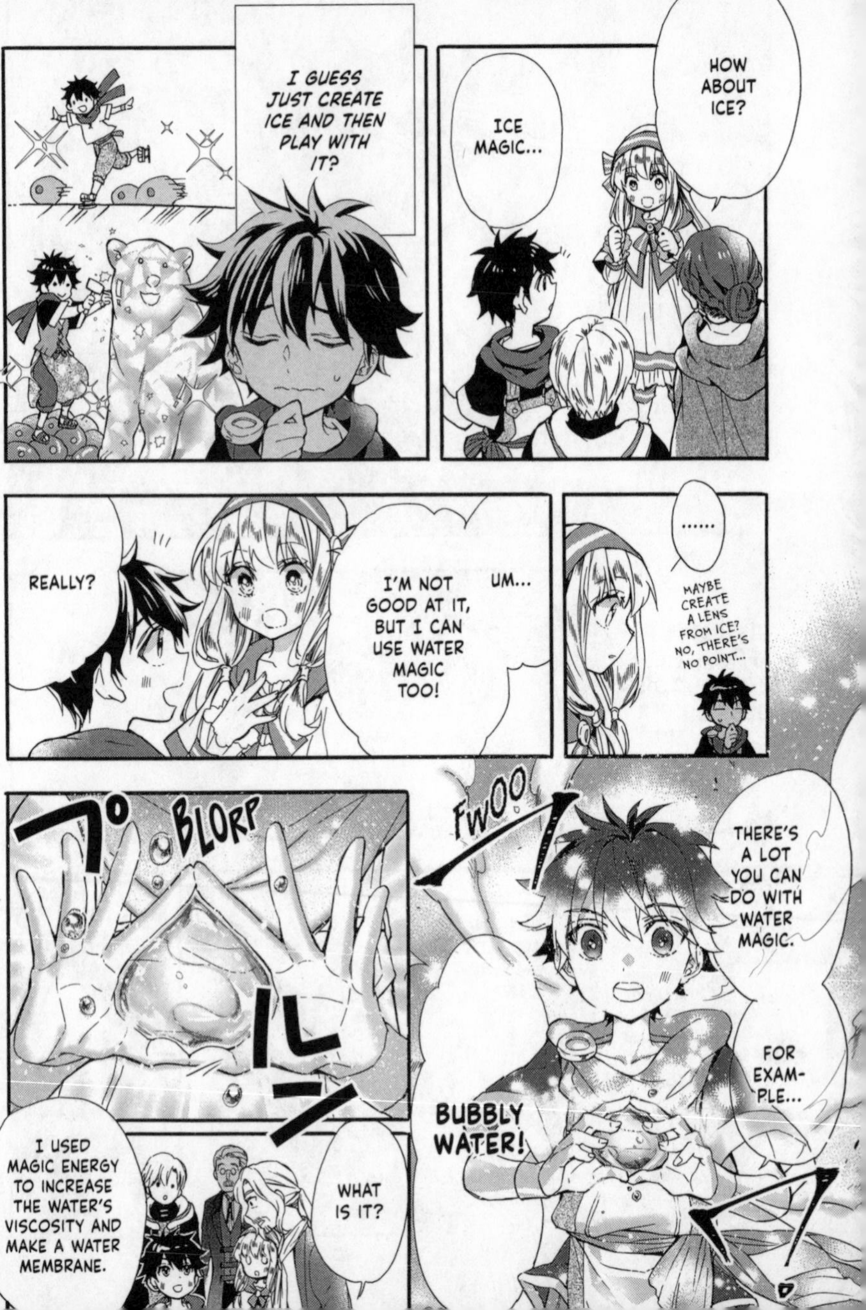
HOW ABOUT ICE?
ICE MAGIC...
I GUESS JUST CREATE ICE AND THEN PLAY WITH IT?
......
MAYBE CREATE A LENS FROM ICE? NO, THERE'S NO POINT...
UM...
I'M NOT GOOD AT IT, BUT I CAN USE WATER MAGIC TOO!
REALLY?
THERE'S A LOT YOU CAN DO WITH WATER MAGIC.
FOR EXAMPLE...
FWOO
BUBBLY WATER!
BLORP
WHAT IS IT?
I USED MAGIC ENERGY TO INCREASE THE WATER'S VISCOSITY AND MAKE A WATER MEMBRANE.

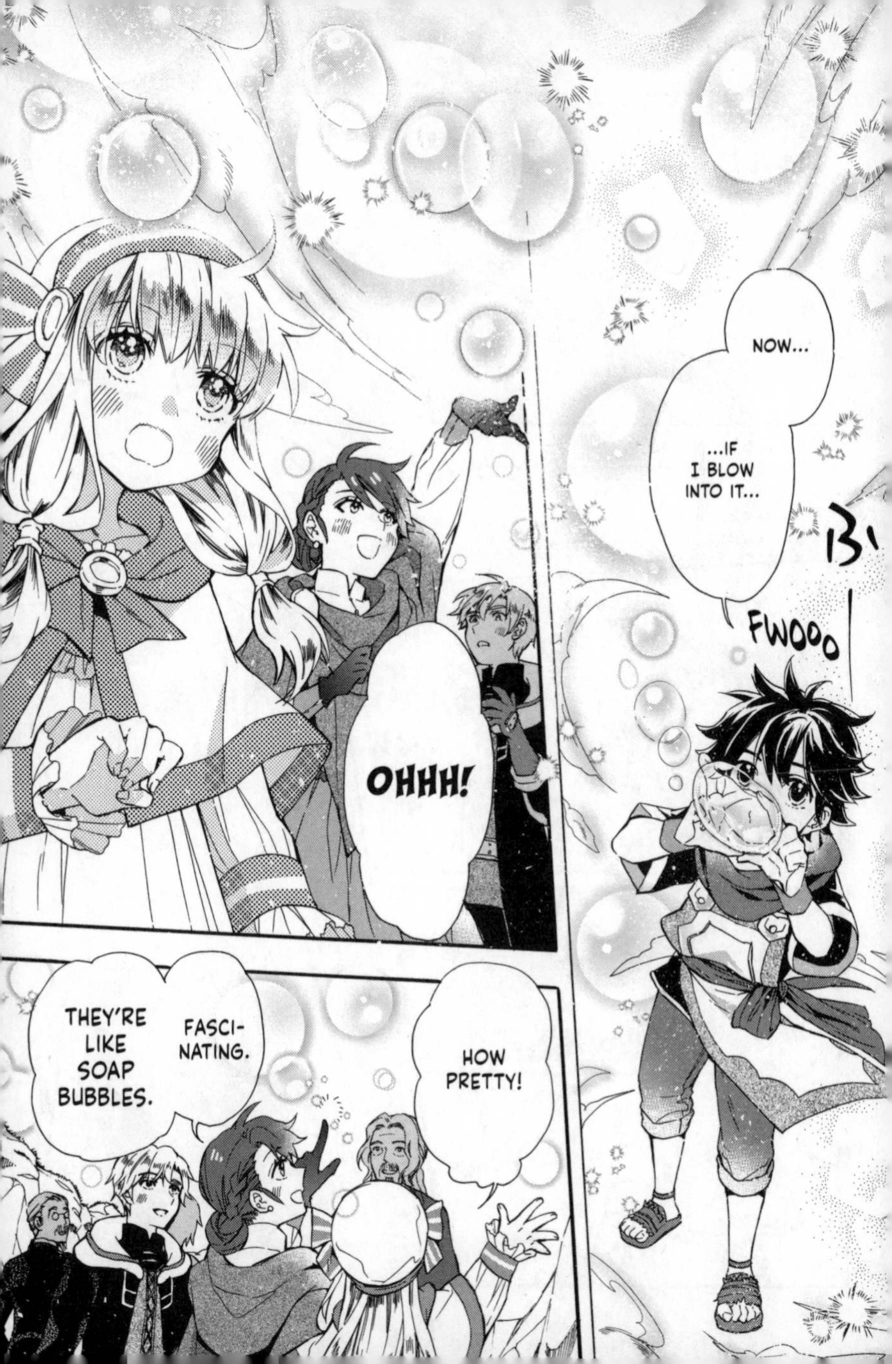
NOW...
...IF I BLOW INTO IT...
FWOOO
OHHH!
HOW PRETTY!
FASCINATING.
THEY'RE LIKE SOAP BUBBLES.

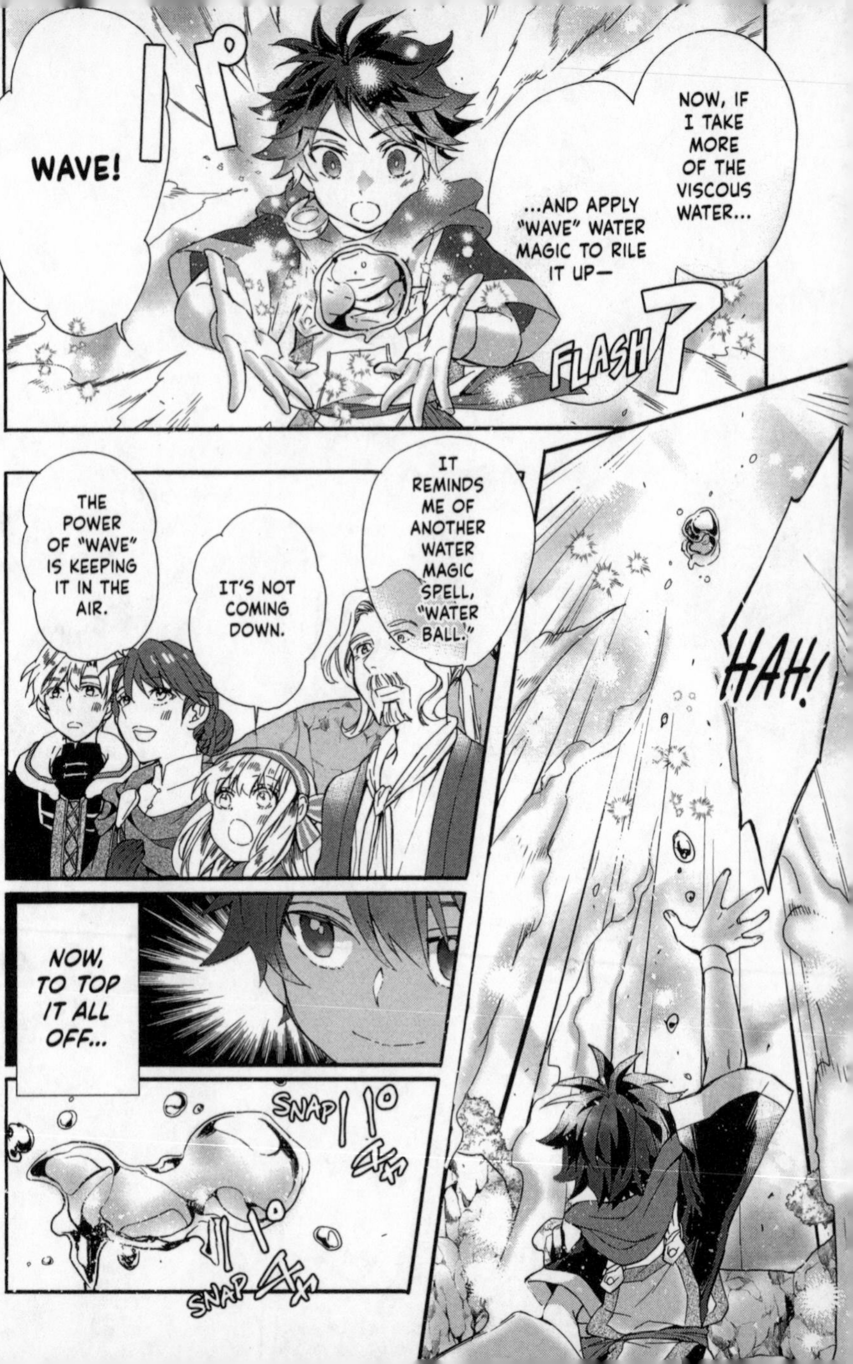
NOW, IF I TAKE MORE OF THE VISCOUS WATER...
...AND APPLY "WAVE" WATER MAGIC TO RILE IT UP—
WAVE!
FLASH
HAH!
IT REMINDS ME OF ANOTHER WATER MAGIC SPELL, "WATER BALL."
IT'S NOT COMING DOWN.
THE POWER OF "WAVE" IS KEEPING IT IN THE AIR.
NOW, TO TOP IT ALL OFF...
SNAP
SNAP

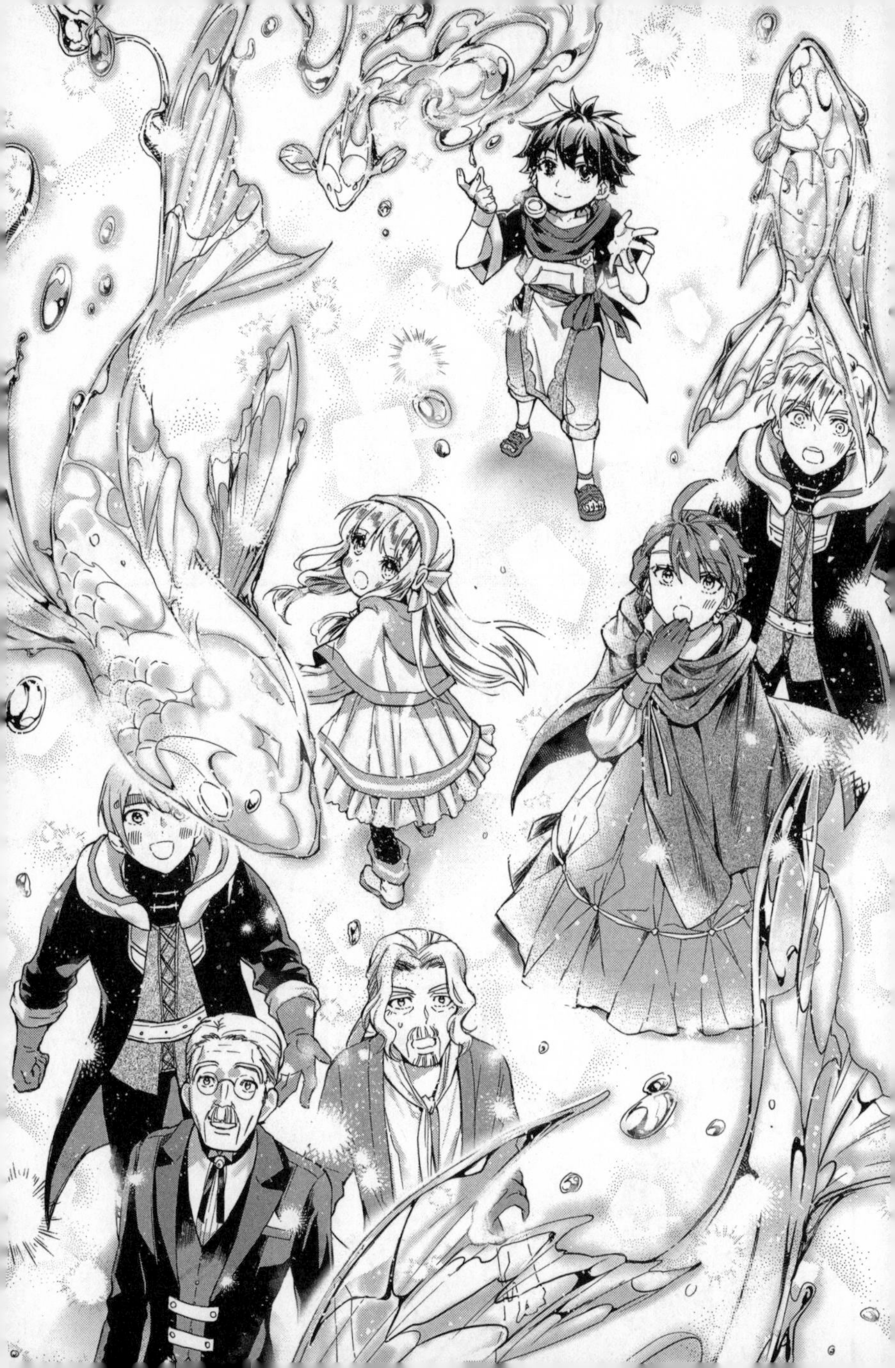

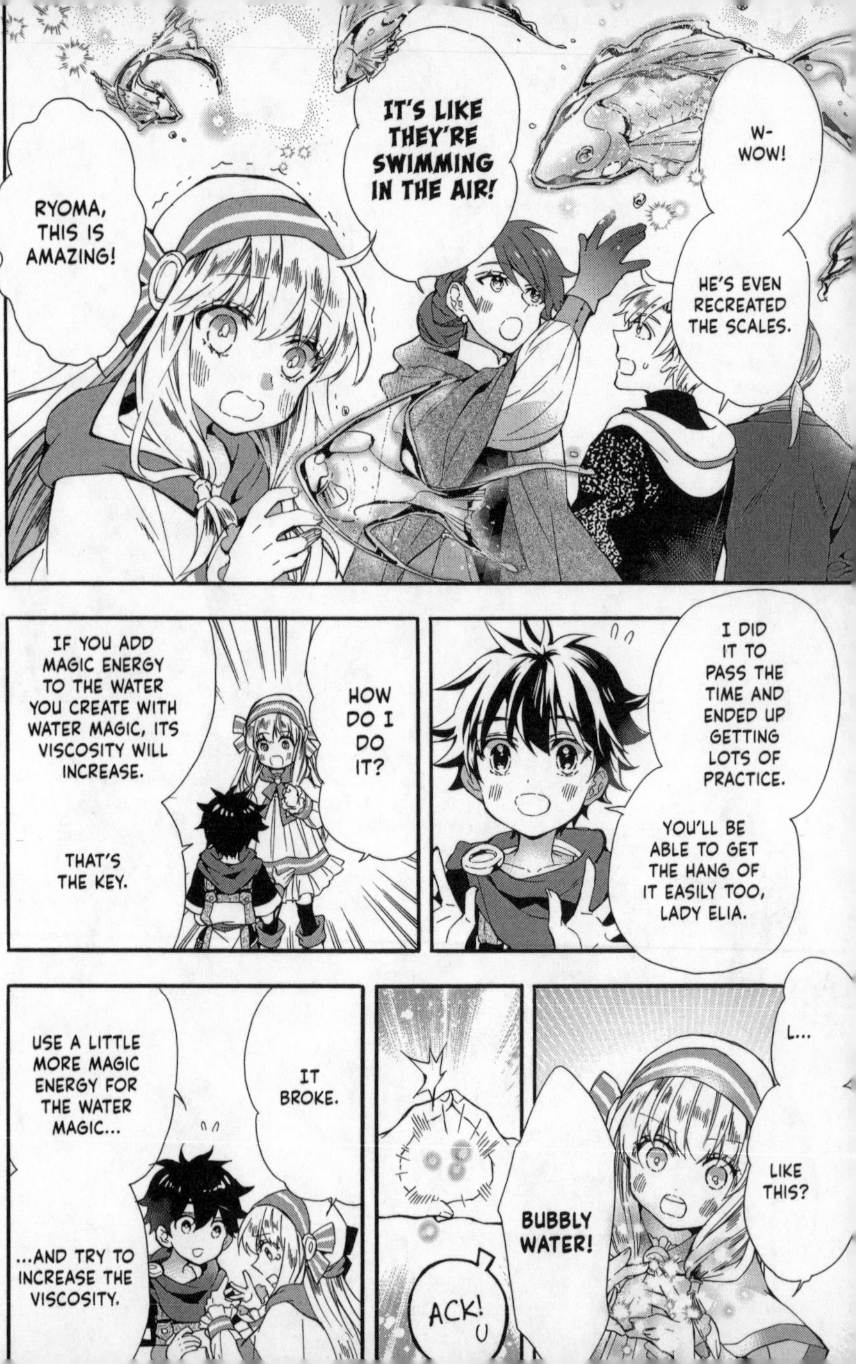
W-
WOW!
HE'S EVEN RECREATED THE SCALES.
IT'S LIKE THEY'RE SWIMMING IN THE AIR!
RYOMA, THIS IS AMAZING!
I DID IT TO PASS THE TIME AND ENDED UP GETTING LOTS OF PRACTICE.
YOU'LL BE ABLE TO GET THE HANG OF IT EASILY TOO, LADY ELIA.
HOW DO I DO IT?
IF YOU ADD MAGIC ENERGY TO THE WATER YOU CREATE WITH WATER MAGIC, ITS VISCOSITY WILL INCREASE.
THAT'S THE KEY.
L...
LIKE THIS?
BUBBLY WATER!
ACK!
IT BROKE.
USE A LITTLE MORE MAGIC ENERGY FOR THE WATER MAGIC...
...AND TRY TO INCREASE THE VISCOSITY.

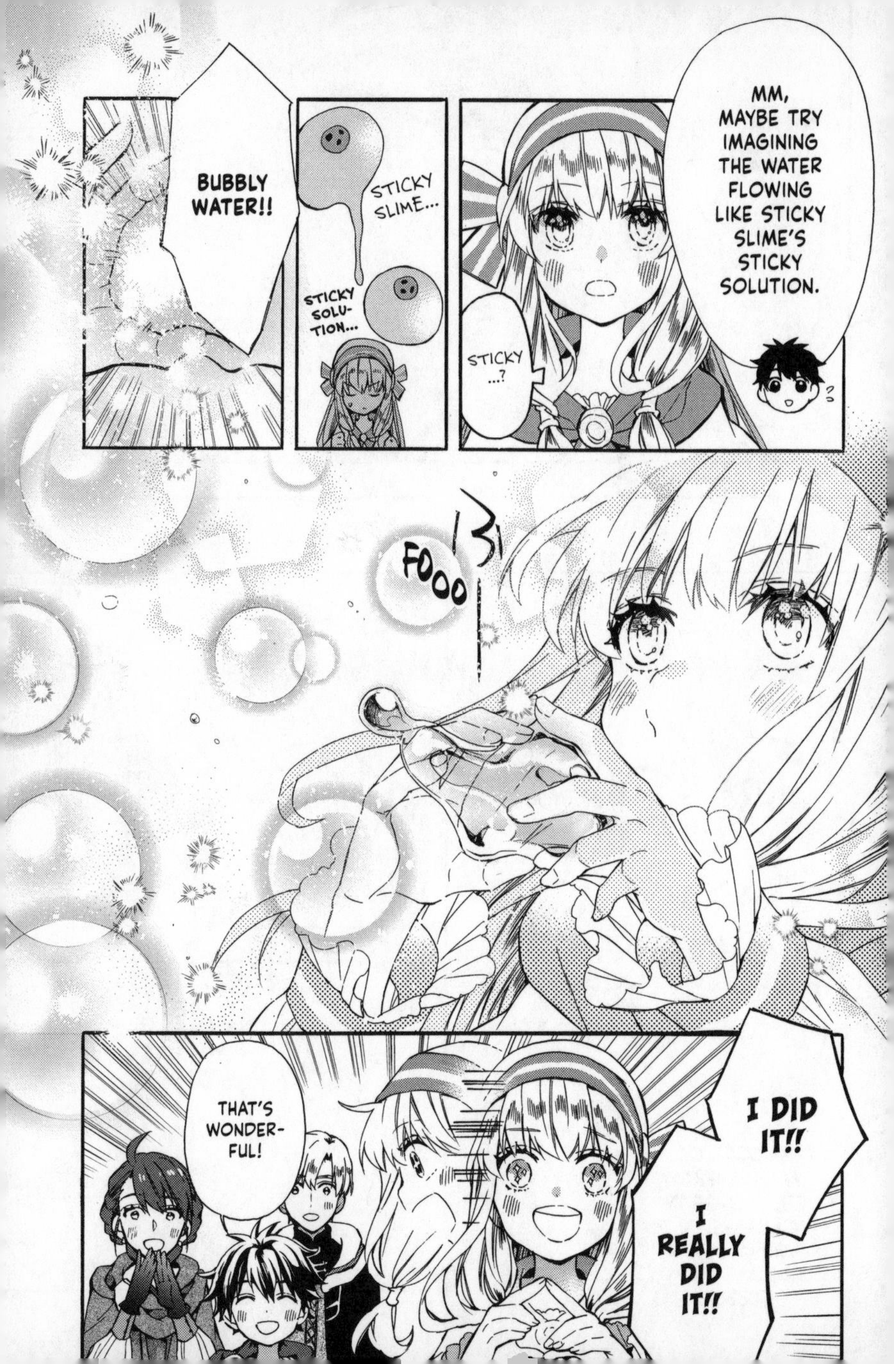
MM, MAYBE TRY IMAGINING THE WATER FLOWING LIKE STICKY SLIME'S STICKY SOLUTION.
STICKY ...?
STICKY SLIME...
STICKY SOLU-TION...
BUBBLY WATER!!
FOOO
I DID IT!!
I REALLY DID IT!!
THAT'S WONDER-FUL!

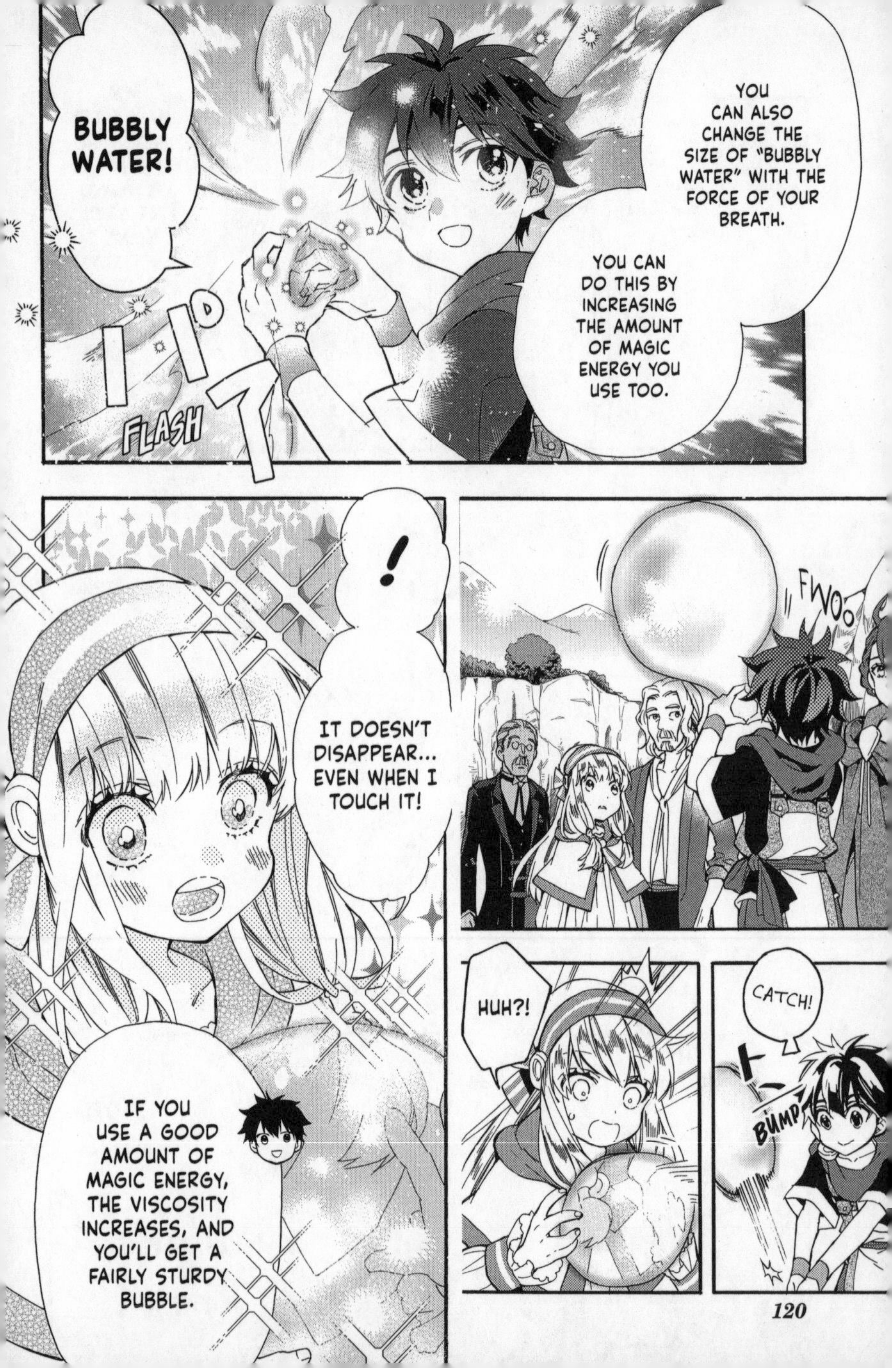
YOU CAN ALSO CHANGE THE SIZE OF "BUBBLY WATER" WITH THE FORCE OF YOUR BREATH.
YOU CAN DO THIS BY INCREASING THE AMOUNT OF MAGIC ENERGY YOU USE TOO.
BUBBLY WATER!
FLASH
FWOO
CATCH!
BUMP
HUH?!
!
IT DOESN'T DISAPPEAR... EVEN WHEN I TOUCH IT!
IF YOU USE A GOOD AMOUNT OF MAGIC ENERGY, THE VISCOSITY INCREASES, AND YOU'LL GET A FAIRLY STURDY BUBBLE.

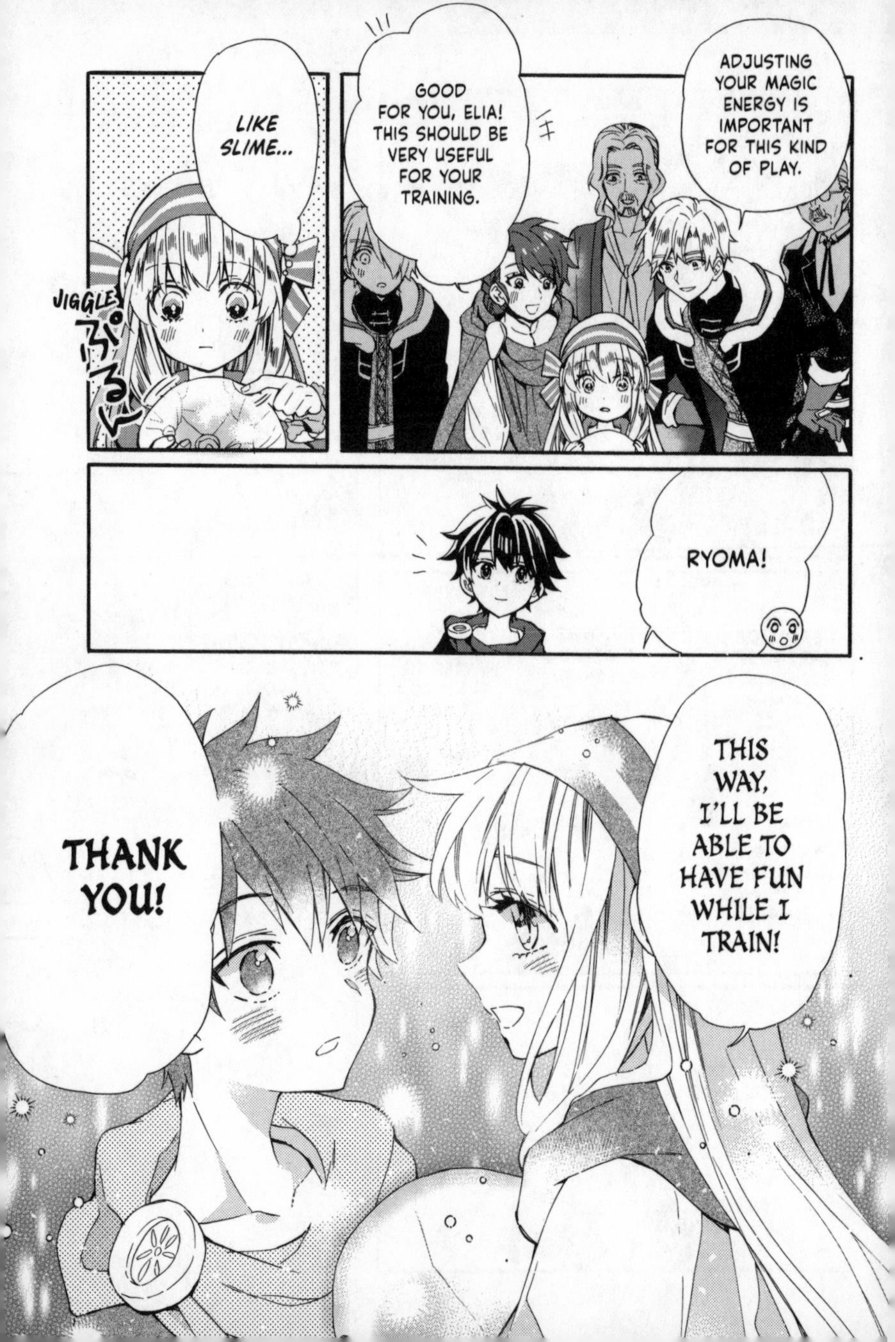
ADJUSTING YOUR MAGIC ENERGY IS IMPORTANT FOR THIS KIND OF PLAY.
GOOD FOR YOU, ELIA! THIS SHOULD BE VERY USEFUL FOR YOUR TRAINING.
LIKE SLIME...
JIGGLE
ぷるん
RYOMA!
THIS WAY, I'LL BE ABLE TO HAVE FUN WHILE I TRAIN!
THANK YOU!

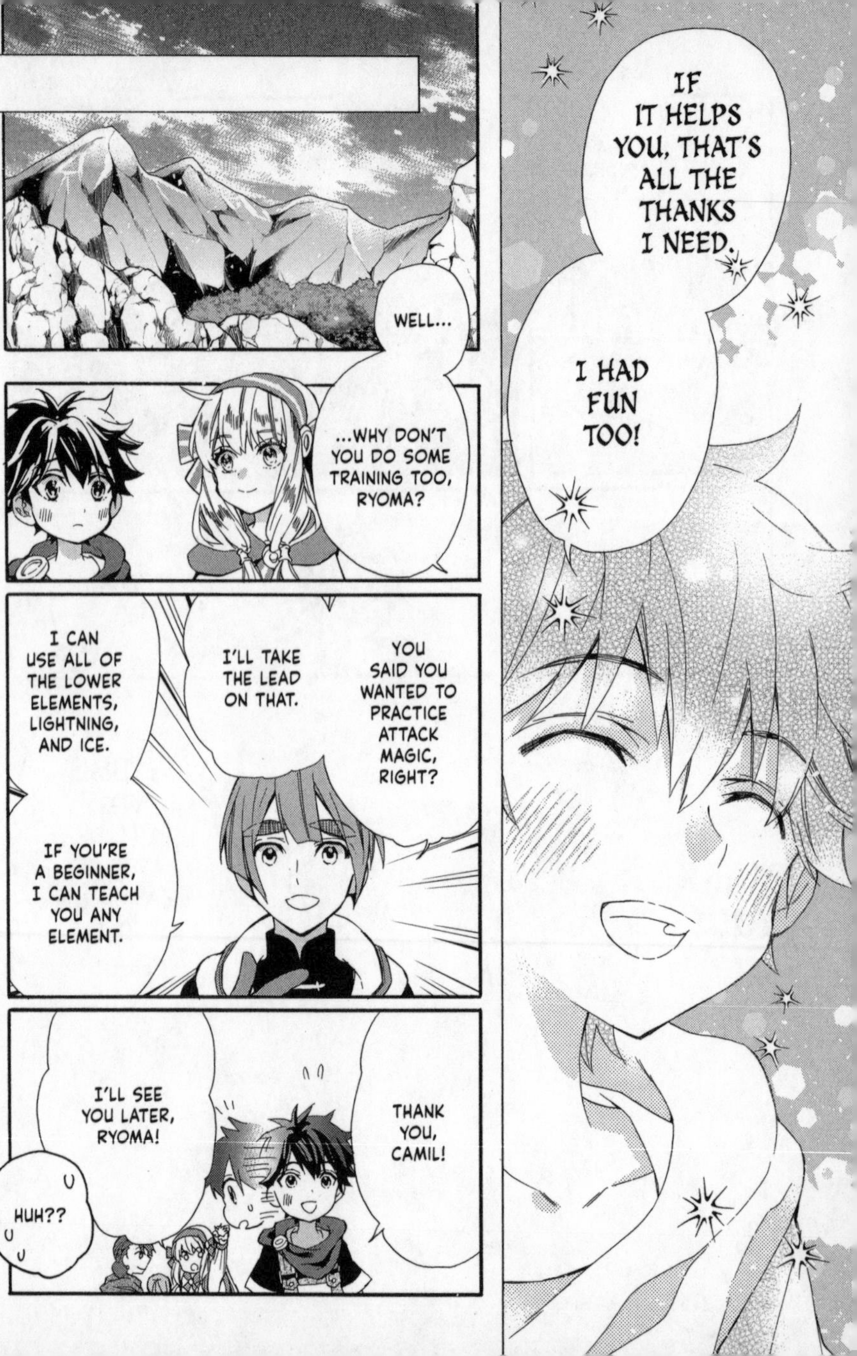
IF IT HELPS YOU, THAT'S ALL THE THANKS I NEED.
I HAD FUN TOO!
WELL...
...WHY DON'T YOU DO SOME TRAINING TOO, RYOMA?
YOU SAID YOU WANTED TO PRACTICE ATTACK MAGIC, RIGHT?
I'LL TAKE THE LEAD ON THAT.
I CAN USE ALL OF THE LOWER ELEMENTS, LIGHTNING, AND ICE.
IF YOU'RE A BEGINNER, I CAN TEACH YOU ANY ELEMENT.
THANK YOU, CAMIL!
I'LL SEE YOU LATER, RYOMA!
HUH??

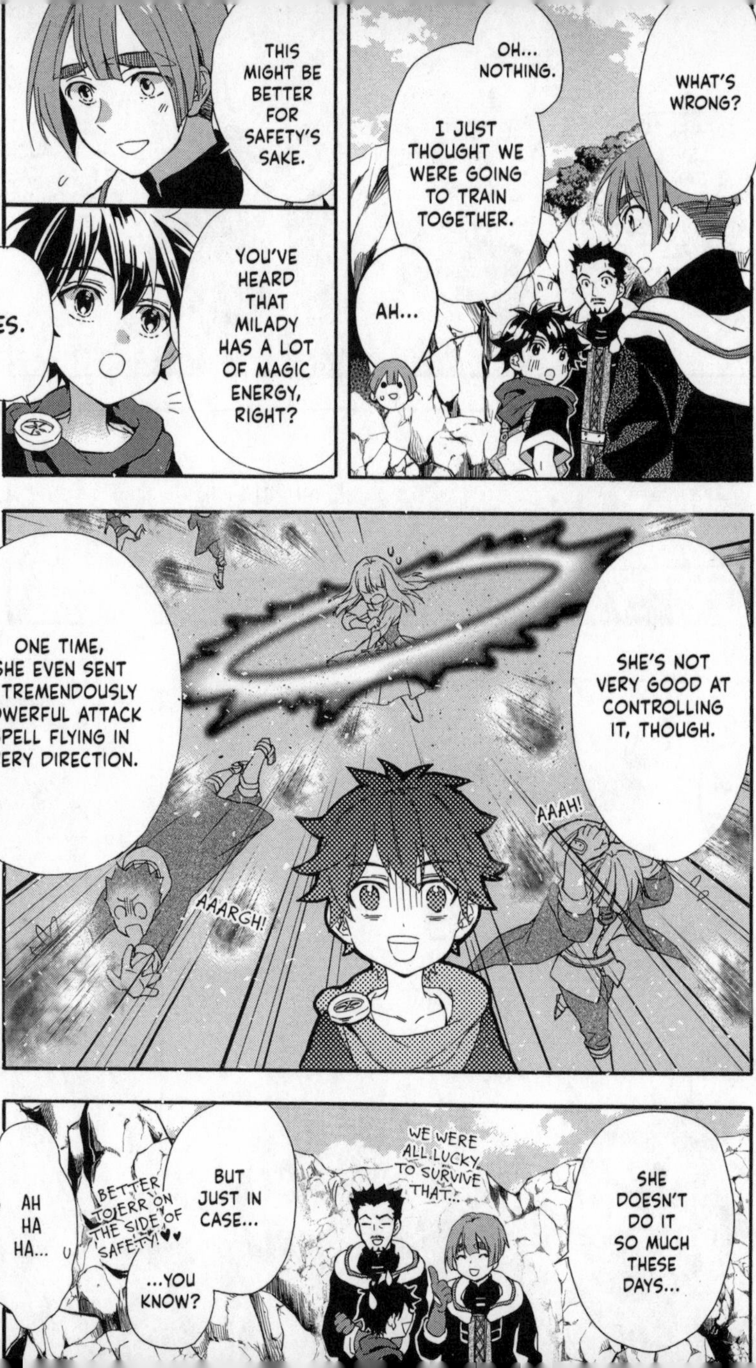
WHAT'S WRONG?
OH... NOTHING.
I JUST THOUGHT WE WERE GOING TO TRAIN TOGETHER.
AH...
THIS MIGHT BE BETTER FOR SAFETY'S SAKE.
YOU'VE HEARD THAT MILADY HAS A LOT OF MAGIC ENERGY, RIGHT?
YES.
SHE'S NOT VERY GOOD AT CONTROLLING IT, THOUGH.
AAAH!
ONE TIME, SHE EVEN SENT A TREMENDOUSLY POWERFUL ATTACK SPELL FLYING IN EVERY DIRECTION.
AAARGH!
SHE DOESN'T DO IT SO MUCH THESE DAYS...
WE WERE ALL LUCKY TO SURVIVE THAT...
BUT JUST IN CASE...
BETTER TO ERR ON THE SIDE OF SAFETY!♥♥
...YOU KNOW?
AH HA HA...

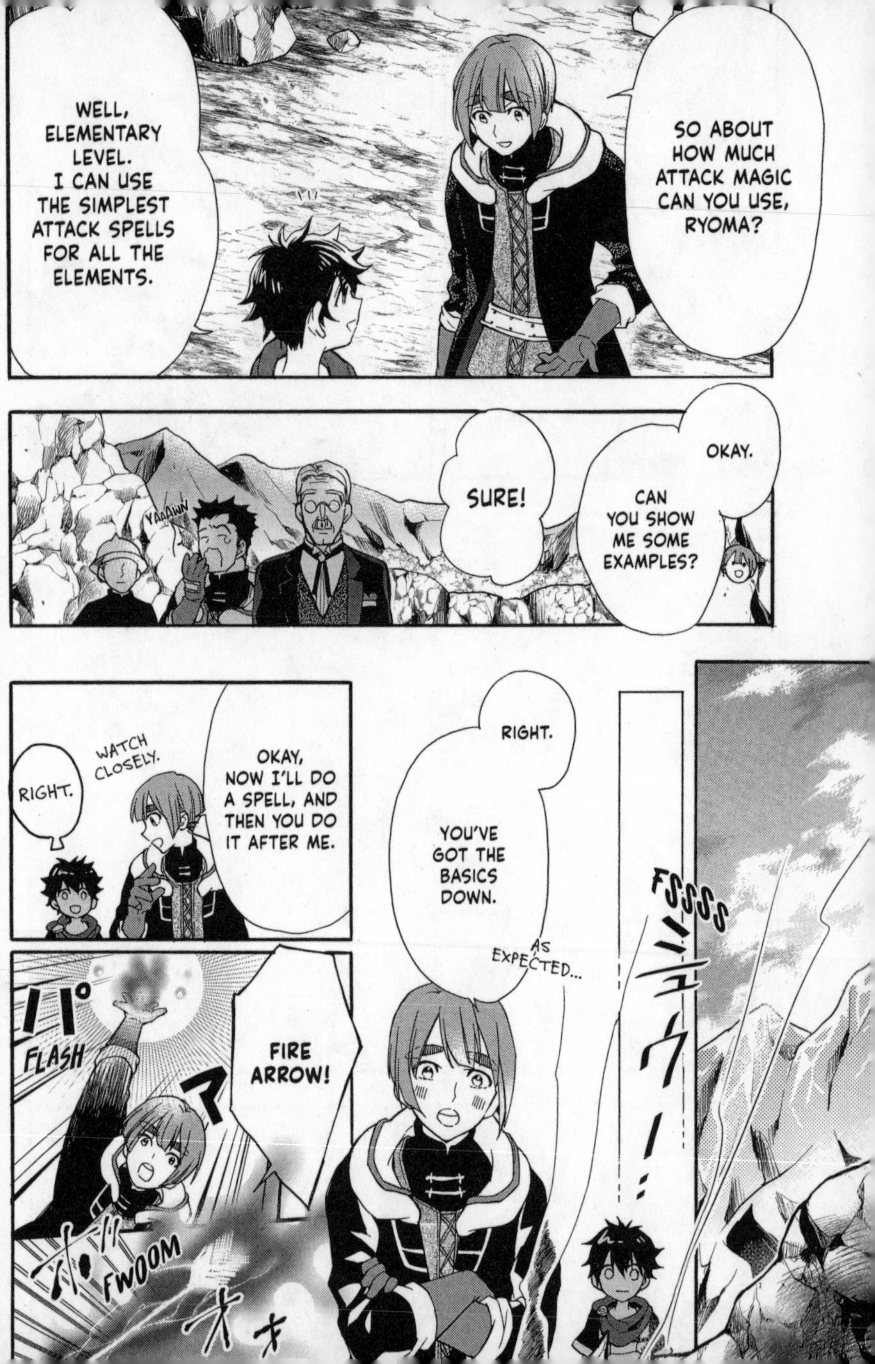

SO ABOUT HOW MUCH ATTACK MAGIC CAN YOU USE, RYOMA?
WELL, ELEMENTARY LEVEL. I CAN USE THE SIMPLEST ATTACK SPELLS FOR ALL THE ELEMENTS.
OKAY. CAN YOU SHOW ME SOME EXAMPLES?
SURE!
YAAAWN
OKAY, NOW I'LL DO A SPELL, AND THEN YOU DO IT AFTER ME.
WATCH CLOSELY.
RIGHT.
FIRE ARROW!
FLASH
FWOOM
AS EXPECTED...
RIGHT. YOU'VE GOT THE BASICS DOWN.
FSSSS

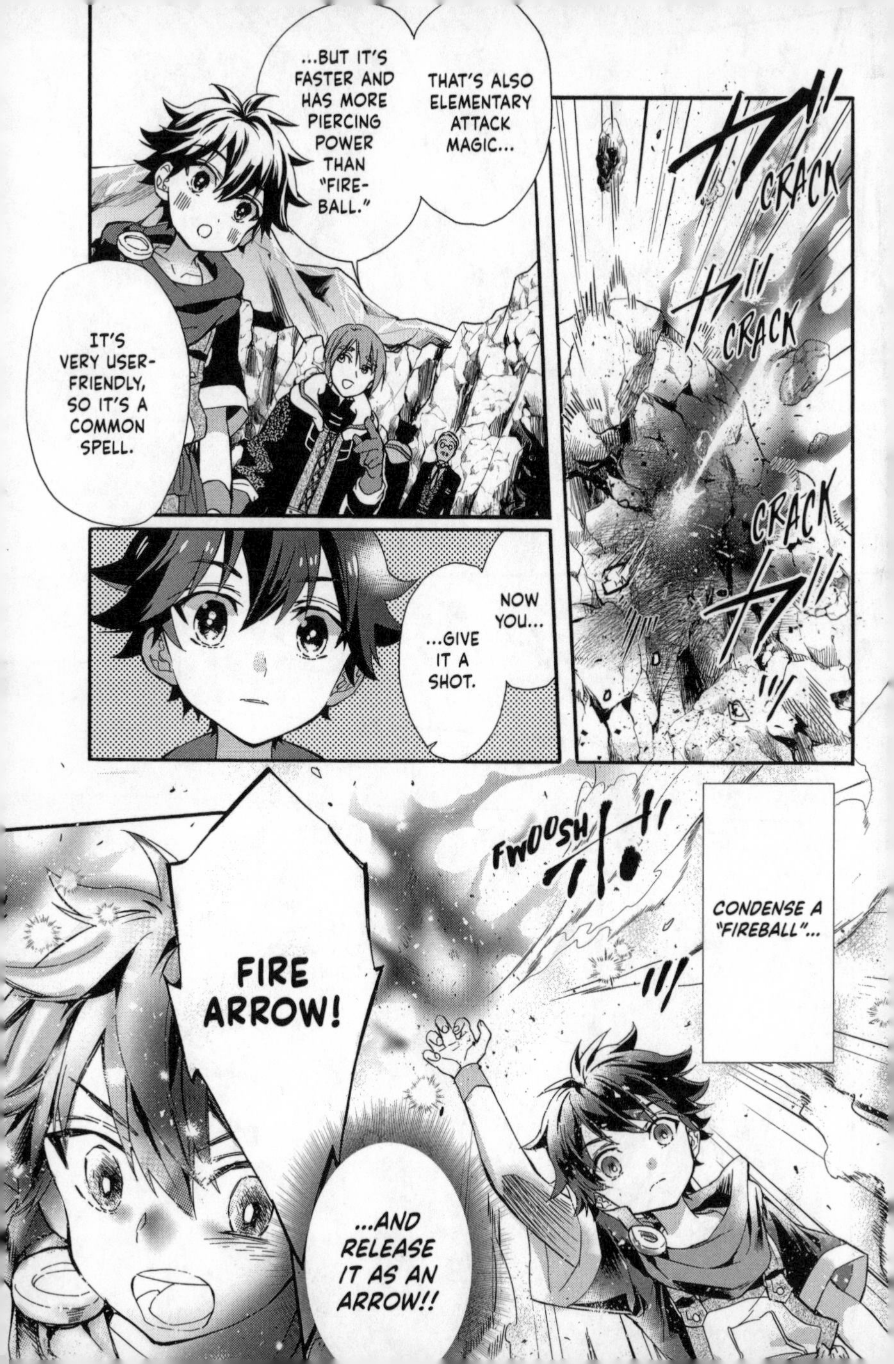
CRACK
CRACK
CRACK
THAT'S ALSO ELEMENTARY ATTACK MAGIC...
...BUT IT'S FASTER AND HAS MORE PIERCING POWER THAN "FIRE-BALL."
IT'S VERY USER-FRIENDLY, SO IT'S A COMMON SPELL.
NOW YOU...
...GIVE IT A SHOT.
FWOOSH
CONDENSE A "FIREBALL"...
...AND RELEASE IT AS AN ARROW!!
FIRE ARROW!

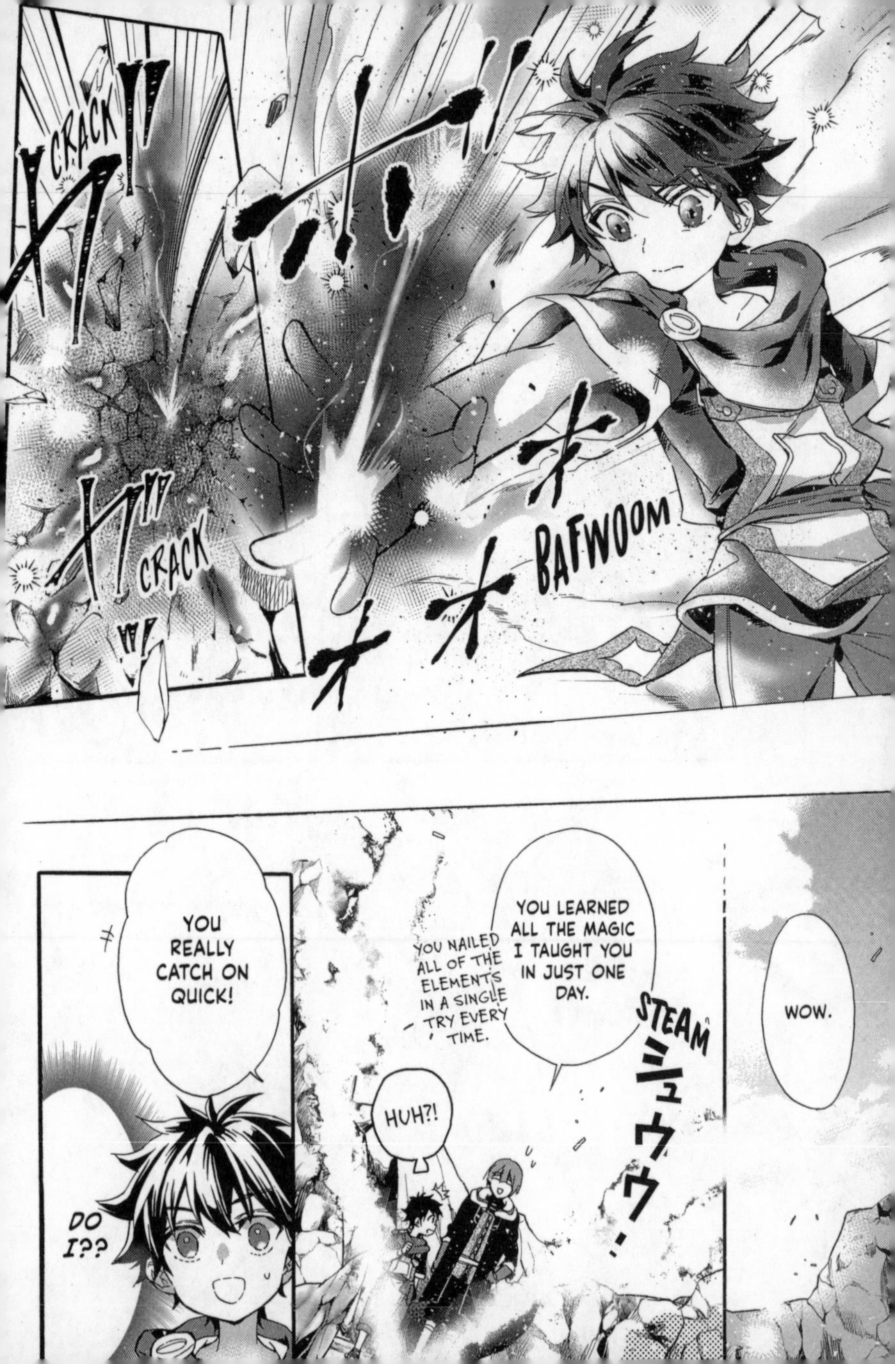
BAFWOOM
CRACK
CRACK
WOW.
YOU LEARNED ALL THE MAGIC I TAUGHT YOU IN JUST ONE DAY.
YOU NAILED ALL OF THE ELEMENTS IN A SINGLE TRY EVERY TIME.
STEAM
シュウウ！
HUH?!
YOU REALLY CATCH ON QUICK!
DO I??

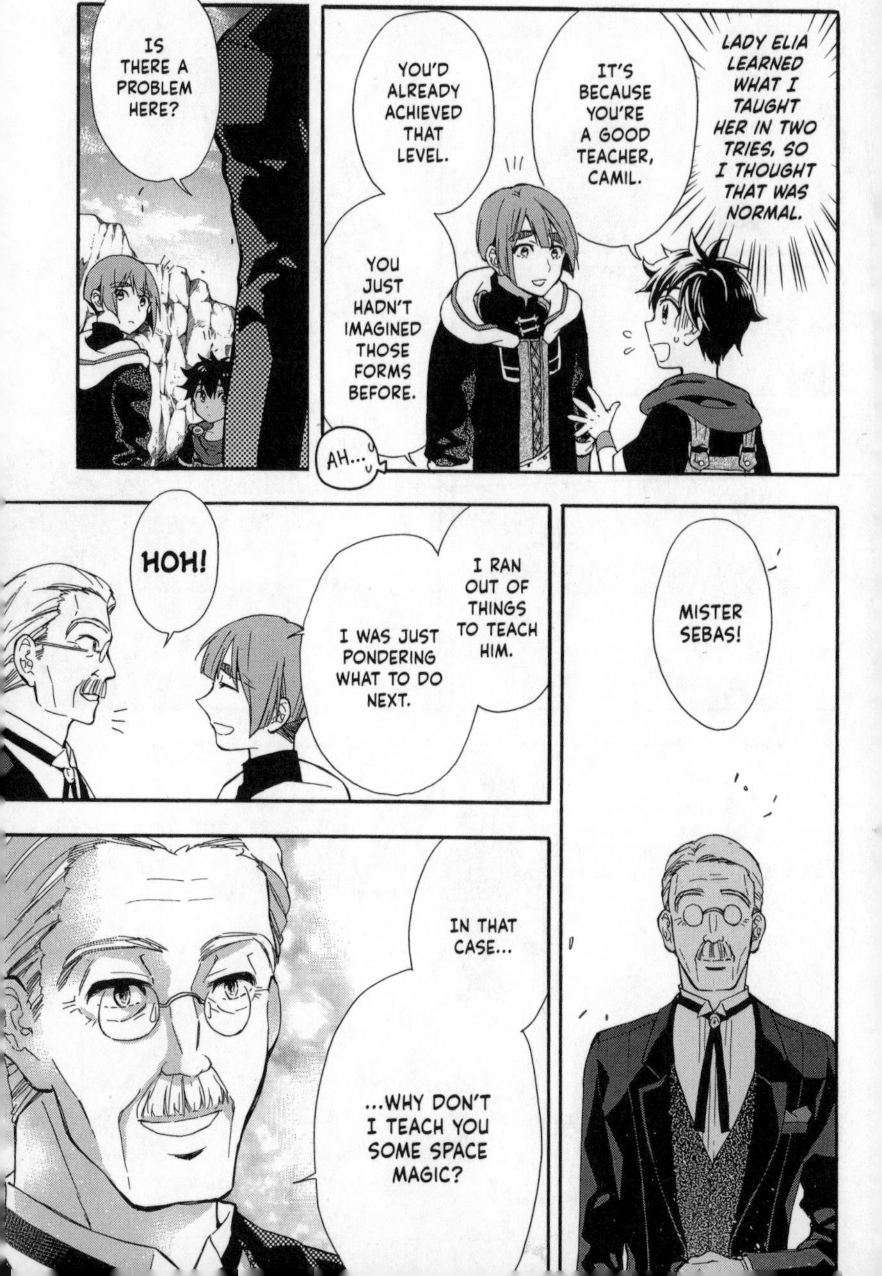
LADY ELIA LEARNED WHAT I TAUGHT HER IN TWO TRIES, SO I THOUGHT THAT WAS NORMAL.
IT'S BECAUSE YOU'RE A GOOD TEACHER, CAMIL.
YOU'D ALREADY ACHIEVED THAT LEVEL.
YOU JUST HADN'T IMAGINED THOSE FORMS BEFORE.
AH...
IS THERE A PROBLEM HERE?
MISTER SEBAS!
I RAN OUT OF THINGS TO TEACH HIM.
I WAS JUST PONDERING WHAT TO DO NEXT.
HOH!
IN THAT CASE...
...WHY DON'T I TEACH YOU SOME SPACE MAGIC?

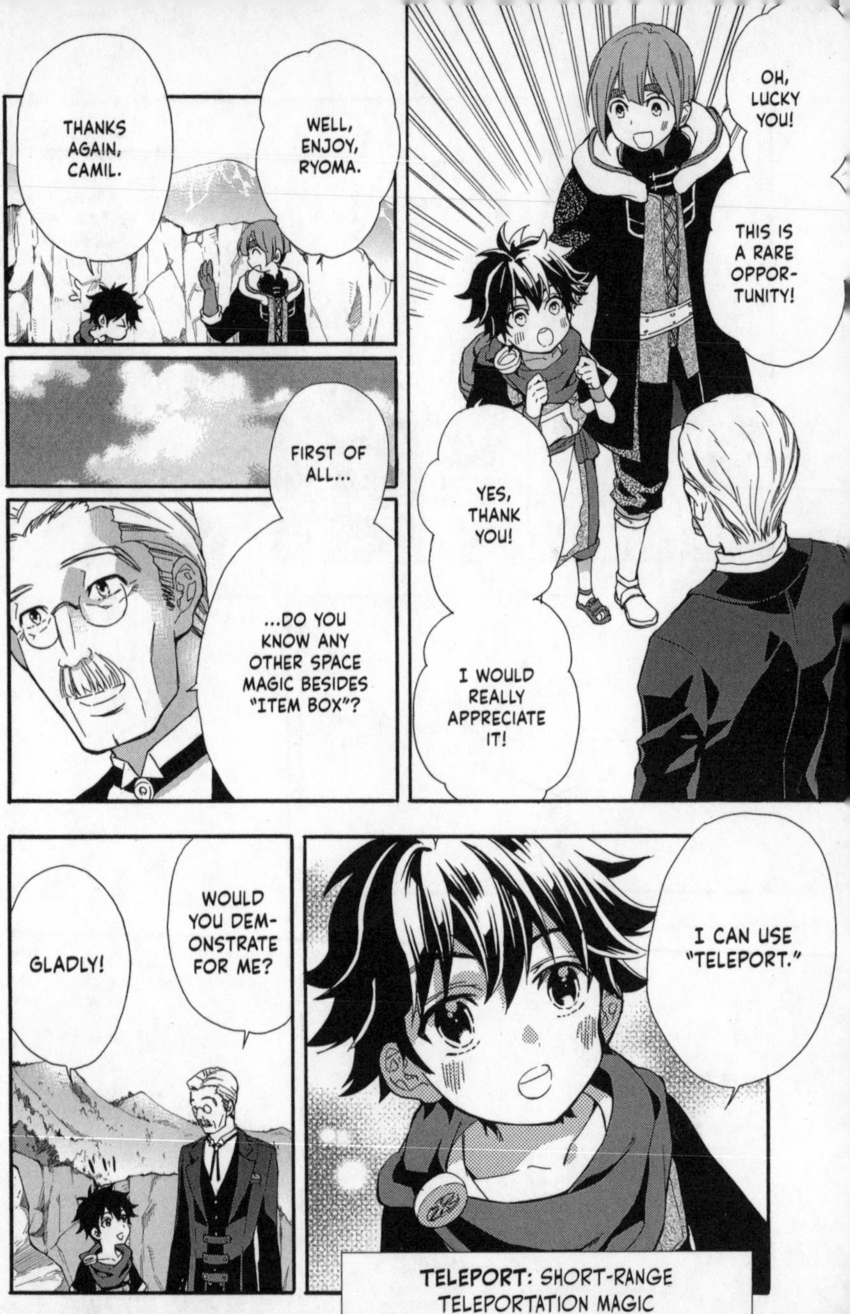
OH, LUCKY YOU!
THIS IS A RARE OPPOR-TUNITY!
YES, THANK YOU!
I WOULD REALLY APPRECIATE IT!
WELL, ENJOY, RYOMA.
THANKS AGAIN, CAMIL.
FIRST OF ALL...
...DO YOU KNOW ANY OTHER SPACE MAGIC BESIDES "ITEM BOX"?
I CAN USE "TELEPORT."
TELEPORT: SHORT-RANGE TELEPORTATION MAGIC
WOULD YOU DEM-ONSTRATE FOR ME?
GLADLY!

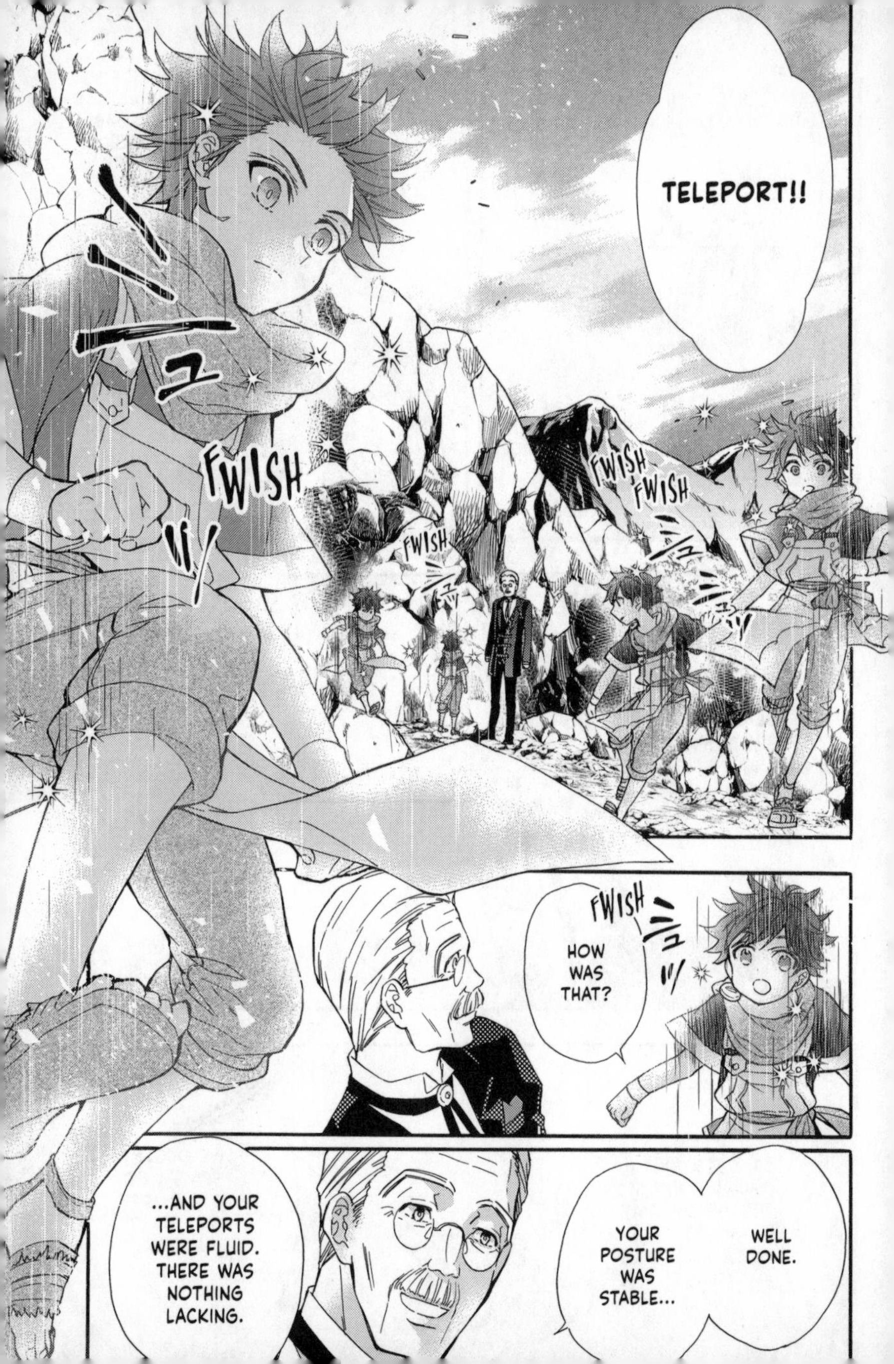
TELEPORT!!
FWISH
FWISH
FWISH
FWISH
FWISH
HOW WAS THAT?
WELL DONE.
YOUR POSTURE WAS STABLE...
...AND YOUR TELEPORTS WERE FLUID. THERE WAS NOTHING LACKING.

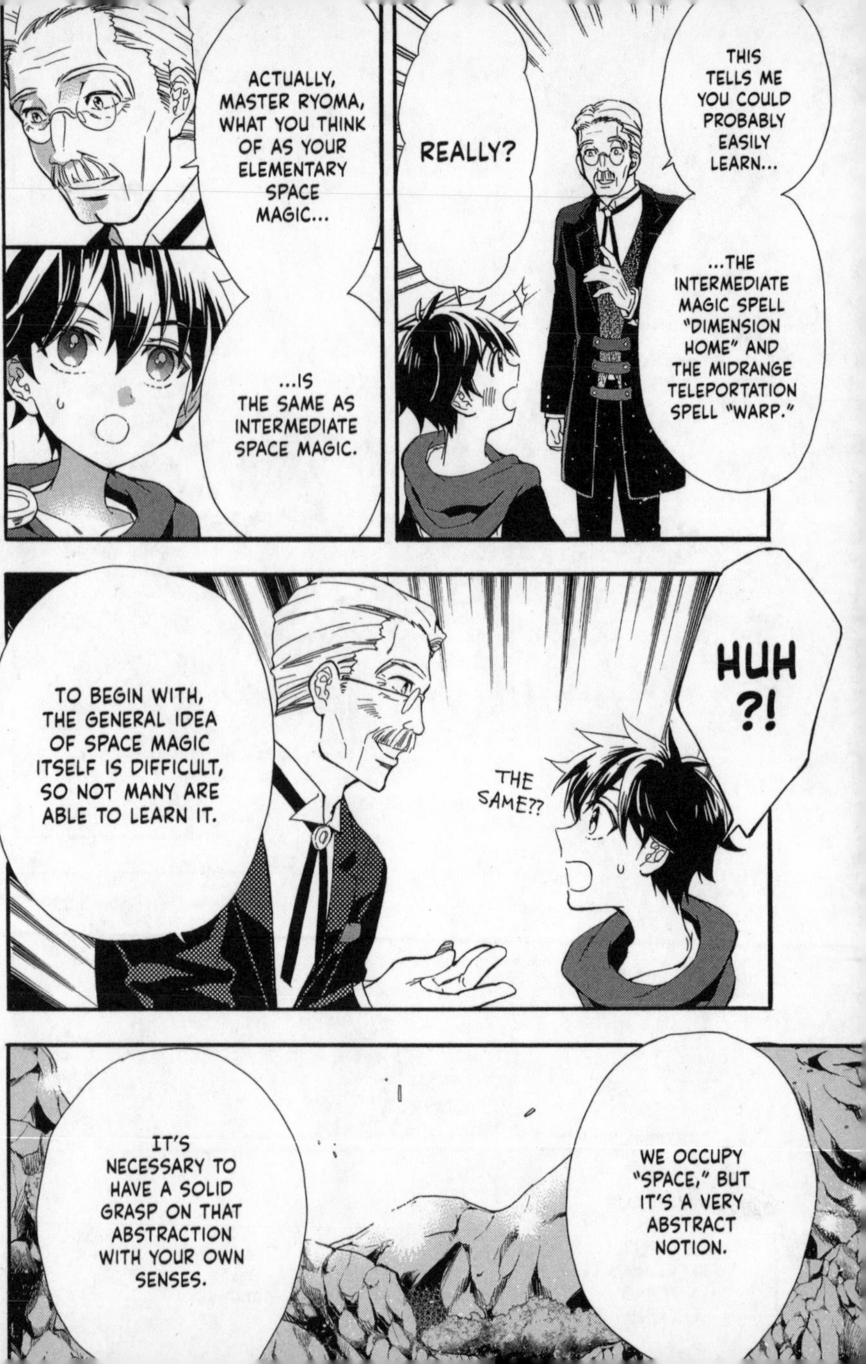
THIS TELLS ME YOU COULD PROBABLY EASILY LEARN...
...THE INTERMEDIATE MAGIC SPELL "DIMENSION HOME" AND THE MIDRANGE TELEPORTATION SPELL "WARP."
REALLY?
ACTUALLY, MASTER RYOMA, WHAT YOU THINK OF AS YOUR ELEMENTARY SPACE MAGIC...
...IS THE SAME AS INTERMEDIATE SPACE MAGIC.
HUH ?!
THE SAME??
TO BEGIN WITH, THE GENERAL IDEA OF SPACE MAGIC ITSELF IS DIFFICULT, SO NOT MANY ARE ABLE TO LEARN IT.
WE OCCUPY "SPACE," BUT IT'S A VERY ABSTRACT NOTION.
IT'S NECESSARY TO HAVE A SOLID GRASP ON THAT ABSTRACTION WITH YOUR OWN SENSES.

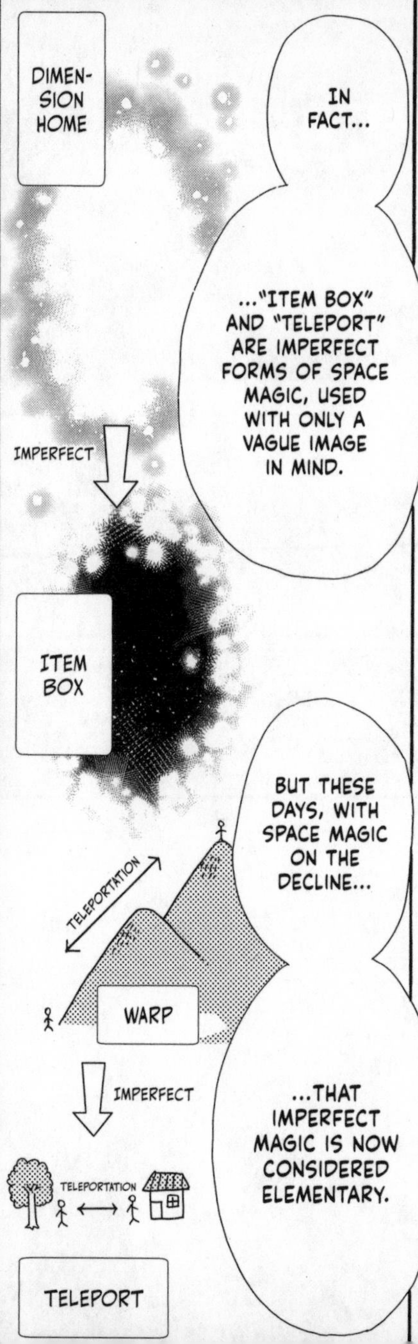
IN FACT...
DIMENSION HOME
..."ITEM BOX" AND "TELEPORT" ARE IMPERFECT FORMS OF SPACE MAGIC, USED WITH ONLY A VAGUE IMAGE IN MIND.
IMPERFECT
ITEM BOX
BUT THESE DAYS, WITH SPACE MAGIC ON THE DECLINE...
TELEPORTATION
WARP
...THAT IMPERFECT MAGIC IS NOW CONSIDERED ELEMENTARY.
IMPERFECT
TELEPORTATION
TELEPORT

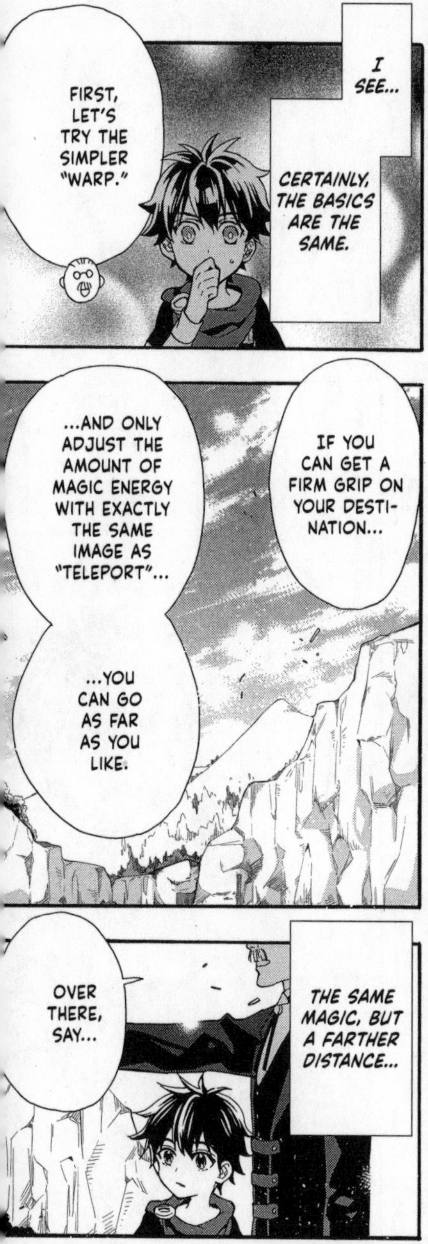
I SEE...
CERTAINLY, THE BASICS ARE THE SAME.
FIRST, LET'S TRY THE SIMPLER "WARP."
IF YOU CAN GET A FIRM GRIP ON YOUR DESTINATION...
...AND ONLY ADJUST THE AMOUNT OF MAGIC ENERGY WITH EXACTLY THE SAME IMAGE AS "TELEPORT"...
...YOU CAN GO AS FAR AS YOU LIKE.
THE SAME MAGIC, BUT A FARTHER DISTANCE...
OVER THERE, SAY...

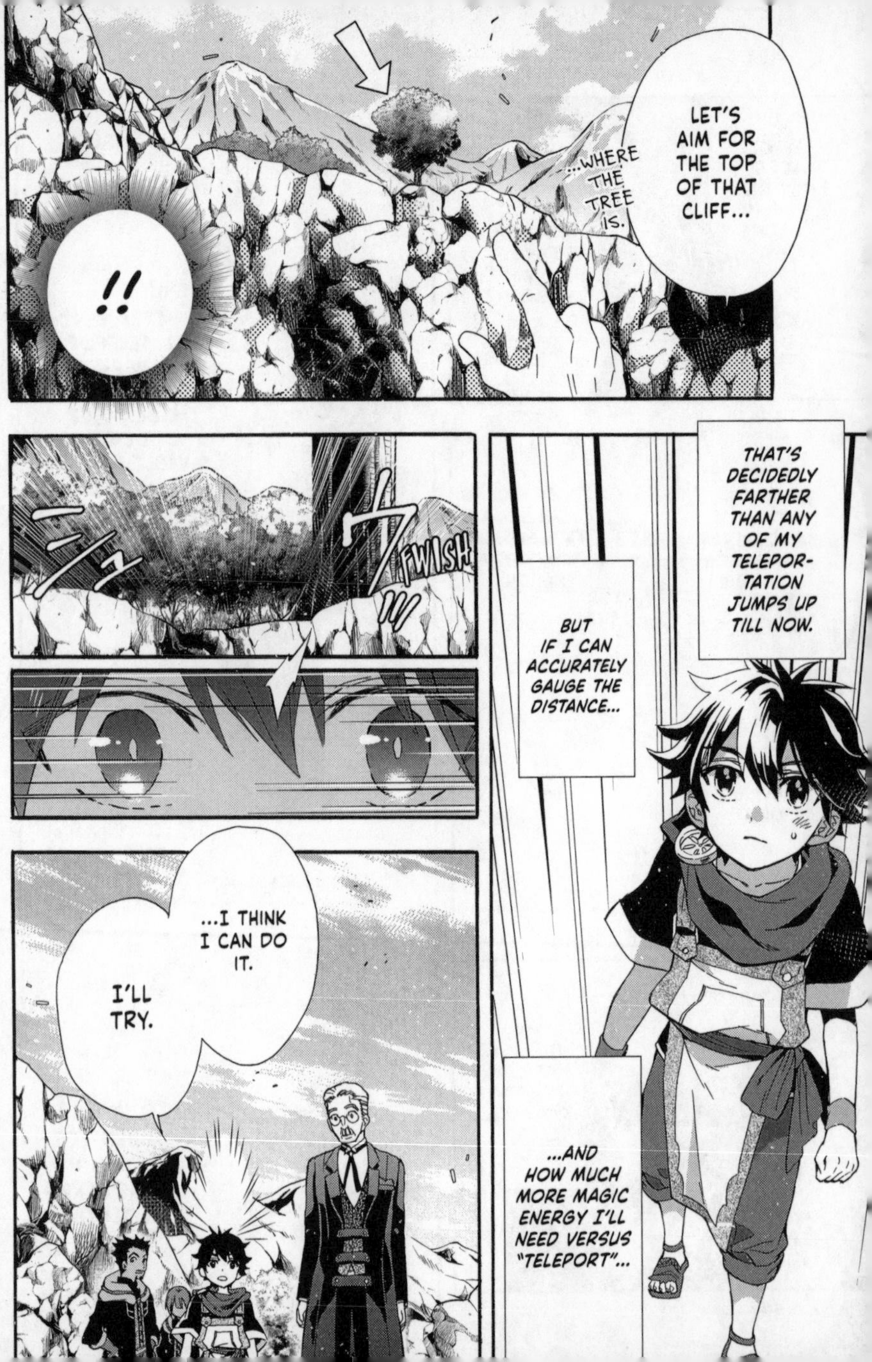

LET'S AIM FOR THE TOP OF THAT CLIFF...
...WHERE THE TREE IS.
!!
THAT'S DECIDEDLY FARTHER THAN ANY OF MY TELEPOR-TATION JUMPS UP TILL NOW.
BUT IF I CAN ACCURATELY GAUGE THE DISTANCE...
...AND HOW MUCH MORE MAGIC ENERGY I'LL NEED VERSUS "TELEPORT"...
FWISH
...I THINK I CAN DO IT.
I'LL TRY.

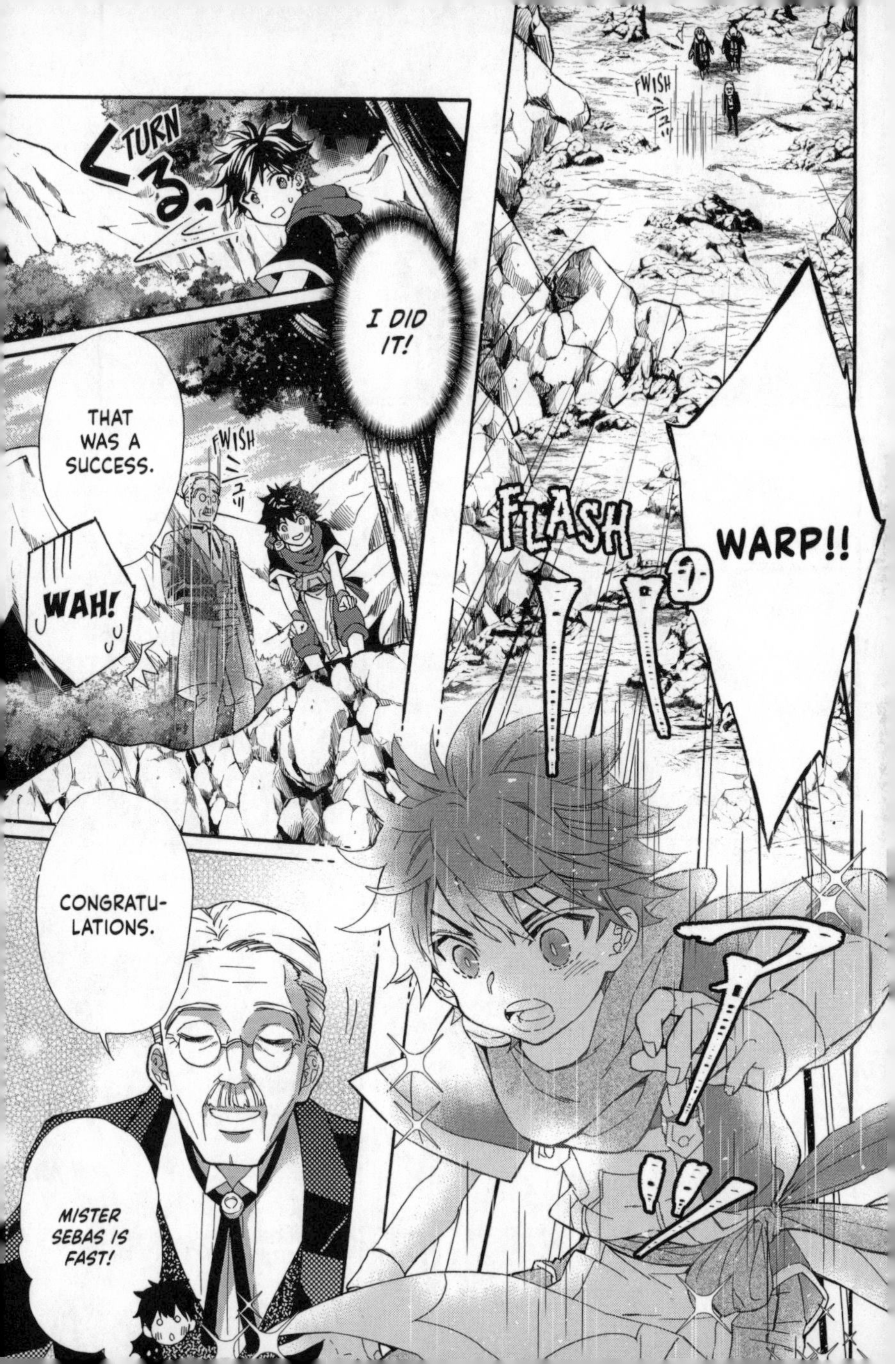
FWISH
WARP!!
FLASH
TURN
I DID IT!
THAT WAS A SUCCESS.
FWISH
WAH!
CONGRATU-LATIONS.
MISTER SEBAS IS FAST!

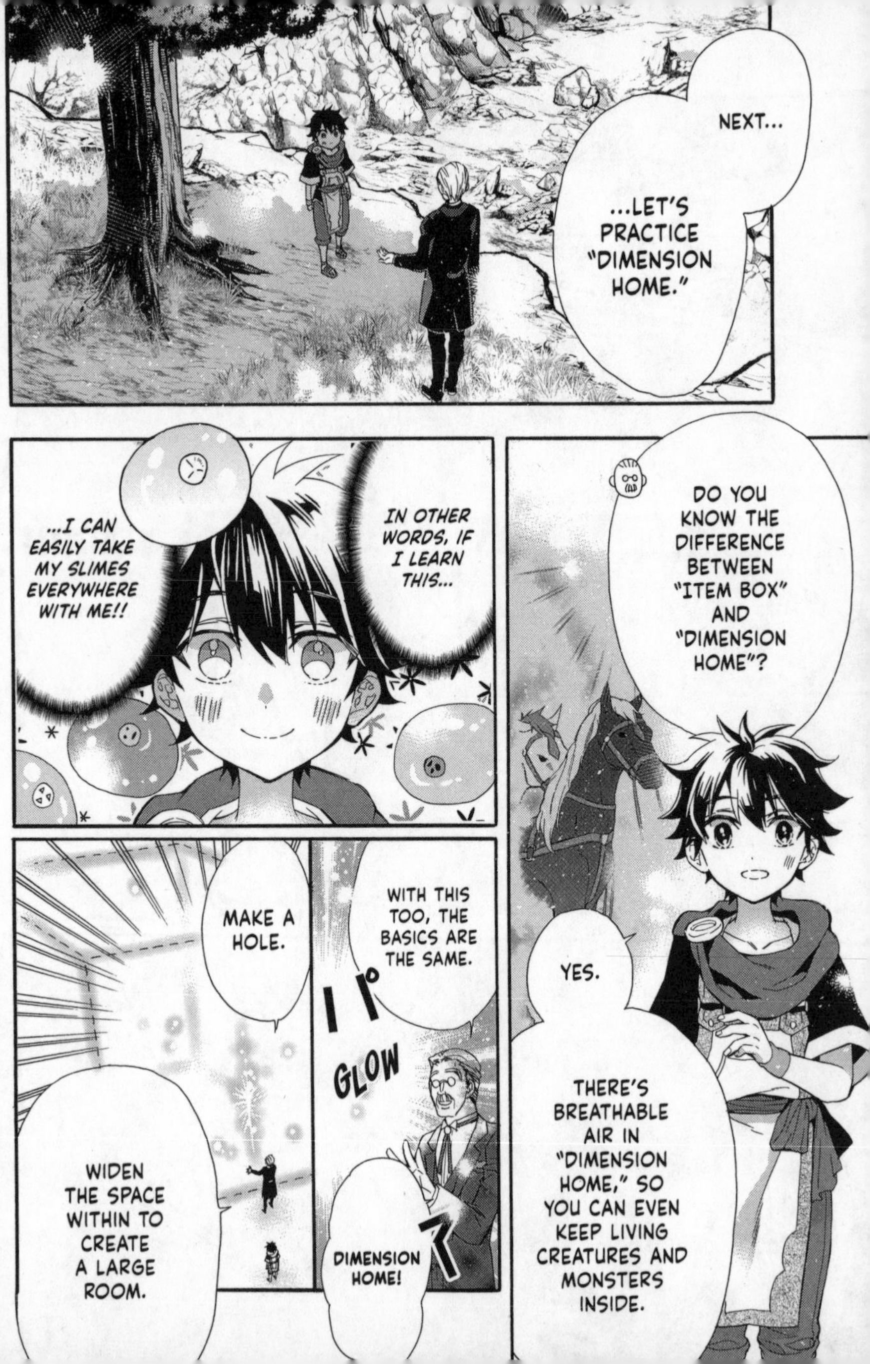
NEXT...
...LET'S PRACTICE "DIMENSION HOME."
DO YOU KNOW THE DIFFERENCE BETWEEN "ITEM BOX" AND "DIMENSION HOME"?
YES.
THERE'S BREATHABLE AIR IN "DIMENSION HOME," SO YOU CAN EVEN KEEP LIVING CREATURES AND MONSTERS INSIDE.
IN OTHER WORDS, IF I LEARN THIS...
...I CAN EASILY TAKE MY SLIMES EVERYWHERE WITH ME!!
WITH THIS TOO, THE BASICS ARE THE SAME.
GLOW
DIMENSION HOME!
MAKE A HOLE.
WIDEN THE SPACE WITHIN TO CREATE A LARGE ROOM.

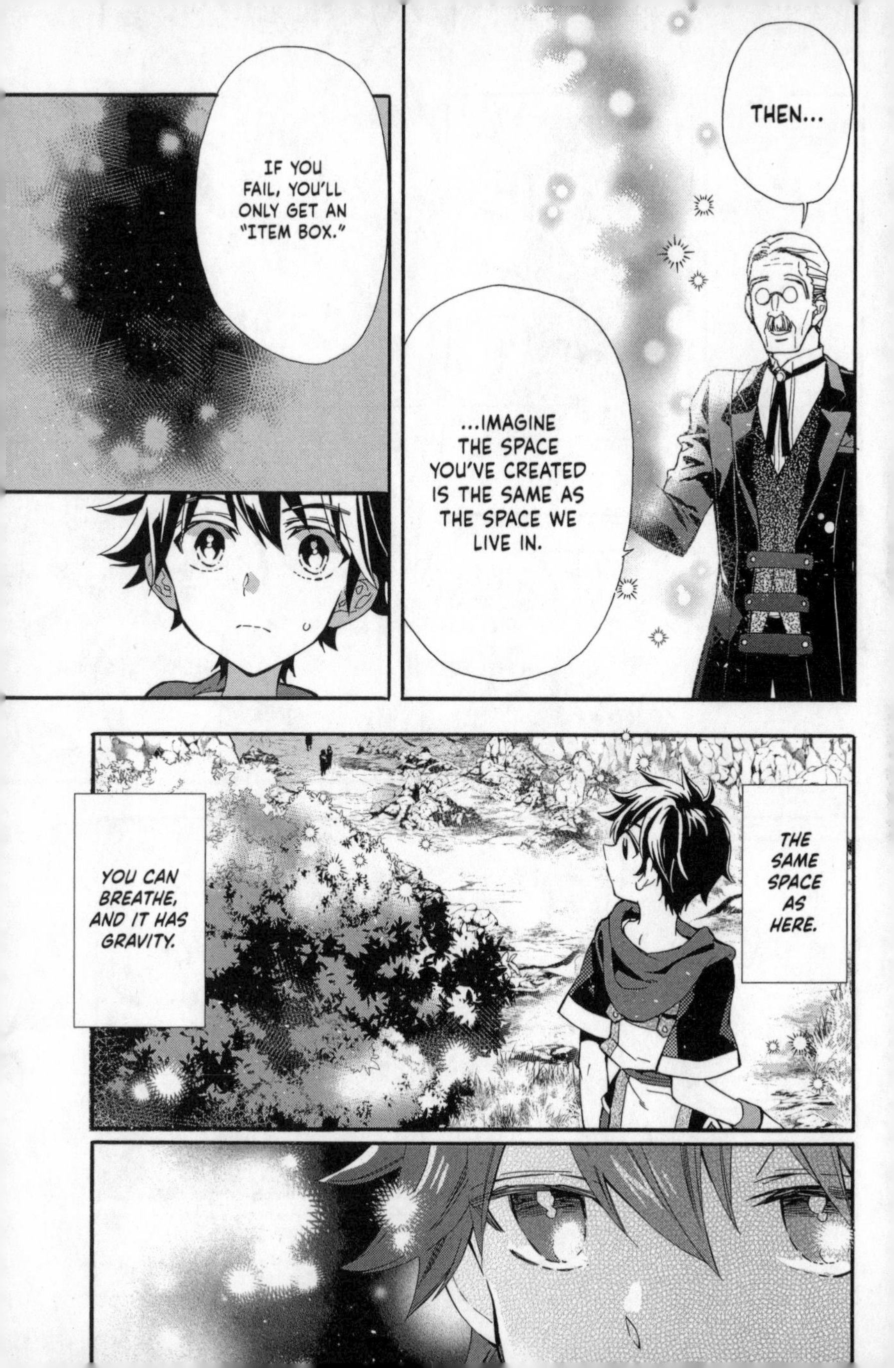
IF YOU FAIL, YOU'LL ONLY GET AN "ITEM BOX."
THEN...
...IMAGINE THE SPACE YOU'VE CREATED IS THE SAME AS THE SPACE WE LIVE IN.
THE SAME SPACE AS HERE.
YOU CAN BREATHE, AND IT HAS GRAVITY.

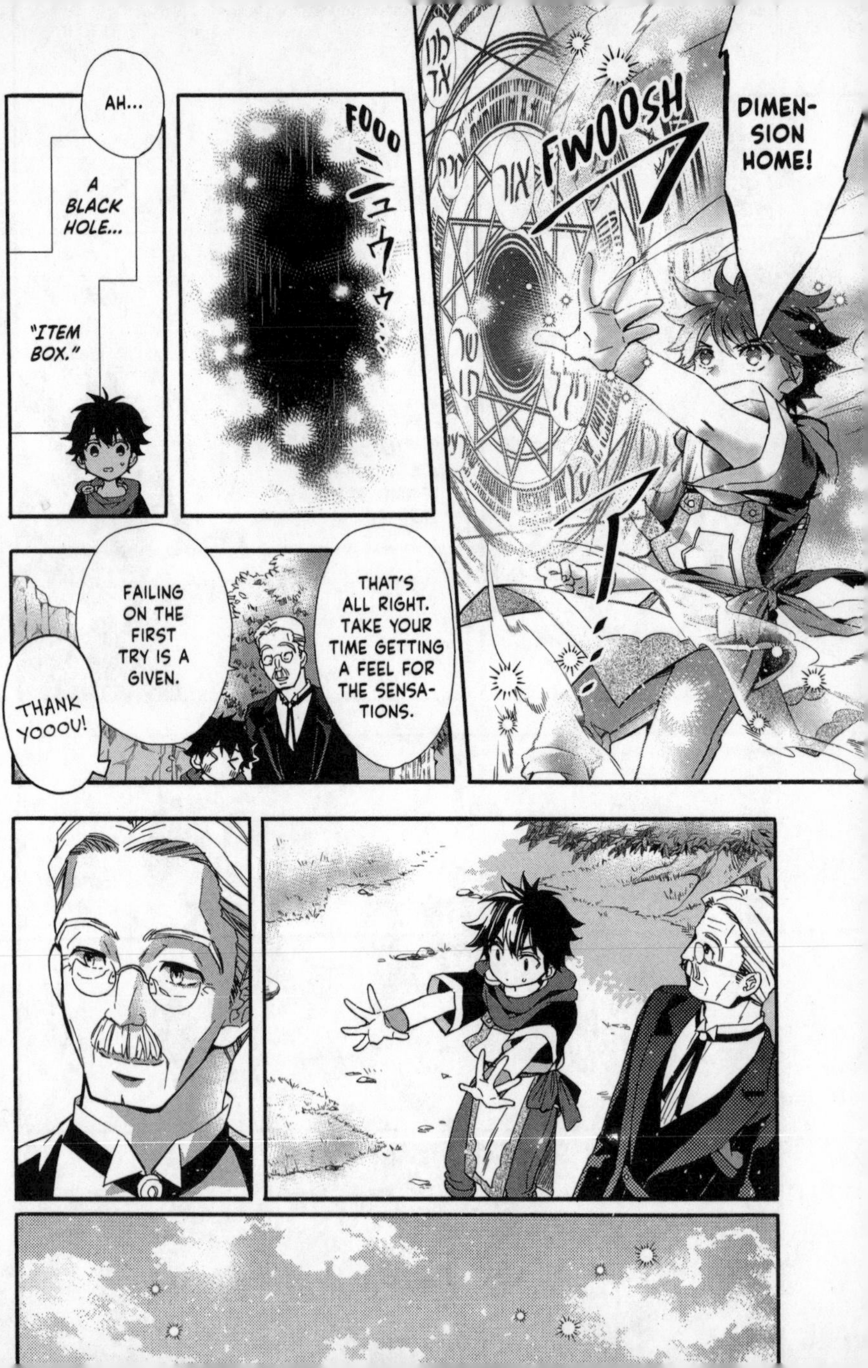
DIMENSION HOME!
FWOOSH
FOOO
シュウゥ…
AH...
A BLACK HOLE...
"ITEM BOX."
THAT'S ALL RIGHT. TAKE YOUR TIME GETTING A FEEL FOR THE SENSATIONS.
FAILING ON THE FIRST TRY IS A GIVEN.
THANK YOOOU!

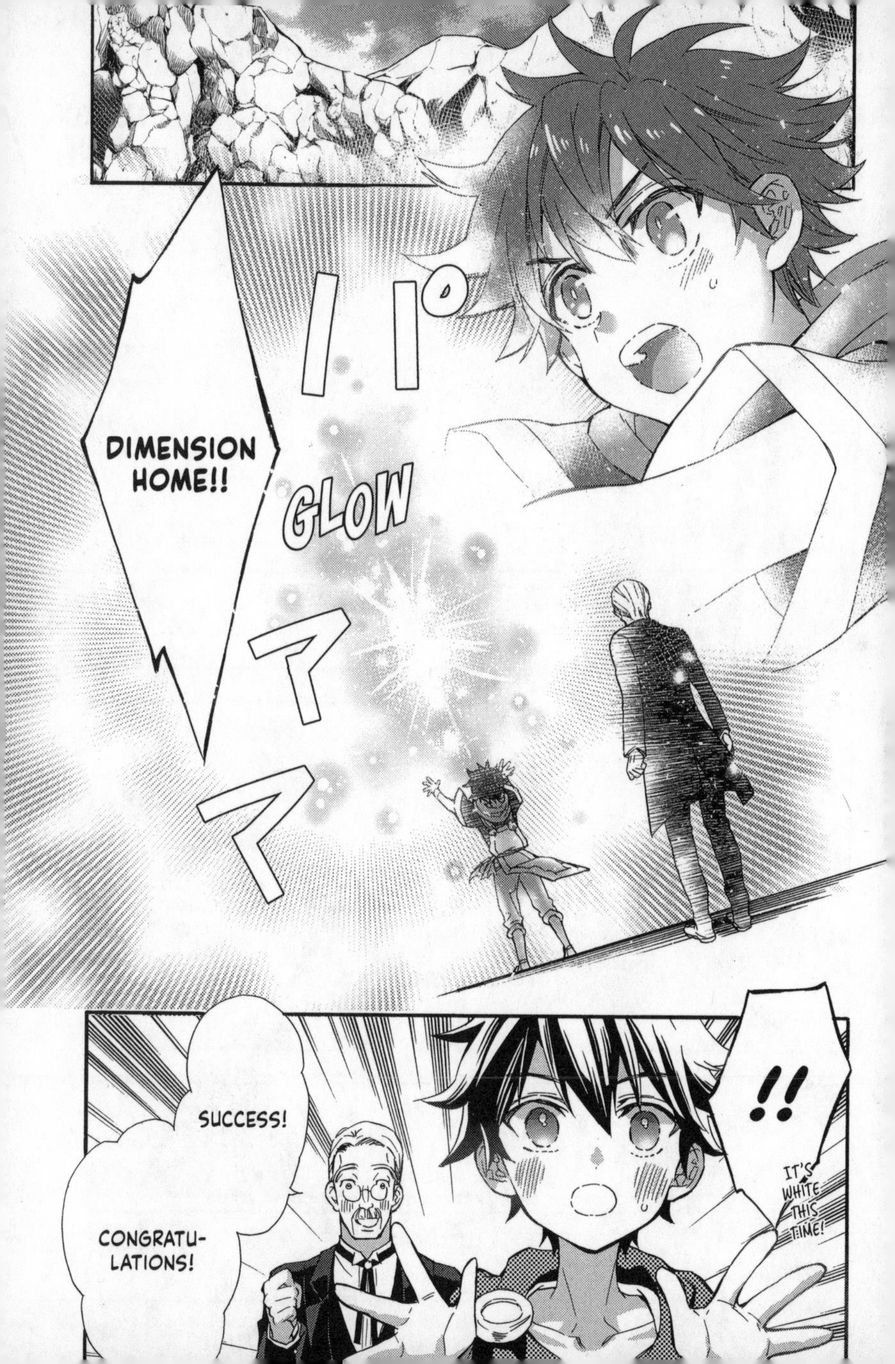
DIMENSION HOME!!
パアア
GLOW
!!
IT'S WHITE THIS TIME!
SUCCESS!
CONGRATU-
LATIONS!

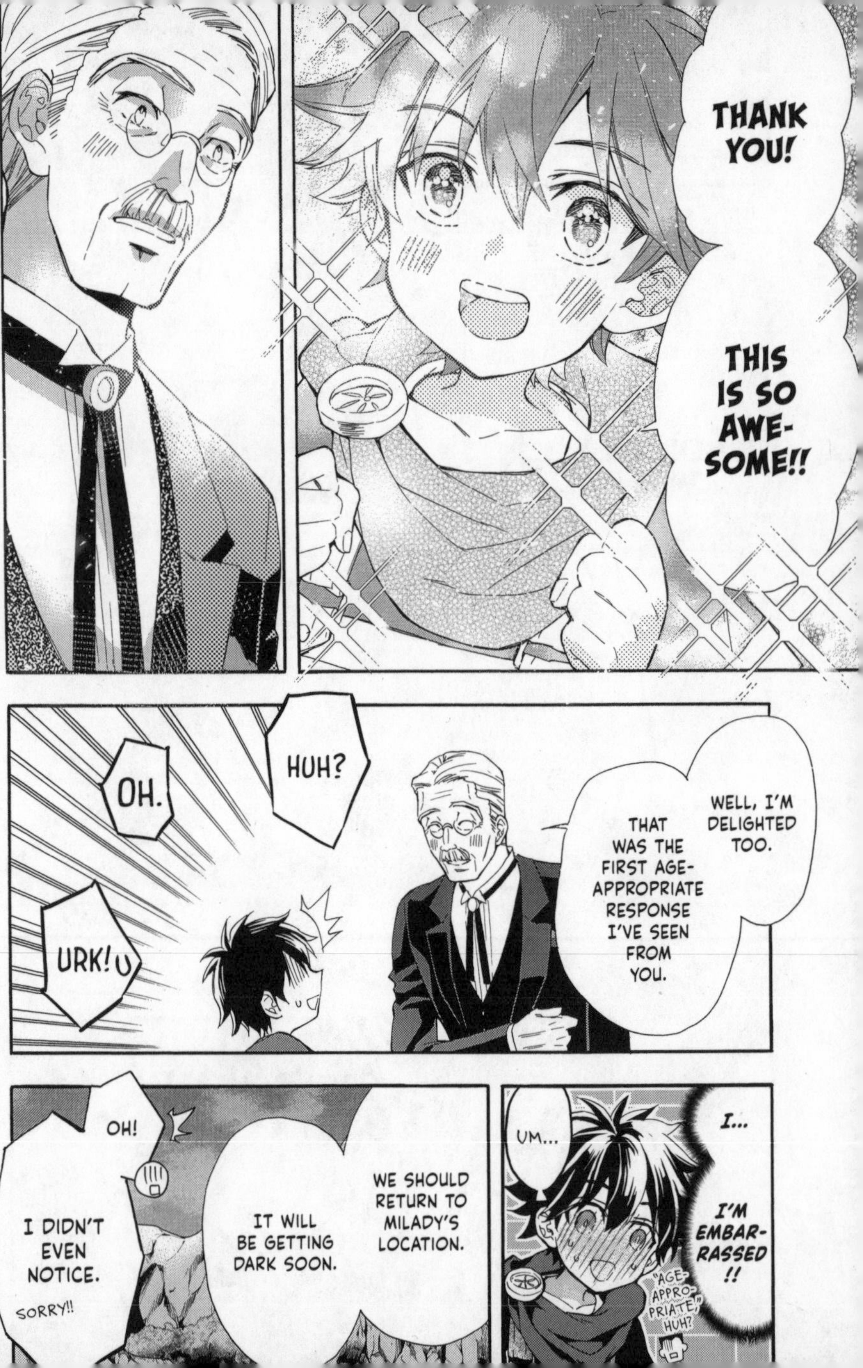
THANK YOU!
THIS IS SO AWE-SOME!!
WELL, I'M DELIGHTED TOO.
THAT WAS THE FIRST AGE-APPROPRIATE RESPONSE I'VE SEEN FROM YOU.
HUH?
OH.
URK!
I...
UM...
I'M EMBARRASSED!!
"AGE-APPROPRIATE," HUH?
WE SHOULD RETURN TO MILADY'S LOCATION.
IT WILL BE GETTING DARK SOON.
OH!
I DIDN'T EVEN NOTICE.
SORRY!!

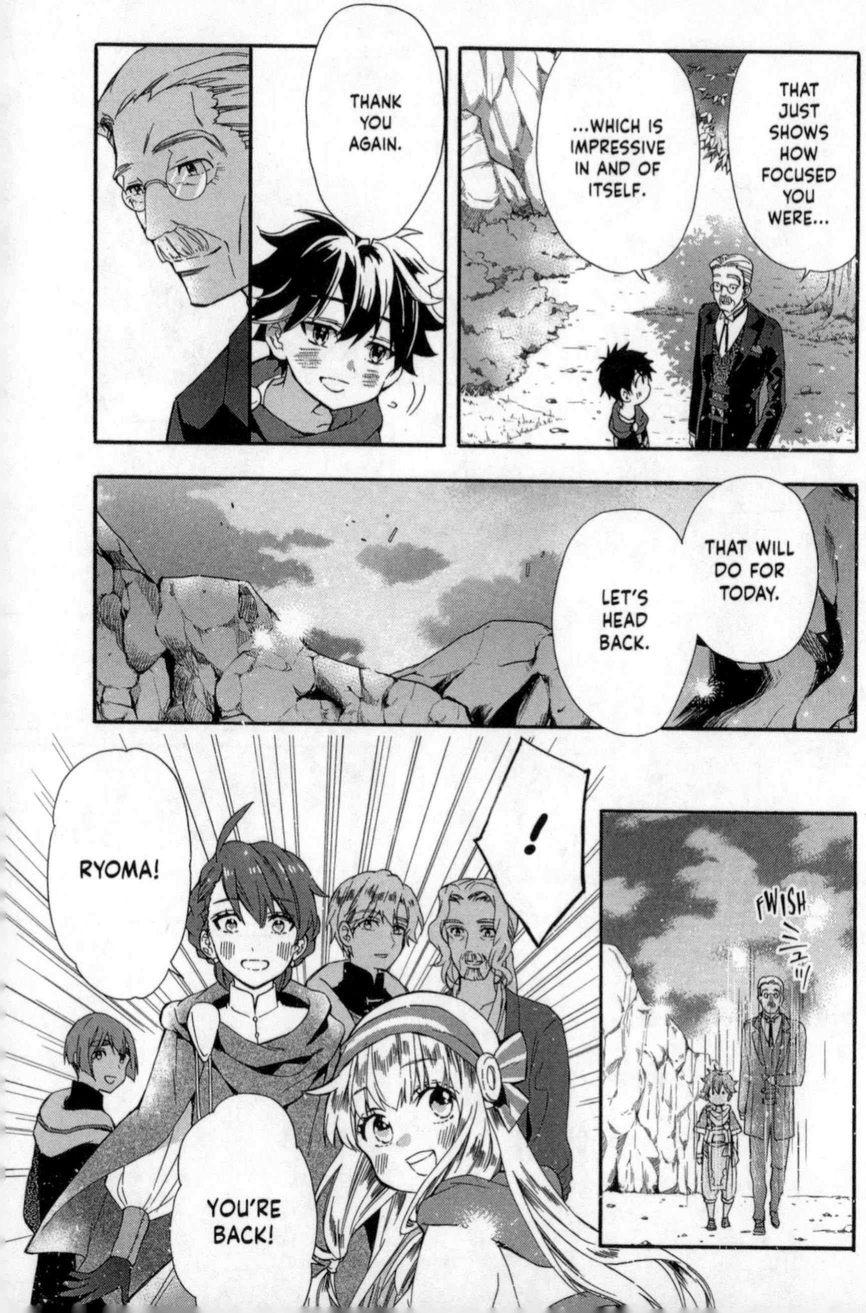
THAT JUST SHOWS HOW FOCUSED YOU WERE...
...WHICH IS IMPRESSIVE IN AND OF ITSELF.
THANK YOU AGAIN.
THAT WILL DO FOR TODAY.
LET'S HEAD BACK.
FWISH
!
RYOMA!
YOU'RE BACK!

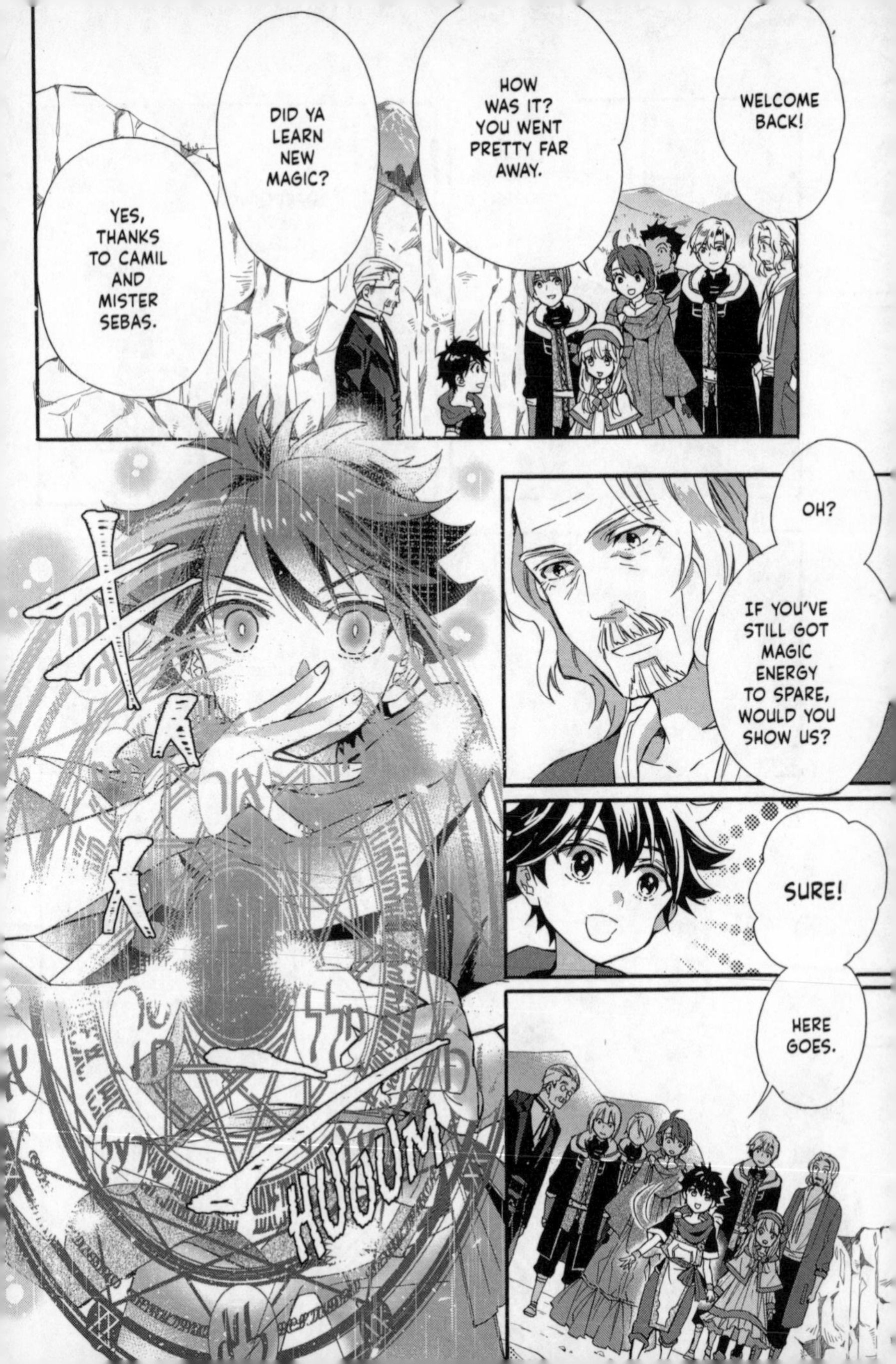
WELCOME BACK!
HOW WAS IT? YOU WENT PRETTY FAR AWAY.
DID YA LEARN NEW MAGIC?
YES, THANKS TO CAMIL AND MISTER SEBAS.
OH?
IF YOU'VE STILL GOT MAGIC ENERGY TO SPARE, WOULD YOU SHOW US?
SURE!
HERE GOES.
HUUUM

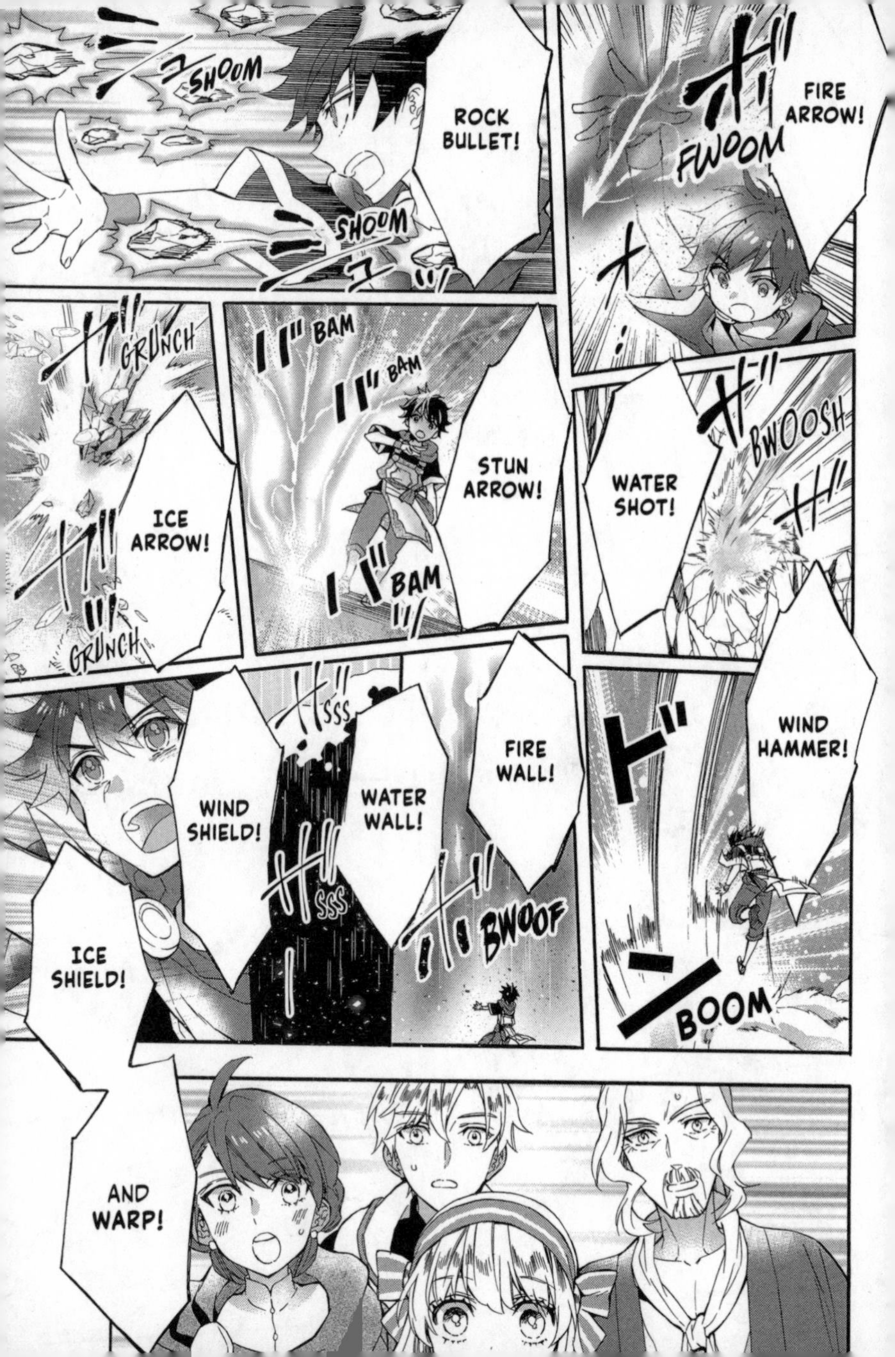
FIRE ARROW!
FWOOM
ROCK BULLET!
SHOOM
SHOOM
WATER SHOT!
BWOOSH
STUN ARROW!
BAM
BAM
BAM
GRUNCH
ICE ARROW!
GRUNCH
WIND HAMMER!
BOOM
FIRE WALL!
BWOOF
WATER WALL!
SSS
SSS
WIND SHIELD!
ICE SHIELD!
AND WARP!

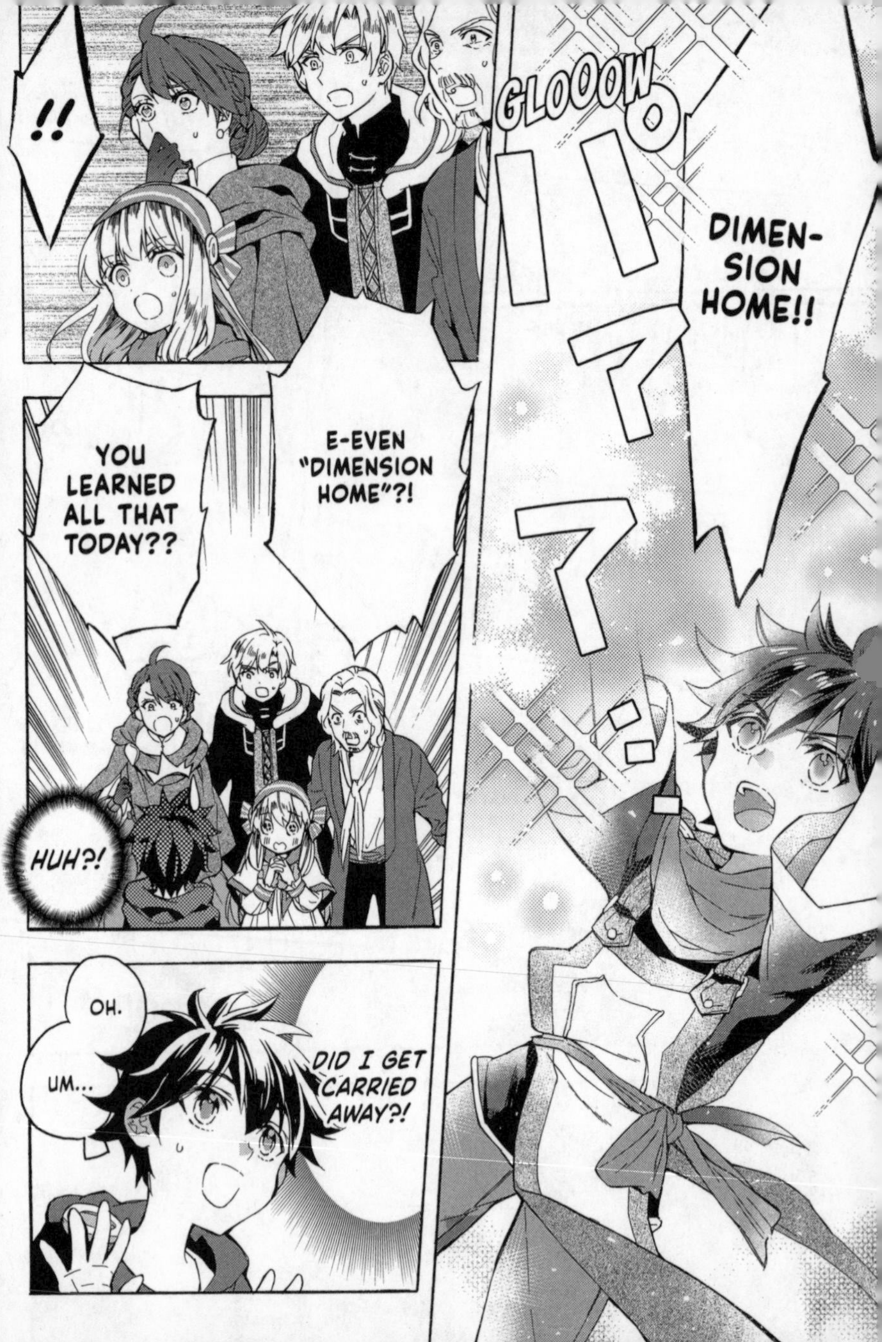
GLOOOW
DIMENSION HOME!!
!!
E-EVEN "DIMENSION HOME"?!
YOU LEARNED ALL THAT TODAY??
HUH?!
OH.
UM...
DID I GET CARRIED AWAY?!

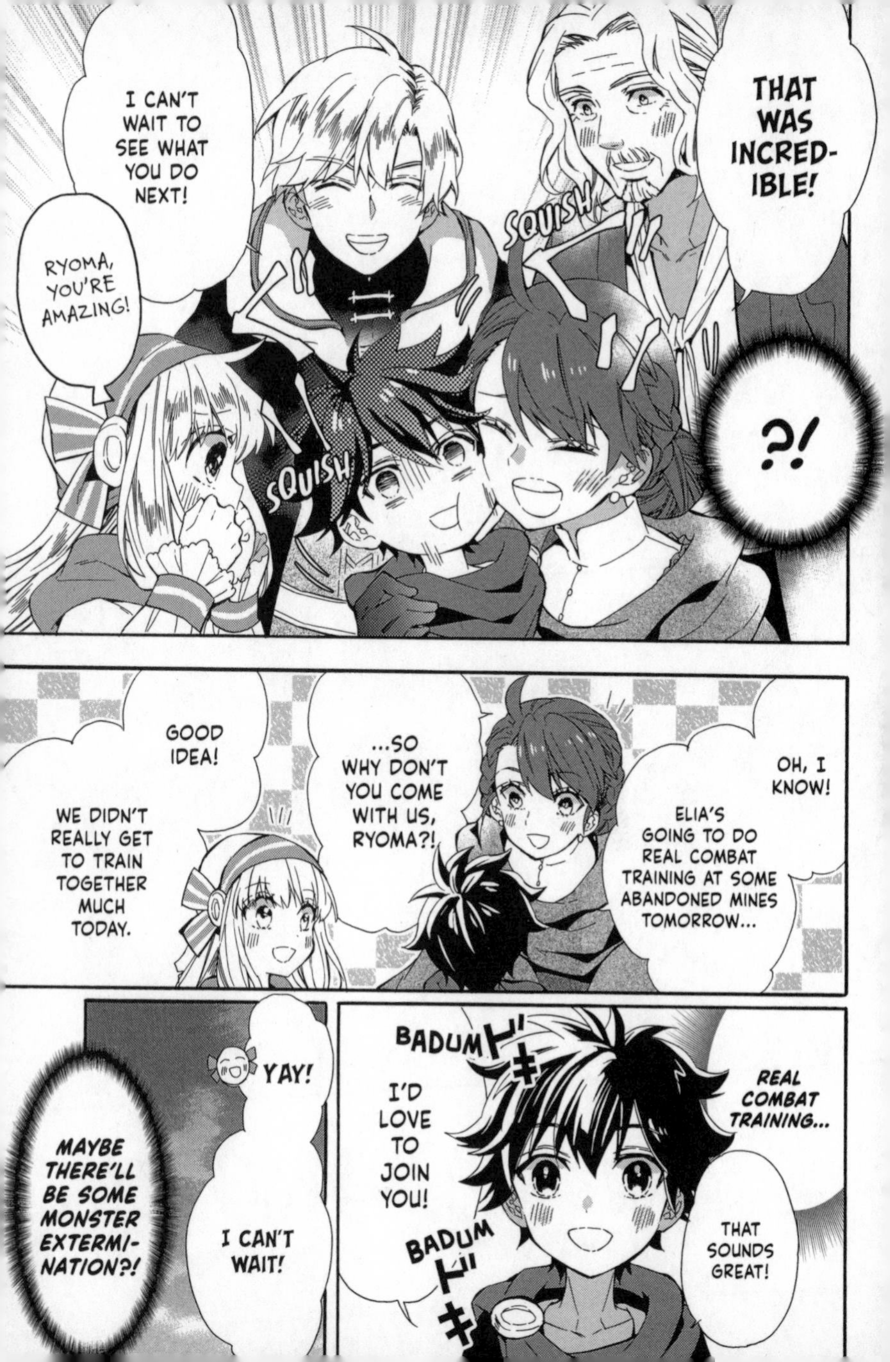
THAT WAS INCREDIBLE!
?!
SQUISH
I CAN'T WAIT TO SEE WHAT YOU DO NEXT!
RYOMA, YOU'RE AMAZING!
SQUISH
OH, I KNOW!
ELIA'S GOING TO DO REAL COMBAT TRAINING AT SOME ABANDONED MINES TOMORROW...
...SO WHY DON'T YOU COME WITH US, RYOMA?!
GOOD IDEA!
WE DIDN'T REALLY GET TO TRAIN TOGETHER MUCH TODAY.
REAL COMBAT TRAINING...
BADUM ドキ
I'D LOVE TO JOIN YOU!
THAT SOUNDS GREAT!
BADUM ドキ
YAY!
I CAN'T WAIT!
MAYBE THERE'LL BE SOME MONSTER EXTERMINATION?!

TALKING...

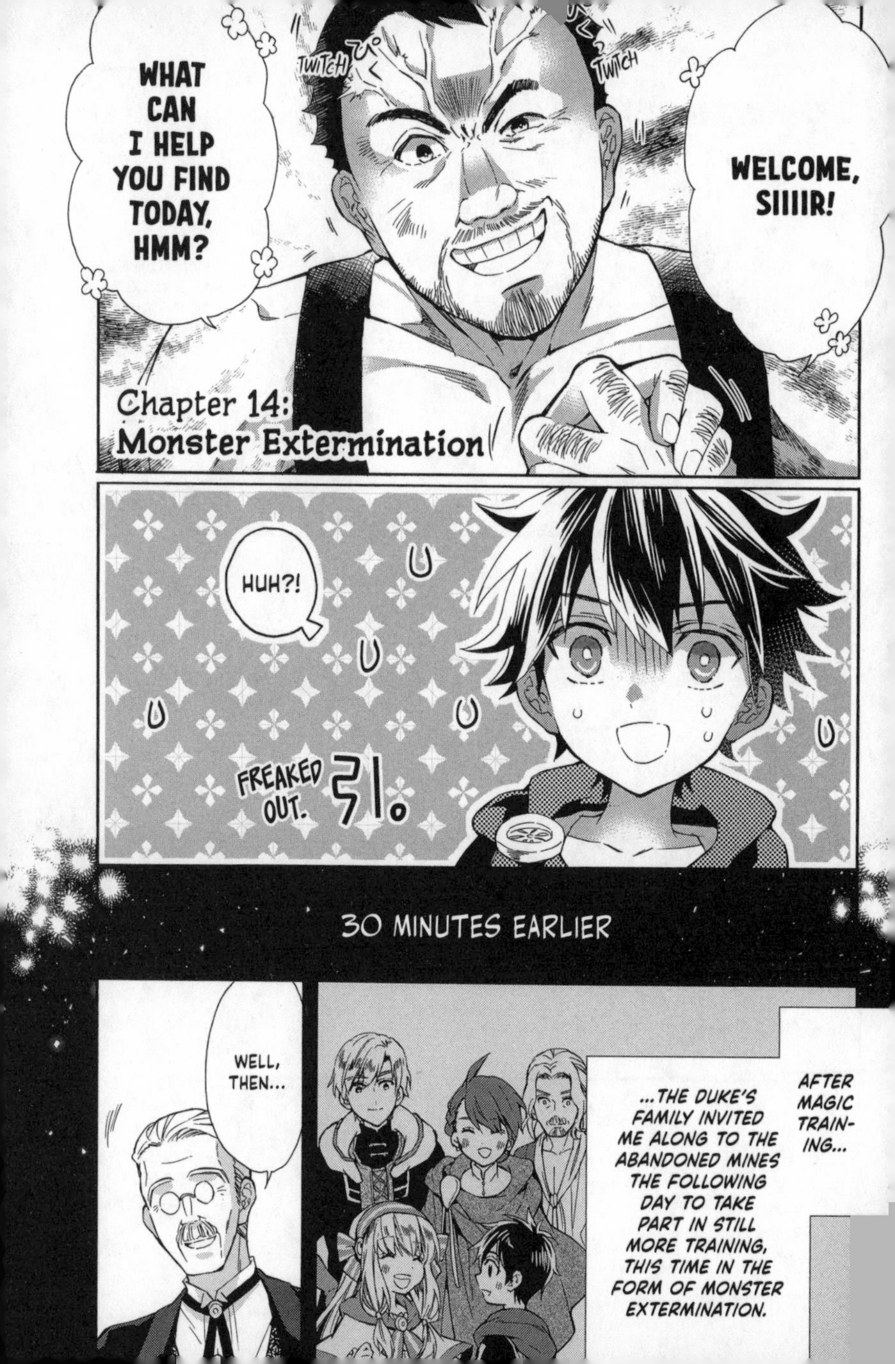
TWITCH
TWITCH
WELCOME, SIIIIR!
WHAT CAN I HELP YOU FIND TODAY, HMM?
Chapter 14: Monster Extermination
HUH?!
FREAKED OUT.
30 MINUTES EARLIER
AFTER MAGIC TRAINING...
...THE DUKE'S FAMILY INVITED ME ALONG TO THE ABANDONED MINES THE FOLLOWING DAY TO TAKE PART IN STILL MORE TRAINING, THIS TIME IN THE FORM OF MONSTER EXTERMINATION.
WELL, THEN...

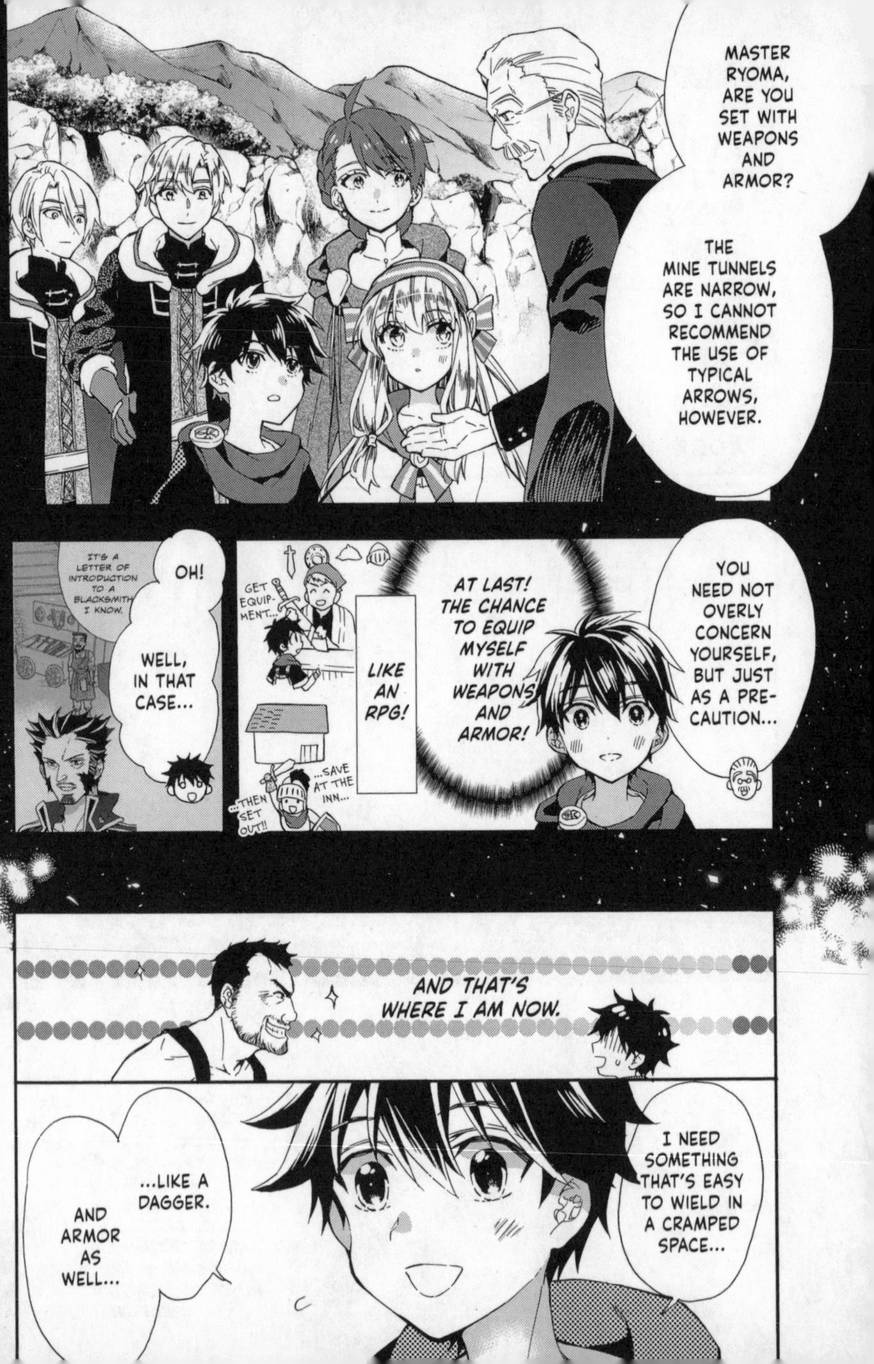
MASTER RYOMA, ARE YOU SET WITH WEAPONS AND ARMOR?
THE MINE TUNNELS ARE NARROW, SO I CANNOT RECOMMEND THE USE OF TYPICAL ARROWS, HOWEVER.
YOU NEED NOT OVERLY CONCERN YOURSELF, BUT JUST AS A PRE-CAUTION...
AT LAST! THE CHANCE TO EQUIP MYSELF WITH WEAPONS AND ARMOR!
LIKE AN RPG!
GET EQUIPMENT...
...SAVE AT THE INN...
...THEN SET OUT!!
OH!
IT'S A LETTER OF INTRODUCTION TO A BLACKSMITH I KNOW.
WELL, IN THAT CASE...
AND THAT'S WHERE I AM NOW.
I NEED SOMETHING THAT'S EASY TO WIELD IN A CRAMPED SPACE...
...LIKE A DAGGER.
AND ARMOR AS WELL...

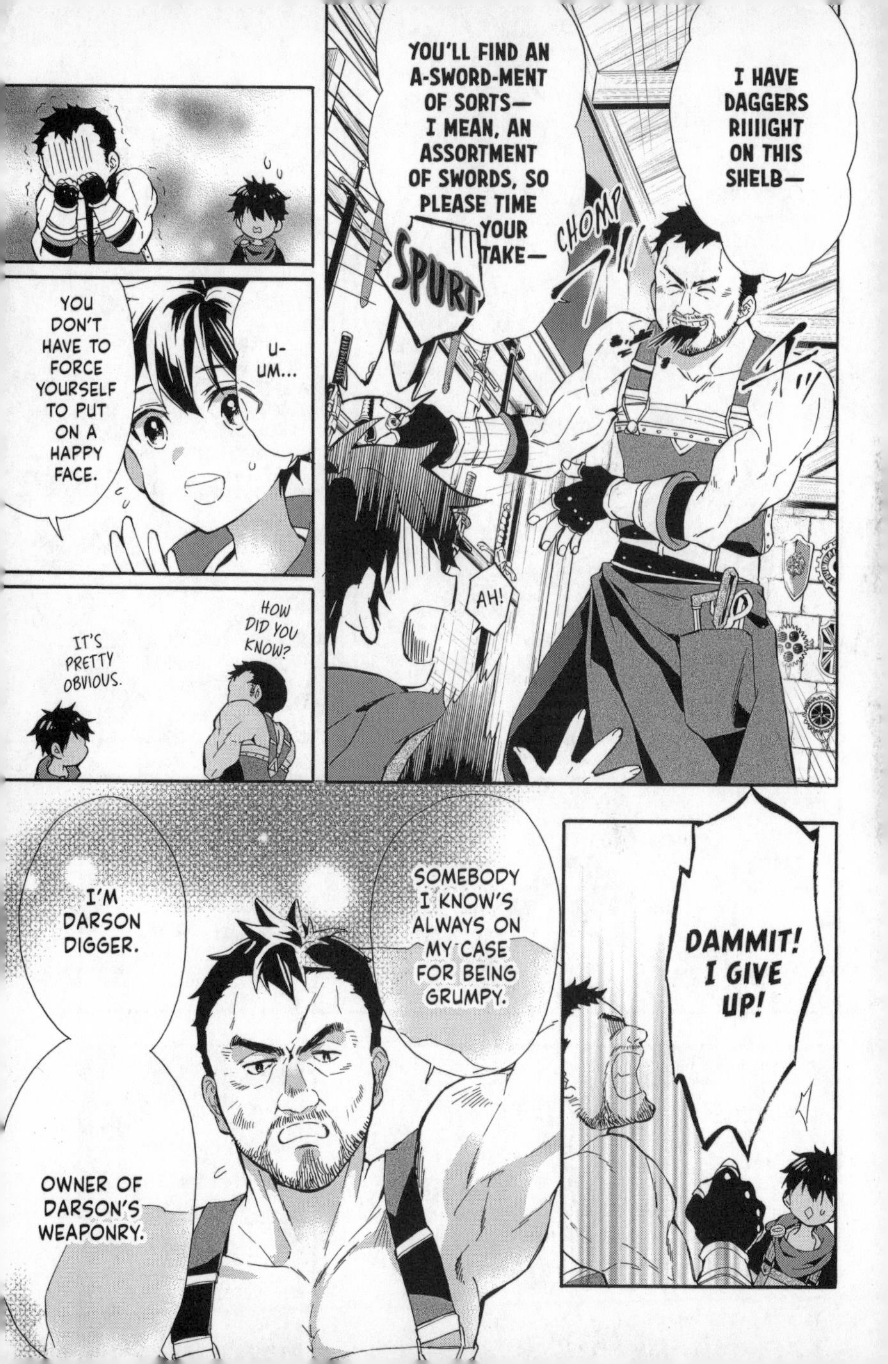

I HAVE DAGGERS RIIIIGHT ON THIS SHELB—
YOU'LL FIND AN A-SWORD-MENT OF SORTS— I MEAN, AN ASSORTMENT OF SWORDS, SO PLEASE TIME YOUR TAKE—
CHOMP
SPURT
AH!
U-UM...
YOU DON'T HAVE TO FORCE YOURSELF TO PUT ON A HAPPY FACE.
HOW DID YOU KNOW?
IT'S PRETTY OBVIOUS.
DAMMIT! I GIVE UP!
SOMEBODY I KNOW'S ALWAYS ON MY CASE FOR BEING GRUMPY.
I'M DARSON DIGGER.
OWNER OF DARSON'S WEAPONRY.

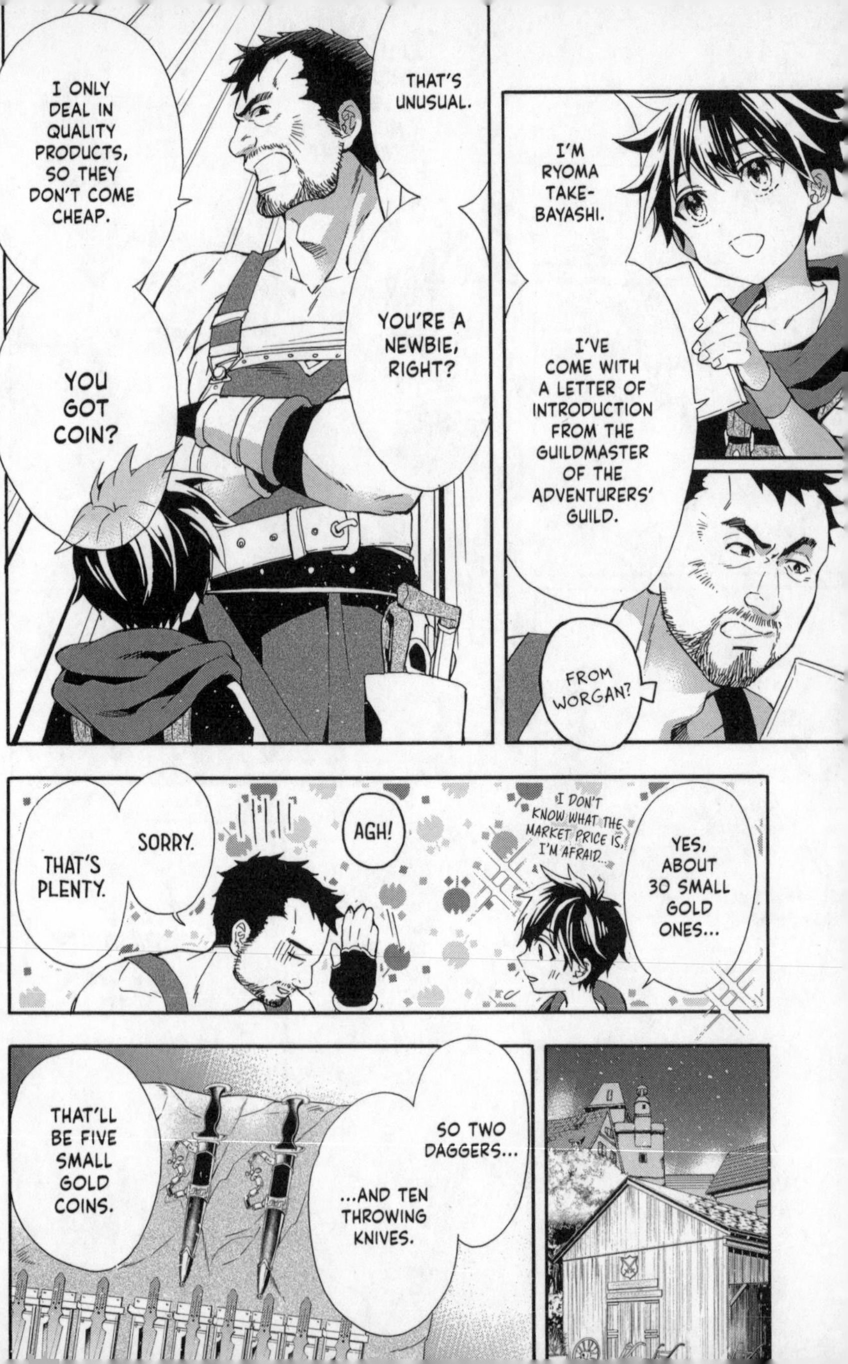

I'M RYOMA TAKE-BAYASHI.
I'VE COME WITH A LETTER OF INTRODUCTION FROM THE GUILDMASTER OF THE ADVENTURERS' GUILD.
FROM WORGAN?
THAT'S UNUSUAL.
YOU'RE A NEWBIE, RIGHT?
I ONLY DEAL IN QUALITY PRODUCTS, SO THEY DON'T COME CHEAP.
YOU GOT COIN?
YES, ABOUT 30 SMALL GOLD ONES...
I DON'T KNOW WHAT THE MARKET PRICE IS, I'M AFRAID...
AGH!
SORRY.
THAT'S PLENTY.
SO TWO DAGGERS...
...AND TEN THROWING KNIVES.
THAT'LL BE FIVE SMALL GOLD COINS.

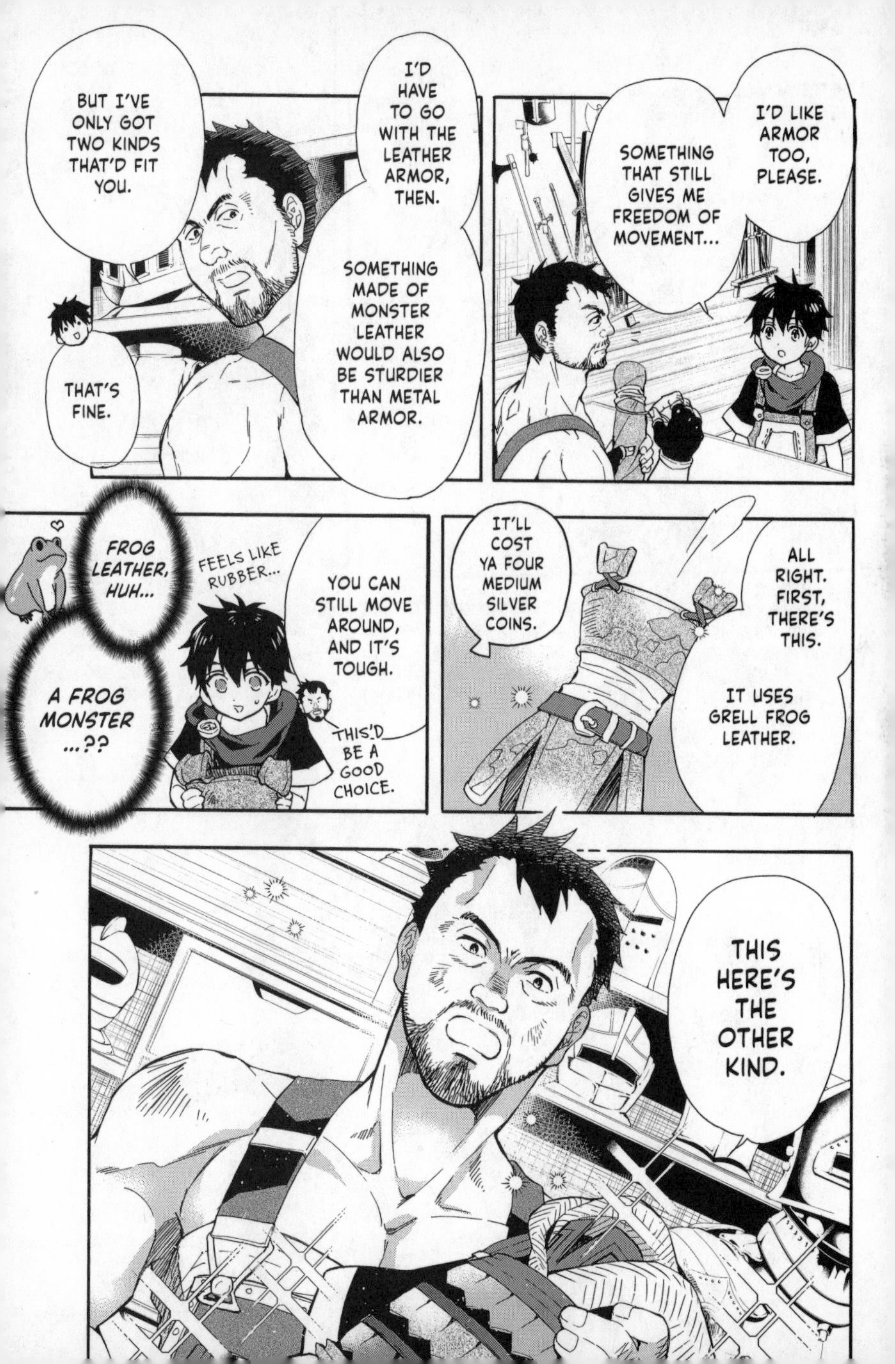
I'D LIKE ARMOR TOO, PLEASE.
SOMETHING THAT STILL GIVES ME FREEDOM OF MOVEMENT...
I'D HAVE TO GO WITH THE LEATHER ARMOR, THEN.
SOMETHING MADE OF MONSTER LEATHER WOULD ALSO BE STURDIER THAN METAL ARMOR.
BUT I'VE ONLY GOT TWO KINDS THAT'D FIT YOU.
THAT'S FINE.
ALL RIGHT. FIRST, THERE'S THIS.
IT USES GRELL FROG LEATHER.
IT'LL COST YA FOUR MEDIUM SILVER COINS.
YOU CAN STILL MOVE AROUND, AND IT'S TOUGH.
THIS'D BE A GOOD CHOICE.
FEELS LIKE RUBBER...
FROG LEATHER, HUH...
A FROG MONSTER ...??
THIS HERE'S THE OTHER KIND.

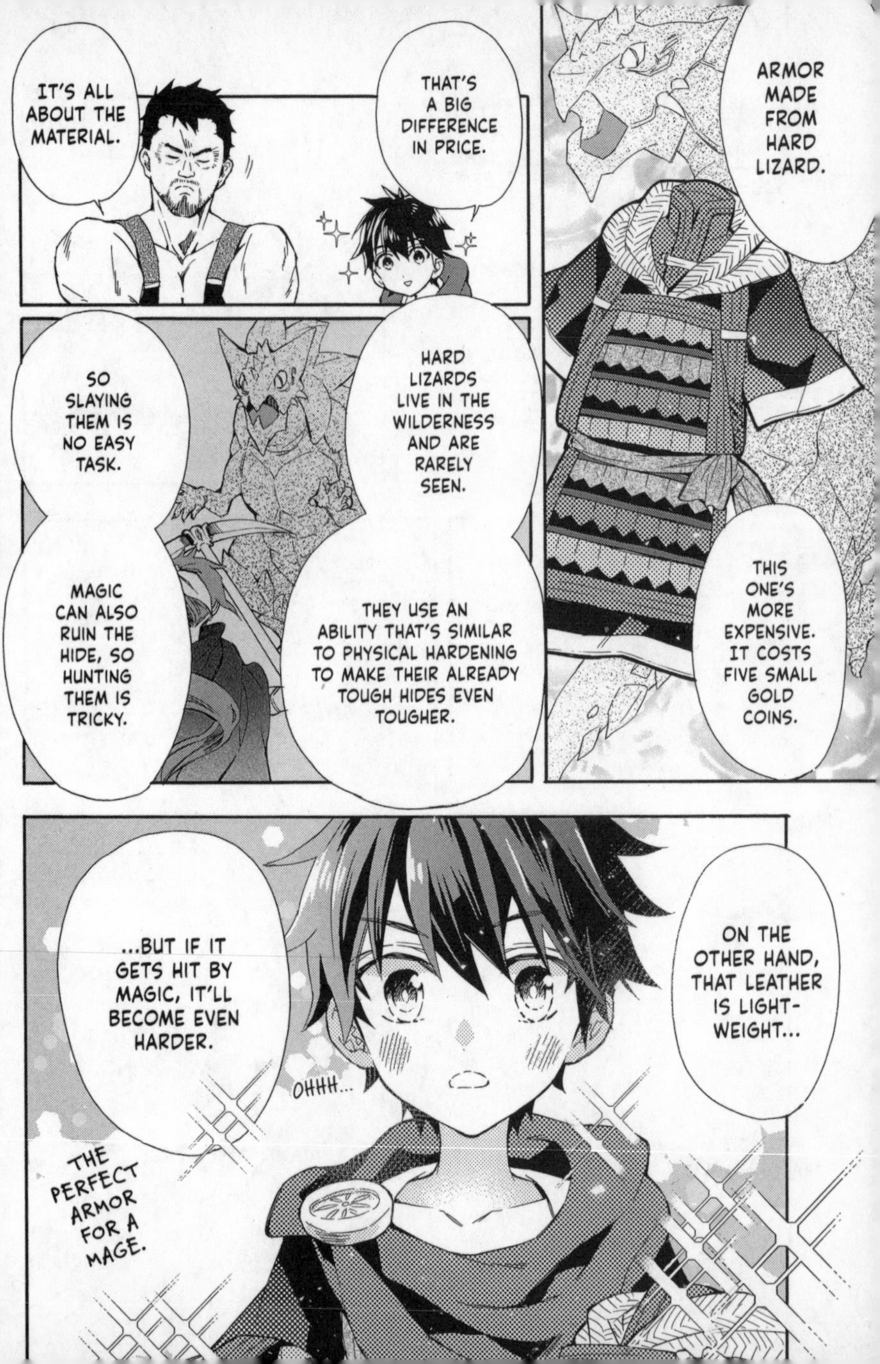
ARMOR MADE FROM HARD LIZARD.
THIS ONE'S MORE EXPENSIVE. IT COSTS FIVE SMALL GOLD COINS.
THAT'S A BIG DIFFERENCE IN PRICE.
IT'S ALL ABOUT THE MATERIAL.
HARD LIZARDS LIVE IN THE WILDERNESS AND ARE RARELY SEEN.
THEY USE AN ABILITY THAT'S SIMILAR TO PHYSICAL HARDENING TO MAKE THEIR ALREADY TOUGH HIDES EVEN TOUGHER.
SO SLAYING THEM IS NO EASY TASK.
MAGIC CAN ALSO RUIN THE HIDE, SO HUNTING THEM IS TRICKY.
ON THE OTHER HAND, THAT LEATHER IS LIGHT-WEIGHT...
...BUT IF IT GETS HIT BY MAGIC, IT'LL BECOME EVEN HARDER.
OHHH...
THE PERFECT ARMOR FOR A MAGE.

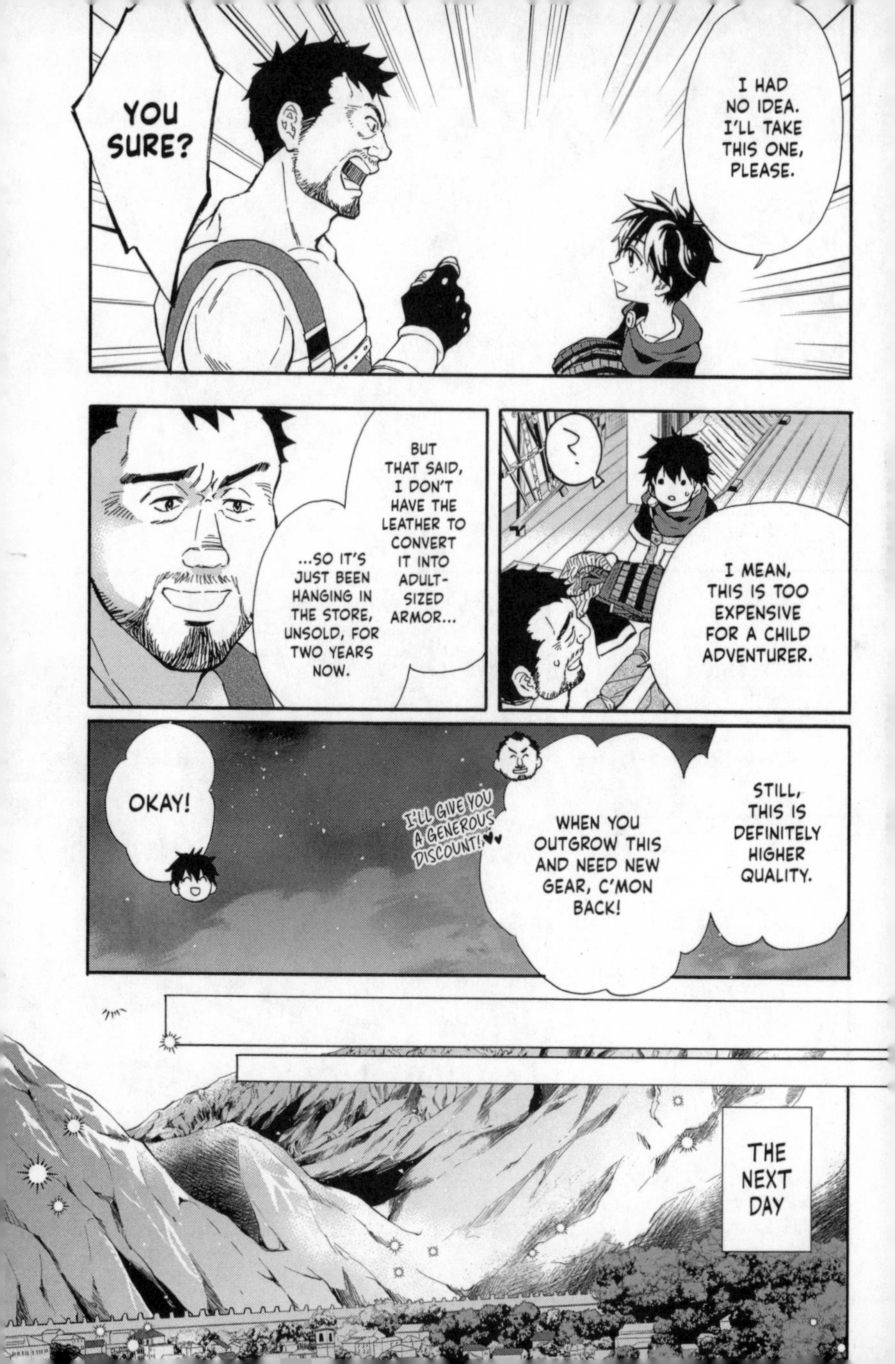
I HAD NO IDEA. I'LL TAKE THIS ONE, PLEASE.
YOU SURE?
?
I MEAN, THIS IS TOO EXPENSIVE FOR A CHILD ADVENTURER.
BUT THAT SAID, I DON'T HAVE THE LEATHER TO CONVERT IT INTO ADULT-SIZED ARMOR...
...SO IT'S JUST BEEN HANGING IN THE STORE, UNSOLD, FOR TWO YEARS NOW.
STILL, THIS IS DEFINITELY HIGHER QUALITY.
WHEN YOU OUTGROW THIS AND NEED NEW GEAR, C'MON BACK!
I'LL GIVE YOU A GENEROUS DISCOUNT!♥
OKAY!
THE NEXT DAY

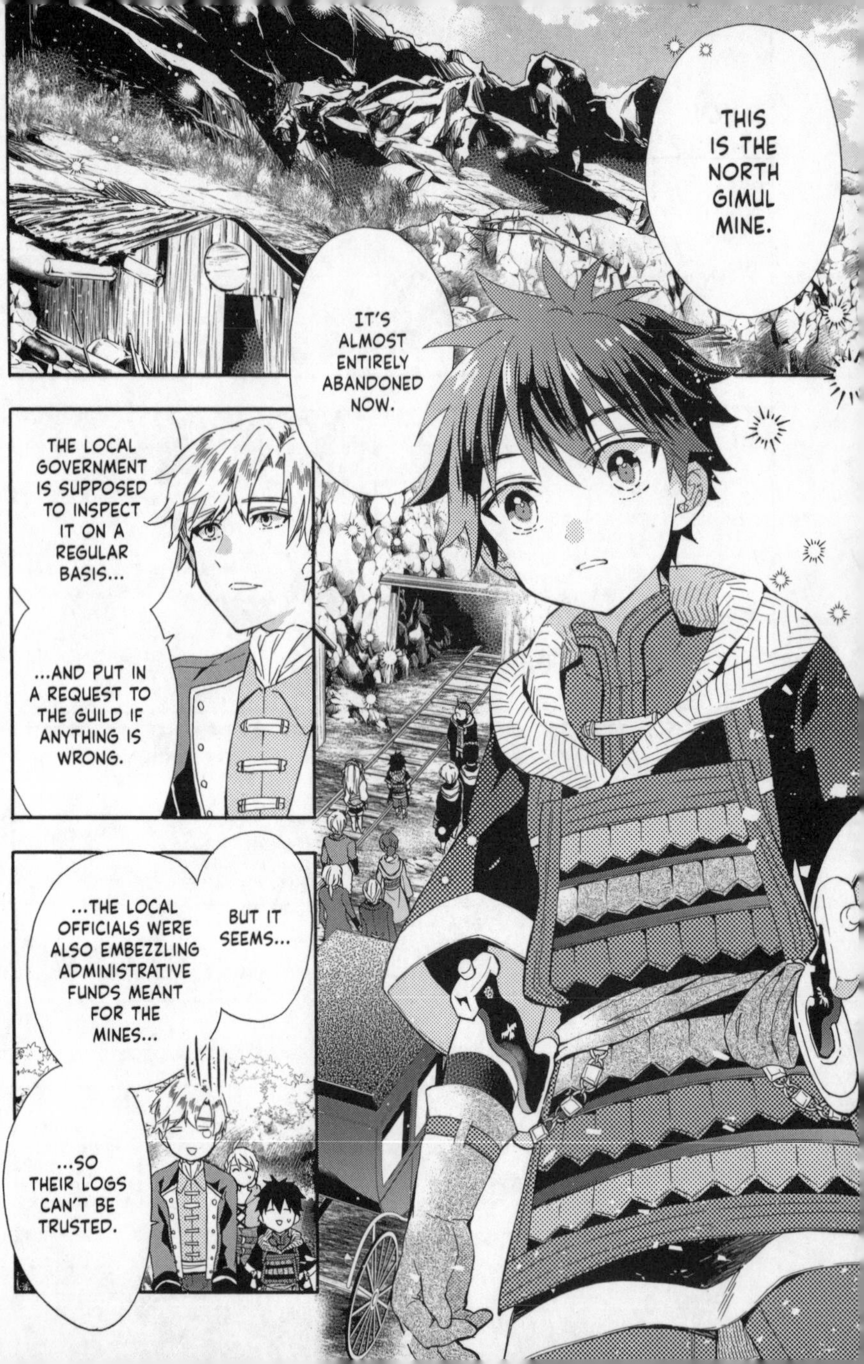
THIS IS THE NORTH GIMUL MINE.
IT'S ALMOST ENTIRELY ABANDONED NOW.
THE LOCAL GOVERNMENT IS SUPPOSED TO INSPECT IT ON A REGULAR BASIS...
...AND PUT IN A REQUEST TO THE GUILD IF ANYTHING IS WRONG.
BUT IT SEEMS...
...THE LOCAL OFFICIALS WERE ALSO EMBEZZLING ADMINISTRATIVE FUNDS MEANT FOR THE MINES...
...SO THEIR LOGS CAN'T BE TRUSTED.

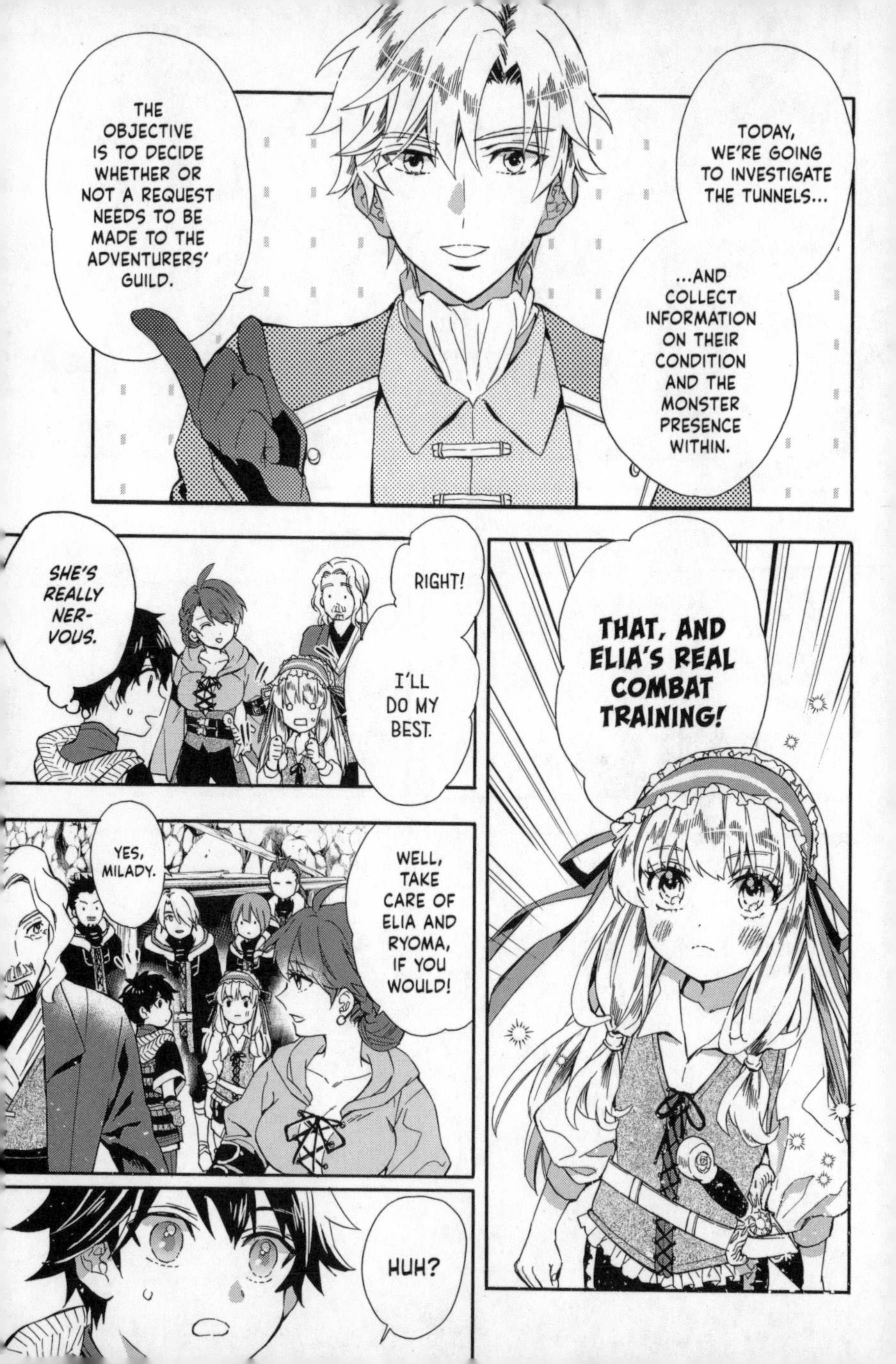
TODAY, WE'RE GOING TO INVESTIGATE THE TUNNELS...
...AND COLLECT INFORMATION ON THEIR CONDITION AND THE MONSTER PRESENCE WITHIN.
THE OBJECTIVE IS TO DECIDE WHETHER OR NOT A REQUEST NEEDS TO BE MADE TO THE ADVENTURERS' GUILD.
THAT, AND ELIA'S REAL COMBAT TRAINING!
RIGHT!
I'LL DO MY BEST.
SHE'S REALLY NER-VOUS.
WELL, TAKE CARE OF ELIA AND RYOMA, IF YOU WOULD!
YES, MILADY.
HUH?

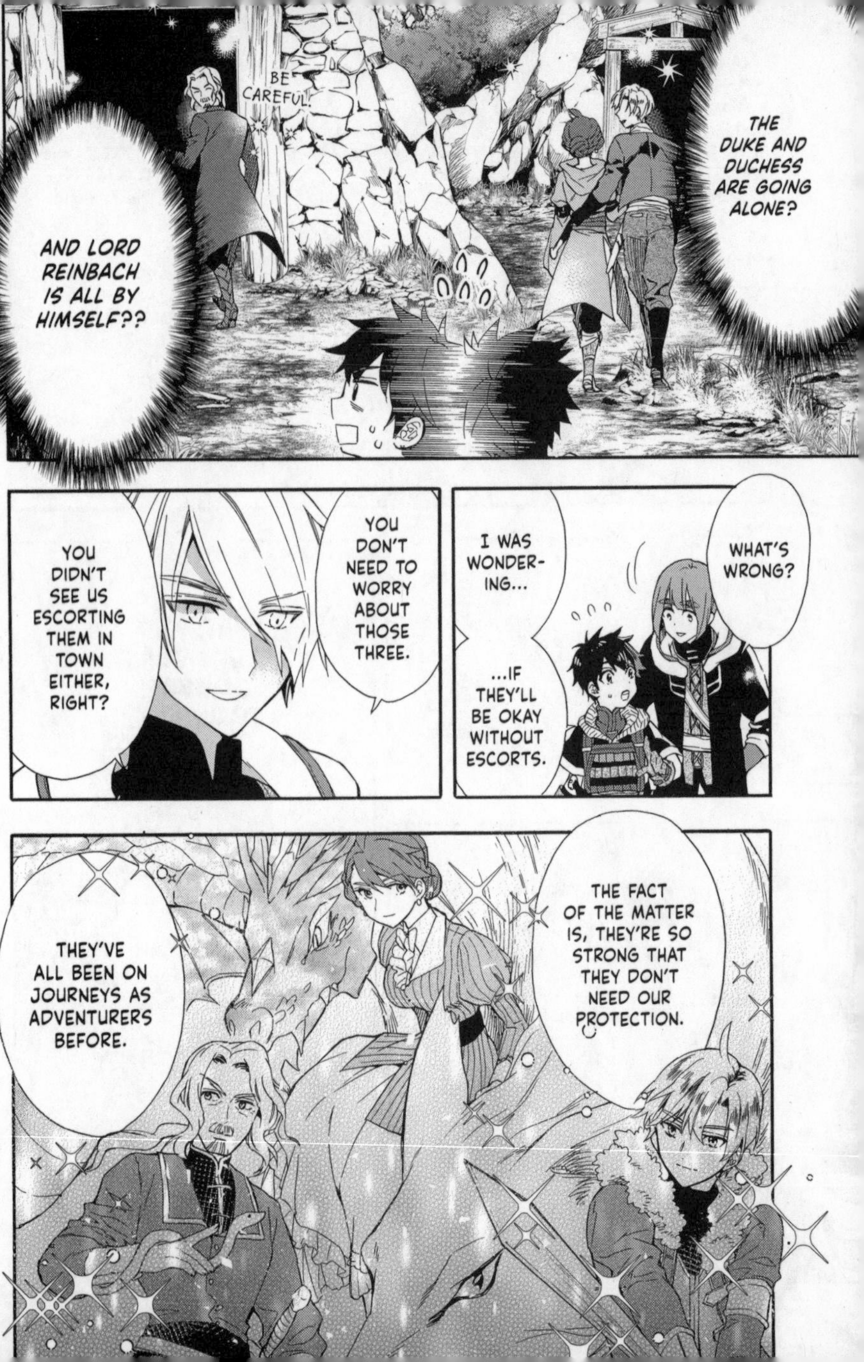
THE DUKE AND DUCHESS ARE GOING ALONE?
BE CAREFUL!
AND LORD REINBACH IS ALL BY HIMSELF??
WHAT'S WRONG?
I WAS WONDERING...
...IF THEY'LL BE OKAY WITHOUT ESCORTS.
YOU DON'T NEED TO WORRY ABOUT THOSE THREE.
YOU DIDN'T SEE US ESCORTING THEM IN TOWN EITHER, RIGHT?
THE FACT OF THE MATTER IS, THEY'RE SO STRONG THAT THEY DON'T NEED OUR PROTECTION.
THEY'VE ALL BEEN ON JOURNEYS AS ADVENTURERS BEFORE.

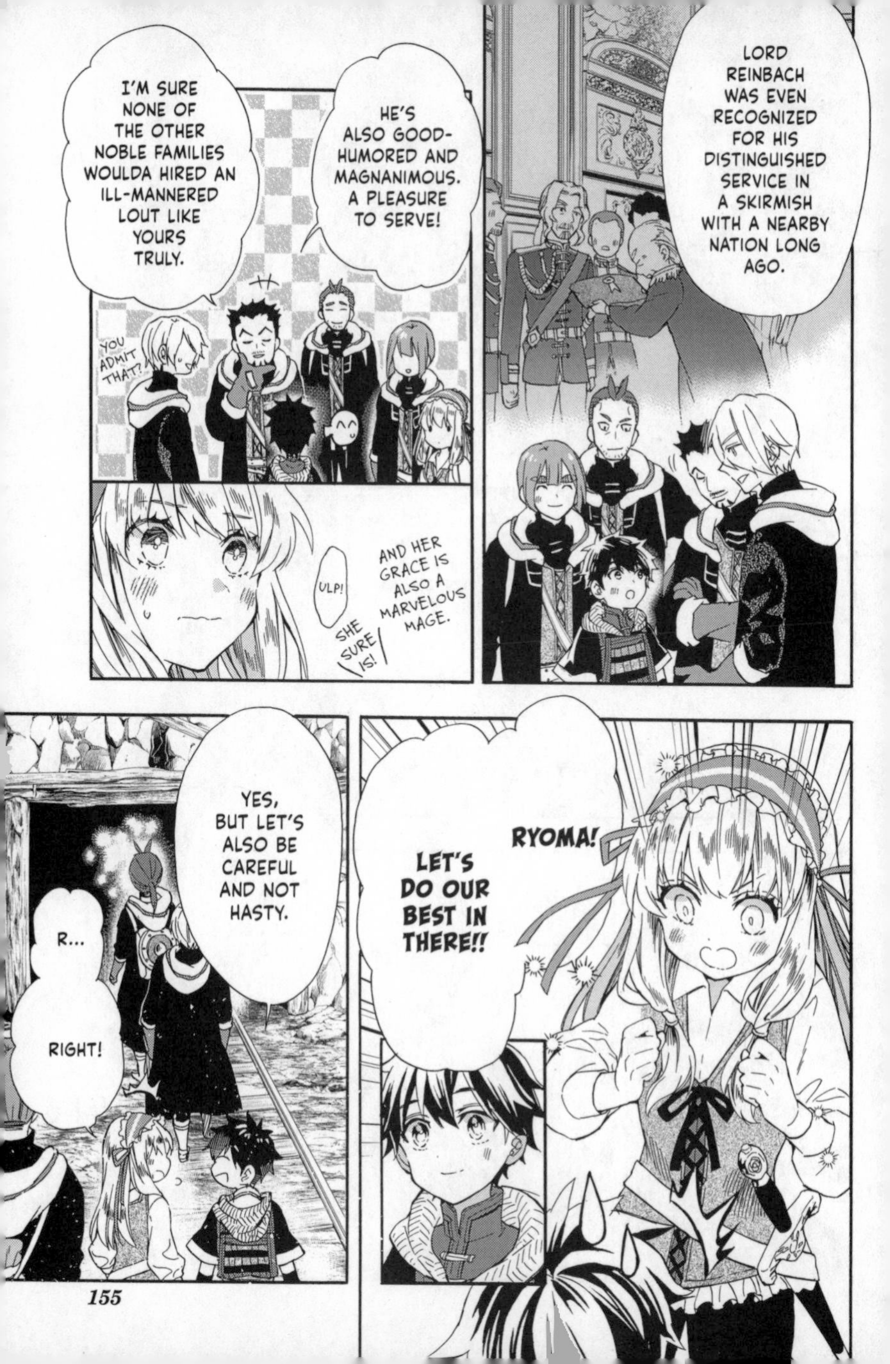
LORD REINBACH WAS EVEN RECOGNIZED FOR HIS DISTINGUISHED SERVICE IN A SKIRMISH WITH A NEARBY NATION LONG AGO.
HE'S ALSO GOOD-HUMORED AND MAGNANIMOUS. A PLEASURE TO SERVE!
I'M SURE NONE OF THE OTHER NOBLE FAMILIES WOULDA HIRED AN ILL-MANNERED LOUT LIKE YOURS TRULY.
YOU ADMIT THAT?
AND HER GRACE IS ALSO A MARVELOUS MAGE.
SHE SURE IS!
ULP!
RYOMA!
LET'S DO OUR BEST IN THERE!!
YES, BUT LET'S ALSO BE CAREFUL AND NOT HASTY.
R...
RIGHT!

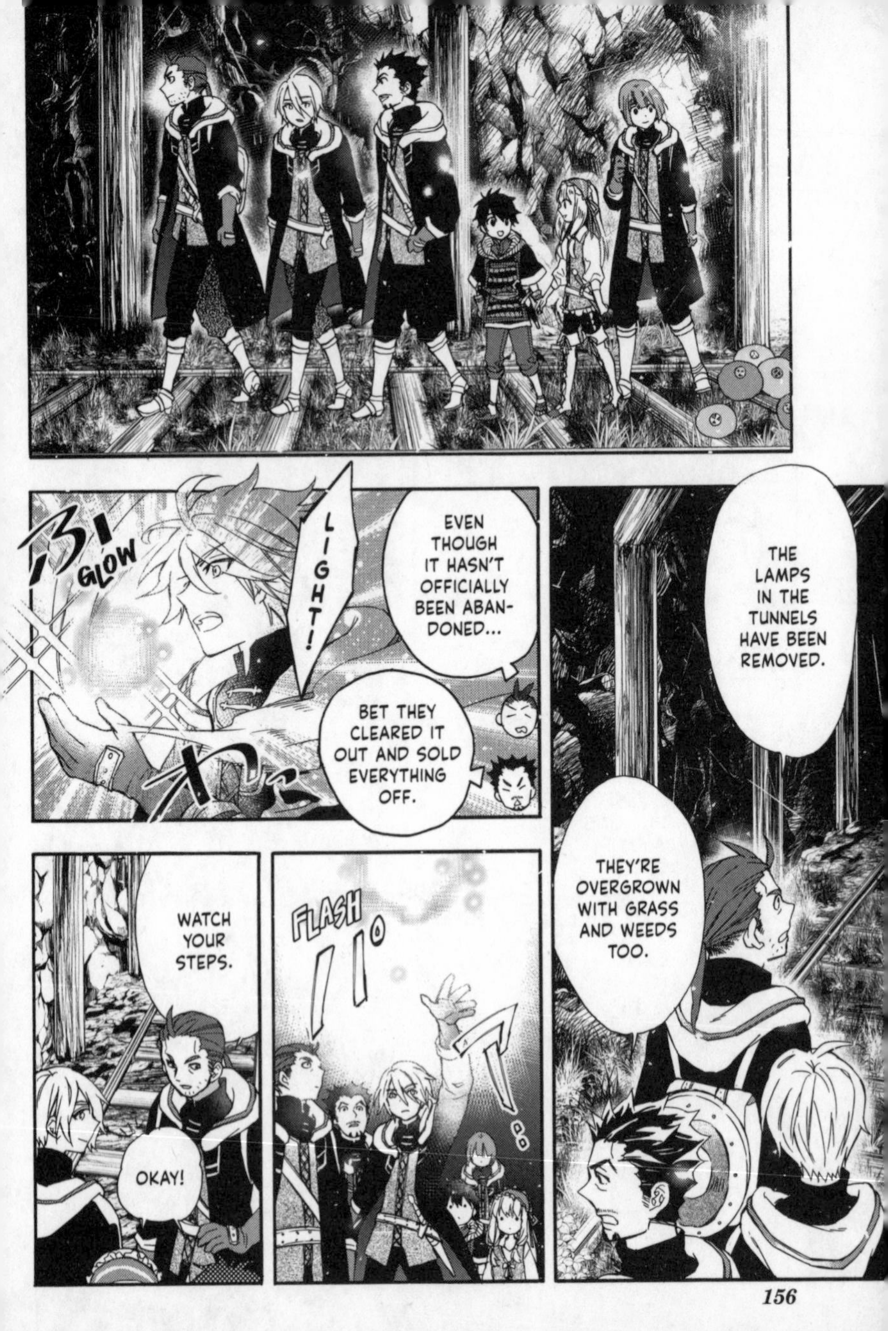
THE LAMPS IN THE TUNNELS HAVE BEEN REMOVED.
THEY'RE OVERGROWN WITH GRASS AND WEEDS TOO.
EVEN THOUGH IT HASN'T OFFICIALLY BEEN ABAN-DONED...
LIGHT!
GLOW
BET THEY CLEARED IT OUT AND SOLD EVERYTHING OFF.
FLASH
WATCH YOUR STEPS.
OKAY!

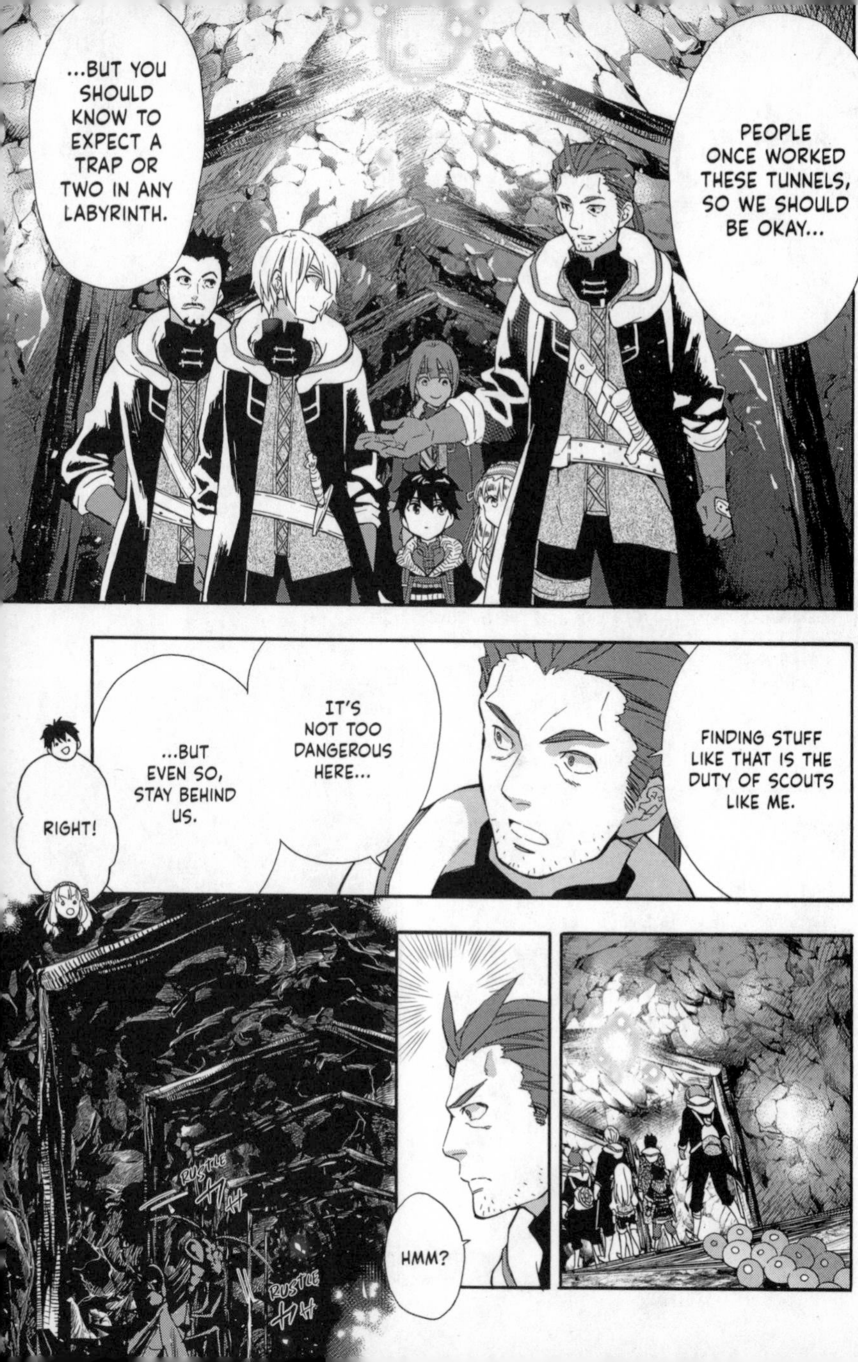
PEOPLE ONCE WORKED THESE TUNNELS, SO WE SHOULD BE OKAY...
...BUT YOU SHOULD KNOW TO EXPECT A TRAP OR TWO IN ANY LABYRINTH.
FINDING STUFF LIKE THAT IS THE DUTY OF SCOUTS LIKE ME.
IT'S NOT TOO DANGEROUS HERE...
...BUT EVEN SO, STAY BEHIND US.
RIGHT!
HMM?
RUSTLE
RUSTLE

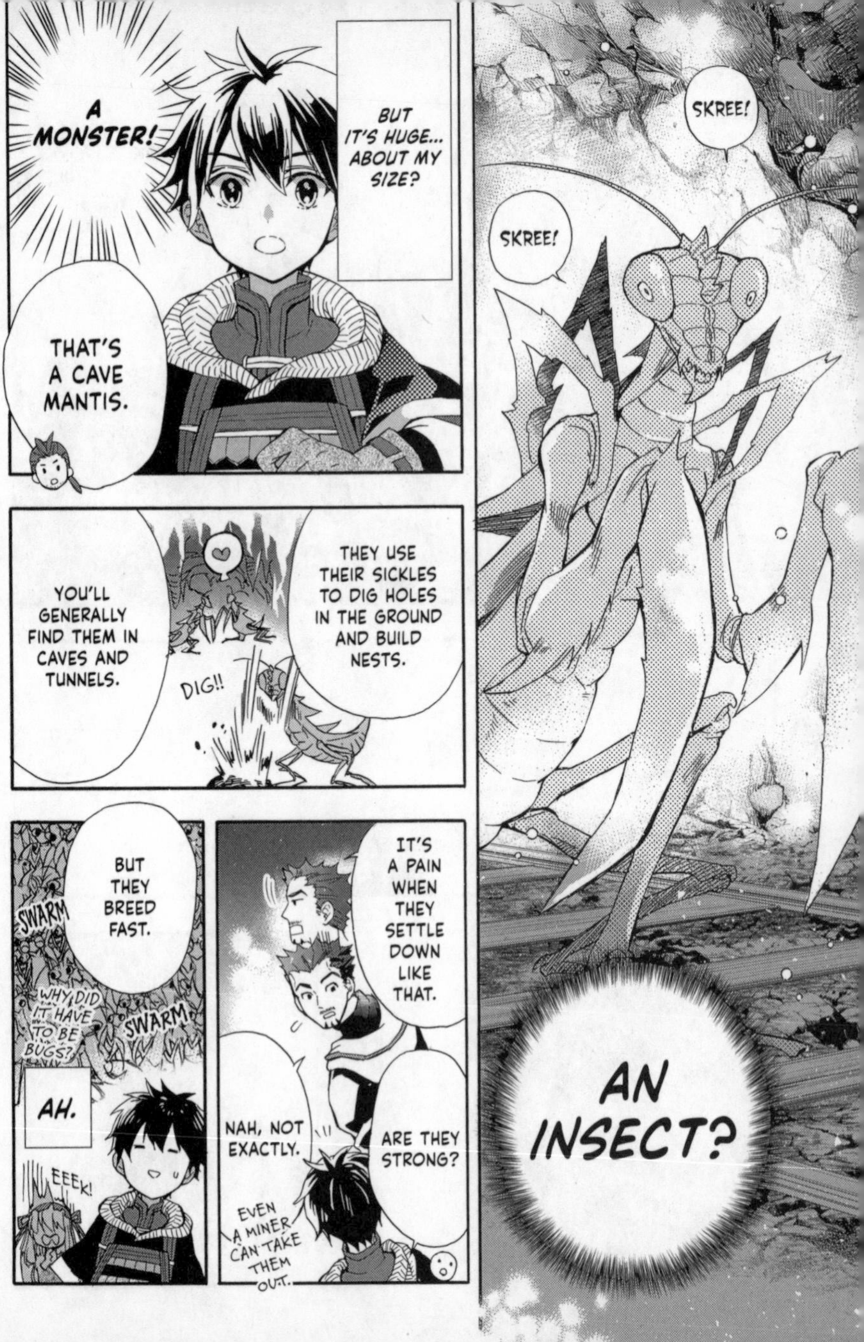
SKREE!
SKREE!
AN INSECT?
BUT IT'S HUGE... ABOUT MY SIZE?
A MONSTER!
THAT'S A CAVE MANTIS.
THEY USE THEIR SICKLES TO DIG HOLES IN THE GROUND AND BUILD NESTS.
DIG!!
YOU'LL GENERALLY FIND THEM IN CAVES AND TUNNELS.
IT'S A PAIN WHEN THEY SETTLE DOWN LIKE THAT.
ARE THEY STRONG?
NAH, NOT EXACTLY.
EVEN A MINER CAN TAKE THEM OUT.
BUT THEY BREED FAST.
SWARM
SWARM
WHY DID IT HAVE TO BE BUGS?
AH.
EEEK!

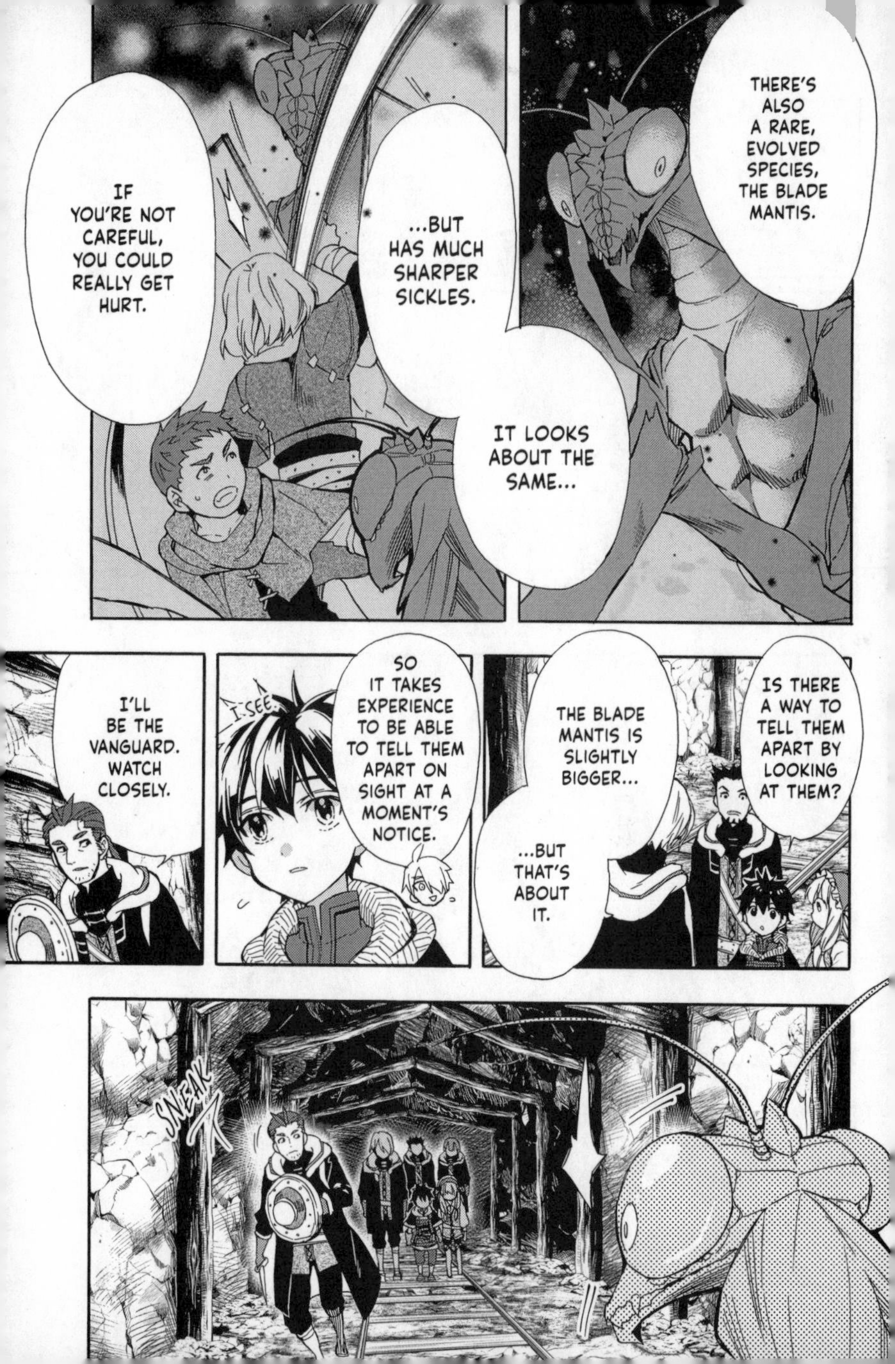
THERE'S ALSO A RARE, EVOLVED SPECIES, THE BLADE MANTIS.
IT LOOKS ABOUT THE SAME...
...BUT HAS MUCH SHARPER SICKLES.
IF YOU'RE NOT CAREFUL, YOU COULD REALLY GET HURT.
IS THERE A WAY TO TELL THEM APART BY LOOKING AT THEM?
THE BLADE MANTIS IS SLIGHTLY BIGGER...
...BUT THAT'S ABOUT IT.
SO IT TAKES EXPERIENCE TO BE ABLE TO TELL THEM APART ON SIGHT AT A MOMENT'S NOTICE.
I SEE.
I'LL BE THE VANGUARD. WATCH CLOSELY.
SNEAK

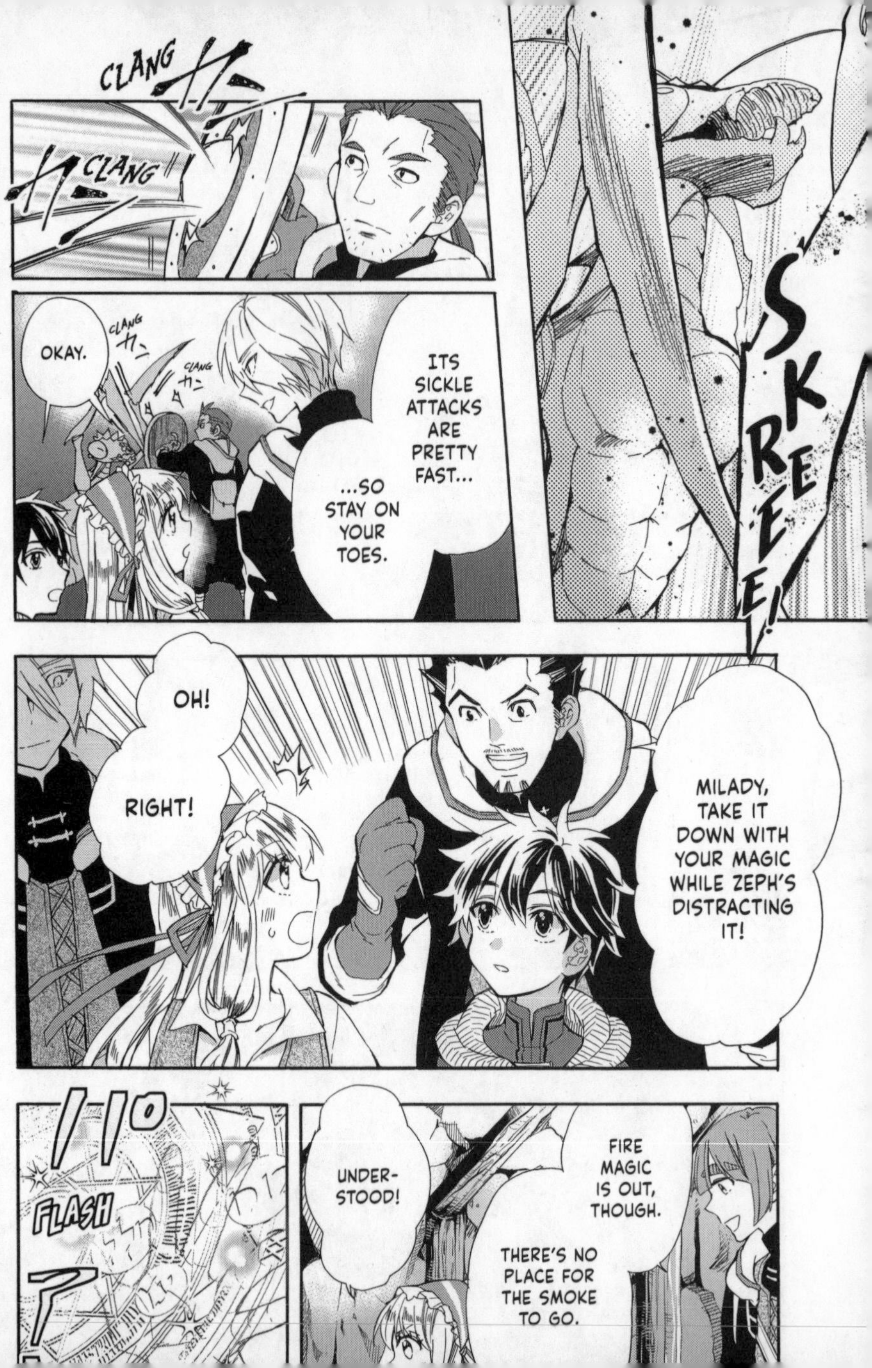
SKREEE!
CLANG
CLANG
ITS SICKLE ATTACKS ARE PRETTY FAST...
...SO STAY ON YOUR TOES.
CLANG
CLANG
OKAY.
MILADY, TAKE IT DOWN WITH YOUR MAGIC WHILE ZEPH'S DISTRACTING IT!
OH!
RIGHT!
FIRE MAGIC IS OUT, THOUGH.
THERE'S NO PLACE FOR THE SMOKE TO GO.
UNDER-STOOD!
FLASH

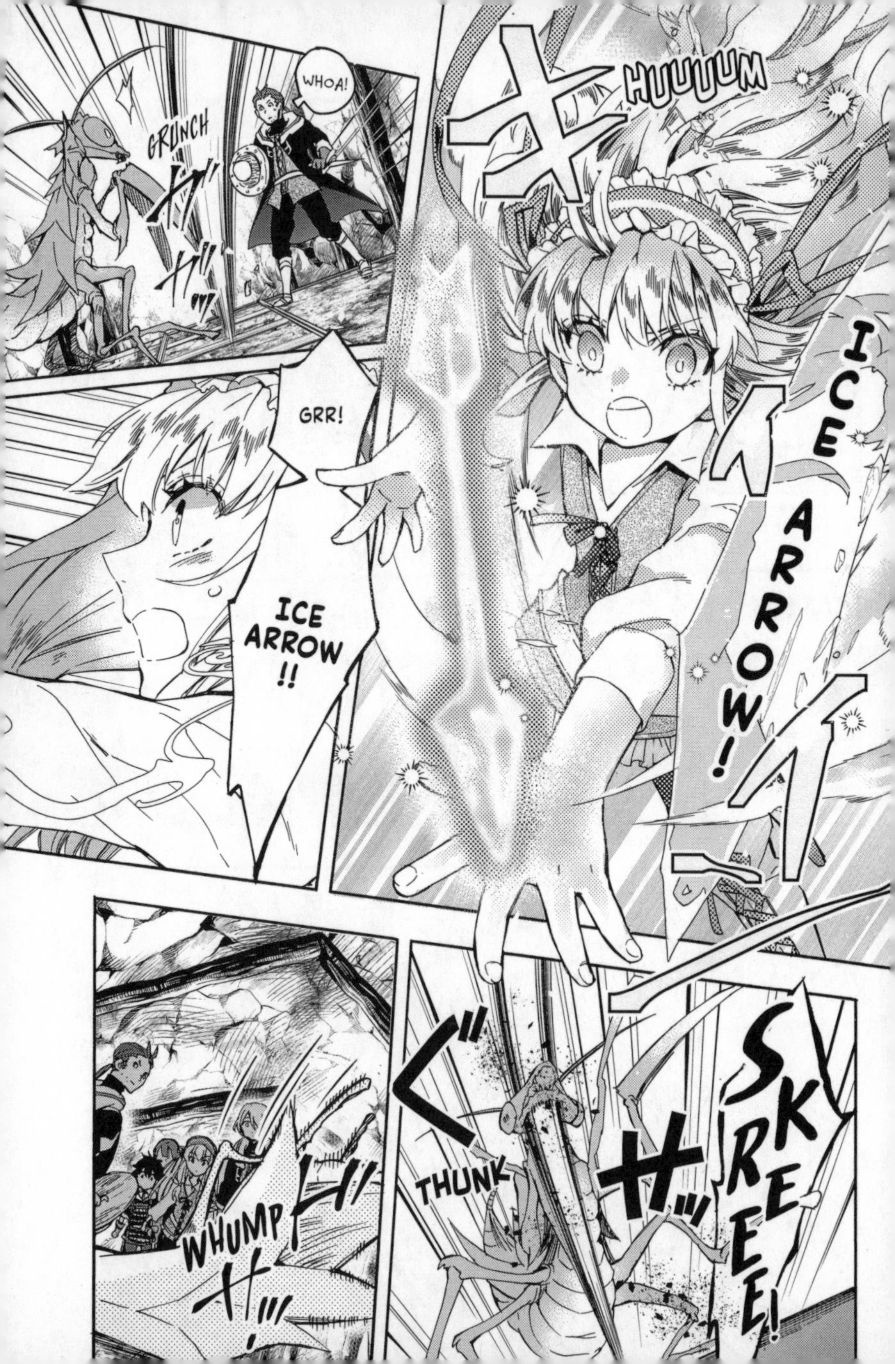
HUUUUM
ICE ARROW!
GRUNCH
WHOA!
GRR!
ICE ARROW!!
THUNK
SKREEE!
WHUMP

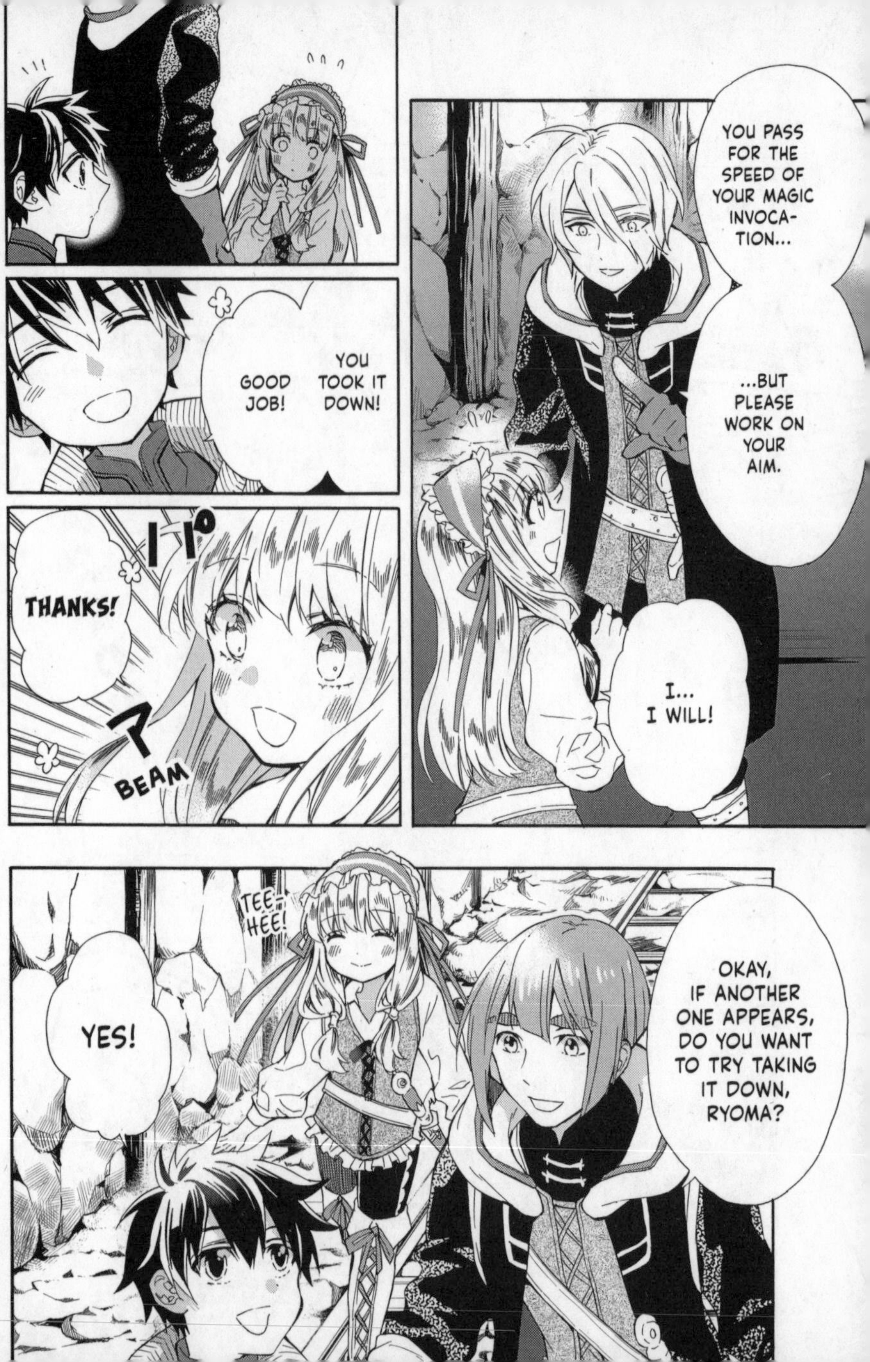
YOU PASS FOR THE SPEED OF YOUR MAGIC INVOCA-TION...
...BUT PLEASE WORK ON YOUR AIM.
I... I WILL!
YOU TOOK IT DOWN!
GOOD JOB!
THANKS!
BEAM
OKAY, IF ANOTHER ONE APPEARS, DO YOU WANT TO TRY TAKING IT DOWN, RYOMA?
TEE-HEE!
YES!

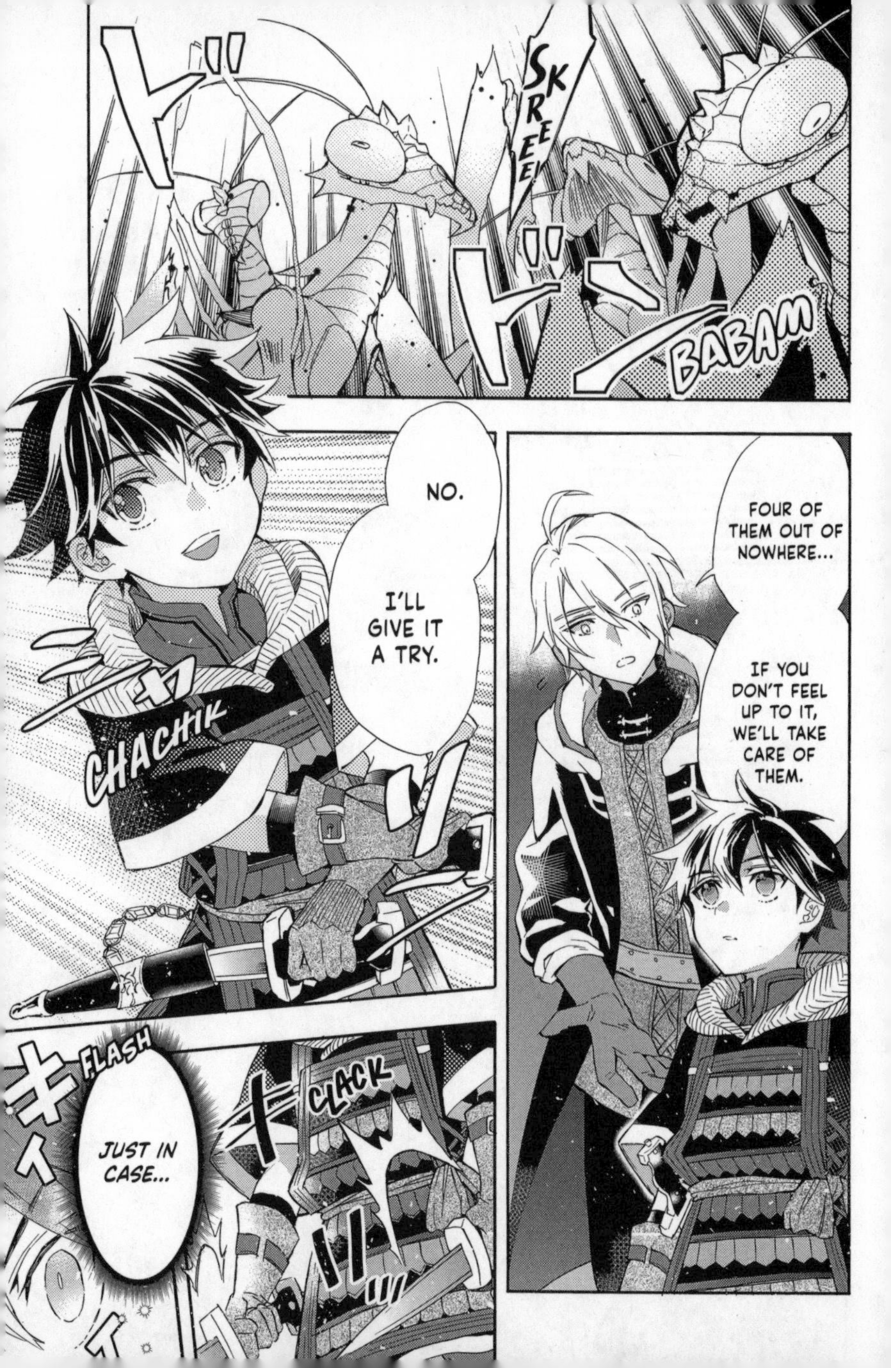

SKREE!
BABAM
FOUR OF THEM OUT OF NOWHERE...
IF YOU DON'T FEEL UP TO IT, WE'LL TAKE CARE OF THEM.
NO.
I'LL GIVE IT A TRY.
CHACHIK
CLACK
FLASH
JUST IN CASE...

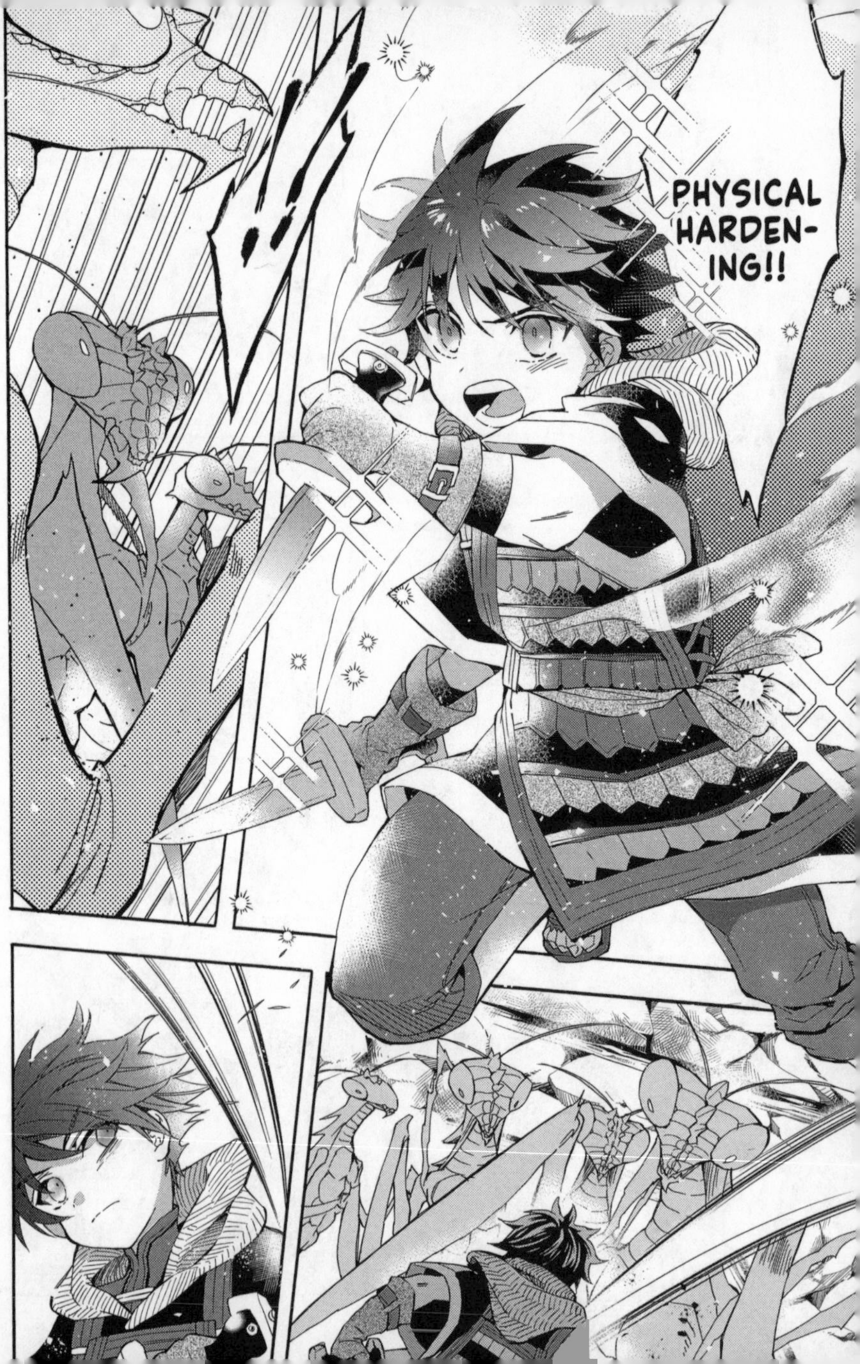
PHYSICAL HARDEN-ING!!

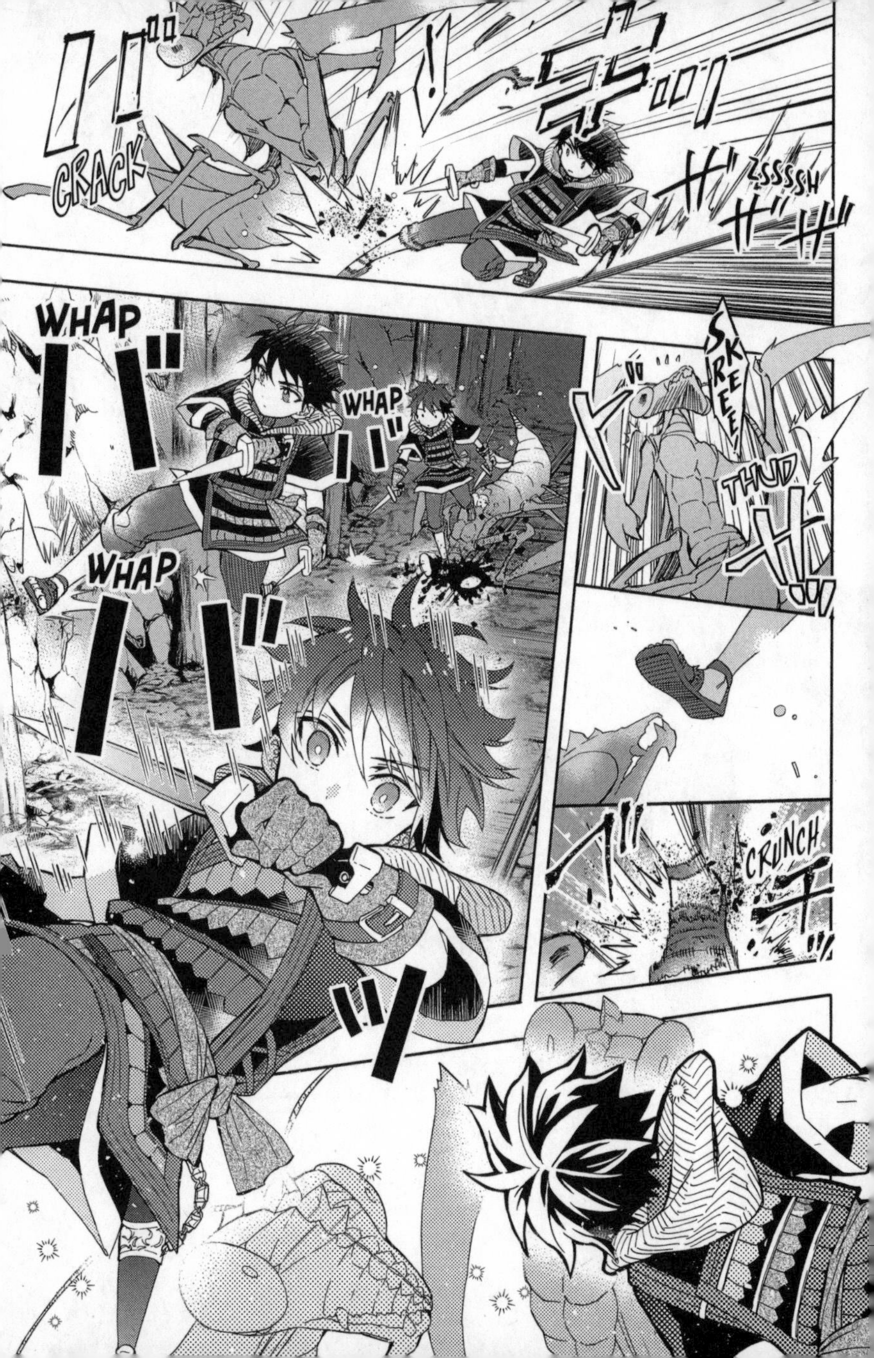
ZSSSSH
CRACK
SKREEE
THUD
WHAP
WHAP
WHAP
CRUNCH

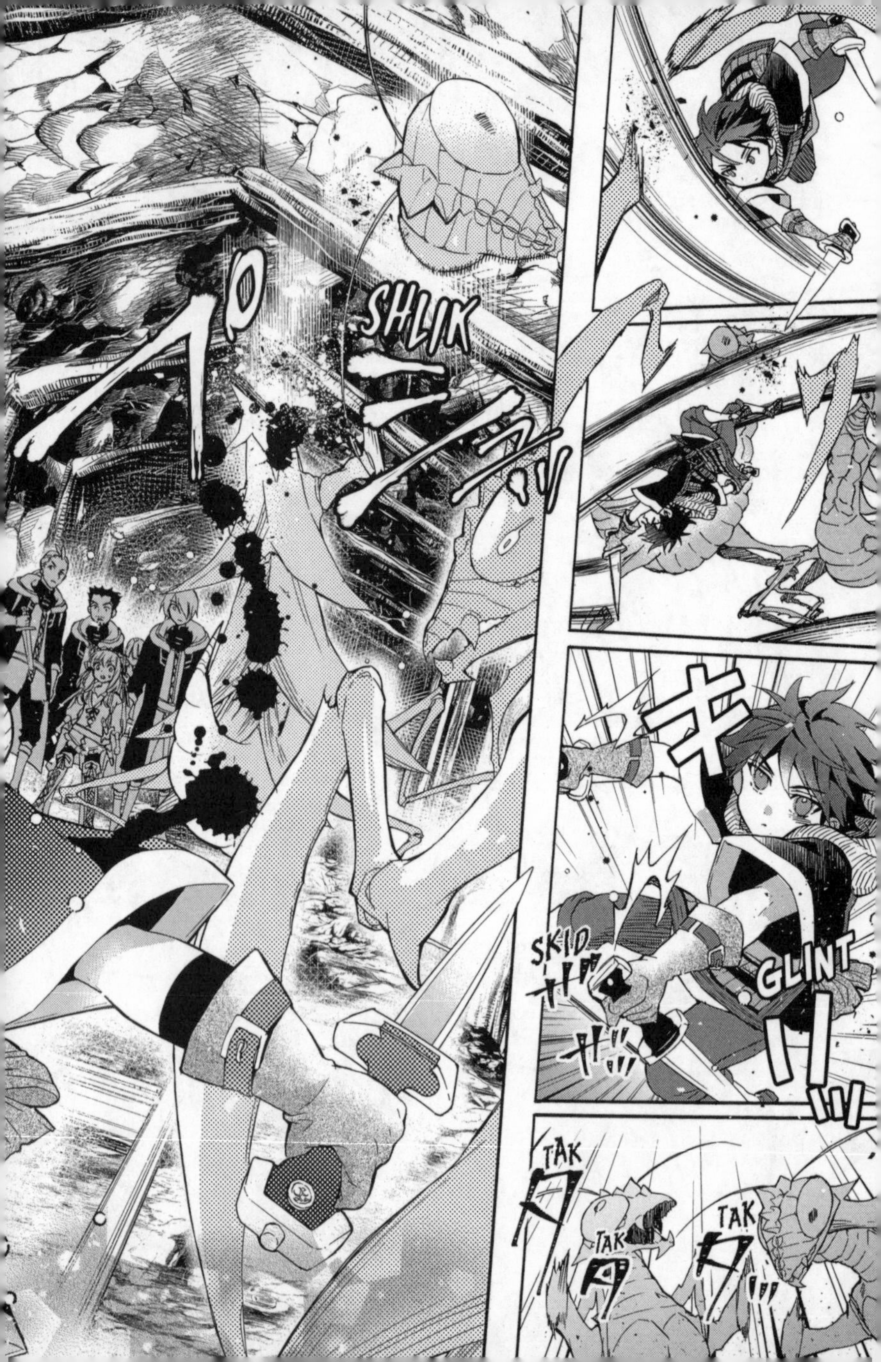
GLINT
SKID
TAK
TAK
TAK
SHLIK

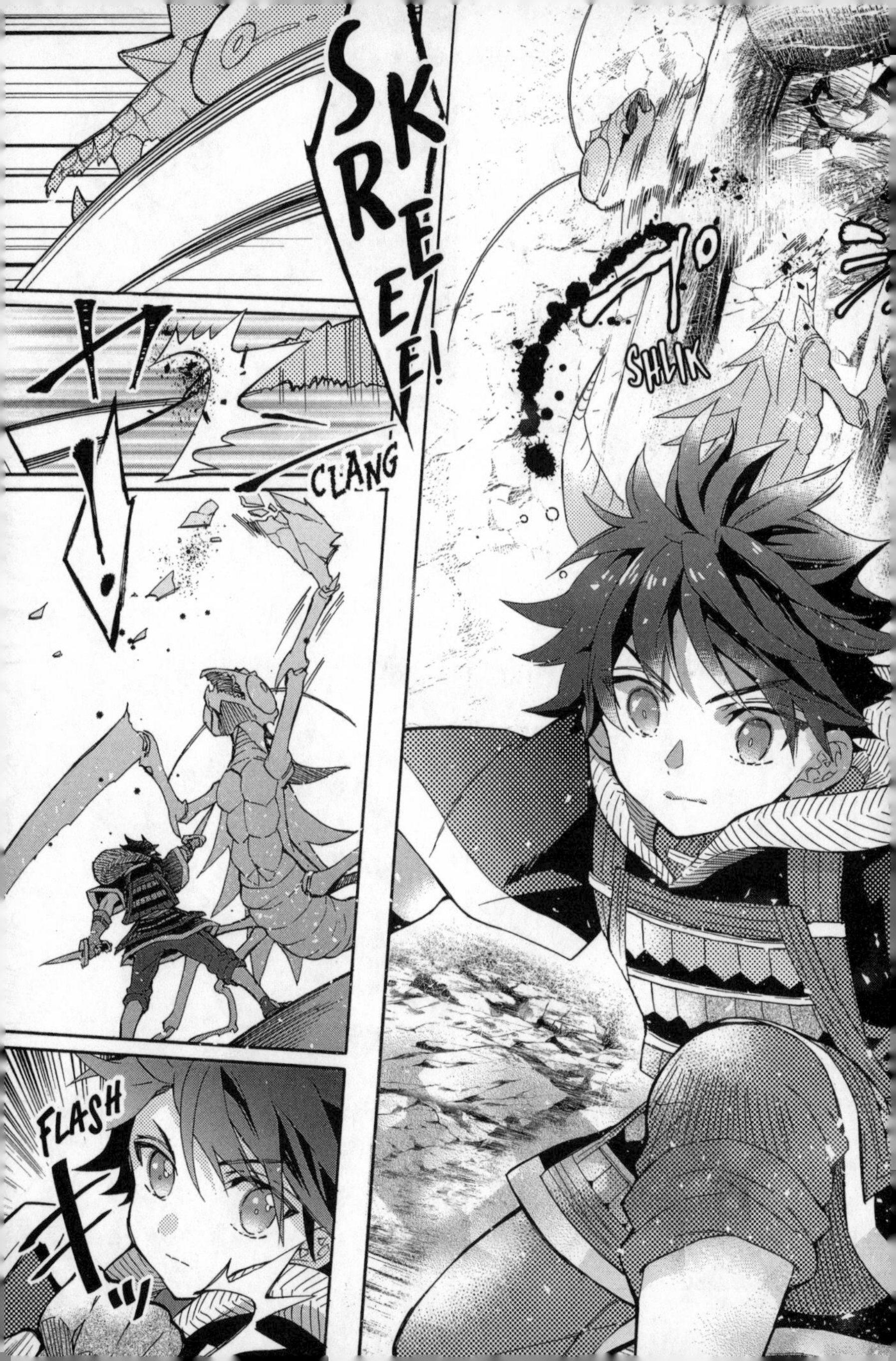
SHLIK
SKREEE!
CLANG
FLASH

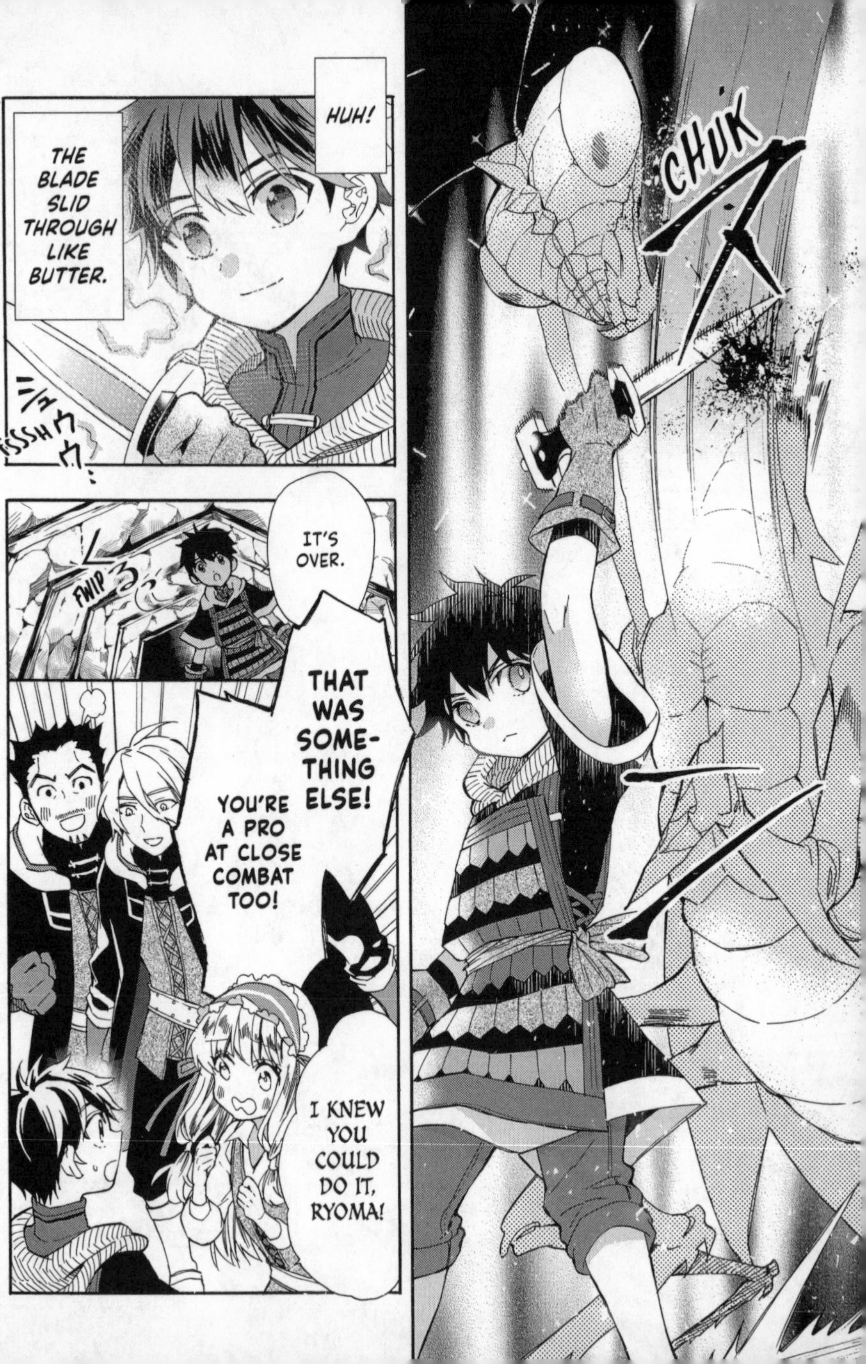
CHUK
HUH!
THE BLADE SLID THROUGH LIKE BUTTER.
FSSSH
FWIP
IT'S OVER.
THAT WAS SOME-THING ELSE!
YOU'RE A PRO AT CLOSE COMBAT TOO!
I KNEW YOU COULD DO IT, RYOMA!

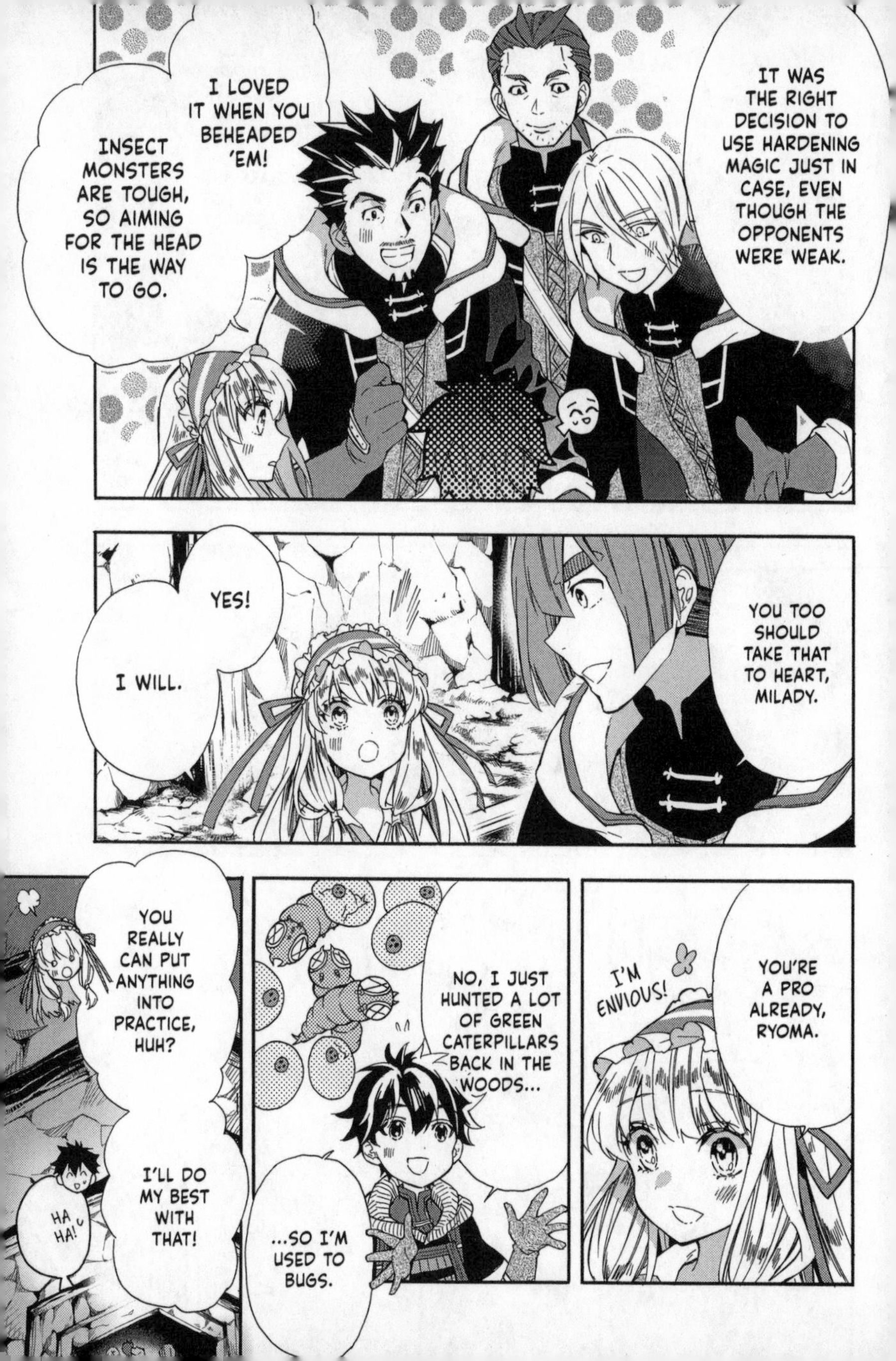
IT WAS THE RIGHT DECISION TO USE HARDENING MAGIC JUST IN CASE, EVEN THOUGH THE OPPONENTS WERE WEAK.
I LOVED IT WHEN YOU BEHEADED 'EM!
INSECT MONSTERS ARE TOUGH, SO AIMING FOR THE HEAD IS THE WAY TO GO.
YOU TOO SHOULD TAKE THAT TO HEART, MILADY.
YES!
I WILL.
YOU'RE A PRO ALREADY, RYOMA.
I'M ENVIOUS!
NO, I JUST HUNTED A LOT OF GREEN CATERPILLARS BACK IN THE WOODS...
...SO I'M USED TO BUGS.
YOU REALLY CAN PUT ANYTHING INTO PRACTICE, HUH?
I'LL DO MY BEST WITH THAT!
HA HA!

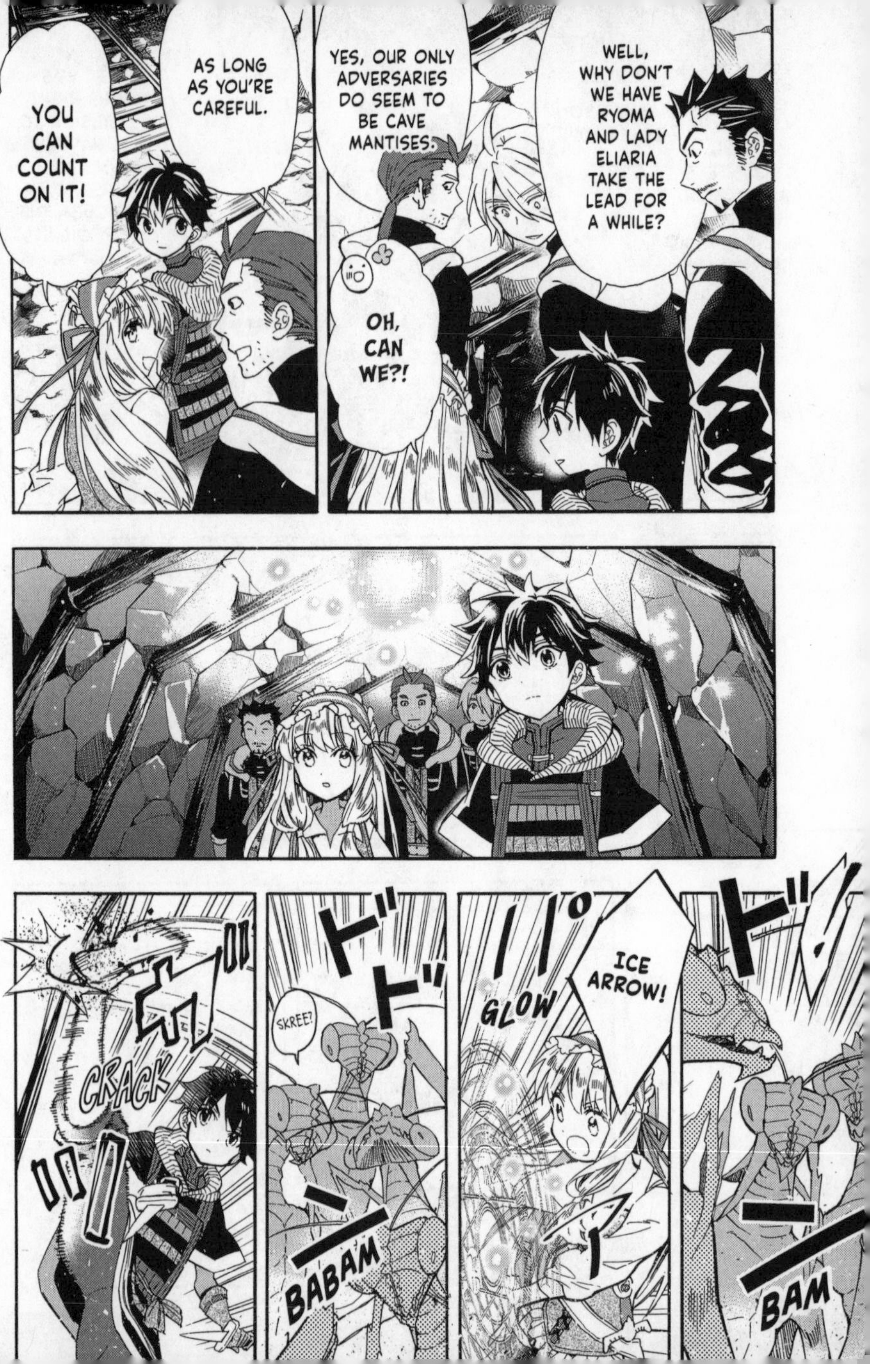

WELL, WHY DON'T WE HAVE RYOMA AND LADY ELIARIA TAKE THE LEAD FOR A WHILE?
YES, OUR ONLY ADVERSARIES DO SEEM TO BE CAVE MANTISES.
OH, CAN WE?!
AS LONG AS YOU'RE CAREFUL.
YOU CAN COUNT ON IT!
BAM
ICE ARROW!
GLOW
SKREE?
BABAM
CRACK

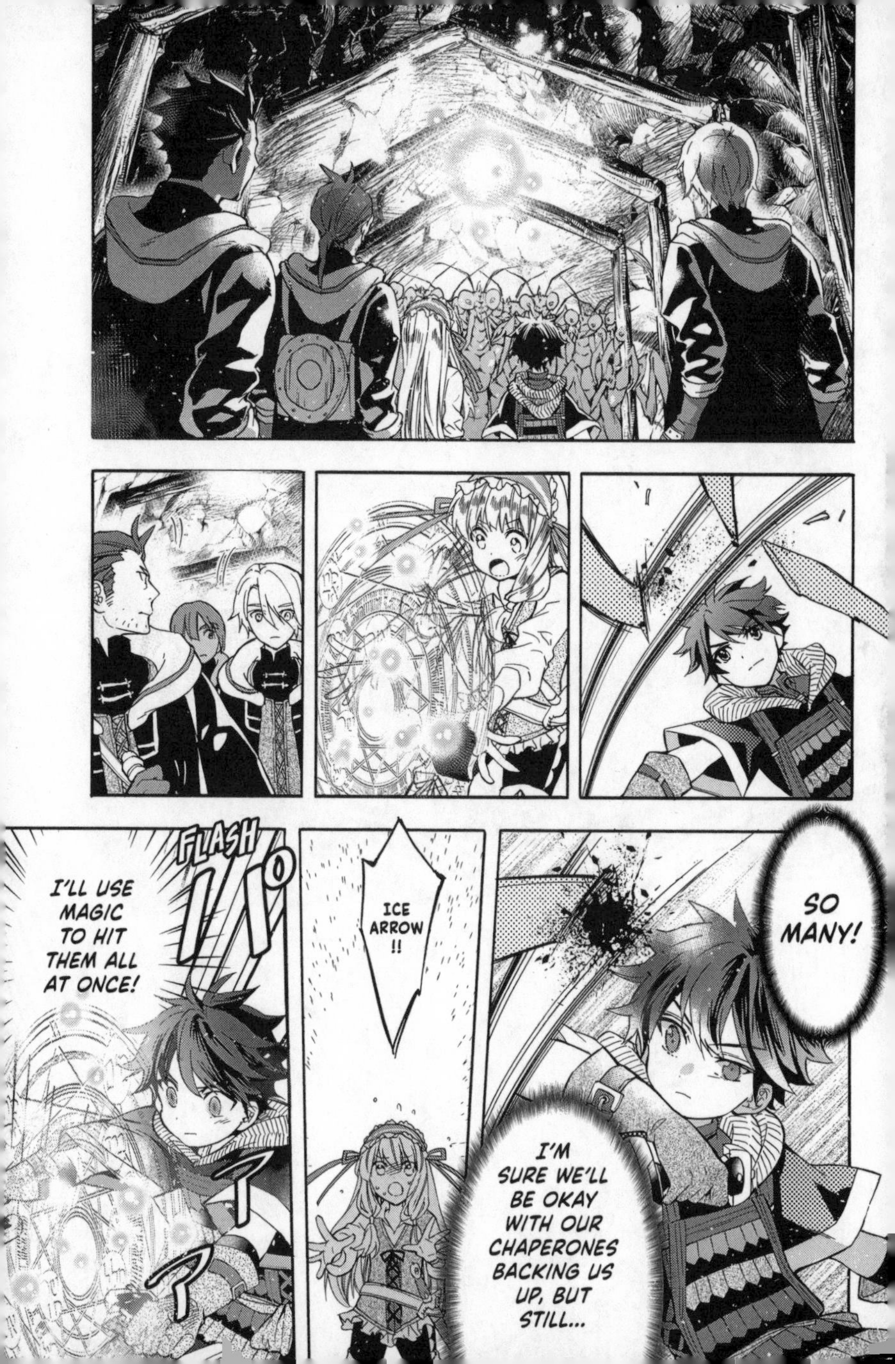
SO MANY!
I'M SURE WE'LL BE OKAY WITH OUR CHAPERONES BACKING US UP, BUT STILL...
ICE ARROW!!
FLASH
I'LL USE MAGIC TO HIT THEM ALL AT ONCE!

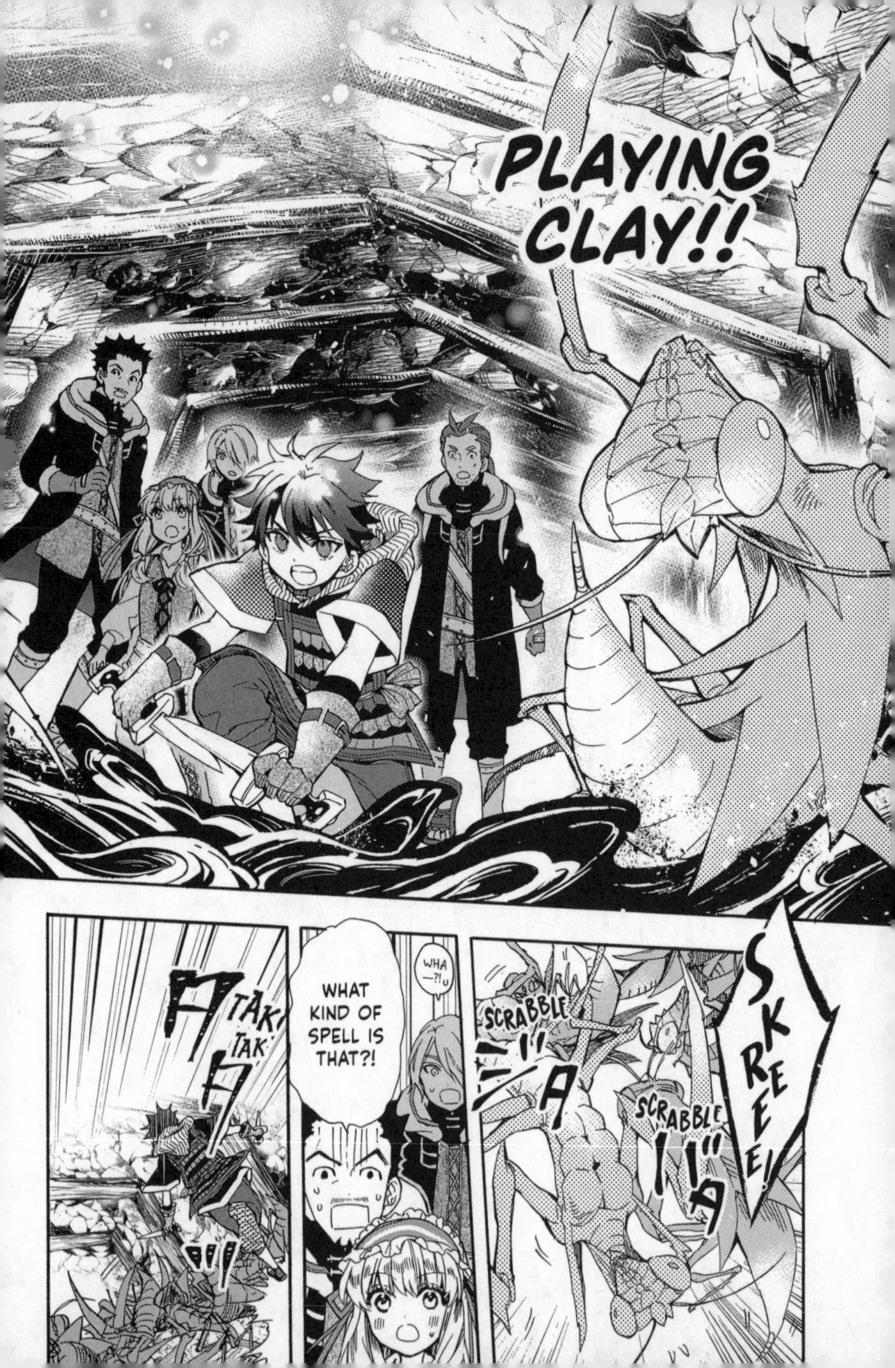
PLAYING CLAY!!
SKREE!
SCRABBLE
SCRABBLE
WHA—?!
WHAT KIND OF SPELL IS THAT?!
TAK
TAK

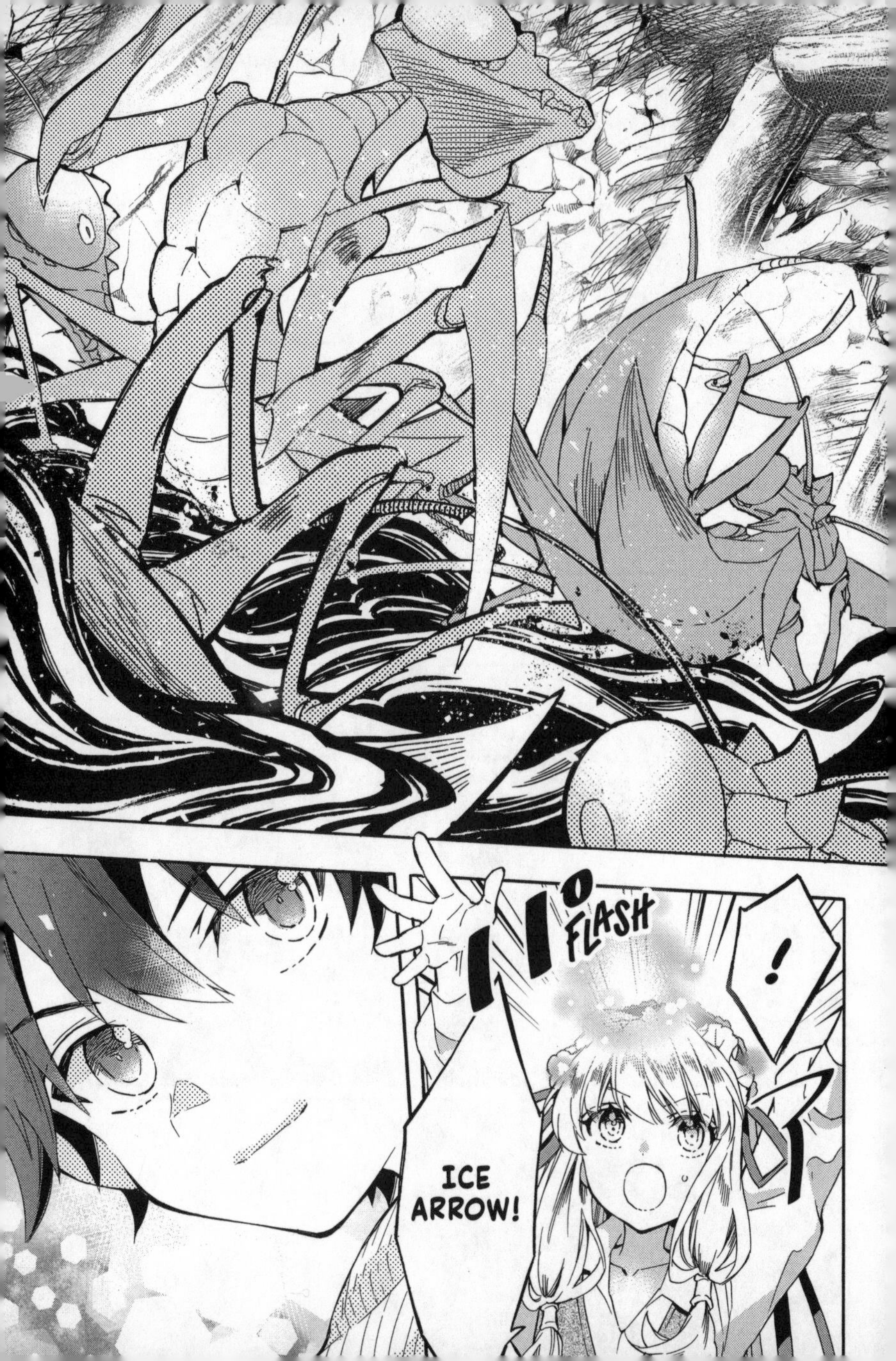

FLASH
!
ICE ARROW!

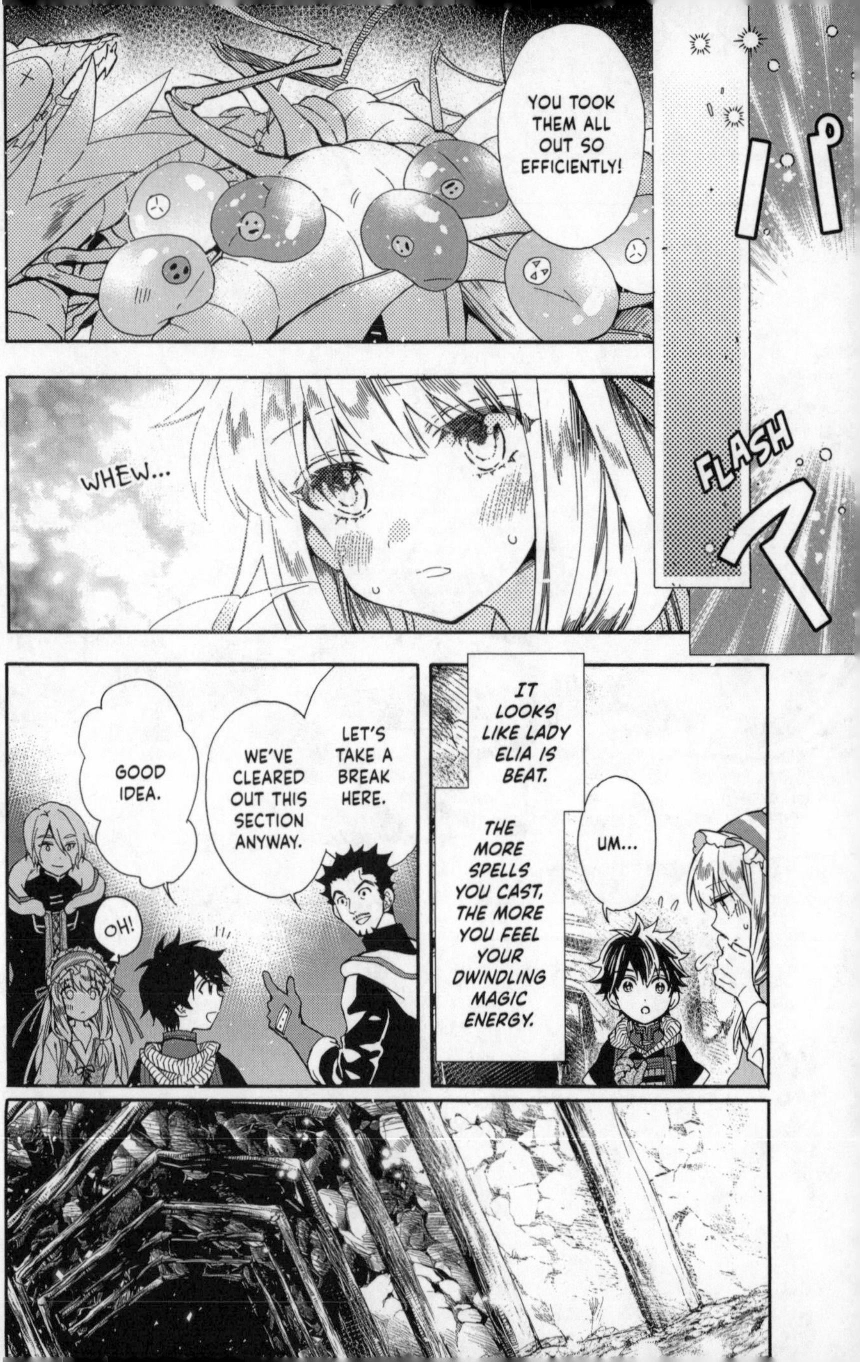
パ
FLASH
YOU TOOK THEM ALL OUT SO EFFICIENTLY!
WHEW...
IT LOOKS LIKE LADY ELIA IS BEAT.
UM...
THE MORE SPELLS YOU CAST, THE MORE YOU FEEL YOUR DWINDLING MAGIC ENERGY.
LET'S TAKE A BREAK HERE.
WE'VE CLEARED OUT THIS SECTION ANYWAY.
GOOD IDEA.
OH!

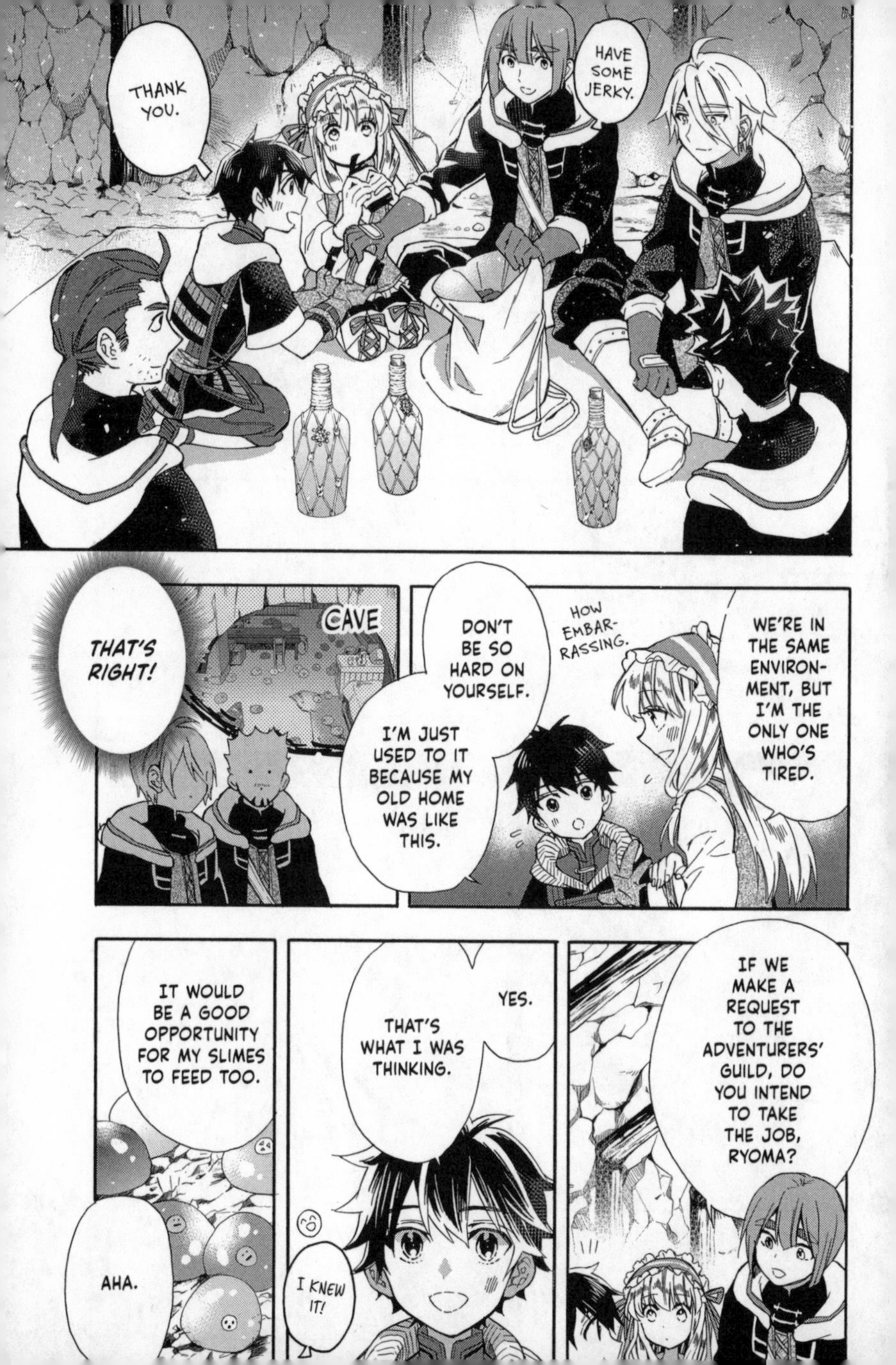
HAVE SOME JERKY.
THANK YOU.
WE'RE IN THE SAME ENVIRONMENT, BUT I'M THE ONLY ONE WHO'S TIRED.
HOW EMBARRASSING.
DON'T BE SO HARD ON YOURSELF.
I'M JUST USED TO IT BECAUSE MY OLD HOME WAS LIKE THIS.
CAVE
THAT'S RIGHT!
IF WE MAKE A REQUEST TO THE ADVENTURERS' GUILD, DO YOU INTEND TO TAKE THE JOB, RYOMA?
YES.
THAT'S WHAT I WAS THINKING.
I KNEW IT!
IT WOULD BE A GOOD OPPORTUNITY FOR MY SLIMES TO FEED TOO.
AHA.

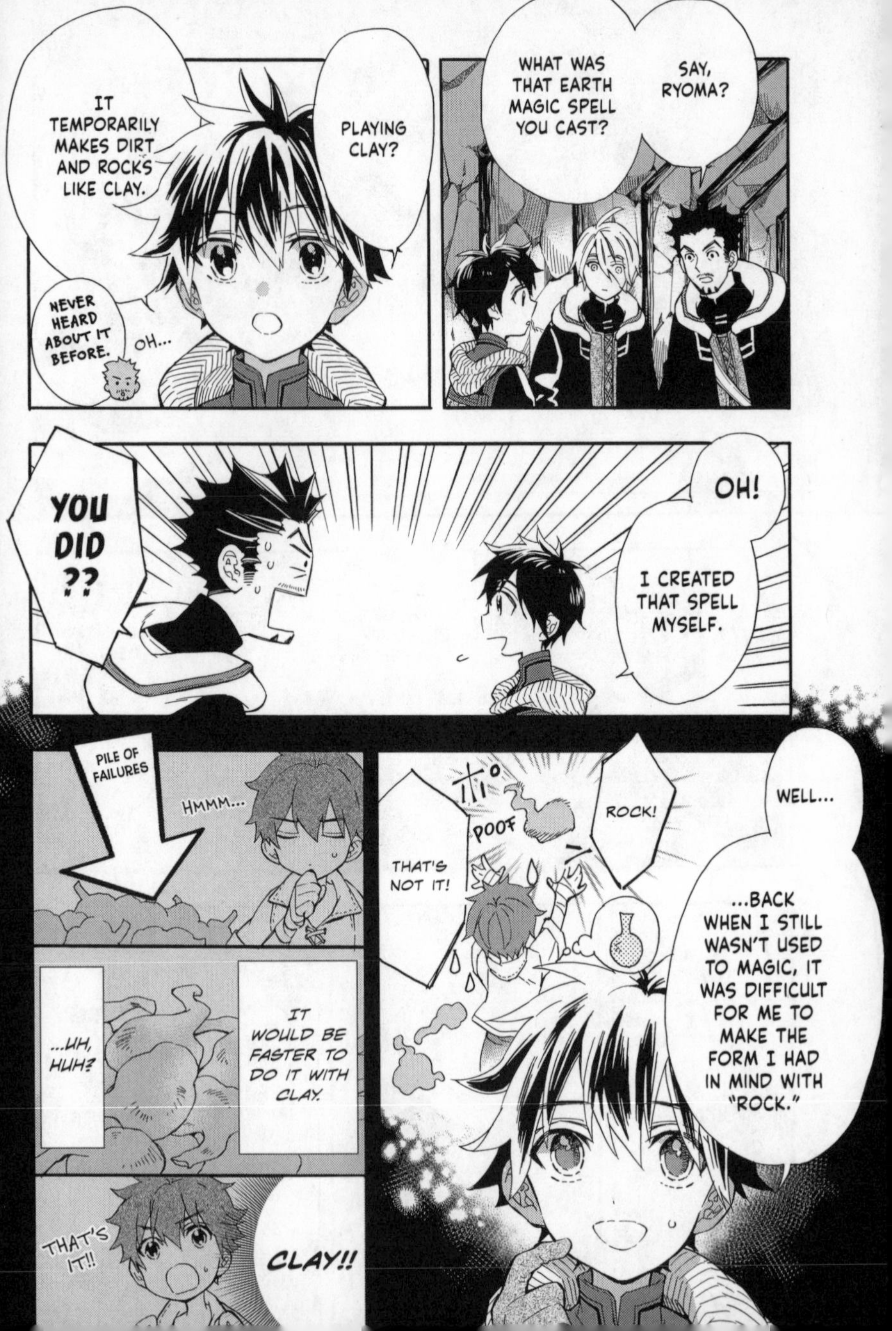
SAY, RYOMA?
WHAT WAS THAT EARTH MAGIC SPELL YOU CAST?
PLAYING CLAY?
IT TEMPORARILY MAKES DIRT AND ROCKS LIKE CLAY.
OH...
NEVER HEARD ABOUT IT BEFORE.
OH!
I CREATED THAT SPELL MYSELF.
YOU DID ??
WELL...
...BACK WHEN I STILL WASN'T USED TO MAGIC, IT WAS DIFFICULT FOR ME TO MAKE THE FORM I HAD IN MIND WITH "ROCK."
ROCK!
POOF
THAT'S NOT IT!
PILE OF FAILURES
HMMM...
IT WOULD BE FASTER TO DO IT WITH CLAY.
...UH, HUH?
CLAY!!
THAT'S IT!!

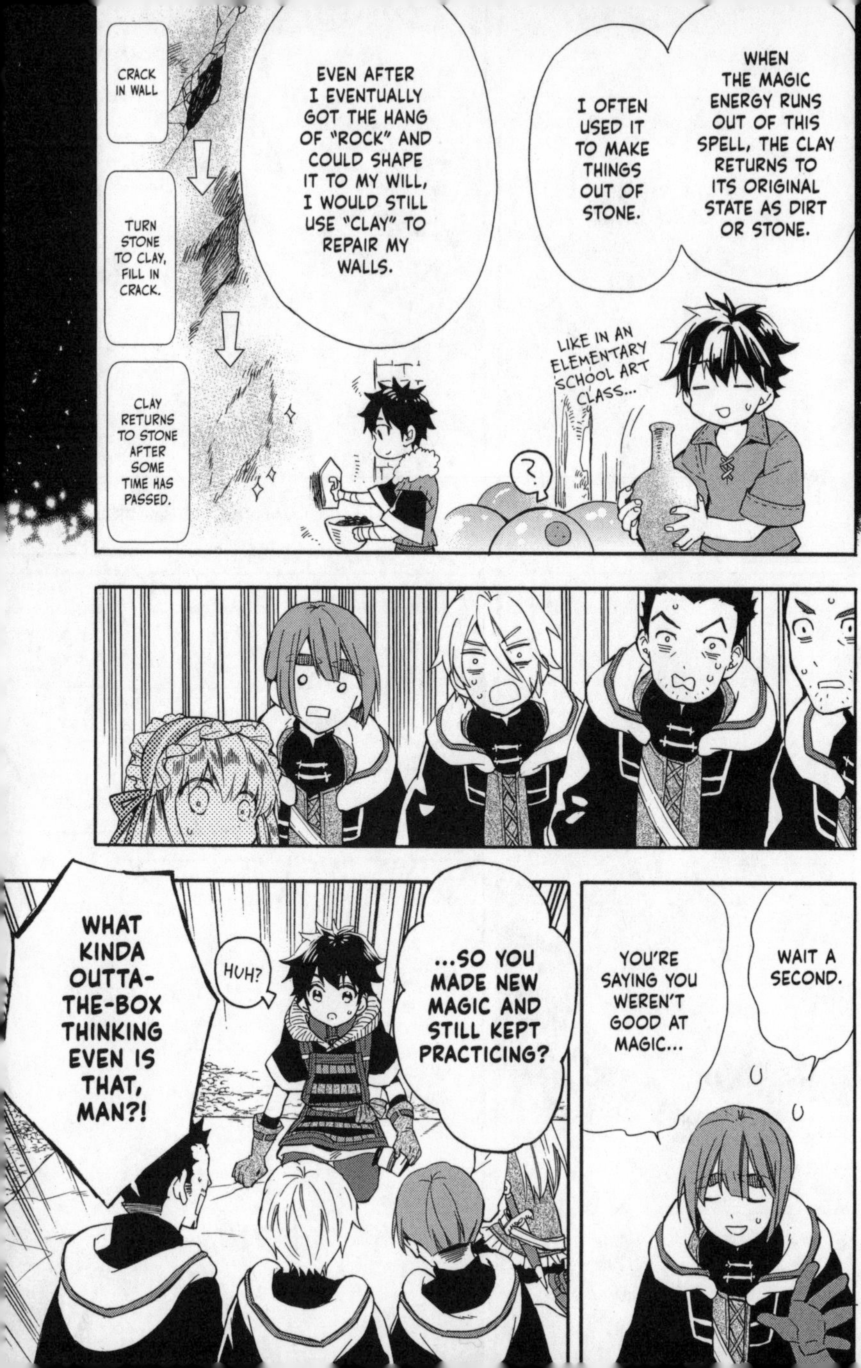
WHEN THE MAGIC ENERGY RUNS OUT OF THIS SPELL, THE CLAY RETURNS TO ITS ORIGINAL STATE AS DIRT OR STONE.
I OFTEN USED IT TO MAKE THINGS OUT OF STONE.
EVEN AFTER I EVENTUALLY GOT THE HANG OF "ROCK" AND COULD SHAPE IT TO MY WILL, I WOULD STILL USE "CLAY" TO REPAIR MY WALLS.
LIKE IN AN ELEMENTARY SCHOOL ART CLASS...
?
CRACK IN WALL
TURN STONE TO CLAY, FILL IN CRACK.
CLAY RETURNS TO STONE AFTER SOME TIME HAS PASSED.
WAIT A SECOND.
YOU'RE SAYING YOU WEREN'T GOOD AT MAGIC...
...SO YOU MADE NEW MAGIC AND STILL KEPT PRACTICING?
HUH?
WHAT KINDA OUTTA-THE-BOX THINKING EVEN IS THAT, MAN?!

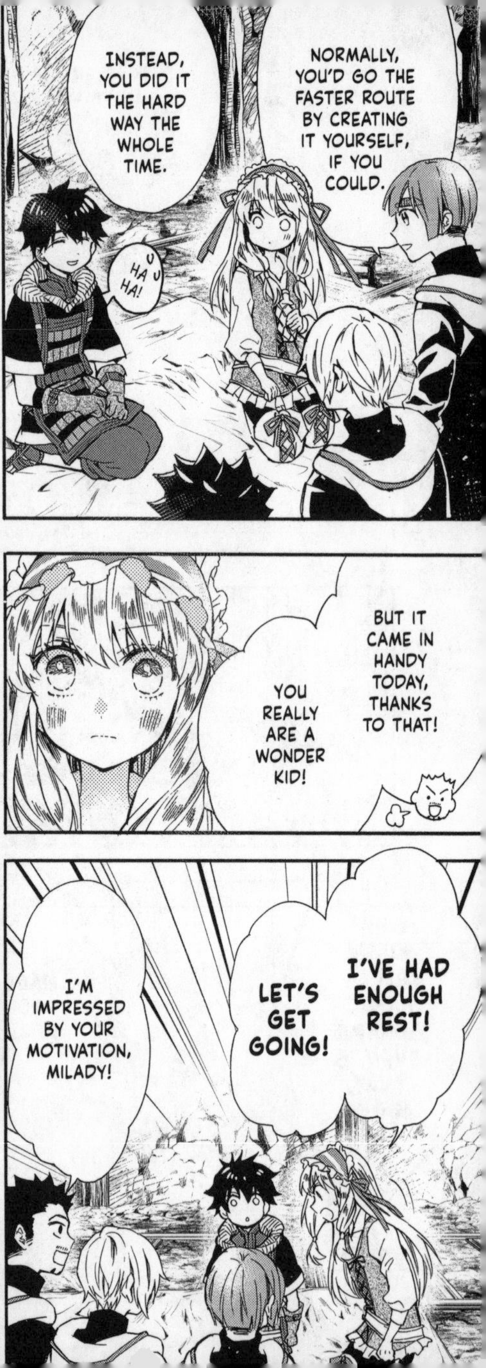
NORMALLY, YOU'D GO THE FASTER ROUTE BY CREATING IT YOURSELF, IF YOU COULD.
INSTEAD, YOU DID IT THE HARD WAY THE WHOLE TIME.
HA HA!
BUT IT CAME IN HANDY TODAY, THANKS TO THAT!
YOU REALLY ARE A WONDER KID!
I'VE HAD ENOUGH REST!
LET'S GET GOING!
I'M IMPRESSED BY YOUR MOTIVATION, MILADY!

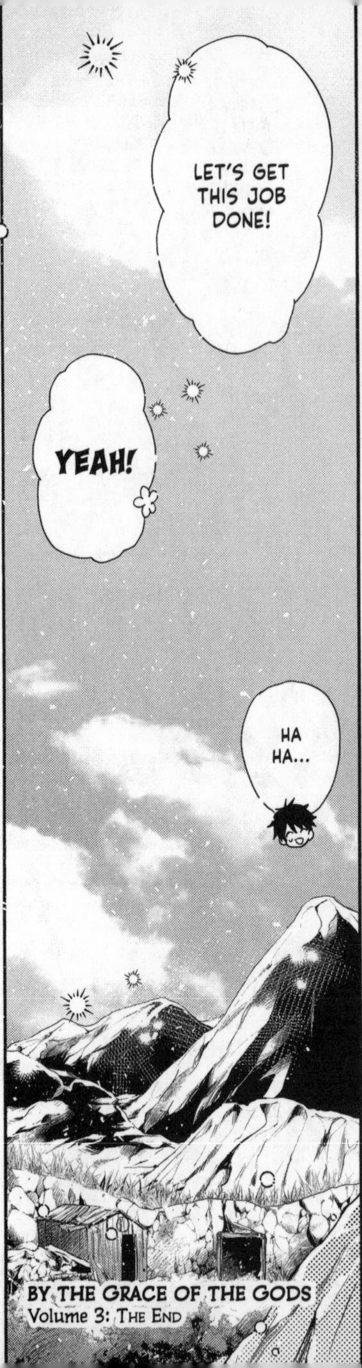
LET'S GET THIS JOB DONE!
YEAH!
HA HA...
BY THE GRACE OF THE GODS
Volume 3: The End

BY THE GRACE OF THE GODS

Tabuchi's Journal

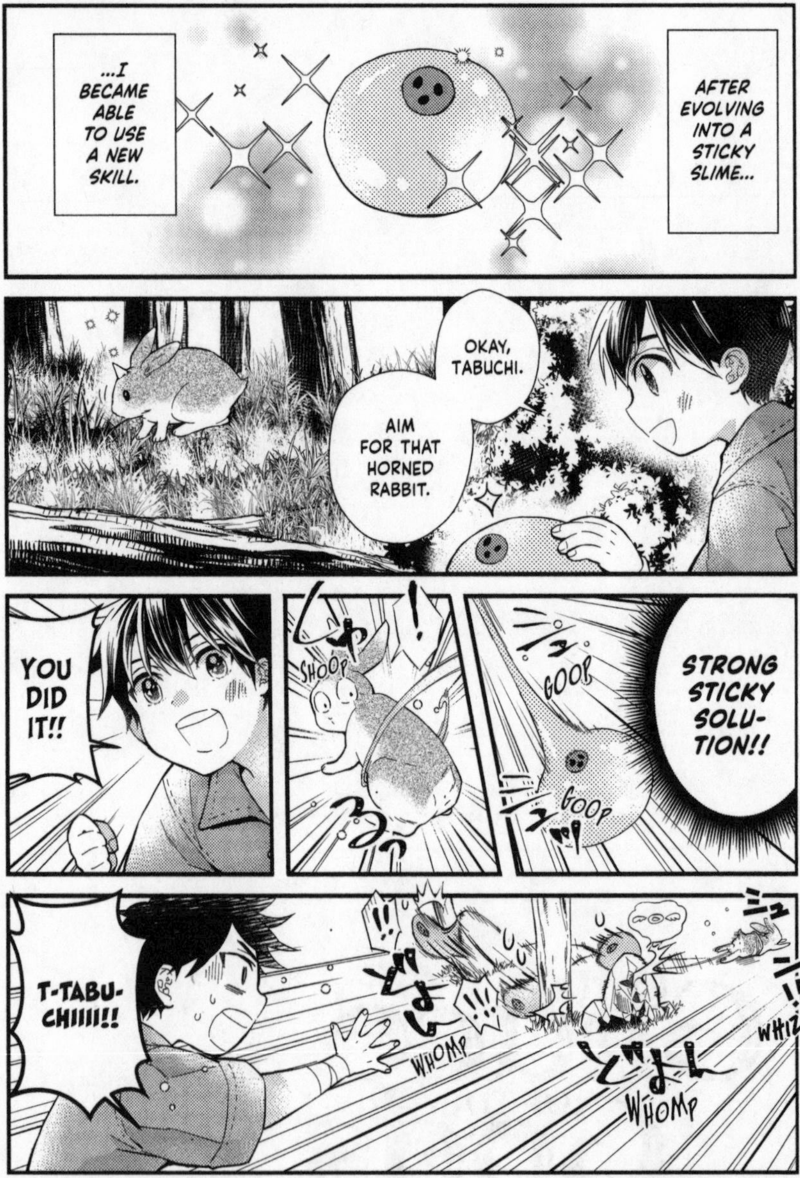
AFTER EVOLVING INTO A STICKY SLIME...
...I BECAME ABLE TO USE A NEW SKILL.
OKAY, TABUCHI.
AIM FOR THAT HORNED RABBIT.
STRONG STICKY SOLUTION!!
GOOP
GOOP
!
SHOOP
YOU DID IT!!
WHIZ!!
WHOMP
WHOMP
T-TABU-CHIIIII!!

LIVE ON, YOUNG TABUCHI!!

BIG STICKY SLIME

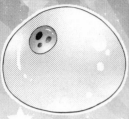

STRONG STICKY SOLUTION (5)
HARDENING STICKY SOLUTION (4)
STICKY STRING SHOT (3)
PHYSICAL ATTACK RESISTANCE (1)
MAXIMIZE (2)
MINIMIZE (4)
JUMP (2)
CONSUME (3)
ABSORB (3)

KING SCAVENGER SLIME

DISEASE RESISTANCE (7)	NUTRIENT REDUCTION (7)
POISON RESISTANCE (7)	PHYSICAL ATTACK RESISTANCE (4)
FOUL FEEDER (8)	MAXIMIZE (5)
CLEANSE (8)	MINIMIZE (6)
DEODORIZE (8)	JUMP (3)
DEODORANT SOLUTION (6)	GLUTTONY (4)
STENCH RELEASE (8)	

To read a brand-new short story by **ROY**,
the author of *By the Grace of the Gods*,
please turn to page 193 of this book,
where you'll find the story presented
in left-to-right reading order.

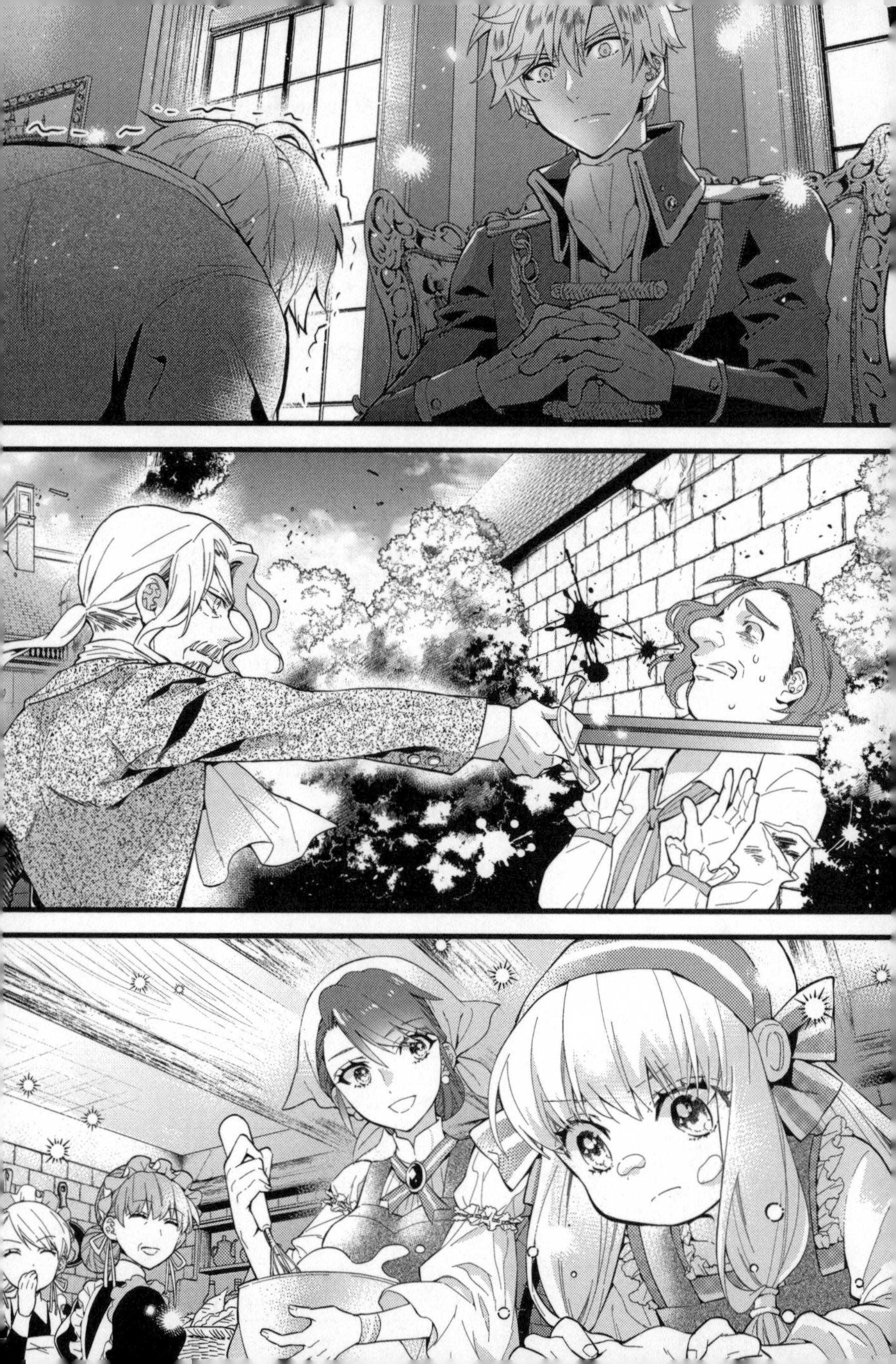

As an experiment, Eliaria put the root between two slices of bread and took a bite.

"Gh!! Ngh…!"

"Have some water, milady."

"Ugh!! Whew… Thank you, Araune. This is no good…"

"It's extremely bitter, so I believe a smaller amount would be better if we do include it."

"Then what about this? Meat and vegetables are common enough, so how about a fish sandwich instead?"

Eliaria next picked up a cured fish.

"This has been cooked over a fire once already, yes?"

Araune quickly got everything together and created a new sandwich based on Eliaria's inspiration.

"Oh, this is quite tasty. A bit salty, but if we add vegetables, it will be just right."

"Let's add this to today's menu!"

After making that pronouncement, Eliaria turned her attention to choosing ingredients to complete the dish that would make the cured fish sandwich taste even better.

And so, the women at home supported their family and friend while waiting for their return.

Unaware she was a topic of discussion in the blazing courtyard, Elia was back at the inn, making a snack with her mother, Elise, and their two maids, to give to Ryoma, who was engaged in the pit toilet cleanup effort.

"Ah...choo!"

"Milady? Are you all right?"

"You keep sneezing. Do you feel unwell?"

"No, not especially."

"Perhaps a bit of wheat flour went up your nose. But don't hesitate to let us know if you do feel poorly."

"I won't, Mother."

"Well, let's get back to the cooking. Lilian."

"Yes, milady. Here are the ingredients."

"A man wants meat after doing a job that takes a lot of physical energy, right?"

"I would recommend a goodly amount of vegetables. I've heard they ward off disease."

"Plenty of meat and plenty of vegetables, then. We'll bring it over, and whenever he gets the chance to take a break, he can enjoy...a delicious sandwich."

"It seems rather boring..."

The four of them had already made several such snacks for Ryoma, who tended to lose track of time and forget about taking breaks while working. Now, the ladies were in a creative cooking rut.

"Can we make him something new and delicious, maybe with different ingredients?"

Eliaria scrutinized what maid Lilian had assembled on the food cart.

"Oh! How about this?!"

"Huh? Isn't that a medicinal root?"

"I read in a book that it's very nutritious. And Ryoma said he cooks with giger too."

"Camil! Zeph! Hughes! Move those arms and legs more than your mouths! That wind is fanning the trees' flames so much, they're likely to jump over to the manor!"

Hughes yelled, "Seriously?! I wish you wouldn't have come raging in here like a whirlwind yourself, Lord Reinbach!"

Just then, a torrent of water fell from the sky right onto the blazing path before them, clearing a way to the house.

"I came to make my report, but it seems a firefighting effort is called for first."

"Sebas! Just the man!"

"Our savior!"

"Hurry, while we have the chance! Get the ones who're still out cold! Carry them into the manor for now, before they're engulfed by the flames!"

"Right!!"

The four cried out, fired up.

Sebas quietly went up to Reinbach.

"Lord Reinbach. Why don't I step out and bring in those of our surrounding guards who can use water magic?"

"Go ahead."

"And if I may... I know how you feel, milord, but please try to rein yourself in. Once his crimes are revealed, we will be able to confiscate the manor and his property. Besides, if the young mistress hears an account of this event later, she may become frightened."

"Y-you're right. I will be more careful henceforth."

Reinbach seemed to casually accept Sebas's suggestion, but in truth, he took it to heart. He trusted his butler, who had been with him much longer than any other servant. His instinct as a grandfather also kicked in, for being shunned by his granddaughter was the last thing he wanted.

"I shall cool my head a bit before doing anything else...and I trust you won't actually tell Elia about this..."

"Playing dumb, are we? Well, no matter. But you'd best come with me quietly. Your manor is surrounded, so there's no sense in trying to flee. I'll be damned if I let you get away, and you certainly can't escape on your own. Your guards there were no challenge, and I'm sure you're far less able than they."

"As I recall, you're a tamer, Your Grace…"

Reinbach snorted at the man's terrified face and his sputtering words.

"Against an opponent like you, a single sword and a little magic are plenty. There's no need for familiars. In fact, the boy could have handled this situation himself."

"The boy?"

"Someone with a promising future in an unforeseen place. You need not worry about him."

Judging that his quarry would not voluntarily surrender, Reinbach closed in with the speed of a much younger man and drove the pommel of his sword deep into the baron's defenseless belly. He looked down as the man slid into a crouch.

"Stay that way a while."

"Lord Reinbach!"

"Oh, good timing."

Four of the duchy's escorts—Jill, Hughes, Zeph, and Camil—came rushing into the courtyard.

"This is the man of the house. Take him and his men away."

"At once, Your Grace!"

Jill answered for them all and quickly bound the baron. The other three went about their orders as well.

"Wow… This one's out like a light…"

"Sometimes I wonder if the duke and his family really have need of us…"

"Well, this is just how it goes. Lord Reinbach always zooms on ahead, leaving a trail of unconscious bodies in his wake, which we then have to load onto the horses. We can't just leave them here, can we?"

While introducing my father into the conversation certainly had the desired effect...it makes me think I'm still a greenhorn in the eyes of the older generation.

Denied the opportunity to make excuses, the official had lost the initiative. At the beginning of the meeting, however, he had asked, "Was anything lacking in the report I gave you the other day?" with a look of feigned innocence. In fact, going in, he radiated confidence. But as the duke slowly moved from vague business to the real issue at hand, the official had begun to pale. And now...

"I have a final order for you. Write down the names of all the others involved, then every wrong for which you are personally responsible and every last detail of the others' crimes. Do that, and I promise I shall spare your life. Surely you would find that preferable to being hanged."

"Y-yes, Your Grace!!!"

The official suddenly bowed his head, smacking it on the table. He swore obedience and begged for mercy, but Reinhart went over it all again just to be sure, demanding the fellow start by writing down the names of everyone else complicit. As the man got busy with his list, Reinhart sighed inwardly.

"Well, that's one task done. I wonder how Father is faring..."

While Reinhart muttered to himself in the office parlor, smoke was rising from a certain residence in Gimul. Traces of a battle were strewn all over the interior, while several incapacitated men had been carried outside. This bevy of brawn now lay unconscious in the courtyard alongside trees that were bright with flame. One of the few men who still had his wits about him had been driven against a wall by Reinbach, the former duke.

"We finally meet, Baron. You do know why I've come here?"

"No, I'm afraid I don't. I never imagined you would pay me a visit like this, Your Grace. In fact, I took you for a burglar."

illnesses. One of them was the establishment of this public utility that you and your colleagues have ruined."

"U-ulp…"

"I believe you know that my father is in this town even now. There are two reasons he himself is not here at the moment. Firstly, I am now the duke, and thus I have a say in various things. My father has already given me all authority. But more importantly, the second reason… He declined to come because he knew he would not be able to control himself in your presence. He may have managed to stay composed in front of his granddaughter upon hearing of the pestilence in the pits, but he was a stern man in his younger days. A government office that has bungled its duty as much as yours might have found itself burned to the ground."

Quarantine was the core epidemic countermeasure. But under circumstances in which treatment was impossible, burning down places where the disease had taken hold— that is, buildings in which there had been infected patients, including hospitals or clinics—had been known to happen as a last resort. Therefore, the possible spread of a plague in town was no joke.

"Forgive me! Please forgive me!"

"We—and you—got lucky. Fortunately, steps have been taken, and we have people on the ground dealing with the situation before the disease has a chance to infect anyone. I had intended to refrain from sharing details, but I hear the decontamination efforts are going very well. My father has also been lecturing me at length on the importance of disease prevention and eradication strategies. However, unlike him, I have not lost my family to an epidemic. So while I don't forgive you and the others for what you've done, I intend to decide your punishment with a calm mind."

The official's eyes appeared to beg for mercy, and Reinhart reined in a bitter smile.

"How so…?"

"Thanks to your reluctance to give the workers their due, upkeep on the toilets fell by the wayside. Have you any idea what state they're in now? Did you never hear a sermon in church about the significance of cleanliness?"

"Y-you don't mean…!"

"Yes, it is just as you imagine. As we speak, the toilets have become a breeding ground for disease, one that could cause an epidemic. And it's all because you lot filled your own pockets while victimizing the poor."

"There must be some mistake! We haven't received any reports about an epidemic or scores of sick people!"

"Miraculously, an exceedingly clever fellow took the job when it was shunted over to the guild. He didn't want to cause a panic, so he reported it to me in private. He's dealing with the problem in what we believe to be the best way possible. That, more than anything, is what made me realize your wrongdoing."

Thus far, no one had been infected. The disease, which could have terrorized the town, had already been identified, while the Adventurers' Guild had begun a secret campaign to wipe it out. There was nothing for the duke and his family to do in that regard. Reinhart continued dispassionately.

"Are you aware, sir, that the Jamil duchy, in ruling its domain, attaches great importance to not only improving the infrastructure and cleanliness of the town in which our citizens live, but also to the reduction of epidemics?"

"I do know that, Your Grace. Ever since your father was the duke, we've been told that is a categorical imperative."

"I see… Of course, there are countless other things that are important. But many years ago, my father lost his own family to an epidemic. From the moment he inherited his title, he was very serious about taking proactive measures against such

"It apparently began with someone lower down the chain: the manager of the site. But you knew the truth all along. As the person at the top, ignorance would not have absolved you of responsibility. The point, however, is that you did know about it, and instead of working to solve the issue, you helped cover it up. By my reckoning, you broke the law this way not once, but two or three times. You even reached out to other departments… I'm afraid we have all the evidence we need."

"H-how…?"

In the face of Reinhart's unshakable manner, the head official unconsciously grew resigned to his fate, and his muttered response admitted his crimes.

"I have inherited my title from my father only recently, so perhaps you think my previous experience and a year in the role leaves me wanting. Perhaps you thought my youth would make me easy to fool?"

"Not in the least, Your Grace…"

"Then why a cover-up if you didn't wish to deceive?"

The contradiction seemed to occur to the official too, as Reinhart's voice became increasingly soft.

"Well, it's true that I'm not as wise as my father. After all, the papers you prepared did fool me for a time. I realized afterward that the documents from that day, as well as other materials, were based on actual records prior to your embezzlement and were compiled for easy digestion.

I feel as if I should kick myself for being gullible enough to take them at face value, however temporarily. At the same time, I am also deeply disappointed at the thought of the clear capability and passion you and your men possess but chose not to apply to your work. That said…"

Reinhart paused, his matter-of-fact tone cutting off. The official raised his head slightly and peered at the duke.

"At this point, the problem has gone far beyond the workers' pay and your embezzlement."

For a moment, it looked as if the official would recover with a prepared excuse.

"But this one…"

However, knowing what the man was about to say, Reinhart cut him off.

"Do you intend to tell me that you did report it? Certainly, I was told by your office that there were a number of trivial problems, all unsurprising given that they were regular occurrences, and that it was possible they were already being dealt with. Your main point, though, was that the issues were minor and not worth the follow-up."

An expression of discomfort blossomed on the official's face as his argument was defanged. Reinhart pressed on.

"The sanitation workers who were hired to clean the pit toilets have not been paid. Furthermore, it seems they were offered recompense far below what regulations demand. As a result, no one has taken on the job since. Thus, the toilets have been neglected for quite some time. This dereliction of duty has given rise to complaints from the citizens. Now the guild has been hired to straighten out the mess. But the very organization of this public service that has long been in place—since my father's time, in fact—has completely collapsed. I can hardly consider that a trivial matter."

"No, Your Grace!"

"At this juncture, I do not care what you think of this project. However, in accordance with policy, your office has an obligation to maintain this public works project, to make every effort to see it through unimpeded, and to report any problems that may arise.

In spite of this, you did not report the situation to me. Not only that, this mess occurred because you both reduced the sanitation workers' pay and then failed to pay them altogether."

"!"

⊹ WHILE YOU WERE CLEANING ⊹

While Ryoma and his adventurer colleagues were working in secret to prevent an epidemic, two men faced each other in a lavishly furnished parlor.

"Would you explain this to me so I may understand?"

Reinhart didn't raise his voice, but his usual gentle smile was nowhere to be found.

A bead of sweat ran down the forehead of the other man—the top official entrusted with the running of Gimul—who sat across from the duke in a fluster.

The cause of the tension lay atop the table between them.

Reinhart had surprised the town hall with a visit, requesting a meeting with the top man. He even turned down the offer of refreshments from the secretary, instead placing a single sheet of paper on the table.

Point by painful point, it described the current state of the town's affairs, including several things that should never have been, issues that had been thoroughly ignored.

"As you can tell from a cursory glance, I have confirmed these issues for myself over the past two days. And yet, when I last visited your office, not a one of these problems was mentioned to me."

BY THE GRACE OF THE GODS 3

Story: **Roy** Art: **Ranran** Character Design: **Ririnra**

Translation: Sheldon Drzka
Lettering: Elena Pizarro
Cover Design: Andrea Miller
Editor: Tania Biswas

BY THE GRACE OF THE GODS Volume 3
© Roy
© 2019 Ranran / SQUARE ENIX CO., LTD.
First published in Japan in 2019 by SQUARE ENIX CO., LTD.
English translation rights arranged with
SQUARE ENIX CO., LTD. and SQUARE ENIX, INC.
English translation © 2021 by SQUARE ENIX CO., LTD.

ISBN: 978-1-64609-082-2

Library of Congress Cataloging-in-Publication
Data is on file with the publisher.

Printed in the U.S.A.
First printing, September 2021
10 9 8 7 6 5 4 3 2 1

SQUARE ENIX
MANGA & BOOKS
www.square-enix-books.com